Looking can be

So let us take care of the finance for you.

As a busy member of the clergy you have enough to do without having to worry about your tax affairs.

TMC is here to help. We were established to provide a tax management service to the clergy and are now one of the largest such specialist advisers in the UK. Our team offers telephone and virtual face to face appointments so that we can discuss your individual needs with:

General tax advice | Completion of tax returns
Tax credits | Payroll administration | Property accounts
Student advice | Annual Diocesan return

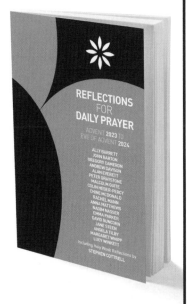
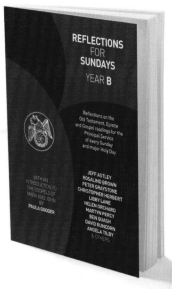

barnabasaid
bringing hope to suffering Christians

...let us do good to all people, especially to those who belong to the family of believers.

Galatians 6:10

Barnabas stands alongside our Christian brothers and sisters around the world, wherever they suffer as a result of their faith.

Donate online at **barnabasaid.org/donate** or call: **01793 744557** Email **info@barnabasaid.org**

The world's most famous hymn book
on your phone, tablet or computer

- Words for all 847 hymns and songs found in *Ancient and Modern* (2013)
- Find hymns by number, first line, author or composer
- Browse the collection by theme or lectionary reading
- Create and edit your own lists of hymns

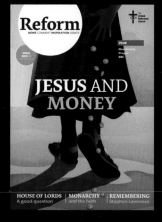

Did you hear the one about the church...

... filled with aid for Ukrainian refugees?
... with an award-winning garden
... celebrating Lent with a sausage?
... that made a ship out of a sofabed?
... with a café where everyone knows your name?.
... that was 'the best afternoon I've had'?
... that started from scratch and grew ever since?

There's so much happening in the URC!

And it's all in **Reform**. Keep informed. Keep in touch.
Subscribe today at **reform-magazine.co.uk/subscribe**

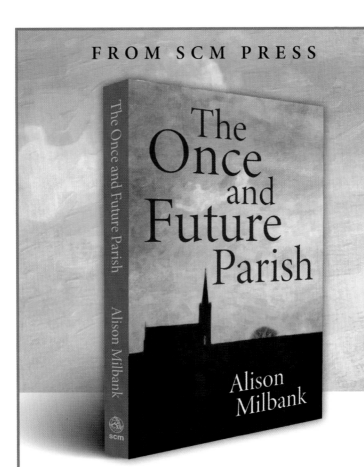

YOU'RE NOT JUST CHOOSING ECCLESIASTICAL YOU'RE CHOOSING THE MOST TRUSTED HOME INSURANCE.

Voted by customers 17 times running* as the most trusted insurer for home insurance, you're choosing home insurance designed specifically for church people.

Our cover accounts for your extra church duties, not only offering discounts for clergy and church volunteers, but also benefiting your church with a £130 donation for every new policy taken out^.

By choosing Ecclesiastical, you're choosing insurance you can believe in.

*Fairer Finance Home Insurance customer experience rating, Spring and Autumn, 2015-2023. ^Terms and conditions apply. Visit: ecclesiastical.com/trust130

www.ecclesiastical.com/homeinsurance

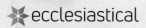 ecclesiastical

Proudly part of the BENEFACT GROUP

Ecclesiastical Insurance Office plc (EIO) Reg. No. 24869. Registered in England at Benefact House, 2000 Pioneer Avenue, Gloucester Business Park, Brockworth, Gloucester, GL3 4AW, United Kingdom. EIO is authorised by the Prudential Regulation Authority and regulated by the Financial Conduct Authority and the Prudential Regulation Authority. Firm Reference Number 113848.
© Ecclesiastical Insurance Office plc 2023

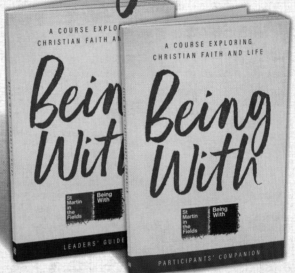

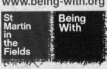

Saint Columba's House

t: 01483 766498
www.stcolumbashouse.org.uk
Maybury Hill, Woking, Surrey GU22 8AB

Situated in beautiful wooded gardens, our urban retreat house offers conference spaces, accommodation, quiet days and retreats.

- 9 flexible, well equipped meeting rooms
- Overnight accommodation for 31 guests
- On site Chapel and Oratory
- Home cooked food
- Easy access from London by rail and road

Contact us:

call: 01483 766498
email: admin@stcolumbashouse.org.uk
web: www.stcolumbashouse.org.uk

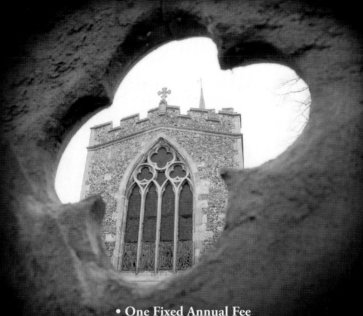

The Canterbury Preacher's Companion 2024

The Canterbury Preacher's Companion 2024

Sermons for Sundays, Holy Days,
Festivals and Special Occasions
Year B

Edited by Catherine Williams

CANTERBURY
PRESS
Norwich

© the Contributors, 2023

First published in 2023 by the Canterbury Press Norwich
Editorial office
3rd Floor, Invicta House
108–114 Golden Lane
London EC1Y 0TG, UK
www.canterburypress.co.uk

Canterbury Press is an imprint of Hymns Ancient & Modern Ltd
(a registered charity)

Hymns Ancient & Modern® is a registered trademark of
Hymns Ancient & Modern Ltd
13A Hellesdon Park Road, Norwich,
Norfolk NR6 5DR, UK

Scripture quotations are from the New Revised
Standard Version of the Bible, Anglicized Edition,
copyright © 1989, 1995 by the Division of Christian Education of the
National Council of the Churches of Christ in the USA.
Used by permission. All rights reserved.

British Library Cataloguing in Publication data

A catalogue record for this book is available
from the British Library

978 1-78622-508-5

Typeset by Regent Typesetting
Printed and bound in Great Britain by
Ashford Colour Press Ltd

Contents

SUNDAYS AND MAJOR FESTIVALS

Unless otherwise stated, the readings and the verse numbers of the psalms are taken from *Common Worship: Services and Prayers for the Church of England* (Church House Publishing, 2000), with revisions, and are for Year B.

2023

Preface

Thank you for investing in the 2024 edition of *The Canterbury Preacher's Companion*. If you are a regular user, you will already know how useful this resource can be, and if this is your first time engaging with this book, you have a treat in store.

At Advent 2023 we enter into Year B of the lectionary, and the voice of Matthew that we have heard for the last year gives way to that of Mark, combined with salient forays into the Gospel of John. This makes for an immediate, rich and deeply theological engagement with the life, death and resurrection of Jesus.

For those new to *The Canterbury Preacher's Companion*, this book contains sample sermons for all Principal and Second Services, together with Saints' Days, Festivals, various special occasions and some all-age material. Sermons for Principal Services are mostly based on the Gospel for the day, while Second Service sermons draw on one or two of the set lectionary readings or the psalm. Sermons for Saints' Days and Festivals comment on the saint or Festival in the light of the lectionary Scriptures. The all-age sermons give lively interactive ways of engaging a multi-generational congregation. Though some of these sermons have been commissioned for this volume, the vast majority have been preached to real congregations in real time during the past few years.

The sermons given here are examples of ways in which preachers have engaged with the Scriptures in their context and from their particular theological, spiritual, cultural and political backgrounds. We continue to diversify the pool of contributors so as to offer a wide and inclusive approach. The word of God is 'living and active', and you have been called by the Holy Spirit to the task of preaching this word from your own background, using your own voice, and speaking within your particular context. Therefore, we would not expect you to preach the sermons straight from the book. We do, however, believe that another's voice within the body of Christ may spark your inspiration and give you confidence to develop your own material – even if your response is, 'Well, I wouldn't do it like that!'

It is a great joy to work with the preachers who have contributed to this volume. Their imagination, passion for the word of God, and creativity is inspiring. It gives me great hope for the future of preaching. Reading through these sermons as I have edited this edition has been a delight, and I encourage you to read both sermons for each week even when you are not on the rota to preach because I believe you will find much material to nourish and grow your faith, as well as good examples of preaching style, and lively and contemporary illustrations.

The introductory article which follows is by Mark Oakley, the Dean of St John's College, Cambridge, and Canon Theologian of Wakefield Cathedral. Mark is a seasoned, articulate and popular preacher with much wisdom to offer us all through his experience of preaching across the UK and beyond, in churches, cathedrals and the academy. In his excellent article, we are encouraged to explore the preacher as poet, prophet and protestor. I strongly commend his words to you.

Entering into the adventure of another year of preaching, may God your Creator bless and guide you, as you make known the Lord Jesus Christ through your words and actions. And may the Holy Spirit counsel and comfort you as she fires your imagination and passion for the vital ministry of preaching to which you are called.

Catherine Williams

The Preacher in 2024:
Poet, Prophet, Protestor

Mark Oakley

When clergy apply for a new job, they know that, if shortlisted, it is highly likely they will have to preach a short sermon to the interview panel. The panel will not want to observe how they anoint the sick, celebrate the Eucharist or chair a meeting. They want to know what they're like in the pulpit, or, perhaps, behind one of those lecterns that look like a posh deckchair. This shouldn't surprise us. The advert most probably said they were looking for a 'good preacher'. Add to this, research endlessly shows that when churchgoers are asked what they look for in a church service, an 'interesting sermon' is always in the top three things. Alarmingly, when they are asked to name what most disappoints them about going to church, the sermon is usually again towards the top of the list.

Feeding a hunger

There is a general hunger for a language like a compass to navigate this life that does not come with subtitles. It appears to be a hunger that is often not fed very well. This can strangely reflect how the preacher feels. We often have a hunger to feed, but feel pretty empty, stressed or at a loose end as to how to go about this in a world of such sensory overload. To preach a sermon is a very different thing from it being heard. At worst, this leads to an unspoken mutual agreement that no one in the parish should expect too much in the sermon slot and that, maybe when the vicar moves on, the advert can mention they want a good preacher.

There is nothing new about this state of affairs. In the nineteenth century, Søren Kierkegaard wrote a parable that imagines a church of geese gathering every Sunday to hear a sermon preached from a high pulpit, where an Old Gander exhorts the congregation that the Creator intended a greater purpose for them. He proclaims that they are strangers there and that their wings were so designed that they might fly to distant lands. Every Sunday the geese would hear the sermon and waddle home, before returning the following Sunday for the same lofty speech about the use of their wings. Whenever one of them asked why no one actually flies anywhere, various geese respond with nuanced arguments about the dangers of what happens to those who attempt it. The following Sunday the Old Gander returns to the pulpit and again preaches about this 'greater purpose' the Creator has for them and their wings, and this cycle of inactivity continues. Kierkegaard's attack is on sermons that lead to nothing and is consequently aimed more at the preacher than at sermons as a form of communication. He writes:

> The trouble is not that Christianity is not voiced ... but that it is voiced in such a way that the majority eventually think it utterly inconsequential ... Thus the highest and the holiest things make no impact whatsoever, but they are given sound and are listened to as something that now, God knows why, has become routine and habit like so much else.[1]

The sacramentality of language

I'm very drawn to Gandhi's image of the evangelism 'of the rose', that is, it is not what we say that draws people but the beauty of who we are, as a person or as a community. It is the attractiveness of our values and integrity that converts. Nevertheless, I believe in the sacramentality of language. Christian people should attend carefully to the words of worship and the words used in their relationships because words can achieve amazing things: life-changing, life-opening, full-stop-into-comma moments, when words arrive at the intellect by way of the heart. I'll be honest – if you are struggling to think about what you might preach about at the moment, if the Sunday slot is a slog, well, frankly, you need to wake up! There is too much that needs exposing, exploring, examining, and too much that needs challenging, correcting, subverting. We are living in a preacher's time. In the same way that Martin Luther King Jr never said 'I have a nightmare', we need to take this opportunity seriously and in hope. The other Martin Luther said, 'Even if I knew the world would end tomorrow I would still plant my little apple tree.' Well, there's a lot of planting to be done. The New Testament scholar Bill Brosend says the preacher's question is always, 'What does the Holy Spirit want to say to these people, in this place, at this time, through these texts?'[2] Walter Brueggemann argues similarly that we are audacious as preachers,[3] we dare to break the silence, and just as the bread of the Eucharist makes us hungrier for God, so must our words seek to deepen our longing for God, showing the famine of our land and the hope of God's horizon.

These are strange times, though. Leaders campaign in graffiti and then govern in tweets. With excited talk of 'fake news' we rather get distracted, it is hoped, from fake politicians or populist slogans, generalizations that smooth over, at best, complexity, and at worst, the truth. It's particularly bad at the moment – and such abuse spreads across our globe very quickly. It leads to confusion in society about what we believe, what we want and what is possible. Consumerism makes words seductive not truthful; technology gives us too many words, and our care for them decreases as they proliferate. The first one to draw a breath is declared the listener. The same ears that listen to politicians, salespeople and news commentators are listening to the Christian and to the preacher.

'Truth decay'

We are living in times when there is a great deal of cynical use of language. It is what has been called society's 'truth decay'.[4] Are we as a society losing interest in truth? Is the idea of there being objective truth – facts – now less important to us than opinions, crisis chatter or infotainment? Is to be interesting more important than being right? Is there a declining value of accuracy as society's reserve currency? Is what matters not veracity but impact? Is dishonesty therefore not held to account as it once was? Is lying just a laugh that amuses by messing up a system of value?

In this chaos, it is tempting to blame some political and state leaders. Some seem to think that what is truthful is merely what reinforces the mood of the crowd, even serving us 'alternative facts'. There is a lot of turning honest complexity into dishonest simplicity. History, thankfully, is peppered with those who warn us about such political manipulation. Alexander Hamilton, for instance, one of America's Founding Fathers, argued for a system of constitutional checks and balances to guard against the possibility, and I now quote him, 'of a man unprincipled in private life' and 'bold in his temper' one day arising who might 'mount the hobby horse of popularity' and 'flatter and fall in with all the non-sense of the zealots of the day' in order to embarrass the government and 'throw things into confusion that he may ride the storm and direct the whirlwind'.[5] Anyone come to mind?

People such as George Orwell and Hannah Arendt warned from experience that totalitarian rule ultimately takes hold by slow injections of falsity that people then begin to repeat. And so for all practical purposes, Orwell concludes, the lie will have become truth. It spreads and leads to a general distrust of experts – the belief that, say, science, if inconvenient somehow, is a conspiracy; and historical studies that don't back up your arguments can just be revised. Journalism begins to reflect a selfie-stick culture, seemingly holding things at an objective distance but only reflecting yourself and your tribe at the end of the day. Religion, too, can hide its darker truths with pious religio-speak or some deference to author-ity and expect the congregations to say 'Amen'. If there is anything to what I'm saying, this is a very dangerous place to find ourselves. This is a preacher's time.

In the Gospel according to St John, Pontius Pilate asks Jesus, 'What is truth?' but he doesn't hang around to find out the answer. After all, the crowd is putting on the pressure outside. Communities of faith, though, are formed to ask the same question but then to stick around, together, to pursue the answer in relationship and worship. A church or chaplaincy should be one of the antidotes to any fashion of falsity, a group of people committed to the pursuit of truth, in dialogue and fellowship, each ready to be corrected, when necessary, passionate about accuracy, fearless in seeing past and present, and researching into the as yet unknown. Tradition is taken seriously but must never become peer pressure by the dead. I have always suspected that religion works best not when trying to answer questions but when it questions answers. A community of faith must be as unafraid to reason vigorously as we are unashamed to adore reverently.

Truth beyond facts

One of the roles of a church is to remind us that truth is found in forms other than facts, that sometimes truth is far too important to be literalistic about. The truths that are expressed artistically, musically, in narrative and myth, are the truths that are always part of the human inner landscape. These include the sense of life as fragile gift, the unignorable intrusions of mystery when love or loss enter it, the intuition that somehow we need saving from ourselves, from self-destruction, by a love both beyond and within. I believe that when we walk into a church we walk into a poem. The liturgy is poetry in motion and we fail to understand its beauty if we miss its density of suggestion, the eavesdropping on the soul, the sensitive state of consciousness that its poetry can prompt. We are not spectators in worship. We pursue the truths that translate into our living. The truths that transform us are embodied in richly suggestive and provocative, often artistic, forms that provoke receptive insight. They are the truths we learn in authentic human encounter when we dare to take off the masks that have worked their way into our skin. Primarily, for Christians, to encounter the person of Jesus Christ is the most freeing and freshest truth of all.

Poet

So, this leads me to my first P: poetry. I've written and said a lot about this so I won't go on too much here,[6] but, as Wallace Stevens said, people ought to like poetry the way children like snow – its thrilling warm-chill, helping us reimagine the world and helping us see our own miraculous, weighted breath. So, any preacher is going to have to be poetic, a shaper of words for the sake of truth, and not to run a spiritual kindergarten but a university of the soul, where we use words that don't just fire off, like ammunition, but that help us hear, distil, and are not stagnant but moving waters. We must use words that are not clichéd but acrobatic, words which hear us and understand us and are there to excite underused imaginations. We need words unafraid of difficulty because difficulty can be important as it pushes us forward into new places. A sermon can be drawn from, like a fountain. It doesn't have to be a river that flows prosaically. If we are to preach in a world of alternative facts and cynical speech we must speak in a fresh and startling way that believes in words, believes in the heart and mind from which they come, believes in the relationships which they seek to build and not fragment. Take words seriously, preacher, or simply help us all diminish.

Prophet

Another 'P'. The preacher today is going to have to be a prophet. This is a word we like to use when we are worked up. But please note: just because you are angry doesn't make you a prophet. A prophet does not just get up, sound off and clear off, feeling a bit better for being so obviously right: 'There! I've told them.' John Donne said that it isn't the wit or the eloquence or the intellect of a preacher that moves his or her listeners, but their nearness. How near is this speaker to my humanity? First, the prophet must be speaking out of a humanity to a humanity. The prophet looks into the future and reports back, warns us who we have become and where it is leading, cattle-prods us into some amendments, not as a fiery, rapid ranter but as someone who wants to help reconcile the world to God, God to the world. This is restoration, not condemnation. Often this still means that the preacher needs to have courage because things need to be said that won't go down well with some. It's really annoying but the gospel gets in the way of trying to keep everyone happy on Sunday morning. The prophetic preacher speaks confidently, with conviction, but not reflecting the poisonous ridicule, sarcasm, demonization and cruelty of the present climate. To be truly prophetic will mean not imitating what you condemn. The prophet is working to dispel illusions without leaving you disillusioned. Hope has two beautiful daughters, says St Augustine: Anger at the ways things are and Courage to put them right. The prophet has passion, a passion for God's justice, and will often be angry, but the purpose of preaching is to bring people home to God, including, of course, yourself.

Protestor

This means that the preacher has another 'P', that of a protestor, protesting against the status quo, protesting on behalf of those who haven't the privilege of a public voice, protesting for change. There's a lot of protesting to be done in this world at the moment, a world in which if you're not at the table you're probably on the menu. It is a world where we exhaust ourselves with competitive and gladiatorial attitudes, where we earn black belts in shopping to impress people we don't like, where a move to the Right is shifting the way we talk about the most important things – asylum, safety, refuge, the poor, the minority, the vulnerable, the other, human rights and equal human dignity. Beware! Many talk as if this shift is of God, or is Christian. A lot of our protest needs to be close to home. Christians need to take the lead in correcting what Christians have sometimes helped bring about. Many will tell us that we should stay out of the political, assuming God, Jesus and the Bible are all apolitical. But as these folk tell us that faith should be personal, protected and pious, we look at the Christ whose execution was not personal, protected and pious, but public, brutal and political. His message had consequences that weren't welcome. Sometimes you might get applause, preacher, but sometimes you will know some cost too. Your spirit might be crucified. In some places in our world, your life might be at risk.

The increasing darkness

There is a fair bit of darkness in this world at the moment. Lives are being ruined, diminished and even ended by militarized regimes, by poverty, by hunger, by terrorism, by hate crime, by an inability in influential people to imagine what it might be like to be someone other than them. The real danger is that we start to fail to notice. We get used to the TV pictures, and we get used to the language that the press and politicians and society at large begin to casually use, where the bombing of a school full of children is referred to as 'collateral damage'; where someone fleeing for refuge, leaving home for their family's safety, becomes an 'immigrant'; where degrading sexualized boasts about behaviour towards women is just 'locker talk'; where God is praised as an execution takes place; where people trying to sleep on streets outside must have 'chosen' to be there, and where upholding human rights based on a belief in equal human dignity is smirked at in pubs and papers, and churches too – unless, of course, they're talking about their own.

All this is increasing the darkness. Who will rescue the victims of it? Who, when society wants to push a person into a dark background out of sight, will shine a light and say 'Don't you dare!' Who will rage at the senseless death of children, at the discrimination and hate shown to the vulnerable, at the convenient casual categorization of human beings into first-, second-, third-class citizens? Who will protest on behalf of a dying planet? Who will always want to rescue us from the suffocation of life? The answer: the one who believes in God – not a God utilized to back a political campaign, not a God weaponized into a big version of our own prejudices, not a God who likes some more than others, but the God who loves equally all he has made, the God who gave us diversity though we tirelessly make division out of it. This is the protest against the darkness of our world's making. As Walter Brueggemann reminds us,[7] Christians have a sub-version, an underground version of reality, a different version, lying there waiting to be made real. God's sub-version means more subversion than we might realize. You don't discover the kingdom of God; you can only live in it or not.

Speak your mind not just your heart

Because we need to keep people in church and pay the bills, and stay liked by the bishop or the church council, we often adopt camouflage in the pulpit and hope to say things between the lines that we hope might be picked up if it verges on being political. But, preacher, they know how you voted. They know. So, what they want to know is do you care for them, are you listening to them – are you as a preacher as keen to listen as you are to speak? Do you love them and the community you serve – and then, if so, you can say what you have to say, why you say the things you say, and we'll see how it goes. Speak your mind not just your heart. Don't make the mistake that everyone cares for something as much as you do. Don't make the mistake of thinking that caring passionately about an issue will automatically translate into preaching convincingly about it. Persuasion is more than passion. But when the gospel needs to protest a state of affairs, it protests and hopes you can see that this is of God and not because I listen to Radio 4 and, therefore, I'm sorry, but I have to turn up the heat. The odd in God has to come out eventually. If we really believe this stuff, there's nothing more important is there?

Resonance, love and longing

If we don't stand for something we might fall for anything. Stand for truth. Not even God can work with unreality. Stand, then, for a reverence of language and its proper use. As Martin Luther King Jr said,

> Cowardice asks the question, is it expedient? And then expedience comes along and asks the question, is it politic? Vanity asks the question, is it popular? Conscience asks the question, is it right? There comes a time when one must take the position that is neither safe nor politic nor popular, but he must do it because conscience tells him it is right.[8]

Luther King was the supreme example of preacher as poet, prophet and protestor. Or, if you prefer your Anglican Divines, remember Donne who said that a sermon should act like thunder that clears the air, or Lancelot Andrewes who said that our charge is to preach 'not what for the present they would hear but what in another day they would wish they had heard'. Resonance rather than relevance, perhaps? As the American preacher Fred Craddock used to say, the question will always be not whether the church is dying but whether it is giving its life for the world.

A sermon is not a text. It is an event. It is inviting us out of the world of consumers into the world of citizens, citizens of God's domain. I love preaching because I discover what I believe when I write a sermon and even more so when I preach one. Theology for me is what happens on the way to the pulpit. Theology is not a hobby, it is survival. To preach, to speak of our faith is so full of love but also of longing, as what is most important to us finally eludes us. We keep going through hints and guesses, glimpses and confirmations, epiphanies and doubts. We shape a collage of God as God shapes the collage that is us. It's beautiful and it's urgent for a thirsty and parched world. To preach is a privilege, to be a poet, a prophet, a protestor and a person, preaching for light in the world, so that others may have that relationship with God that you only wish you had yourself.

Contributors

Mark Amos is Associate Chaplain at The Abbey School, Reading, where he also teaches philosophy and theology. He has recently started a PhD at the University of Leeds with a focus on how intimacy might be understood within the divine–human relationship.

Kate Bruce is an RAF chaplain. She has spent many years teaching preachers, running training events and writing books and articles on preaching. Her latest book is co-authored with Liz Shercliff, *Out of the Shadows: Preaching the Women of the Bible* (SCM Press, 2021). She is currently working with Liz on a second volume. She preaches regularly in a wide range of contexts. Alongside her love of preaching she has an interest in performing stand-up comedy.

Chris Campbell is the Rector of Ashwell with Hinxworth and Newnham, three rural parishes in North Hertfordshire. Before ordination, Chris was a maths teacher in London and a children and families' minister in Cambridgeshire, and she has retained a passion for storytelling and preaching to all ages.

Kat Campion-Spall is an Anglican parish priest currently serving as Rector of the Bristol Harbourside Churches. Kat, influenced by feminist biblical interpretation, tries to listen carefully for, and bring to light, the voices that have been silenced by received interpretations of the Scriptures.

Tom Clammer ministered in the diocese of Gloucester before serving as Precentor of Salisbury Cathedral. He is now a freelance theologian, educator and spiritual director, and a novice brother of the Anglican Order of Cistercians. Used to full cathedrals or half a dozen in a rural church, Tom preaches regularly, mostly in the dioceses of Salisbury and Gloucester.

Esther Elliott is a Church of Scotland Workplace and Community Chaplain in Edinburgh. She is also a Reader at St Mary's Episcopal Cathedral in Edinburgh. Previously she preached regularly in an Anglican parish in Nottingham and taught preaching, doctrine and mission for ministers in Derby Diocese.

Isabelle Hamley is an Anglican priest, author and broadcaster, with a passion for the Old Testament. She has been a parish priest, university chaplain, Old Testament lecturer and chaplain to the Archbishop of Canterbury, and now works as theological adviser to the House of Bishops.

Mariama Ifode-Blease is Assistant Curate at St James's Church, Piccadilly. She combines this with a leadership role in the charity sector. Prior to this, as a lay chaplain, Mariama has been blessed to preach to different congregations and in a variety of contexts.

Jonathan Lawson is Vicar of St Gabriel's Church in Newcastle upon Tyne. He has served and preached in many different contexts from retreat houses to cathedrals, and ministered for ten years as a university chaplain. He has a particular interest in vocation and spiritual direction.

Rachel Mann is a priest, poet, novelist and broadcaster. Author of 12 books, she is passionate about literature, every aspect of culture, as well as ensuring that those traditionally excluded from the life of the church have an honoured place. Her preaching reflects these passions and commitments.

Sandra Millar is Interim Director of Mission and Ministry in the diocese of Gloucester and preaches in a wide range of contexts from cathedral to country church. She is interested in making Scripture connect to the realities of contemporary culture and everyday life.

Peter Moger is a priest in the Scottish Episcopal Church at St Peter's Stornoway on the Isle of Lewis. Prior to this he has served as a parish priest in the Church of England, as Secretary of the Liturgical Commission, and as Precentor of York Minster. He is also the editor of the *Common Worship Lectionary* (Church House Publishing) and of *Reflections for Daily Prayer* (Church House Publishing).

Mark Oakley is Dean of St John's College, Cambridge, and Canon Theologian of Wakefield Cathedral. He is the author of several books on the relationship between faith and poetry, including *The Splash of Words: Believing in Poetry* (Canterbury Press, 2016). He is an admired speaker and preacher, and a collection of his sermons, *By Way of the Heart*, is published by Canterbury Press (2019).

Catherine Okoronkwo is Vicar of All Saints and St Barnabas churches in Swindon and is the Bishop of Bristol's Adviser on Racial Justice. A poet and writer, she is interested in the use of the creative arts in ministry and mission. Her debut collection of poetry, *Blood and Water / ọbara na mmiri* is published by Waterloo Press (2020).

Andrew Rudd is a Reader in Frodsham, Cheshire. As well as preaching, he leads writing workshops, retreats and quiet days, and teaches aspects of spirituality and reflection on various formation courses within the diocese. He is Poet-in-Residence at Manchester Cathedral, and also offers spiritual accompaniment.

Michael Sadgrove has been a parish priest, theological educator and cathedral precentor. He was Dean of Sheffield, then Dean of Durham before retiring in 2015. A selection from his preaching was published as *Christ in a Choppie Box: Sermons from North East England* (Sacristy Press, 2015).

Arani Sen is Rector of St Olave, Hart Street, and Area Director of Ministry for the Two Cities, Diocese of London. Previously he ministered in inner-city, multi-ethnic parishes in Leeds, Southall and Islington. He is of Bengali heritage, his family coming from Kolkata. He is passionate about racial justice and social action. He is the author of *Holy Spirit Radicals: Pentecost, Acts and Changed Society* (Malcolm Down Publishing, 2018)

Karen E. Smith is a Baptist minister who taught church history and Christian spirituality at Cardiff University and served as pastor of a church in South Wales. She publishes in the area of spirituality and has been a regular contributor on BBC radio. Now retired, she is an Honorary Senior Research Fellow of Cardiff University.

Liz Shercliff is a writer, speaker, researcher and preacher. She is author of *Preaching Women: Gender, Power and the Pulpit* (SCM Press, 2019), and co-author of *Out of the Shadows* (SCM Press, 2021) and *The Present Preacher: Discerning God in the Now* (Canterbury Press, 2021); founder of an annual conference for women, Women's Voices, and of the North West Preaching Conference.

Catherine Williams is a spiritual director and writer. She contributes to spirituality resources such as *Pray As You Go* (Jesuit Media Initiatives), *Reflections for Daily Prayer* (Church House Publishing), and *Fresh from the Word* (International Bible Reading Association), and is the lead voice on the Church of England's *Daily Prayer* and *Time to Pray* Apps (Aimer Media Ltd). Licensed to the Bishop of Norwich as a Public Preacher, Catherine preaches regularly in a variety of contexts.

Paul Rhys Williams is the Rector of the Sandringham Group of Parishes which encompasses ministry on the Sandringham Estate. Paul is a Commander of the Order of St John and Vice Dean of the Priory of England and the Islands. These and other settings provide stimulating contexts in which to minister and preach.

Year B, the Year of Mark

(Year B begins on Advent Sunday in 2023, 2026, 2029, etc.)

Advent

First Sunday of Advent   3 December
Principal Service   **The Widest Horizon**
Isa. 64.1–9; Ps. 80.1–8, 18–20 [*or* 80.1–8]; 1 Cor. 1.3–9;
Mark 13.24–end

It's only 22 days until Christmas Day. For many of us, our vision will have focused and our horizon narrowed to a preoccupation with cards and cake, presents and parties, family and food as all our energies are consumed by getting ready for one of those truly immovable dates in the calendar. In the church, we are now focused on numerous carol services, the demands of hospitality, decorating and deadlines as everything now tunnels towards one moment: the arrival of the baby in the manger. This is the coming of the Christ-child into our world, Emmanuel God with us, and surely Advent is now the countdown to prepare us for that day.

The widening horizon

But our reading from Mark has no mention of stables or shepherds or kings. There is nothing about a baby. Instead, we are given a big vision, the very widest horizon of all. Jesus is talking to his followers about the end times, all that will happen when he comes again, when skies are darkened and stars fall, and Christ returns in power and glory. It's an extraordinary vision and one that can make us squirm uncomfortably. It is a challenge to read the signs of the times and pay as much attention to the changing spiritual seasons as we do to the signs of the natural seasons. How much easier if these days of Advent can just be about making ready once again for a baby, doing all the things that are familiar and safe, rather than being prepared to experience the unknown.

Mystery and adventure

Wide horizons are full of mystery and uncertainty, but also adventure, and interestingly the word adventure contains the word 'advent'. The word advent means the arrival of a significant person or event, and the word 'adventure' means engaging with something risky, even dangerous, to make something happen or find something new. *Great Circle* is a novel by Maggie Shipstead, which draws on the lives of pioneer women pilots to describe the fictional heroine, Marian Graves.[9] Marian is transfixed by a desire to go beyond limits, not just the limits of society, but the limits described by geography, always pushing to fly beyond the horizon, even if she risks death on her great adventure to circumnavigate the globe around the poles. The great Christian author C. S. Lewis has a wonderful description of the mystery and awe of the wide horizon at the end of the book *The Voyage of the Dawn Treader*, one of *The Chronicles of Narnia*.[10] The ship's crew are coming to the end of the world, discovering 'whiteness, shot with the faintest of gold, around them on every side', longing to press on into the unknown, the world of Aslan himself. It's the big horizon of Advent, the great adventure, the return of Christ himself.

Living the tension

In her poem 'Watchet Auf', Anne Lewin names the dual tension of Advent. She identifies the escalating demands of Christmas Day and the insistent, often unheard, solemn theme of Advent to repent and be ready. She ends the poem with the question, 'And will he find us/ Watching?'[11] This is directly alluding to the task that Jesus sets his followers in response to all that he has spoken about. In the midst of escalating anxiety, a changing world and a sense of doom, we are simply to be watchful. We watch as we reflect on Scripture, as we notice the way we can act to include and bless those around us; as we pray more deeply for the world that God loves. This is the Advent call: the call to lift up our eyes and see the very widest horizon, the horizon that speaks of the return of Christ as judge and Lord. Let's begin our Advent adventure, not just preparing for a baby to be born but making ready for the day when the whole world will be renewed, a day when all will be restored and reconciled in and through Christ, who will come again. May our Advent prayer be the watchful words: 'Come, Lord Jesus.'

Sandra Millar

Hymn suggestions

Hills of the North, rejoice; Come, thou long expected Jesus; Lo! He comes with clouds descending; Christ, whose glory fills the skies.

First Sunday of Advent   3 December
Second Service   **Mood Swings**
Ps. 25 [*or* 25.1–9]; Isa. 1.1–20; **Matt. 21.1–13**

The crowd

As I write this in August 2022, the Lionesses have just won the European Cup Final. There have been quite literally days of partying and exuberant celebrations. The sense of exhilaration and joy is tangible. Like a champagne cork flying out of a bottle, there has been so much energy and effervescent joy. We gain a similar sense from today's reading from Matthew's Gospel, as Jesus enters Jerusalem sitting on a donkey. There is no doubt that people were pleased to see him. There is something about a crowd, isn't there? A crowd that is jubilant is one thing, but a wise person knows how quickly a crowd's mood can change. 'Sometimes they strew his way, and his sweet praises sing; resounding all the day Hosannas to their King: then "Crucify!" is all their breath, and for his death they thirst and cry' – to quote the hymn 'My song is love unknown' by Samuel Crossman.

Pedestals

I can never work out if this is a purely British disease, but there is definitely a delight in the United Kingdom in bigging people up and then an enjoyment in watching their demise. It feels like a kind of blood sport. I suppose it comes from a longing for someone to be better than ourselves, and then the relief in discovering that they are human after all. I find it noticeable that Jesus, as depicted in the Gospels, is often what you might call 'camera shy'. He often slips away from the public gaze and appears keen to avoid the cult of celebrity. Indeed, at times, he seems to go out of his way to wind people up, as we'll see later. Today is therefore a rare, almost unique, vignette, of the Jesus who plays to the crowd. His riding into Jerusalem is very symbolic and has all sorts of suggestions of kingship and of being the anointed one. This is a politically sensitive

4

action – some might say provocative. Just preceding this passage Jesus has helped two blind men to see again. Now everyone can see Jesus, and who he is: their anointed one.

Rage

In the Scrovegni Chapel in Padua are a whole set of wall paintings by Giotto, depicting Jesus' life. They are quite something to see and I have a book of the pictures at home. One of them depicts Jesus cleansing the Temple, the story that we are invited to ponder today, and if you look at the picture you'll find it hard to see a meek and mild Jesus. Jesus looks furious and his hand is clenched as a fist, ready to hit someone. Our images of God play an important part in how we relate to God. Victorian stained glass has a lot to answer for! We are presented here with an interesting image, a single human being amid the vastness of the Jerusalem Temple, causing havoc. Overturning tables and driving people out. Something is not right here.

I hate you

There are various and many temptations in the spiritual life. One is to over-formalize prayer, such that it becomes staid and lifeless as if you were talking to a relic in a long-lost language. The other can be so chummy and so upbeat that there is no room for sadness or melancholy. I guess that what we are searching for is an authentic relationship with God, one where we can be real and honest and true. In such a relationship, which the psalms excel in demonstrating, we can say anything to God: from adoring him to telling him that we hate him, if we do. What we see in Jesus is someone who is authentically himself, who wasn't carried away by the crowds, who could cope with being unpopular, who spent time by himself. Someone who could call things out, if needs be.

Advent

As we start a new church year, I guess these matters raise some interesting questions for us, both individually and corporately. We might wonder about our place in the crowd. How easily (or not) are we swayed by the opinion of others, by the masses, be it in person or on social media? We might wonder about what makes us rage. What tables would we like to turn over and what people might we want to drive out – and why? Then in solitude or in silence or with a trusted friend we might consider what God is saying to us in this, and what his invitation is to us as we journey through this new year with him. Can we perhaps ask for the grace to be authentically ourselves with him?

Jonathan Lawson

Hymn suggestions

Jesus Christ is waiting; Ride on, ride on in majesty; O come, o come, Emmanuel; You are the King of glory.

Second Sunday of Advent 10 December
Principal Service **The News is Good**
Isa. 40.1–11; Ps. 85.1–2, 8–end [*or* 85.8–end]; 2 Pet. 3.8–15a; **Mark 1.1–8**

It is a truth universally acknowledged that the church in possession of the good news must be in want of those to exclude from it. The gospel according to Jesus Christ presents a radical and inconvenient truth: an inclusivity that is formed by the breath of the Holy Spirit and that holds the blood pouring out from the side of a man who dared to say, 'You belong.'

A table of belonging

Belonging is a deep psychological, emotional and social need. We all want to belong; we all want and need to feel safe. And that is why it is necessary to remember the table, the table, set before us, the table where Abraham welcomed and ate with three visitors in Genesis 18, the table at which Jesus ate his final meal, and at which he washed the feet of his disciples, the table masterly presented in Andrei Rublev's fifteenth-century icon. We need to remember the table and recognize Jesus there as the disciples did on the road to Emmaus, at the table, in the breaking of the bread. It is a sad reality that some would like us to think that the table is only for the selected few, those whom another self-appointed group has deemed worthy of belonging, or not, as the case may be.

We can probably recall examples of exclusivity that do not chime with the truth rooted in the transformation of the wilderness of our human failings into the fertile ground of God's welcome. We read in Isaiah 40 of the 'herald of good tidings'. This is the good news for which we should lift up our voices. The displacement of exile referenced by Isaiah is recognized but there is good news too. As one commentator writes: 'Jerusalem is the place of divine self-revelation.'[12] As followers of Christ we read this as the place in which Jesus died, was buried and rose again. These historical moments capture a transcendental reality: at the table of the Last Supper, here is our God. The integrity of the table, therefore, has not been set by us. It is not up to us to decide who can be at the table and who should stand aside. Our job is to protect and promote the integrity of the table.

An authentic invitation

In the Gospel reading, we anticipate meeting this Jesus. Mark's Gospel is like listening to and watching a mini-series on the telly, written, I am told, in a fast-paced Greek that isn't necessarily sophisticated, but is real and visceral and captivating. The beginning of Mark's Gospel echoes the passage from Isaiah. John the Baptist is introduced with a mix of references from the Hebrew Bible, speaking into the hopes of the of the Jewish people at the time. Mark moves us out of Jerusalem only for John the Baptist to point us back towards it, towards a sense of exilic return to the source of all life, and the source of all love. Jesus is not even on the scene yet, but we know that he is not coming alone: 'He will baptize you with the Holy Spirit' (Mark 1.8). We are asked to get ready; we are asked to watch and wait.

A table for life

And so we come to Advent, to the deep questioning of our relationship in, and with, time during this season. To the sense that our place at the table of this eternal banquet has been prepared and remains through time and space. To the confidence that the invitation is authentic and the calling to be at the table is constant and consistent. We come to this table through pain, and suffering, and rejection, and loss, loneliness and labelling, betrayal and anger. And Jesus gets all of that because he lived all of that.

The church has so much to learn, so much for which to repent and lament, and so much work to do to remember that the news is *good*, that the good news is Jesus Christ, and that his table is a non-negotiable space of belonging. Before, and as, we preach the gospel we need to interrogate the effects of our words and our interpretations. Because we preach Jesus Christ, crucified. We preach about the table, and the resurrection, and the life.

God knows it is not easy to be a follower of Christ. Yet we remember and hold on to the image from Isaiah 40.1–11. We worship a God who is safe. Safe and steady, loving, kind and understanding. We can come home to God at the table and let it all hang out, because God will feed us through the love, light and healing of God's Son, Jesus Christ. It is here we belong. This is our feast, this is our fire, this is our resting place.

Mariama Ifode-Blease

Hymn suggestions

I have decided to follow Jesus; Come to the table (Sidewalk Prophets); Come, thou long expected Jesus; I will feast at the table of the Lord (Chris Tomlin).

Second Sunday of Advent   10 December
Second Service   Tell Me Lies
Ps. 40 [*or* 40.12–end]; **1 Kings 22.1–28**; Rom. 15.4–13; *Gospel at Holy Communion*: Matt. 11.2–11

Power and truth. Religion and politics. All of this in a marvellous story from the First Book of Kings …

Ahab, the king, has surrounded himself with special advisors: 400 prophets, to help him discern what to do next. Part of his country has fallen into enemy hands and he wishes to recapture it. Is that a good idea? So, he asks his 400 prophets. They say with one voice: 'Go for it, Ahab, get it done! The Lord will give it to you.'

But really?

But oddly the king is not convinced. He has a niggle of doubt. He remembers another prophet, Micaiah, who is not part of his inner circle and who 'never prophesies anything favourable about me, but only disaster'.

So finally, the king asks Micaiah what to do, and Micaiah tells him: 'Yes, go along with everybody else, go along with all the other prophets.' And this doesn't work either. The king senses that this is wrong – Micaiah is stringing him along. He presses Micaiah until he does give him a bad prophecy, a prophecy of doom. He forces it out of Micaiah because that's the truth he knows deep in his heart.

It's a voice Ahab hears but hasn't learned to trust. He throws Micaiah in prison as if that will stop the truth. As if silencing the voice of truth will make it better. And the escapade does go badly, all his fears are justified.

The voice of God

Why do we find it so hard to listen to the voice of God? Even if it's speaking clearly deep down in our heart? Why do we prefer church structures, systems of belief, majority views and the peer pressure of the crowd? Why is *that* so much easier than listening to a voice that we knew all along, the voice we recognized? Why can we not follow the instructions that are written, here within us?

One reason might be that we listen to too many voices. The king surrounds himself with this echo chamber. Everybody around the king says exactly what they imagine the king wants to hear. A soothing mirror of his own wishes amplifies his every whim. And so the truth gets twisted and distorted by confirmation bias, by the growing unreality of this group of people. This seems so topical – every day we see it played out around us in social media. The truth vanishes away.

Religious certainty

And of course, these are *prophets*. The saddest aspect of this story is the claim of these prophets to hear the word of God. We need to be very careful with the word of God. We need to be so aware that the word of God is always mediated through our fragility. We will, and do, get it wrong. Often the best we can see, as Paul says, is partial dim reflections in a mirror. We do not see face to face, we do not have exclusive access to the story. Our discernment needs to be humble and tentative in the face of the word of God.

The *word of God* – of course, there's a clue in the title! – the word of *God* is not the word of *me*. It never actually belongs to me. It's always a word that stands beyond my words, it's always inadequately expressed in my word. The Word of God can never be pinned down to a text, but the Word becomes flesh and lives among us. God can never be reduced to a set of words, which I can then agree or disagree with, assent to or dissent from.

Of course, we need our holy words. It's a lifelong task, to find some way to talk about God. We try our best with these words, but all too easily we elevate them to the status of idols and give them more credibility than the one who speaks them.

Among the prophets and experts of religion, among the conflicting voices of power, among the noise of our echo chambers of relationship, we can listen for that word. That small voice of direction or correction, comfort or challenge. We do not *own* the word of God but, still, we can recognize it. There is something in us, deep in the silence, that connects with the voice that brought us into being. Something, someone, who calls us to follow.

Andrew Rudd

Hymn suggestions

Be thou my vision; O come, o come, Emmanuel; Will you come and follow me; May the mind of Christ my Saviour.

Third Sunday of Advent 17 December
Principal Service **'I am not the Messiah'**
Isa. 61.1–4, 8–end; Ps. 126, *or Canticle*: Magnificat;
1 Thess. 5.16–24; **John 1.6–8, 19–28**

The usual picture of John the Baptist is a loud, disruptive and socially inappropriate preacher. Yet, in our Gospel reading, John is anything but this. He is quietly respectful and says what he is not: he is not the Messiah, he is not Elijah, he is not the prophet. John's vocation has been a long time coming. He was made for this moment. So, if you know you are called, the only question left is 'Called for what?'

I am not the Messiah was a kind of prayer that enabled John to centre himself in a world that would attempt to pull him apart. I would like to suggest that we consider the possibility that many of the moral failings of our leaders have some root in their failure to pray the prayer of John the Baptist. 'I am not the Messiah' too easily becomes 'I might be the Messiah', and, before you know it, 'I am the Messiah'. From there, it's all too easy to cross ethical boundaries if you believe that you are more than you are.

Because John the Baptist begins with a threefold renouncing, no to Messiahship, no to being Elijah or one of the prophets, he is then able to say something just as bold. I know who I am. I see myself in God's story. God is doing a new thing and I can play my part in the new thing that is to come. And John can do that once he is clear about what he will not do.

Masks for the kingdom

John's renouncing invites us to consider how we can also say 'no' to the false selves and false roles we take on, especially when we believe we are taking on those roles and putting on those masks for the kingdom of God.

We live in an age which tempts us with marketing pitches, intended to make us believe that everything is possible for us: that I can do anything I set my mind to do. With that approach, there is not enough time in the day for all the things to which we should say 'yes'. This is not setting our sights too low. This is living in reality, in real time, recognizing that daydreaming can keep us from saying 'yes' to our true calling, to our true vocation. Being able to say 'no' makes our 'yes' more meaningful. That's true for our own character and personality as it is for our management of time.

Called to be yourself

John the Baptist renounces the calls that are not his in order then to tell the religious leaders what his call is to be and do. He is called to be a voice, to baptize with water, and to recognize his own unworthiness before the one who is to come.

This renouncing three times before affirming three times is echoed in the baptismal liturgy. Each time we baptize, those to be baptized say 'no', 'no', 'no' before saying 'yes', 'yes', 'yes'. Our life in Christ begins by saying what our life will not be ruled by – not by Satan or evil powers or sinful desires. Those renunciations bring clarity to the call we affirm in our life in Christ.

Moving the spotlight

Did the religious leaders expect to hear from John that he was the Messiah? Were they expecting to find a man doing his best Elijah imitation? Were they hoping to see the prophet that Moses promised would come? If so, they were about to be disappointed. In this exchange, John is already decreasing so that the one to come could increase. He is already moving the spotlight from himself to the Word that John proclaimed.

There are plenty of Messiahs who will tell you what to believe, how to behave and what to say. They will have the right answer and offer you a quick fix and a sure way to salvation. You will find them not only in the world but also in the church. They prey on our anxiety and in our anxiety; it is tempting to look for quick salvation, for the flashy programme that will bring the people back, or the right branding that will secure a flourishing future. In desperation, we could so easily reach for a new Messiah or dress up a new Elijah or one of the prophets, but with better computer graphics.

Working for God's new thing

This is where the more contemplative side of John the Baptist is helpful to us now. Remember, he was not always shouting 'Prepare!' He was not always making a scene. This Advent, he is saying 'no' to all the calls that are not his. He is praying, again and again, I am not the Messiah, in order to perform his true work on behalf of God's new thing.

So, this is the opposite of an altar call. What are you not called to be or do this year? How many times do you need to say 'no' in order to find with clarity and confidence the true 'yes' placed in you by God for which the Way of Jesus awaits?

Paul Williams

Hymn suggestions

On Jordan's bank; Restore, O Lord, the honour of thy name; Beauty for brokenness, hope for despair; Wait for the Lord (Taizé).

Third Sunday of Advent   17 December
Second Service   **Leap Like Calves**
Ps. 68.1–19 [*or* 68.1–8]; **Mal. 3.1–4; 4**; Phil. 4.4–7;
Gospel at Holy Communion: Matt. 14.1–12

A patch of colour

Imagine this reading from Malachi as a film. The camera pans back from a tall, ancient building, which dramatically fractures and falls, and then quickly we move to a different scene where fire rages through crops; we hear the distant sound of thundering as an army advances. The slash of a whip cuts through the air, fast. Darkness seeps in from every corner. Then the camera zooms in on a patch of colour, a sudden contrast, a scene of lively, unexpected energy, as into full view comes … a calf, a skipping, curious, joyful calf.

It's just so incongruous. What is a calf doing in the middle of this imaginary scene? Indeed, what is a calf doing in the middle of this reading?

It's a grim picture. Forget the build-up to Christmas happening out there, the anticipation of the lights being turned on, the Coca-Cola van driving across our screens, and every shop, every advert exhorting us to be ready. Forget all of that, and focus instead on this story, the story that prepares hearts and minds for the coming king, rather than the cuddly baby lying in a manger. This is about the warrior king, the mighty one, coming in glory and power and wonder. He is the one who is going to return and bring all things into order. In the midst of this a calf leaps from its stall.

The joy of the Lord

What is this calf that skips – or more than skips – into this picture of judgement, disaster and decay? The word translated as leaps is a word that encompasses all the strange frolicsome actions of calves released to pasture for the first time. You can watch a film of it happening on YouTube, and see the lively curiosity, the hilarious lamb-like hops, the skips and the runs and the jumps. As they are released, the calves come bucking and tumbling and running, looking silly.

The prophet Malachi says that those who revere the name of the Lord shall go out leaping like calves from the stall. Sometimes those who follow God seem silly in the face of disaster, whether communal or personal. Their actions, their words, seem laughable. In her book *The Hiding Place*, the Dutch Christian, Corrie Ten Boom, tells of how her sister Bessie prayed for those who persecuted her in the horrors of a concentration camp – and gave thanks for the fleas.[13] But those who revere the Lord will leap like calves: joy was her strength and those fleas kept the worst of the persecutors outside the door. Sheila Cassidy, a British doctor, was tortured in Chile during the terrible Pinochet years and wrote of courage and kindness that seemed laughable in the face of all that was happening.[14] In the midst of disaster, the focus shifts and those who revere the Lord somehow find the courage to hold firm.

Love, joy and death

People also seem a bit silly as they wait for their own death. In a discussion about death, composers, writers and others talked of the beauty of music, the riches of poetry and the language of love, which, in the face of death, inspire and strengthen. They recalled that although love may have fewer words, when we come to the end it is love that matters most. Love often looks silly, yet in the face of the unspeakable, it enables us to leap like calves.

For human love is the echo of the great love of God, the love which Malachi is referencing. For although God is a God who is going to cleanse and restore the earth, God is also the God who loves his creation. And for those who revere his name, the sun of righteousness will arise with healing in its wings. It is because of that promise that we have the courage to leap like calves from the stall, leaping in spirit with joyful confidence, ready to explore all that God has for us.

Sandra Millar

Hymn suggestions

I cannot tell how he whom angels worship; Purify my heart; Restore, O Lord, the honour of your name; Judge eternal, throned in splendour.

Fourth Sunday of Advent 24 December
Principal Service **God's Coming Home**
2 Sam. 7.1–11, 16; *Canticle*: Magnificat, *or* Ps. 89.1–4, 19–26
[*or* 89.1–8]; Rom. 16.25–end; **Luke 1.26–38**

Teetering on the brink of Christmas. We're nearly there, just one more sleep to go. I wonder if you have family coming home – or whether you are going home to your family sometime during this season. Tonight, in the small hours, Jesus will be born. God is coming home, to dwell with us, and we will celebrate God's home-coming tomorrow.

In our Bible readings today we trace how God chooses to make a home with and in creation. With David and Mary, God chooses to make a home, in God's time and on God's terms.

A home for YHWH

The people of Israel had become settled and at home in the land, and under David's leadership were becoming a great nation. They were no longer nomadic and were winning the skirmishes against the local tribes. David feels settled too and begins to feel guilty that, though he lives in a solid wooden house, the ark of God is still in a tent. It's time to make God a splendid temple where he can be worshipped and where the other tribes around can see just how great a God is YHWH.

But God is having none of it and tells the prophet Nathan to remind David that the God of the Israelites has always lived in a tent – has always been on the move from the time when the people were brought up out of Egypt to the present day. At no point has God ever asked to be 'housed'. God will not be pinned down or confined by David. God declares that it isn't David's job to make God a house. Rather, it's God's decision to make David a house – not a wooden one, but a great dynasty, the House of David, a motif that will be a rallying cry for generations to come. It will carry hope for the people in exile; it will be a sign and symbol for the coming of God's Messiah, God's special chosen one. God says to David, 'Your house and your kingdom shall be made sure for ever before me, your throne shall be established for ever' (2 Sam. 7.16).

Mary the home

Hundreds of years later, another person was plucked from obscurity: Mary, a young girl living in Nazareth, engaged to a skilled and honest carpenter. She has an encounter with the Archangel Gabriel which changes her life for ever. God chooses Mary to be God's house and home, the place where God the Word will become incarnate, will be made flesh, will be Emmanuel, God with us. Mary will bear Jesus and will grow and nurture him in her body. God chooses this time to be confined and pinned down – not in wood and stone, but within humanity.

Mary is not chosen for anything she's done, she doesn't earn the right to be the mother of Jesus – it is God's decision, which she agrees to after some considered thought. It's hard to comprehend that the impossible will happen – she has to let go of doubt and confusion and submit to God at work in her life. Gabriel reminds her, 'Nothing will be impossible with God.' God is coming home.

Where God dwells

Tomorrow we'll celebrate the birth of Jesus, the Messiah, born into the house and lineage of David, in the city of David, Bethlehem, which means 'the house of bread', and Jesus of course will be the bread of life. Can you hear all these echoes coming together down through the centuries? It always makes me tingle, the way the threads come together.

The analogy goes further. We, the church, are the body of Christ and the temple of the Holy Spirit: the place where God dwells. The church, like Mary, is called to bring Jesus into the world – to birth Christ for those around us, for the communities we serve. God has a plan for us as the body of Christ, and as the plan unfolds we may be perturbed, scared, and feel inadequate at what we are called to do. God's plans are often beyond the expectations of our abilities. Humbly we place ourselves into God's hands and believe that through our obedience God's will for the world will be realized. God will be at home with us.

God's homecoming

Christmas reminds us that God chooses to dwell within humanity. God chooses to be at home with us. God chooses to work through humanity, however inadequate, and this should make our whole lives resound with echoes of God. People should see within us something different, something whole and special and true because God has come home to us.

Remember this Christmas that you are the house in which God chooses to dwell. God chooses to be at home with you and in you, not because of anything you have done, not because you've worked hard, not because you are wealthy or famous, but solely because God loves you and chooses to be born within you. Your task is to grow and nurture God within you, bringing Christ forth for the world.

As you teeter on the brink of Christmas today and as you prepare your home for the celebrations starting tomorrow, give thanks that the Lord chooses to dwell in you just as God chose to dwell with and in David and Mary. Allow God's homecoming to change, shape and transform you, your family and your home this Christmas.

Catherine Williams

Hymn suggestions

For Mary, mother of our Lord; Come, thou long-expected Jesus; Let us build a house; Born in the night, Mary's child.

Fourth Sunday of Advent 24 December
Second Service **A Presence that Will Fill the Earth**
Ps. 85; **Zech. 2**; Rev. 1.1–8

Villages without walls

Villages without walls; the glory of God filling the earth. This is the hope ventured in this passage. The bias of Scripture seems to be against the finality of walls. God's people have never been called to protectionism. Yes, God established a community as they filled the earth and promised to be their God. Yes, God protected Israel, but provision was always made for those beyond the walls, beyond the territory. You see, we cannot keep the presence of God to ourselves. We are called to be lights in the world. What a wonderful thing to be called to on the night before we celebrate the light who came into the world.

The prophet Zechariah presents to us a man with a measuring line, working out the dimensions of Jerusalem. A fairly logical thing for someone to do when returning to their home and finding it in tatters. Most of us can't begin to imagine what a return like this feels like. But God has plans for these people that will not be thwarted either by exile or by the desolation of the land. Did the land matter? Of course. God promised it in covenant faithfulness. Do people need a land to make their home? Yes, definitely. Geographical displacement is a burden borne by far too many. But God wants this particular land to grow, to cover, in fact, the whole earth.

Zechariah was speaking both to the people who had started to leave Babylon and return home and to those who remained in the North. But would God go with them? Would they know God's presence? Into these questions, Zechariah speaks of a great hope for the people. And not just for God's people, but for all people. The vision is of a multitude: 'Many nations shall join themselves to the LORD on that day, and shall be my people; and I will dwell in your midst.' Among this mass of people, God's presence was coming.

The presence of God

There is one wall spoken of in the passage. God promises to be a wall of fire around the people. It is a wall of protection, but also of mercy, invitation and justice. Why is it each of these things? Because fire is associated with the very presence of God. We know, of course, what the presence of God looks like. When Christ came, people gathered around him as though he was the presence of God – we see this at his birth and for the rest of his life. And what did they find? Protection, mercy, invitation and justice. Christ is the presence of God. He is the flaming wall. In gathering to Christ, we gather in the presence of God.

Each Pentecost, everyone came together, from different tribes, tongues, cultures and places of origin. At the Pentecost spoken of in the book of Acts, the Spirit of God – the glory of God, the presence of God – came in power. Really, this passage from Zechariah sees no greater climax than at this later Pentecost. There was even fire, not as a wall around but resting upon people. This wasn't a fire to divide but a fire that would fill people from all over the earth, who would then in turn fill the earth. The Spirit is still doing this filling in our midst today.

No more walls

There will be a time when all people will know the presence of God. The Bible talks about a heavenly Jerusalem coming from above in which all will dwell in the presence of God. There will be no walls in this heavenly Jerusalem, so let's not make them now. Let's not put up walls around the church that keep people out, or even that keep people in. As we wake up among the familiar closeness of our Christmas activities, let's be careful not to raise up walls between ourselves and others. Instead, let's embody the protection, mercy, invitation and justice of God.

We should do all that we can to tear down walls. What can we do to tear down walls between people? What can we do to counter-act injustice? How can we bring reconciliation, peace and hope to those at enmity with each other? How can we break down divisions of race, socio-economic status and religion? How can we receive from others and give to others as though walls are not final? As we ask these questions, we invite the presence of God among us; we invite the infant in the manger. As we work for these things, we acknowledge that we are building towards a future that is imperish-able and will last for ever.

Spirit of God, come and fill the earth.

Mark Amos

Hymn suggestions

Light of the world; O come, divine Messiah; Over all the earth; O come, O come, Emmanuel.

Christmas and Epiphany

Christmas Day   25 December
Set I   **Thank You**
Isa. 9.2–7; Ps. 96; **Titus 2.11–14; Luke 2.1–14 [15–20]**

A Christmas dilemma

A few weeks before Christmas, a newly ordained Christian minister was struggling to write a sermon for the Christmas morning service. The problem, it seems, was that she felt the Christmas story was already so well known. After reading the story from Scripture and singing carols that echoed the text, surely there was no need to repeat the story yet again in a sermon. So, what should she do?

In some ways, I suppose she was not alone in her quandary. Many people do know the story and perhaps, generally, some of the themes of the Christian faith that arise from the story. For instance, we might reflect on the obedience of Mary and Joseph or the birth of the saviour among the poor. We could focus on the longing of the shepherds for the coming of the Messiah or their surprise to hear the angels' songs. Or, we might think about how they left their flocks to go to Bethlehem when they were told of the birth of the long-awaited saviour. Or, perhaps, just reflect on the angelic 'glad tidings' for the world.

The gift of grace

In one memorable reflection on Christmas, the German writer and theologian Helmut Thielicke spoke of Christmas as a time when we can remember that God comes to us all 'in the depths'. To illustrate this point, he described a photograph that he kept in his study of a group of prisoners who were taking part in a nativity play. In the picture, some of the prisoners were dressed in white robes as 'angels' and holding candles, they offered light to another group of prisoners dressed as very frightened 'shepherds'. Thielicke explained that one young man was in prison because he had killed his friend in a fight over a wristwatch. Year after year he played the same part in the nativity play. Kneeling before the manger, he would say: 'I lay in fetters groaning; You came to set me free.'[15]

Reflecting on that scene, we are reminded that the heart of the Christmas message is, 'The grace of God has appeared, bringing salvation to all.' No one is beyond the grace and love of God. All may discover the forgiveness, freedom and peace even 'in the depths' when we meet the saviour. Thinking of such love and grace beyond measure, perhaps today our best response is simply to say to God, 'Thank you'.

Saying thank you

Thank you for coming as a baby – born as one of us.

Thank you for the stories we have in Scripture that remind us that we may all know your love and experience new life in Christ.

Thank you for your presence, not just in worship, but day by day in all of life.

Thank you for being with us in joy and in sorrow.

Thank you for standing by us in disappointment.

Thank you for rejoicing with us – for sharing with us moments of laughter and fun.

Thank you for making yourself known through friends and family, and within the church family.

Thank you for the smiles of children, the care of friends, and the kindness of strangers.

Thank you for forgiveness when things have gone wrong – when we have made bad choices, or even deliberately gone our own way.

Thank you for coming to us even when we have turned away.

Thank you for not giving up on us.

Thank you for your gift of peace – the deep lasting peace of your presence – when the whole of life seems to be spinning out of control.

Thank you for grace upon grace, light in our darkness, and comfort in our sorrow or fear.

Thank you, God, for being there when we thought we could not go on.

As we think of the birth of Jesus in Bethlehem so long ago, I imagine that each of us could make a long list of things for which we are thankful to God. For the story is a reminder that we do not worship a God who stands afar off, but one who stooped to be born among people. He suffered and died on the cross and rose again, and even now comes to us and shares in all of life with us. Indeed, 'the grace of God has appeared, bringing salvation to all'.

So, with angels and archangels and all the company of heaven, at this holy festive season, we offer to God our thanks and praise. To God be all praise and honour and glory and thanksgiving, now and always.

Karen E. Smith

Hymn suggestions

Where do Christmas songs begin?; Shepherds watch and wise men wonder (Iona); O little town of Bethlehem; Once in royal David's city.

Christmas Day   25 December
Set II   **God With Us**
Isa. 62.6–end; Ps. 97; Titus 3.4–7; **Luke 2.[1–7] 8–20**

You may have received many beautiful Christmas cards by now. Many of our cards depict an idyllic picture of the holy family, radiant faces, domestic bliss and angelic harmony. The reality was very different and rather a surprise. Certainly, a surprise to the people waiting for a Messiah, a king in royal robes, who would sweep away the Romans and all signs of oppression, through an uprising or revolution. Christmas is full of surprises: surprise gifts, cards, guests, but the greatest of these is the birth of the Son of God into humble circumstances, visited first by the social outcasts, the filthy shepherds. The birth of Jesus into this broken, fractured, hurting world is God's gift for all humanity, that the Son of God will dwell with his people. This is the surprise we will unwrap together this Christmas.

The surprise of the stable

The reality of the birthplace of Jesus Christ, the saviour of the world, was very different to the perfectly choreographed crib scenes of our Christmas cards. The place where Jesus was born was probably a damp cave, a place where animals were kept. The smells would have been intolerable – rotting hay, animal excrement, rancid air. The Christ-child was laid in a manger, an animal feeding trough, on a bed of prickly straw.

Now, this is surprising; surely God could have chosen anywhere on the planet for his son to be born. No one would have expected a king to be born in a smelly, unhygienic stable. When the magi came to look for Jesus, they knew they were looking for a king, so they headed straight for Herod's palace, only to be told that the new king had not been born there. Kings are surely born in palaces. God chose to act in a totally surprising way; Jesus was born in poverty, which shows that he has come to earth for every single human being, the homeless, the displaced, the refugee, the unloved, the damaged, the rich and the powerful. You and me. All of us.

The surprise first visitors

The first people invited by heavenly emissaries to the stable reiterate this message of hope for every single human being, whatever their circumstances. Shepherds were socially despised and looked down upon by the religious leaders; they were seen as unclean and even as crooks; their lifestyle of watching their sheep day and night, and living outside, made them smelly and socially excluded. They were seen as unfit for Temple worship as their lifestyle prevented them from ceremonial and purification laws. Yet it was to shepherds that God sent a choir of angels to invite them to visit the saviour born in David's city.

This reiterates that Jesus is for everybody, whoever we are, whatever we think of ourselves, even if we think we are not good enough; there is a message of 'good news', of joy, of new beginnings. Jesus is the saviour of the world, and our church communities are for everyone. Like the shepherds who rose and responded to the angel's invitation, we too are invited to meet with Jesus the saviour. God accepts us as we are. The Christmas message is that nobody is excluded from the open arms of God.

The surprising new kingdom

We observe the birth of Jesus in a dirty stable; his first visitors were among the most despised in Jewish society. A new upside-down kingdom is being heralded in, a kingdom where all are welcome, where there are no social barriers, no racism, no discrimination. Through encountering Jesus, we are totally transformed. St Paul's letter to Titus, read today, sums up the grace of God beautifully: 'But when the goodness and loving-kindness of God our Saviour appeared, he saved us, not because of any works of righteousness that we had done, but according to his mercy' (Titus 3.4–5).

In his love and mercy, God is reaching out to a hurting, suffering world. Jesus is God's gift to each one of us; this is what St Paul calls God's grace, a gift of new life, a life to set us free from the pains, the guilts, the sufferings, the hurts that haunt us. This is the most wonderful surprise to celebrate at Christmas.

The Christ-child is a gift we can each receive, a gift freely offered, a gift we have to be willing to unwrap. This Christmas we offer gifts to one another, as acts of love. As we unwrap our gifts, the surprises waiting for us, let us think on the gift of God for each one of us, this helpless baby, the Christ who came into this world to reveal to us God's purposes, mercy and hope. '"Look, the virgin shall conceive and bear a son, and they shall name him Emmanuel", which means "God with us"' (Matt. 1.23).

Arani Sen

Hymn suggestions

While shepherds watched; It came upon a midnight clear; Come, thou long expected Jesus; Hark, the herald angels sing.

Christmas Day   25 December
Set III   The Voice of the Word
Isa. 52.7–10; Ps. 98; Heb. 1.1–4 [5–12]; **John 1.1–14**

In the beginning ...

In the beginning, before there was light and darkness, day and night; before there was sky and earth and sea; before there was vegetation: plants yielding seed, and fruit trees of every kind; in the beginning, before there was sun, moon and stars, before there were sea creatures and birds of the air; before there were living creatures of every kind: cattle and creeping things and wild animals; in the beginning, before there was humankind, was the Word.

In the beginning, before there were lungs and larynxes, lips and tongues to speak, before there were ears to hear and brains to interpret; before vowels and consonants; before adjectives, nouns and verbs; before clauses and conjunctions, in the beginning, before there were words, was the Word.

In the beginning, was the Word, and the Word was with God, and the Word was God.

In the beginning, God had no body, no brain, no lips, no larynx. When God spoke, it was not by the vibrating of vocal folds, causing vibrations in the air, reaching eardrums, being interpreted through a common language – none of which had yet come into being. No. The Word was not that kind of word.

The Word was spoken

The Word was God, and when God's Word was spoken it burst out with an explosion of creative force whose echoes still reverberate across the universe. When God spoke, it was not with a word, but with the Word. And when that Word burst forth from God, suddenly there was something that was not God, as all of creation came to life. Light and darkness, day and night; sky and earth and sea; vegetation, sun, moon and stars, creatures of the waters and the air, living creatures of every kind, and us, humankind. We were all brought into being by the Word that was spoken.

And now there were bodies and brains, mouths and ears, words and language. But the Word was still not that kind of word. God still had no lips, no larynx, no lungs. The Word was in the world, and the world came into being through him; yet the world did not know him. Although God had spoken, human ears did not all hear, did not recognize God's voice in the language of creation.

The Word spoke

Until that dark and wondrous night when a girl and a man took shelter in a stable. The girl in whom the Word had been growing, bones and blood and flesh, slowly, secretly, until the time came for him to be birthed. And the Word had lungs and breathed his first breath, and the Word had a voice, and for the first time lifted his voice ... and cried.

The Word voiced bewilderment, or exhaustion. Pain or hunger. The need for comfort, for love. The Word voiced a sound heard every night in every nation – from refugee camps to private hospitals, in city slums and wealthy suburbs and the remotest outposts of human civilization. A sound that unites all of humanity.

The Word voiced a sound that signals a new life beginning, whether it is wanted or not. And, whether we like it or not, it is a sound that gets inside us. It may cause us to feel joy or grief, nostalgia or regret, anxiety or relief, yearning or indifference.

The Word speaks

However it provokes us, moves us, stirs us, whether we want it or not, God speaks to us. God speaks to us with our own voice, in our own language. God cries for the bewildered and the exhausted, for the suffering and the hungry, for the comfortless and the unloved. God cries for the refugees and the rich, the scared and the overwhelmed, the poor, the comfortable and those on the very edges. God cries for the humanity that God now shares with us – God became one with what was not God.

Through this birth, this child, God gives us power to become children of God, born not of blood or of the will of the flesh or of the will of man, but of God. And with this child, the Christ-child, who stirs our hearts so strangely, we are called to lift our voices too, to cry out with him, to know that we are inextricably united, that we are related through our shared humanity. That first cry was you, was me, was those who did not, could not, cry, was every human life lived.

The Word has another beginning as he is brought to birth on that holy night, to speak with our voice, to share our cries, whether we want him or not. But if we listen, we will hear him, speaking with our voice, with the voice of the bewildered and the exhausted, the suffering and the hungry, the comfortless and the unloved, the voice of the refugee and the rich, the scared and the overwhelmed, the poor, the comfortable and those on the very edges. We will hear the voice of the Word made flesh who lives among us.

Kat Campion-Spall

Hymn suggestions

Before the world began; O come, all ye faithful; Of the Father's heart begotten; See, amid the winter's snow.

Christmas Day   25 December
Second Service   **An Icon of Christmas**
Morning Ps. 110, 117; Evening Ps. 8; Isa. 65.17–25; **Phil. 2.5–11**,
or Luke 2.1–20 (*if it has not been used at the Principal Service of the day*)

We're probably familiar with icons of the nativity from the Eastern Churches. Often, they contain a bewildering variety of scenes: angels and animals, shepherds approaching the crib, the magi on their journey, women attending to the birth, Gabriel with the Virgin Mary, Joseph meditating, even the tempter disguised as a shepherd, all set in a harsh rocky landscape. Right in the centre of all this activity the infant Christ is lying in his crib, wrapped in a cloth that is startlingly white against the dark background.

The rustic characters, the lack of perspective, the kaleidoscope of biblical episodes all crowded together haphazardly in one image: written (for you *write* an icon, you don't paint it) perhaps by someone with few pretensions to great artistry, yet with complete conviction and fervour. It is, simply, an act of devotion to the Christ-child – as every icon in the Orthodox Churches is an act of love, blessed by the prayers of its writer and of the faithful. You do not *look at* an icon. You are drawn *into* it, as through a window on to heaven; you are led along the way of knowing and loving and praising God.

These different stories – compressed into a single image – can feel busy and disorientating. Until your eye travels to the heart of the icon and to that diminutive figure, so white, so compelling, so still, the centre that holds it together and tells us that it all has a focus. And we begin to understand.

There are two pictures of Christmas here. At one level, all this activity stands for the world in its limitless diversity. The star speaks of the universe, the landscape: our world. Into this flow and flux, Christ comes: powerless, innocent, small. He is the axis around which the vast energies of the cosmos surge, the fulcrum where the huge forces and counter-forces of creation are in balance. He is the pole star towards which the world is orientated and its hopes and longings directed. He is the true bearing by which all positions are triangulated, all inclinations and directions defined and corrected. He is the centre of gravity towards which all things ultimately fall to their rest, the point of focus where rays of light converge. He is the source and destiny of creation and cosmos, nature and nations, our planet and its peoples. He is little, yet he bears the weight of the universe; weak, yet he walks among the galaxies; helpless, yet he holds the forces of the universe. For he is the Word incarnate who was in the beginning, and through whom all things were made. The centre holds!

At another level, the icon stands for something on a more human scale. For in the birth of Jesus, God not only inhabits the vast spaces of the universe but comes to us as a presence that is both intimate and personal. The icon tells many stories all at once in a way that when we first look at it seems confused. Yet there's a point of connection: the child at the heart of this crowded image, the still, small point of rest. Here is where all those stories converge. In the incarnation, our own stories with their dignity and bathos, their tragedies and triumphs, their longings and fears and hopes, are taken up into his and given ultimate value and worth, for God has deemed it worthwhile to come among us. Graham Greene says in *The Power and the Glory* that God is 'all loves and relationships combined in an immense and yet personal passion'.[16] Christmas proclaims that at the heart of all life lies the mystery of God, and it is towards this mystery that our whole beings should be bent, like the magi and shepherds drawn to the manger and to the infant who is our life and source and end.

For the icon writer, faith was probably untroubled by questions and doubt. For us, things are more elusive in a complex world of shifting values where Christianity has to compete in a postmodern marketplace of ideologies and beliefs. Yet Christmas beckons us with an invitation to a new simplicity, a new humility, a new love. For in the precariousness and vulnerability of the crib we see everlasting love and power emptied and robed in the swaddling cloths that betoken the form of a servant in St Paul's great hymn in Philippians. It is foolishness, yet wiser than any human wisdom. It is weakness, but stronger than any human strength, this 'God contracted to a span, incomprehensibly made man'.[17] For in our well-loved Christmas images, we see nothing less than the glory of the only-begotten Son incarnate among us amid the beauty and pain of the world, and in every human heart.

> ... Christ plays in ten thousand places,
> Lovely in limbs, and lovely in eyes not his
> To the Father through the features of men's faces.[18]

Michael Sadgrove

Angels from the realms of glory; The Son of God his glory hides; Thou who wast rich beyond all splendour; Love came down at Christmas.

First Sunday of Christmas 31 December
Principal Service **Circumstance and Mud**
Isa. 61.10—62.3; Ps. 148 [*or* 148.7–end]; **Gal. 4.4–7**;
Luke 2.15–21

One human thing

What do you and I have in common with every other human being? And what do we have in common with Jesus? Paul emphasizes it in our reading from Galatians. Luke has already told us of it, and in today's reading reminds us of it. 'God sent his Son,' Paul tells us 'born of a woman.' This birth, like every other birth, was messy and painful. None of the Gospel writers tells us who cleaned up afterwards. Nobody mentions that first cry as Jesus entered the world and took his first breath. Did Mary or Joseph check Jesus' body for some physical sign that he would be special? We have no idea. But one thing we do know, one thing that is central to Paul's gospel is that Jesus was born of a woman – he was human, with all that that entails.

Tidings of …

Half a millennium ago, town watchmen sang to the gentry at Christmas time 'God rest ye merry gentlemen'. In return for their 'tidings of comfort and joy', they received the equivalent of a Christmas bonus. Five hundred years on, Christmas is still a season of goodwill – to those we like; of comfort – apart from for those we ignore; of joy – unless you have lost someone this year, or you are in pain, or you simply can't afford the stereotypical Christmas. I heard the story of a nativity play put on by a small church. The church didn't have many children, so one child played all three magi. The child walked on to the stage at the right moment, turned to the baby Jesus and his parents and said, 'Behold, I bring you gold, circumstance and mud.'

I wonder whether that is closer to the truth than the sanitized versions of Christmas that surround us. I don't mean that surrounds us in the shops and on TV; I mean the sanitized Christmas that we have here in church. The baby Jesus who 'makes no crying'. The new mother, still sore and emotional as all new mothers are, who manages to give birth silently. The calm-looking mother with a new baby still learning to feed who welcomes strangers into her … well, wherever she has given birth, with equanimity. That first Christmas, I suggest, was far more like circumstance and mud than a silent holy night.

Circumstance and mud

Circumstance and mud are an essential part of the Christian gospel because they are an essential part of being human. Birth and life are both messy. Circumstances happen. When Prime Minister Harold Macmillan was asked what his greatest challenge was, he apparently replied 'events'. Events happen, and circumstances are where we are. Perhaps we too often ask God to intervene in events and forget that Jesus is with us in circumstance.

Arsène Wenger, one-time manager of Arsenal Football Club, said, 'Christmas is important, but Easter is decisive.' A Twitter follower replied, 'Don't forget the destiny of the Christmas baby.' That kind of thinking sanitizes Christmas too. Jesus was born not only to die but also to be part of human circumstance and mud – to be one of us. God did not enter the world *disguised* in flesh; God *became* flesh. God did not become flesh so we can get out of the world, God became flesh so God could enter into it. Jesus is God in circumstance and mud.

Christmas is revolutionary. Christmas changes the world.

God in flesh, hope for the world

Christmas offers hope that other elements of Jesus' story do not. It refreshes the parts others cannot reach, in the words of what used to be a well-known advertisement. Jesus' life shows us how to live, Jesus' friends tell us about who we might be, Jesus' death shows us the suffering of the world, and Jesus' resurrection shows us that death is defeated. But Jesus' birth shows us that Jesus is one of us, knows our human experiences and feels our human joys and pains. Christmas tells us that Jesus not only knows what it's like to be marginalized, ignored or oppressed, but he also knows why those of us who are not, allow it to happen. Jesus understands what it is to be human because Jesus was born of a woman. That's why it matters that after all the glory of the angels singing on a hillside, Luke tells us the shepherds went and found a child.

The Christmas hope for the world is the humanity of Jesus. The presence of Jesus in circumstance and mud.

Liz Shercliff

Hymn suggestions

Hark, the herald angels sing; Joy to the world; A world awakes; As the old year passes.

First Sunday of Christmas   31 December
Second Service   **At the Turn of the Year**
Ps. 132; **Isa. 35**; Col. 1.9–20, *or* Luke 2.41–end

'Say to those who are of a fearful heart, "Be strong, do not fear! Here is your God. He will come with vengeance, with terrible recompense. He will come and save you."' (Isa. 35.4).

The prophet might have been speaking to us on this last day of the year as we take down our old calendars and replace them with new ones.

We look back on the past year and ask ourselves (if we are wise) what has been really significant for us and for the world during these 12 months. And even more, we should love to know what is to happen in the future, what the new year will bring to us by way of opportunity and threat. We wouldn't be human if we didn't have foreboding about the risks and dangers facing our world as it continues to face a climate emergency, not to mention war and conflict, and the scale of human poverty and need that is always with us. The prophet's fierce language speaks of vengeance and recompense. What awful consequences of our human sowing will the year's harvest yield?

The world of the prophet's time was just as threatening. He was writing to exiles who had lost hope of ever seeing their homeland again. They were trying to keep themselves alive against what they saw as threatening, destructive forces that were partly outside them-selves and partly within. How to be faithful to God and his covenant in this corrupting environment, how to 'sing the LORD's song in a foreign land'? Those were the issues. And when the prophet spoke to them, they were on the point of giving up for good.

When he spoke to them ... or rather, perhaps, when he sang to them. For this prophet, whose writings are bound up in the Bible with the words of the great Isaiah who lived more than a century before him, is the Old Testament's great bringer of hope to the hopeless, the forlorn and the forgotten. His message is simple. God is about to do a new and wonderful thing: to act as in the days of old when the Hebrews were delivered out of their slavery and led on their long march towards the Promised Land. It will happen again, only more gloriously. Another journey is in prospect, this time from Babylon back to the land of Canaan where the exiles will rebuild their lives. 'A highway shall be there,' says the prophet, a holy way for the people to return home. And the desert shall rejoice because of it.

The despondent picture of fierce landscapes, the parched and arid wilderness, was embedded in the Hebrews' memory. There, they learned how to lament and cry for help. And in a metaphorical sense, it was no doubt true of their experience of exile too, so far from the solace of home and all that spoke of safety. But the stories of their desert journey also told how streams of water had broken through thirsty ground when Moses struck the rock with his staff. This is the memory the prophet builds on when he promises a future filled with promise. So glorious is it that the blind see and the deaf hear, the lame dance and those without speech find their voice. So complete is this transformation that it can only be spoken of as a manifestation of God's majesty: 'They shall see the glory of the LORD.'

As Christians, we see prefigured in all this the glory of the incarnate Son in whose words and works the ancient promises begin to find fulfilment. We are celebrating his coming in these days of Christmas. Whatever deserts we have had to endure in the past year, whatever exile we still find ourselves living in, whatever our winters of desolation and despair, Christmas has come round again to bring us joy. And with it the strength and resolve to face the coming months with hope in the one who – says the gospel – is our Emmanuel, the God who is with us to the end of the age.

The gods we make for ourselves will always let us down. They may bring hopes of a kind, but they are illusions, a false dawn. Only the living God can strip us of fantasy and give us back our hope. If, like me, you are sometimes tempted to wonder whether the world has a future, go back to Isaiah and his vision of the blossoming desert. Entrust our times to the God who bids us to be strong. For Christmas has brought our *Sol Invictus*, the Unconquered Sun who has come into the world to enlighten every human heart, take away our fear and give us a hope by which to live and die.

Michael Sadgrove

Hymn suggestions

O little town of Bethlehem; Awake, awake, fling off the night; Longing for light, we wait in darkness; Christ be the Lord of all our days.

Baptism of Christ (First Sunday of Epiphany)
7 January
(For Epiphany, see p. 284.)
(For Epiphany All Age, see p. 354.)
Principal Service   Enter Baptism
Gen. 1.1–5; Ps. 29; Acts 19.1–7; **Mark 1.4–11**

The New Year sales are all around us, and at such times it's very obvious that we live in a world dominated by logos. Designer clothes, expensive sportswear and must-have trainers all with their exclusive trademarks intend to make a statement about who we are. Adverts and social media saturate us with the importance of upgrading our image and sharpening our identity.

The image we project is important and in our culture in the West is often defined by the place we live, the car we drive, the clothes we wear, the sport we follow and the music we listen to. Today's feast – the Baptism of Christ – challenges all this posturing by reminding us loud and clear that our identity is as children of God and through baptism we enter into the body of Christ.

Enter John

For the Jewish people in the Older Testament, ceremonial washings in rivers and pools were commonplace. An expression of the desire to turn one's back on a murky past and make a fresh beginning with God. Baptism was John's way of strengthening the resolve of those who heard him preach and were anxious to reform their lives. The ceremonial washing in the Jordan marked a return to the Lord and a day to remember. Nevertheless, John was at pains to point out that the best was yet to come: 'I have baptized you with water; but he will baptize you with the Holy Spirit.'

Enter Jesus

The first glimpse we have of Jesus in Mark's Gospel is as 'one of the crowd' at the river Jordan. The 30 years up to that point were preparation for this moment. Living a private and obscure life in Nazareth, Jesus had been deepening his relationship with God. Baptism was a significant turning point in his life. It marked a change of direction: an end of his time of waiting and the start of his public ministry of service to God's people. This gesture emphasized Jesus' desire to be associated with his people and exercise a ministry in the midst of human brokenness. The baptism of Jesus marks God's new way of relating to humanity, through his son.

As the heavens opened and the Spirit descended on him, Jesus came to experience his true identity as God's beloved Son. Perhaps too he began to glimpse what a life of service and ministry might mean – becoming aware of the responsibilities ahead. At his crucifixion, Jesus would take on the full consequences of baptism.

Enter us

Celebrating the baptism of Jesus reminds us to reflect on our own baptism and what it means to us. I can remember my baptism: I was a teenager at the time. Most of us probably can't remember the moment when, as babies in our parents' arms, we were brought to the font to be baptized. Baptism is not a magic charm or merely a rite of passage, it is a sacrament; a means by which God acts within our world and touches our life with grace. That grace happens whether we can remember it or not. Heaven is opened to earth, and earth to heaven.

Our parents and godparents made public declarations about their faith on our behalf. That needs to be validated in our everyday lives by our personal decision. The reality is that we can often take our spiritual rebirth for granted and lead our lives with no reference to the gospel and the life we are called to live, made in God's image and carrying the identity of Christ within us.

Our once-and-for-all baptism began a lifelong process of sanctification, of being made holy. A pilgrimage that has its ups and downs, its wrong turnings and spiritual cul-de-sacs, but a process strengthened by many epiphanies of the Spirit, revelations of God that throughout our life build upon our baptism and enable us to live as children of God and members together of the body of Christ.

Enter the Holy Spirit

The Holy Spirit active in creation is the same Spirit who brings new creation in our baptism, transforming us and the world as we go about loving God, helping our neighbour, being compassionate, showing forgiveness and living the justice values of the kingdom. Through our baptism, we are invited to continue the mission of Jesus. Our calling is to be Christ-like, to journey with Jesus from Galilee to Jerusalem, to assume his values, his attitudes, and to adopt his manner when dealing with each other.

This is a day to give thanks to God for the people who have shared their faith with us, who have walked with us and brought us up to understand that we are precious in the eyes of God. At the same time, we have to ask ourselves if it is obvious from the kind of lives we lead and the type of people we are that we are baptized members of Christ's church in whom God's grace is working to re-create his word. Do our lives in Christ make a difference to those around us wherever we are?

The only logo we need, the logo that others will judge us by, is the one placed on our forehead at baptism, the sign of the cross, the symbol for the Logos – the Word made flesh, Jesus Christ our Lord.

Remember your baptism, give thanks for it, and make a New Year's resolution to grow more and more into the likeness of Christ this year.

Catherine Williams

Hymn suggestions

Lord, when you came to Jordan; When Jesus came to Jordan; Be thou my vision; I'm ready now (Wash over me).

Baptism of Christ (First Sunday of Epiphany)

7 January

Second Service   **But God …**

Ps. 46 [47]; Isa. 42.1–9; **Eph. 2.1–10**;

Gospel at Holy Communion: Matt. 3.13–end

I wonder how you feel about the world we live in? Watching the news does not really promote hope. Looking at events unfolding around us, locally and globally, it is easy to agree with thinker Hegel that the only thing human beings seem to learn from history is that they do not learn from history. Which isn't very cheerful, I have to admit! And if we look back a little further, at the stories recorded in Scripture, this has been the case from the beginning. It is exactly the kind of repetitive, fragile human story that the apostle Paul is considering in the chapter we read from the Letter to the Ephesians. In this chapter, Paul takes stock of human nature.

On the one hand, Paul makes a dim assessment of humanity left to its own devices. They are objects of wrath. But then he goes from the worst of the human condition to the height of hope in God and reminds us that, whatever mess we make, we are not left to deal with it alone.

There is a fascinating combination of the deepest pessimism and the shiniest hope in Paul's words, a vivid contrast between what human beings are by nature and what they can become by grace. It isn't an easy, carefree kind of hope; it isn't wishful thinking. It is hope that is borne out of everything that Paul knows and has experienced about God. It is a costly hope, which rests on what Jesus did on the cross, and on human beings choosing to let God change their lives in response, in ways that are rarely comfortable.

So, what are Paul's prescriptions for the world he lived in?

Being honest

Well, first, he prescribes honesty, about how bad things are, and how powerless we are to change them. Paul's prescription isn't about looking primarily at the world outside of ourselves – the world in the news, 'others' we can look on in judgement or con-demnation. Instead, Paul encourages his readers to look not so much at the darkness out there but at the darkness within. He prompts the Ephesians to look at themselves – and let themselves be seen by others. Not just think, how do I think I am doing, but what do those looking in on to ourselves, our families, our church, our working life see? It is only when we look at ourselves honestly that we can take the next step: taking responsibility.

Taking responsibility

He says, 'All of us once lived … [like this] and were by nature children of wrath.' This is strong language! Paul does not say that we are all the same, but that all of us contribute to the brokenness of the world around us, and that all of us must face our own vulnerabilities and failings. This is what we do when we say the words of the confession: together, we acknowledge our share in the state of the world, from our personal choices to being caught up in systems we have little power over. The enormity and complexity of the brokenness of humanity make the next step a logical one: letting go of the idea that we know better – better than our neighbour, better than God.

Letting go

Paul argues that we are so used to the way things are, that we simply cannot imagine what life could and should be like. We need outside help. We need God. We need one another. The only way to change is for our imagination of what is good, right, but also possible, to be transformed from the outside in.

But God …

Honesty and responsibility could easily be crushing were they not held within a much bigger picture. This is where two little words change everything: '*But God …*'

Time and again in Scripture, things seem dire, dark, hopeless even. And then God's presence bursts into the darkness.

Here, God interrupts the power of sin and brokenness with salvation. But God … has loved, has saved, and acted with grace and invited us into new life. God has opened the way in Christ: shown us how to live.

God has saved us. It is done, it is on offer. All we have to do is accept it. Though of course the notion of being saved is not always popular. Many of us would prefer to do the saving, to be Prince Charming rather than Snow White. But this isn't something we can do for ourselves. It is all about grace, and we can only accept it when we are honest with ourselves about our need for God.

Paul reels out word after word to talk of God's action: grace, love, mercy and kindness. Salvation is not primarily about blame and condemnation. It is about truth, love and new life. So, when we look at the headlines and feel the weight of brokenness, we can say, 'But God ...' God made the light to come in the darkness, and the darkness has not overcome it. Our part is simply, and amazingly, to respond to the call to let God transform our lives and communities – and join in, with truth and grace.

Isabelle Hamley

Hymn suggestions

Love divine, all loves excelling; My hope is built on nothing less; This is my prayer in the desert; There's a wideness in God's mercy.

Second Sunday of Epiphany   14 January
Principal Service   **Put on Your Specs and See**
1 Sam. 3.1–10 [11–20]; Ps. 139.1–5, 12–18 [*or* 139.1–9]; Rev. 5.1–10; **John 1.43–end**

During the season of Epiphany, I often find myself recalling a scene from an advert for a leading chain of opticians. My favourite, in the series of adverts, is when the shepherd accidentally shears the sheepdog instead of the sheep. Then comes the catchphrase, which has received the rare distinction of passing into everyday usage: 'Should have gone to Specsavers.' (There are many other opticians to choose from, of course.) Epiphany challenges us to discover what it means to see Jesus and to be seen by him as well, but with a deeper, different kind of seeing that is nothing to do with physical vision.

Jesus is the Christ

We are still in the first chapter of John's Gospel, and right from the first words we listened to a few weeks ago at Christmas, we have known who Jesus is. There is no doubt in John's telling of the story: Jesus is the Christ, the Word made flesh, the one who has come into the world. Already people are leaving everything to follow him. And already those who have met him are rushing off to find their friends, with the words, 'Come and see.' This is not simply an invitation to look at a view or notice an interesting scene. John is using the word 'see' in the way that we sometimes use it, to mean understanding. We might go further and suggest that this kind of seeing is experiential and requires us to get involved. It is so much more than just looking.

An immersive experience

Contemporary technology has begun to open up famous art in whole new ways. A couple of years ago I went to an immersive Van Gogh experience, which included virtual reality, and I wasn't just seeing the art, I was inhabiting it. I was able to notice the sky changing, the rain falling, the breeze moving the curtains. It was amazing. Come and see had turned into come and be in this experience. This is what Philip wants to convey to his friend Nathaniel, traditionally depicted as an old man seated under a fig tree. In this scene in John's Gospel the revelation, or epiphany, that comes to Nathaniel is that Jesus can see everything about him. This is the Christ who knows us intimately, the God of Psalm 139 who has been with us since we were formed in the womb and is acquainted with all our days. We have come a long way from admiring a baby in a manger. Now, in this short episode, we are being shown another way in which Jesus is so much more. Another aspect of God is revealed. The invitation is to go and be in the experience as we also decide to follow and discover more of the reality of Jesus.

Back to Advent, forward to Lent

Jesus hints to Nathaniel of all that is to come – and in tones that might fit with Advent as much as Epiphany, he suggests that Nathaniel will come to realize fully that Jesus is the Christ, the one in whom all things will be reconciled. Slowly it will become clear to all who follow Jesus that this is a different way of living from all that they had expected. This is a kingdom about people, relationships, love and belonging for all people. This will become the everyday reality of following Jesus, and discovering more about what it means to see him and to be seen by him. As the days and weeks go by, all of those who follow will discover that this is the way of the cross. It almost sounds as if we are getting ready for Lent, that season when we think about how often we fail to grasp the purpose of Christ, the fullness of who he is, and are reminded once again that we need to ask God to grant us clearer vision.

As those who have heard Jesus' call, we don't want to be like those adverts. Instead, we echo the great thirteenth-century prayer of St Richard and ask that we see more clearly and follow more nearly each day the one who knows us so very well. Epiphany is the season of revelation and the season of response. It is a time for us to pray that we might see more and more of the truth of Jesus. And it is time for us to respond to all that it means to be a follower of Christ, safe and confident in the knowledge that Jesus has already seen all that we are, and yet still calls us to be his friends, and loves us more than we can ever know.

Sandra Millar

Hymn suggestions

Will you come and follow me; Just as I am; May the mind of Christ my Saviour; Dear Lord and Father of mankind.

Second Sunday of Epiphany   14 January
Second Service   **Promise in the Wreckage**
Ps. 96; **Isa. 60.9–end**; Heb. 6.17—7.10;
Gospel at Holy Communion: Matt. 8.5–13

Haunted by destruction

Photography and film have incredible power. Indeed, their inventions fundamentally changed our relationship with reality. For they can vividly capture moments in time that painting, say, cannot match. In the two centuries since the invention of photography, there have been countless memorable images. Equally, there are others which haunt the human imagination: cities ravaged and destroyed, sometimes by a single bomb; lives and communities devastated by hate and greed and power; human beings and societies hollowed out and turned to ruins. I cannot be alone in being especially haunted by images of destruction drawn from that most terrible of centuries, the twentieth.

I am haunted by these images even as I can't, in my privilege, quite imagine what it must have been like to grow up in the aftermath of destruction. I sometimes wonder how on earth people had the hope to rebuild post-war Hiroshima or Berlin or even parts of bombed-out London. In the case of some cities and societies, the destruction was total. How did communities hold on to visions of hope? Of course, such tragedies are not restricted to the past. In our own time, countless people find themselves forced to make sense of what a future might look like in shattered communities in Syria, Ukraine and too many other places.

Hope in the ruins?

The words and images of the closing sections of Isaiah can seem very far away from such modern horrors. In the final part of Isaiah, God says, through the prophet,

> I will make you majestic for ever,
>   a joy from age to age.
> You shall suck the milk of nations,
>   you shall suck the breasts of kings;
> and you shall know that I, the LORD, am your Saviour
>   and your Redeemer, the Mighty One of Jacob.

Indeed, while the passage acknowledges the trials faced by the people of God, the words of Isaiah are almost torrential in the lavishness with which God's promises will be conferred on his people:

> the LORD will be your everlasting light,
>   and your God will be your glory.
> Your sun shall no more go down,
>   or your moon withdraw itself;
> for the LORD will be your everlasting light,
>   and your days of mourning shall be ended.

Despite the seeming distance between the context of Isaiah and our own world, it is worth reminding ourselves that for all the incredible promises we read here, they are written in the aftermath of disaster. They were written for a community that had returned to Judah from exile in Babylon. This is a community that has not only been transformed by captivity but one in which the Promised Land lies, effectively, in ruins. Those who had been left behind during the exile and those who had returned would have been strangers to one another. The human and social ruins generated by exile were, of course, not the ruins of total war; nor had any bomb gone off which had laid waste to Jerusalem or the communities of Judah.

Wreckage no more …

Nonetheless, the Temple of Solomon had been destroyed. In the exile, the people of God – the covenant people of the living God – had been humbled, with their leaders taken off in captivity. Perhaps it is not too much of a stretch to say that psychological heavy ordnance had gone off in the psyche of the Jewish people. In short, this is the chosen people of God living in the seeming wreck of the covenant. Into this wreckage God speaks:

> Whereas you have been forsaken and hated,
>   with no one passing through,
> I will make you majestic for ever,
>   a joy from age to age.

It would not have been unreasonable for those returning from exile and for those who greeted these returnees to have laughed at these words of God. The ancestors of those who had wept in Babylon would certainly have been stunned by the words of Isaiah.

If there are relatively few, in a society like Britain's, who know first-hand what it is to find themselves in a totally wrecked society, forced to build anew on the basis of a dream, most of us know what it is to live in the midst of wreckage: the wreckage of relationships, or the collapse of dreams, the loss of home and security and so on. In the face of the wreckage of our own lives and communities, it would be easy – tempting at least – to despair. Still, God invites us to live on his promises. We have centuries, millennia, of forebears who have gone before us and faced the utter wreckage of the world. Can we do less in such a time as this? God says,

> I will appoint Peace as your overseer
>   and Righteousness as your taskmaster.
> Violence shall no more be heard in your land,
>   devastation or destruction within your borders;
> you shall call your walls Salvation,
>   and your gates Praise.

In Christ, God offers it, yesterday, today and tomorrow.

Rachel Mann

Hymn suggestions

Glorious things of Thee are spoken; Lead, kindly light; As with gladness; Hear what God the Lord hath spoken.

Third Sunday of Epiphany 21 January
Principal Service **Transforming the Ordinary**
Gen. 14.17–20; Ps. 128; Rev. 19.6–10; **John 2.1–11**

Images and expectations

We all have images of God. Inner pictures shaped by experiences, often rooted deep in childhood. Is God the clockmaker who winds up creation and disappears to some distant heavenly realm? Is God a get-out-of-jail-free card to be cashed in post-mortem? Perhaps God is a fairy godmother, called on to fix things in rough moments? Such images will shape our expectations, which will shape what we see.

Our reading today points to a different picture. Jesus is the God inside human experience who comes to do something new: transforming the ordinary. Now perhaps you want to object. Perhaps, your instinct is to say, 'Yeah, right … water into wine. Nice if you can pull it off, but I've never seen that. I don't see the connection between that old story and the world today.' That's a fair objection and one I want to take seriously.

John's story – what jumps out?

Right from the outset, in this first sign in John's Gospel, Jesus is in the midst of human ordinariness – at a wedding, with his mum and some friends. There's a problem – the wine's run out. Embarrassing, but it happens. Mary knows Jesus can solve the problem and encourages the servants to do what he tells them. There seems to be a bit of relational tension between Mary and Jesus. There is nothing too out of the ordinary, yet.

Notice how Jesus takes the ordinary to bring about extraordinary transformation: the waiting staff at the wedding, water and jars. Given his power, he could have clicked his fingers and wine would have materialized – but that's not what he does. He transforms the ordinary, working with people, instructing the staff to fill the jars with water. The steward draws out liquid and finds it is fine wine, and there are gallons of the stuff. In the first of John's signs pointing to his glory, we see the ordinary transformed. This is reinforced again and again in his ministry. The feeding of the 5,000, in John 6, resonates with the Cana miracle – when Jesus uses the little lad's five barley loaves and two fish to feed a multitude. The transformation of the ordinary; he's at it again!

Expectation leading to perception

Now, back to the objection that the story in John doesn't seem to have much connection with our ordinary everyday. No. I've never seen water turned to wine, but then do I really need to experience this to grasp the relevance of the sign? Can we see God's transformative power at work in the ordinary today? If we can't see it maybe we are holding on to unhelpful images of a god far away, disinterested and uninvolved. Perhaps we are looking for the god of party tricks to keep us entertained. Maybe we are not expecting to find God at work at all in the mundane everyday.

There is something here about expectation leading to perception. Mary expected Jesus to do something extraordinary in the ordinary. After all, since the promise of his birth this has been her experience: her elderly cousin pregnant too; shepherds, angels, visitors from far away; the prophecy of Simeon in the Temple when Jesus was a baby; Anna's inspired teaching about him. Mary has been shaped as a seasoned spotter of the extraordinary eliding with the mundane. She expects it and so perceives it.

The ordinary transformed here and now

We too experience the ordinary transformed here and now:

- in the strange coincidences – the phone call at the right time; the unexpected encounter; encouragements coming from different sources at the same time; God is always working in the ordinary if we open our eyes to see.
- in unexpected provision – resources were depleted, and then there is enough after all. Someone leans in at the right time. Help arrives unexpectedly just at the moment of crisis.
- in the odd lightness of heart that skips in the unlooked-for – like the shaft of light bursting into the gloom. Hope coming unbidden, pushing back the darkness.
- in the new beginning when life seemed consumed with grief; the surprise of discovering what seemed a cul-de-sac turns out to be a through road.
- in the discovery that when we offer the little we have to God – be that in terms of time, effort, resource, even willingness – God transforms this and makes of us so much more than we could ever ask or imagine. Not a thimble full of blessing but gallons of it.
- watery faith suddenly has body and depth; a more robust character and complex shape.

Images and perceptions

The images we have of God will influence our expectations, which will influence what we see. If I think God is far away, disinterested and mostly grumpy, then I have no expectation of encountering God in the ordinary. But if I have schooled myself at Mary's feet, I will know that Jesus is the God in flesh, God with fingerprints, God in the midst of us: shoulder to shoulder, cheek by jowl, heart to heart. This is the God who transforms the ordinary.

Every. Single. Day.

Kate Bruce

Hymn suggestions

Be still, for the presence of the Lord; Let us build a house; Longing for food, many are hungry (Christ be our light); Open the eyes of my heart, Lord.

Third Sunday of Epiphany   21 January
Second Service   **Worship!**
Ps. 33 [*or* 33.1–12]; Jer. 3.21—4.2; Titus 2.1–8, 11–14;
Gospel at Holy Communion: Matt. 4.12–23

Why worship?

In some churches, a 'new song' means one written in the last couple of years. In others, it's anything more recent than Charles Wesley! The feel of this psalm is that a song is bubbling up on the lips of the author right in the moment. It's a joyful, skilful, musical sound, with many instruments and words of adoration.

The idea of a God who requires worship seems strange to those outside the church and sometimes those within. Should we be a worshipping community? What would that say about God? The first thing to get straight is that God doesn't need our worship. It adds nothing to God that God does not already have. In fact, God's love for us does not demand a return as such. It turns out, though, that this is all the more reason to worship. It turns out too that in giving God praise, we honour the gift already given most appropriately.

Our Psalmist knows something of who God is and what God has done. The tone is praise to a God of justice, a God who sets things right, and a God who shows mercy and love. The writer trusts this same God. Has God shown faithfulness to the author? Likely, yes. The hint is that God has been faithful through times of war and its consequences. War, of course, leaves no one untouched. It uproots, devastates and divides. It not only kills the spirit but kills real people in real time. But the Psalmist can recognize God's faithfulness even in such times. Has God shown faithfulness to us? Yes. God, we are reminded, has steadfastly loved us, in covenant, word and deed. Does the earth shake sometimes? It certainly does. Do people know extremes of pain and suffering? Often. We may be going through such times even today. So what faithfulness of God is this which gives birth to song, dance and instrumental delight, even in such demanding times?

God is faithful

Israel had known a covenant partner who had gone before them, surrounded them and acted as their advocate. Of course, they did not always recognize this God as being for and with them. Likewise, we don't always recognize that God is indeed for and with us, and thus many of us can find it hard to sing praise. But we probably believe, too, that God is faithful. We have known God's justice in this, that the Creator of all that is, from all eternity, willed to become human in Christ Jesus. We know that justice has a centre and that righteousness has a face. We know that love became incarnate in complete identification with a people. And we know, too, that this saviour, of which our Psalmist had perhaps only captured a glimpse, will set the world right in compassion, justice and righteousness.

There is much reason to praise. The psalm gives us some reasons: we have been delivered; we have received God's steadfast love. This same love was breathed out into the world at creation, breathed out through the mouth of Jesus in word and deed, breathed out by the Holy Spirit on all flesh. This love demands nothing in return. It is gratuitous, gracious and without lack. Indeed, nothing can separate us from this love that we have seen in flesh and bone through Christ Jesus.

What kind of worship?

We can be those who, like this Jesus, walk faithfully alongside each other. We too can give ourselves to each other in steadfast love: in word, deed and fellowship. God's covenant love will not break if we don't do this, but worship will inevitably take this shape in our lives when we catch what God is about. Let's recognize and reflect outwards the God who has poured out love on us and given us a future, a hope and a mission in this world.

Can we raise a shout of praise to this God who loves us beyond any other love? Can I hear an 'Amen' in the place? You'd better believe it! We are a people richly blessed by God. We will face adversity, we will face trauma, just as we will experience joy and fullness of life. Through it all, we have a God who faithfully walks alongside us, who is our advocate, who indeed is worthy of our praise. Call to that same God now. Let the 'breath of his mouth' give you life again. Allow this same God to raise up in you a song of praise, recalling the covenant faithfulness that took flesh in Jesus Christ and which stretches throughout the earth.

Amen, and hallelujah to our faithful God.

Mark Amos

Hymn suggestions

Great is thy faithfulness; Praise, my soul, the King of heaven; Here is love vast as the ocean; Blessed be your name.

Fourth Sunday of Epiphany   28 January
(For Candlemas, see p. 291.)
Principal Service   **One with Authority**
Deut. 18.15–20; Ps. 111; Rev. 12.1–5a; **Mark 1.21–28**

I wonder which of your teachers had the most impact on you. Which teacher do you remember most clearly? And why? Did they have a particular teaching style that worked for you? Were they very strict, or very lenient? What was it about them that impacted you so strongly that you remember them all these years later?

Amazing teaching

Mark's Gospel frequently tells us that Jesus was teaching and that the people were amazed at his teaching and said that he spoke 'as one with authority', and yet Mark tells us very little of what Jesus actually said. There may be a clue in this passage though. The people are amazed at his teaching, then he sets a man free from the grip of evil, and the people are even more amazed 'at his teaching'. We are seeing enacted teaching; embodied teaching. What Jesus does is a direct outworking of who he is and what he's been saying, and when the people see it happening in practice, they recognize it as more than mere words but as teaching 'with authority'.

With integrity

First, the people are astounded because Jesus 'taught them as one having authority'. This suggests that Jesus' style of teaching seemed more authoritative than that which the people were used to. The most common style of the rabbis in Jesus' day was to teach by continual reference back to earlier authorities. In other words, authority was 'derived'. In much the same way that we might back up our argument by saying, 'As St Thomas Aquinas said ...' or 'As Evelyn Underhill wrote ...' Rabbis would teach by assembling and presenting the teachings of authoritative teachers who had gone before them.

However, the impression we gain from the Gospels is that Jesus didn't usually do that. Instead, he taught as though the truth of what he said was self-evident. He taught 'as one having authority' rather than as one who needed to appeal to an external authority, to someone else. Jesus knew who he was – he was confident in his identity. This was confirmed by God at his baptism: 'You are my Son, the Beloved' (Mark 1.11), and tested by Satan in the wilderness: 'If you are the Son of God ...' (Luke 4.9). Now his character and teaching come together with integrity. He is integrated.

So too with us, are we ready to give an account of the hope that is within us, not appealing to the past but rather living the Christian life now, with all its joys and sorrows, confident in the people we are called to be as part of the body of Christ?

With impact

Second, after Jesus has healed the man with an unclean spirit the issue of authority comes up again. This time it is the teaching itself that is described as having authority. When Jesus speaks, things happen. There is authority in what he says. Jesus speaks to the people, and his words have an immediate impact in front of their eyes – the man is healed. His message is a message of freedom from oppression, and his words have the authority for that to happen. Jesus walks his talk. Is this true for us? Do our words follow through in our actions; do our actions proclaim our faith?

Jesus' authority

The whole focus on Jesus' authority is related to what he says and does, not to some badge of office that he wears. There is no suggestion that Jesus has authority because he is a properly ordained rabbi. People do not listen to him because he has been vested with authority. They declare him to have authority because they have listened to him and found what he says and does to be authoritative. His authority is earned. And it is earned by the fact that his message is a message of freedom and hope that is backed up by people being set free at his word and touch.

So too with us and the ministry that we have each been given. We need to know who we are, our identity – God's beloved children, part of the body of Christ and filled with the Holy Spirit. We are God's chosen people from the foundation of the world, dearly loved, confirmed in our baptism and strengthened by word and sacrament as we worship together week by week. We are God's chosen people who are integrated so that who we are and what we say and do in our everyday lives hold together and have validity. Do our words and actions bring freedom, healing and wholeness to those around us? Do they bring the kingdom of God, as we faithfully follow Jesus the teacher, the one with authority?

Paul Williams

Hymn suggestions

Christ is the world's true light; May the mind of Christ my Saviour; Be thou my vision; I speak the name of Jesus over you (In Jesus's name).

Fourth Sunday of Epiphany   28 January
Second Service   **Use Your Minds!**
Ps. 34 [*or* 34.1–10]; 1 Sam. 3.1–20; **1 Cor. 14.12–20**;
Gospel at Holy Communion: Matt. 13.10–17

Faith at risk

Twice in my life, I've prepared to go to a church college. The first time was as a trainee teacher when I had a place at a Roman Catholic training college. The second was as a trainee priest when I had to go to a Church of England theological college. At first sight, the colleges, and the reasons for going there, seem very different. But the two occasions have something distinctive in common. On both occasions, Christian friends warned me against going. 'You'll lose your faith,' they said.

It seems to be a common worry that if you think about your faith, and study it seriously, you will lose it. But Paul is very clear in his letter to the Corinthian church – pray with the mind, praise with the mind, in thinking be adults. Think! Use your mind!

Use your mind

Faith is not wishful thinking. Faith is not blind hope. Faith engages our minds. Instruction is important, says Paul.

In this first letter to the Corinthian church, Paul addresses something like 15 different issues. There are rival leaders and divisions in the church. There are various forms of immorality. There are problems inside marriage and outside it. Worship and theology are chaotic. Women and slaves are being denigrated. I notice one thing in common among all these problems – the treatment of others. Isn't it strange that in a letter talking about how to treat other people, Paul includes this section on thinking and using your brain?

I wonder if Paul is telling the Corinthians to think about what they are doing. There's an example in chapter 11.33: 'When you come together to eat, wait for one another,' says Paul. Why? The early churches met in homes – specifically, homes that were large enough to hold them. Wealthy people's homes. It seems that some people arrived early and ate as soon as they arrived, leaving only leftovers for latecomers. Who might the latecomers be? Those who had to work. Possibly servants in the very house where the church was meeting. The wealthy, who didn't work, arrived early and ate first. The poorer members of the church arrived later and had to eat what was left. 'Think about what you're doing,' says Paul.

'I want you to understand'

In some Bible versions, chapter 15 begins with 'Now I want you to understand'. Paul wants the Corinthians to understand the good news, not just accept it or pass it on, not be children in their thinking, but understand. Be adults in their thinking. In today's reading, Paul has already demonstrated how to do that by exploring the implications of speaking in tongues: it doesn't engage the person's own mind, and it doesn't benefit other people, therefore pray to be able to interpret, or choose to pray with your mind.

Paul clearly does not agree with any of those who counselled me against going to colleges where I would explore my faith. In fact, I think he would have encouraged me to go. Because he encourages all of us to engage with our faith, to grow in understanding; in short, to grow up.

'I would rather speak five words with my mind'

Paul specifically asks the Corinthians to think about the doctrines and practices of their faith – what does it mean that Jesus died, was buried, rose and appeared, he asks in chapter 15. What does it mean that Jesus took bread and broke it with his disciples on the night that he was betrayed, he asks in chapter 11. In this reading, 'you are eager for spiritual gifts, so strive to excel in them'. Paul's reason for this is not so that you look smart, though. It's for the benefit of others. 'If you say a blessing with the spirit, how can anyone in the position of an outsider say the "Amen"? ... You may give thanks well enough, but the other person is not built up ... in church, I would rather speak five words with my mind, in order to instruct others also, than ten thousand in a tongue.'

Use your minds

Where is the challenge in this, then? Paul wrote his letter in response to questions from the church in Corinth and some things he had heard about them. I wonder whether the thinking we are called to do is in answer to a question something like this: what does the church, or the Christian faith, have to say about the issues of today? Climate change, wars around the world, and the abuse of women and girls, for example. Or local issues – lack of affordable housing, the need for foodbanks. It's time to respond with our minds.

One final thing Paul does throughout this letter is to turn to Jesus, and Jesus' dealing with people. Paul's gospel can be summarised like this: Jesus did this, therefore you …

Use your minds.

Liz Shercliff

Hymn suggestions

May the mind of Christ my Saviour; Let this mind be in you; Be thou my vision; Light of the world, you stepped down into darkness.

Ordinary Time

Second Sunday before Lent   4 February
Principal Service   **Faith: A 'Leisure Pursuit'**
Prov. 8.1, 22–31; Ps. 104.26–end; **Col. 1.15–20**; **John 1.1–14**

Recently I received a National Survey from the Consumer Research Bureau – perhaps some of you had one too. If I fill it in and return it, I might win a million pounds.

The survey is huge, with hundreds of questions about my house, my car and my investments. About the newspaper I read, where I shop, and which shampoo and deodorant I use. Question 45 asks me what I feed the cat. Section 8, subsection 4, asks if I'm saving for a Christmas hamper. Question 59 asks how many bottles of whisky I buy each year.

But what really grabbed my attention in this survey, and the reason I'm sharing it with you, is in the section marked 'leisure pursuits'. There is a list of 66 sports and activities to enjoy in your spare time – activities like snowboarding, and betting, hair and beauty, wines, and 'men's interests' (whatever those are!).

Nestling between railways and retirement in section 35 is 'religious activities'. This is what the world perceives people of faith to be up to; faith is a 'leisure pursuit', something we do in our spare time, on a par with train spotting (apologies to the train buffs among you!). How is it that 'religious activities' have found their way into 'leisure pursuits'?

A matter of life and death

It was a very different story for the early church – for communities like the one at Colossae to whom Paul was writing. To be a Christian in the first century meant adopting a completely different lifestyle from those around. It was dangerous to be a Christian. At the least Christians were ridiculed, but they were also persecuted and martyred. Being a Christian might lead to an early and painful death – but it was worth it, for belonging to Jesus Christ meant everything: it was a matter of life and death. It was not something to be done in your spare time or to fill up a dull Sunday when there was nothing more interesting going on. So today is a good time to be considering what we believe about Jesus Christ and what his presence in our lives really means.

Who is Jesus?

John in our Gospel talks of the Word – who was with God and who was God. John is picking up here on the idea of Wisdom in the Old Testament being integrated throughout creation. God spoke, 'Let there be light', 'Let there be life' – and there was. Creation speaks of God. We hear God through the beauty, diversity and cycles of life we see all around us.

At the time appointed by God, the Word pre-existent before creation came into the world and was made flesh – became one of us – Jesus Christ. We've just celebrated that at Christmas when this very well-known passage from John is often read. In Jesus – the Word – we see and experience the fullness of the glory of God. We hear from God through the wonders of creation and we learn what God is like by looking at the life, death and resurrection of Jesus.

Using words is one of the ways we communicate. Jesus – the Word – is God's communication to the world. We are each made in the image of God and when we accept Jesus Christ as our saviour, the one who calls us to follow him, to be like him, then we find the image of God within us grows and blossoms and we become more Christ-like. We are 'little words' of the Word. This affects the entire way we live our lives.

Jesus – first in all things

Back to the Colossians, who recognized the importance of Jesus. Paul writes to tell them not to keep searching for the next exciting thing because Jesus is the one they need, the one in whom all things hold together. Everything needed to fully belong to God can be found in following Jesus Christ. Paul describes Christ as the beginning, the origin, the firstborn from the dead – the one in whom we see that eternal life with God is not just possible but promised and fulfilled. We don't have to make our way to God or do good things to make God love us. We don't have to be good enough to be acceptable to God. In Jesus, God loves us as we are, comes to us and brings us home. Nothing and no one is outside the range of God's love and reconciliation. This is huge and life-changing for the whole of creation. This is so much more than a 'leisure pursuit'.

So, to be a Christian is to recognize that Jesus Christ comes first in our lives – is our primary relationship, from whom all other relationships are formed. If we don't put Christ first, as our origin and goal, then many other things will take our attention and pull us away from God. It's at those times that worship, prayer and our faith are in danger of becoming a leisure pursuit, a take-it-or-leave-it hobby, which we may drop away from when life is challenging, or church isn't as we'd like it to be, or justice issues seem too demanding.

It's ten days until Ash Wednesday and the beginning of Lent. Lent is traditionally a time for digging deep into our faith, as we prepare for the drama of Holy Week and the great celebrations of Easter and Pentecost. Perhaps some good questions to be asking ourselves at this time are:

- Who is Jesus for me?
- How is Jesus shaping my life, my decisions, my words and my actions?
- What can I do to show others that the Christian faith is more than just a 'leisure pursuit'?

Catherine Williams

Hymn suggestions

Jesus is Lord, creation's voice proclaims it; My Jesus, my saviour; In Christ alone; From the highest of heights to the depths of the sea (Indescribable).

Second Sunday before Lent 4 February
Second Service **Tales of the Unexpected**
Ps. 65; Gen. 2.4b–end; Luke 8.22–35

The disruptive power of grace

I have a fascination with lighthouses, their innovative designs of brick and glass, their risky construction and the creative myths, legends and stories that surround them. Most of all, though, I feel the attractive pull of a life of routines in the face of wildness. Polishing the brass and ensuring that the light shines with predictability while the storm rages can be acts of denial, diversion or defiance. They can also be quiet acts which celebrate the power of disruption. At some point the storm will cease; the turmoil and chaos will be disrupted by an unknown, unpredictable power.

The theologian Walter Brueggeman calls Psalm 65 a 'Psalm of new orientation'.[19] Some of the psalms, he suggests, affirm the stability of the world created and maintained by a trustworthy and reliable God. These are 'psalms of orientation', useful to the successful and powerful as a means of celebrating their achievements or as a means of social control of others. Then there are 'psalms of disorientation', which describe the reality of life when it is hard, disordered, dark and ragged and the God who is there acquainted with the sorrows and the grief. Finally, there are these psalms of new orientation which bear witness to the surprise of new life and possibility just when none had been expected. The disrupting power of grace. These psalms are not there to explain how this happens; they simply give expression to it. They tell it, they testify to it, they take pleasure in it.

Creation out of chaos

Psalm 65 tells, testifies and takes pleasure in God who crucially doesn't just control the chaos but who rather uses and employs the watery chaos for good. God silences the roaring of the seas and the roaring of the waves (verse 7) and then provides water which softens the earth so that it can provide grain which feeds the people and animals and makes even the valleys and meadows shout and sing for joy (verses 9–13). Creation of something good out of something chaotic and wild.

The wisdom held and enjoyed in this psalm could be said to be ancient and long established. The reading from Genesis 2 can be understood as the story of life being gradually brought out of chaos. God may very well have created the world out of nothing, as traditional interpretations of the world as a 'formless void' would have it. But the 'formless void' can also be understood to be 'the waters' that God broods and hovers over. Creation out of the waters of chaos: the disrupting, unexpected, unpredictable power of grace and love and kindness to which we can only respond with 'wonder, love and praise'.

Transforming candour and silence

There are two details in Psalm 65 which are worthy of a closer look. First, this is a community song of thanksgiving. This is a community which has been overwhelmed by deeds of iniquity, injustice and sin. They have previously shared a common sense of complaint and grievance about that and now they are a community who feel forgiven, saved and chosen. They want to testify, tell and take pleasure in the God of grace and power who has brought that about. Second, in this context, the psalm starts with an extraordinary phrase, sadly hidden by most English translations. 'Praise is due to you, O God, in Zion; and to you shall vows be performed, O you who answer prayer!' 'Praise waiteth for thee, O God' is the translation of the King James Version. A more literal translation would be, 'For you, a still silence and praise in Zion, O God.'

This is the song of a community which has talked to God about how life really is without pretence or cover-up. They have spoken truth to the power of all the things which have disorientated them. That, in itself, is transformative. The cat is out of the bag, so to speak, the problems are called out, candour has been exercised and its effects cannot be undone. Life will never be the same again. And then something inexplicable happens to transform the situation for good. But before that is celebrated, the community keeps still and silent for a moment. It waits. It quietly tarries.

What does that silence hold for the community? Perhaps a sense of settling. Perhaps a sense of shared awe. Perhaps a sense of not being able to find quite the right words. Perhaps a deep breath for courage or trust. Perhaps a sense of respect for the God who has done these things. Perhaps a hope that this is just the start and eventually all will be well, all manner of things will be well.

Esther Elliott

Hymn suggestions

All my hope on God is founded; Through the love of God our Saviour; Eternal Father, strong to save; Love divine, all loves excelling.

Sunday next before Lent   11 February
Principal Service   **Transfigured and Transformed**
2 Kings 2.1–12; Ps. 50.1–6; 2 Cor. 4.3–6; **Mark 9.2–9**

Valentine's Day is approaching. In Thomas Hardy's novel *Far from the Madding Crowd*, Bathsheba Everdene, a young, headstrong woman, has inherited a sizable farm and is determined to make it work. Her neighbour, the older single wealthy landowner, Mr Boldwood, has not taken her seriously as a farmer. Partly in playful revenge but largely in jest, Bathsheba sends Boldwood a Valentine's Day message: 'Marry me'.

Boldwood, of course, takes it seriously and Bathsheba's frivolity leads to tragedy. Yet her flaw, her gross misjudgement, also leads to Bathsheba's own transformation, as she recognizes her mistakes and reappraises her life and purpose.

Let's reflect on the meaning of Jesus' transfiguration and what it may mean for us to be transformed into the likeness of Christ.

Mountain-top experiences

Peter, James and John are taken by Jesus to a mountain top. Mountain-top experiences are awe-inspiring moments, the elation of reaching a summit, the sensation of wonder at the breathtaking views. The disciples are perhaps feeling privileged at being chosen to accompany Jesus up to the mountain top, yet they are totally unprepared for what will happen next.

Jesus is transfigured; his clothes seem dazzling white; Elijah and Moses appear in company with Jesus. The three disciples are totally perplexed by their experience, completely baffled. Peter is petrified and talks gibberish.

Puzzles to solve

Not so long ago, Peter responded to Jesus' question, 'Who do you say I am?' with the answer, 'You are the Messiah.' Yet, he cannot grasp this fully; it is a puzzle that is incomplete; one conundrum after another, the final solution so elusive that no cerebral skills will resolve this. To hear the Messiah, the long-expected saviour, foretell that he will be led to trial and be crucified is too much for Peter; he rebukes Jesus.

Yet the experience of transfiguration takes Peter a step closer to understanding the Messiah. These three get a glimpse of the glory of God, yet they and the disciples will not be able to solve the puzzle until they have witnessed the suffering and death of Jesus. The final solution will be revealed three days later – the miracle of resurrection and the glory of God, the reign of Christ over all things will be revealed and all will make sense. The long-expected Messiah has triumphed over death and the way to the kingdom of God is open to all.

Our transformation

On Wednesday we begin Lent. Lent marks our own journey to the cross, travelling slowly and deliberately with Jesus before we reach the mountain top. Christianity does not end in pain and suffering but in the transfigured glory of resurrection.

St Paul explores this in today's Epistle. St Paul speaks of our unveiled faces. The veil is something that provides a sense of mystery, a sense of anticipation of what is to come. In many cultures, brides wear veils. When my parents got married in India, they had never met. I wonder what they experienced when my father lifted the veil from my mother. In the wedding photos, there is something beautiful yet also a sense of nervousness, some anxiety. Over the next 57 years, much will become unveiled: character, personality, hurts, joys. Similarly in our journey of faith, unveiling is a sign of opening up, of opening ourselves up to be transformed by the light of Christ.

Moving into Lent

As we enter Lent, we are given opportunity to be transformed – drenched in the light of Christ, overwhelmed by his glory. Meditation on the Bible can give us space to look deeply within ourselves, to let our reading of the word of God slowly seep in and transform us from within. In our busy, frenetic lives, Lent provides us with an opportunity to slow down, to be deliberate in our spiritual disciplines, to allow the glory of God to make us more Christ-like.

Pray, reflect on your priorities, meditate on what needs to change. If today you spend time with your loved one, or if you enjoy a meal with a family member, your relationship is cultivated and deepened. The same principle applies to a life in God; rethink, reconfigure, slow down. A walk can be a good place to pray. Read a Lent book, cultivate new patterns of prayer.

The transfiguration points us towards the suffering of Christ and on to the triumph of the resurrection. In our own lives, our prayer is that we might be transformed into the likeness of Christ.

Arani Sen

Hymn suggestions

Be thou my vision; Meekness and majesty; Be still, for the presence of the Lord; God is love, let heaven adore him.

Sunday next before Lent   11 February
Second Service   **The Reality of God**
Ps. 2 [99]; **1 Kings 19.1–16**; **2 Peter 1.16–end**;
Gospel at Holy Communion: Mark 9.[2–8] 9–13

The reality of our God is that God does not appear or speak to us when or in the way that we would necessarily expect. And we are all the better for it. In our relationship with God, we develop an intimacy of the heart that makes us realize that God is with and for us, even when things seem not to be the case.

God shows up

When Elijah fled for his life, it is clear that he was facing a desperate situation. He felt isolated and defeated, and asks 'that he might die'. For some of us, we may have never reached these depths of despair. For others of us, Elijah's words reflect a moment in our lived experience. Yet God enters into the narrative to give Elijah a new path and purpose, to give him new hope.

Perhaps it is because of this, or the memory of the stories of old, that we find that Elijah's expectations about God do not match our reality. Here we must ask: what kind of God do we imagine and carry with us each day? For Elijah, his was a God of high drama, of wind, earthquake and fire. But he discovered God in none of these things. Instead, it was the 'sound of sheer silence' through which the presence of God could be heard. If our God can be present beyond our expectations, then it is to this God that we can lay our troubles, our fears, our deepest hopes and dreams.

God transforms

In the space where there is so much lacking, there we find the provision of God. There is food and drink and nourishment, from what seemed to be out of nothing. Is there an area of our lives or a part of our life story that we feel that God needs to transform? We know that God can do extraordinary things. Out of the journey in the wilderness, Elijah is called to anoint a king over Israel. From a man on the run to being placed in a royal court. Elijah's identity as a prophet remains and the fear of persecution is no more. We do not know if there was an argument between God and his chosen prophet. Did Elijah say, 'God, this is a turn-up for the books! Do you know what I have already suffered?!', or did he simply say, 'Yes, I will do this'? The reality of God is that when we feel that there is no way out or for things to improve, God can and often does offer something new.

In 2 Peter 1.16, we hear of the story of the transfiguration, which Peter witnessed and is recorded in the Gospels. Peter is confident in the one we are called to follow because he saw Jesus transformed on the mountain. He saw the light of God and was in the presence of the divine. Peter recalls Jesus' baptism in the River Jordan and the voice of God claiming Jesus as God's own. In this, we too must recognize our place as children of God, named and held through baptism, and be reminded of the reality of God as our maker, who delights in us and our lives.

God gives

We are seeing a pattern here of calling, of surprise and of constancy. God does not abandon Elijah, and God will not abandon us. Peter makes clear that the God he follows in the person of the Lord Jesus Christ is real. He is not talking of 'cleverly devised myths' but of a story that has changed his life and the lives of those around him. The reality of God is that we are given Jesus Christ not only as an example of how God can be present in our lived experience but as a promise of how God works to remind us of to whom we really belong.

Peter reminds us that, though he cannot fully explain it, this is not the end of the story. We are told that because of what he has witnessed in his life we can be sure that there is more to come. We have already been reminded earlier on in the chapter of our calling to build and grow our faith so that we can deepen our knowledge of Jesus Christ. In doing this, we will be able to see more of what it is we can become in the reality of the love of God. We are already known to God, claimed as God's for the higher purpose of a life lived infused by that very love and rooted in a greater glory that is yet to come.

Mariama Ifode-Blease

Hymn suggestions

Dear Lord and Father of mankind; Immortal, invisible, God only wise; Be still, my soul, the Lord is on thy side; Majesty, worship his majesty.

Lent

Ash Wednesday 14 February
Principal Service   **Parched Places**
Joel 2.1–2, 12–17, *or* **Isa. 58.1–12**; Ps. 51.1–18;
2 Cor. 5.20b—6.10; Matt. 6.1–6, 16–21, *or* **John 8.1–11**

Lent is a season of parched places. A season of journeys in the desert, of stripping back, soul-searching, fasting, giving and praying. A season of turning and returning to the divine as we recognize our deep need for God. A season of travelling with Jesus from the desert to Jerusalem. A season of see-sawing between life and death and life again.

Fasting: a serious matter

Isaiah is strident in his warning about outward shows of repentance and contrition that change nothing. Isaiah majors on the practice of fasting. Fasting is not a game, not a tick-box spiritual exercise. Giving up treats and luxuries for a short while. Fasting is a serious matter. There is no point in fasting says God if you continue to do nothing to relieve the parched places in other people's lives.

Feeding the hungry, offering hospitality to the homeless, clothing the naked and seeking peace and reconciliation is what the Lord desires of us. Watering the parched places and speaking life. Stop pointing the finger says God, stop speaking evil. Rather recognize that God is leading and guiding – helping us to grow strong in faith and love for others, as we put their needs above our wants.

Into the desert

Jesus, beginning his ministry, is drawn by the Spirit into the desert, that parched place, and undertakes a long period purging himself of

63

everything so that he might be filled with God. He's tested and comes through, to be that watered garden, that spring of water which never fails, of which Isaiah speaks. Jesus enters into the parched places of peoples' lives bringing living water. The oppressed, the poor and the downtrodden come high on his agenda. He is guiding continually and satisfying needs in parched places. As disciples of Christ, we are called to follow and imitate.

St Paul writing to the Corinthian church shows how life imitating Jesus Christ – life as the body of Christ – leads to reconciliation with God. Through his death and resurrection, Jesus is that 'repairer of the breach' mentioned in Isaiah. Walking in his light means we are called to be repairers and restorers of relationships and communities. Bringing life into those parched places where relationships have broken down. St Paul gives us a huge list of the difficulties and dangers that following Christ may bring, but throughout all we are in Christ and called to be Christ-like – in the midst of death, to bear life. If we have nothing (the ultimate parched place) our only possession is Christ, and therefore we have everything.

Living water

We see that modelled in the story in John's Gospel of the woman caught in adultery. She's in a parched place: paraded publicly and shamed, in danger of being stoned to death, of losing everything. The religious leaders are in a parched place too, caught in their desire to shame, to grab the moral high ground, teetering on the brink of murder.

Jesus, with intelligence and grace, brings calm and order out of a potentially explosive situation. Jesus listens, ponders and writes in the sand – taking the heat out of the moment, bringing order, calm, depth. Just feel that living water flowing through this situation. His judgement when it comes is brilliant: the pointing of the finger, the speaking of evil has been diffused, the breach has been repaired. Grace and life have watered the parched places.

The way of the cross

The cross in ash we may receive on our foreheads today reminds us that we come from dust and will return to dust, and the journey from one to the other may be through parched and dusty places. Where are the parched places in your life? What is dry or dusty, gasping for breath, or spiralling out of control? Where do you need the Lord's guidance? Where do you need the Lord's life? In your prayers tell Jesus about that, and ask for the gifts and graces you need.

Jesus walks the journey with us, ahead, beside, within, around and throughout. He gives his life on the cross so that all our dust and sin might be made clean and whole – the parched places watered so that our wildernesses may blossom and burst into song. And we need that so much at this time – for ourselves, for our communities, for our world.

As we enter into Lent, recognize and name your own parched places and the parched places of the world around you. Recognize what you need to let go of, to strip away, to empty so that Jesus – the living water – may replenish you, filling you to overflowing with his life. Then raise your eyes and look around for where you can bring that living water, which you carry as Christ's disciple, to the parched places of those around you.

Catherine Williams

Hymn suggestions

Forty days and forty nights; Lord Jesus, think on me; Father, hear the prayer we offer; Ashes to ashes (Dan Schutte).

First Sunday of Lent   18 February
Principal Service   **Into the Wilderness**
Gen. 9.8–17; Ps. 25.1–9; 1 Peter 3.18–end; **Mark 1.9–15**

Lent is upon us. We're in a season that leads from Ash Wednesday to Holy Week and Easter. It's a season that grows in intensity as we join in the events that lead to the crucifixion and resurrection of Jesus.

During Lent, the church traditionally plays down celebration. Colours are muted. The seasonal colour – purple – is the colour of preparation, repentance and mourning. There are no flowers in church. We don't use the Gloria or Alleluias. We sing less, we pray more (hopefully). We take time to reflect on and order our relationships with God, with each other, and with our world. We take stock of our faith and take a long hard look at our Christian believing and practising. We might give up something for Lent, going without favourite treats. Or we might take something on that builds our faith, through spiritual discipline.

Forty days

In this season Jesus spends 40 days in the wilderness. Immediately following his baptism by John, the Holy Spirit drives him into a hostile and difficult environment, where he is tested and tempted. He is being prepared for what's to come as he enters into his calling.

Significantly, the period is 40 days. Noah spent 40 days in the ark on the floodwaters. Moses and the Israelites spent 40 years in the wilderness after their liberation from Egypt. Elijah, broken and dejected, escaped into the wilderness for 40 days. Forty days is symbolically a time of testing and preparation, a time to trust in God's faithfulness and provision.

Time spent in the wilderness leads to renewed trust and faith, and a fresh expression and realization of God's graciousness and love towards his people. In the story of Noah, the rainbow symbolizes God's promise to save the people. The word for 'bow' in the passage from Genesis is the same word in Hebrew that is used for a bow as in 'bows and arrows'. The writer of Genesis is suggesting that the rainbow is God's symbol of disarmament. God's bow is hung up. God turns from anger and renews the covenant of love with creation. Likewise, at the end of 40 years in the wilderness, the people of Israel enter into God's inheritance: the Promised Land. Jesus, as he comes out of the desert, proclaims the good news, saying, 'The time is fulfilled, and the kingdom of God has come near; repent, and believe in the good news.'

Wilderness experiences

Most people have some sort of wilderness experience in their lives. Being a Christian, being faithful to Jesus, does not protect us from difficult times and places. Baptism is not an immunization against adversity – though it is strength and preparation for the journey.

What is wilderness for you? Is it a place of grief, loneliness or isolation? Is it a place of addiction, characterized by denial, guilt or self-loathing? Is it a place of competition: the need to be the biggest or best, the longing for status? Is it the downward spiral of negativity and cynicism that means that you are always complaining? Is it the place of ageing and impending death? Is it unemployment or the threat of redundancy? Is it financial loss and the fear of fiscal collapse? Is it the wilderness of leadership with difficult or impossible decisions to make? The wilderness is a place where one is at risk, endangered, frightened, vulnerable, lonely. What is your wilderness?

Jesus in the wilderness

In his wilderness, Jesus encountered Satan, wild animals and angels, and he emerged stronger, focused and holy. Though we may not be able to avoid wilderness experiences in our lives, we can prepare for them, we can survive them and we can emerge stronger and holier from them, recognizing that the good news of God can be encountered and lived out in the desert too. Preparation comes by walking closely with Christ – not calling on God only in emergencies but by being daily in fellowship with Jesus. Our baptism was the beginning of that journey, but we need to remain on the road and not just be there when it suits us.

It's heartening too to know that the wilderness contains angels. We need to have our eyes open to these – the positives and gifts that occur amid desolation. And God may use us as angels – as God's messengers – from time to time. A loving word or action in season or out of season may make a significant difference to someone in the wilderness, enabling them to catch hold of hope and be strengthened.

Wilderness, of course, isn't restricted to Lent. We may find ourselves in it at any time, and sometimes with very little notice. This period of Lent reminds us of that fact and encourages us to put down deep roots in Christ, to prepare ourselves for desert times. And as with Jesus, it may be the Spirit who drives us into a wilderness place, testing and strengthening our faith and trust in the one who loves us, provides for us and promises never to let us go.

Most of all, let's remember this Lent that Jesus is in the wilderness. He goes before us, is alongside us, behind us, and through his suffering and death has triumphed and saved us. Whatever happens, whatever wildernesses we endure, God, in Jesus, will be there.

Catherine Williams

Hymn suggestions

Forty days and forty nights; Guide me, O thou great Redeemer; Lord Jesus, think on me; In the desert, in the darkness (Through the wilderness).

First Sunday of Lent 18 February
Second Service **Starting with the Solution**
Ps. 119.17–32; Gen. 2.15–17; 3.1–7; **Rom. 5.12–19**,
or Luke 13.31–end

Who's to blame?

This story of Adam and Eve from Genesis is often approached from an accusatory angle. Whose fault was it, really, that we all ended up in this mess? Who brought sin into the world and ruined it for everyone? Who can we blame? And it represents something extremely significant, and profoundly true, about our relationship with God and with each other. But how would it look to think about Adam and Eve not through the eyes of accusation but of forgiveness? To ask not what the impact of Adam's sin is on us, but what the impact of Jesus' forgiveness is on Adam? Because the other way of looking at Adam and Eve is not that they were the first to sin, but rather they were the first to recognize their need for forgiveness. So perhaps a better question is, not whose fault was the sin, but where does that forgiveness come from?

This passage from Romans contains a lot of accusatory language. A lot of judgement. 'For the judgement following one trespass brought condemnation … one man's trespass led to condemnation for all … by the one man's disobedience the many were made sinners.' But Paul's point here is not to find someone to blame. Because Paul's overarching narrative is one of grace. Being the rhetorician that he is, he is very much enjoying the force of this parallel and contrast between the one man, Adam, and the one man, Christ. But the main thrust of the passage is a message of forgiveness, of abounding grace, of free gift.

Distorted desires

The sin committed by Eve and Adam is to allow their desires to become distorted by the envy and rivalry of another. Before the serpent came along, they were quite happy to live within the limits set by God and quite comfortable with their nakedness. The one tree is not a problem for them, as they have all the other wonderful trees in the garden to eat from. But the influence of the serpent begins to open their eyes to look at the world in a different way, as the serpent himself says. The desire for the forbidden fruit becomes unbearable because Eve starts to see it through the eyes of the serpent. And once they both eat, they see themselves not through the eyes of their loving God, who sees in their nakedness beauty and innocence, but through the eyes of another, which brings shame and fear.

Perhaps it is the promise of becoming like God that is the strongest temptation – not necessarily from a desire for power or worship or glory, but perhaps simply from a desire to be like the one they love the most. They try to achieve it not through imitating God, but through desiring, and taking, what rightly belongs to God.

In need of forgiveness

And so Paul sets out the path of human history, with a fractured relationship with God, in need of forgiveness and walking in the footsteps of our earliest ancestors who realized that trying to take God's place doesn't bring us closer to God but separates us further. They understood that they were sinners in need of forgiveness.

Until another moment in human history when something changed in our relationship with God and with each other. The moment when Christ came to us as a free gift. Not like the trespass, the transgression, the fruit, taken without permission, grasped from misplaced desire, but given with no conditions, no expectations, no constraints. Paul talks elsewhere about Jesus as the second Adam – this is clearly his theme here even if he doesn't say it in so many words. And what he means when he says this is that, as God created humanity in Adam, so in Jesus God is recreating humanity.

A new way of being human

In Jesus, we see a new way of being human, living as ones who are forgiven. Our need for forgiveness is still real, our sin is still real, but our forgiven-ness is our primary reality. And in Jesus we see a way of becoming like God not through grasping for what is God's, but through imitating God. We don't look through the eyes of the serpent, with envy and rivalry, but can learn to look through the eyes of Christ, the eyes of God, with love and forgiveness.

Our forgiveness is made possible by Jesus' gratuitous self-giving, which results in the new life of the resurrection. For us to live as forgiven is to imitate this gratuitous self-giving, to imitate Christ, to look at the world through his eyes and to be his hands and feet. To do that is not to live accusatorily, seeking out sinners, apportioning blame. It is to start with the solution – to approach the world with a readiness to forgive, and to love.

Kat Campion-Spall

Hymn suggestions

Dear Lord and Father of mankind; Praise to the holiest in the height; There in God's garden stands the tree of wisdom; To be in your presence.

Second Sunday of Lent   25 February
Principal Service   **The Eve of Something Better**
Gen. 17.1–7, 15–16; Ps. 22.23–end; Rom. 4.13–end;
Mark 8.31–end

Lent focuses our minds on prayer, for others and their needs, for ourselves to hear the quiet call of the season to resist, not an ever-increasing amount of our favourite snacks and treats but something altogether more serious.

The trademark of Lent is a call to resistance, to resist pinning our hopes on what we can see, and instead trust in what we cannot see. And that is simply because we are on the eve of something better. Praying can sometimes feel as if we are speaking into a void, but our voices are received and held, and honoured. God listens and God understands.

Keep following

In the reading from Genesis 17, we note that, at the heart of it, God is simply saying to Abraham and Sarah that they are on the eve of something better. What kind of God, you may ask, waits 99 years for a farmer, shepherd and landowner to give him another son? At 99 years of age, and with the longing for a child piercing his wife's, Sarah's, being, neither Abraham nor Sarah probably felt that they were on the eve of something better. God renames them both and speaks to Sarah's soul by saying that she will become a mother, whether she believes it or not.

In the Gospel reading, instead of saying, 'You, my dear disciples, are on the eve of something better', Jesus tells his followers something like this: 'You know this journey we are on together? Well, it's going to continue to be like this, only much worse.' After feeding the 4,000, rebuking the Pharisees who had asked for a sign, and healing the blind man at Bethsaida, Jesus' words in Mark 8 are shocking to his disciples. So, on the one hand, we have a God who says we are on the eve of something better, and, on the other, we have that same God in the person of Jesus who says the future is like this, but only much worse. Who are we to believe?

Perhaps the answer lies in Jesus' words a little later: 'If any want to become my followers, let them deny themselves and take up their cross and follow me.' Jesus does not say, 'If any want to become my followers, let them deny themselves and take up their cross and believe in me.' The weight of our cross may threaten to erase our very being, and our faith may wax and wane, but our aim is to keep on the path, to keep on following Jesus.

Heavy is the cross

The foretelling of Jesus' own death and resurrection before urging people to follow him makes our path as Christian pilgrims incredibly lucid. There will be suffering but there will also be hope and the promise of something better. The weight of this truth of the journey ahead shakes Peter to his core. The humanity in Peter is confronted with the realization that this, what Jesus has just revealed, is something bigger than his person; it is something that Peter will neither be able to stop nor control.

In Peter, we see the manifestation of the trademark of Lent: a call to resistance. This is a call to resist the fall into a reliance on human things, on the human gaze, and instead turn our hearts and bodies towards God. This is the call to go back to God, within the wilderness wandering of Lent, and tell God what it has been like, what it *is* like, what it *really is* like, being me, being you, living in our bodies, *loving* in our bodies and waiting in our souls.

The greater promise

The call of Abraham and Sarah reminds us that God does not really care how old we are, how old we feel or what state we feel our body or mind may be in, because God speaks to our place in the boundlessness of eternity, to our naming and being held beyond this earthly plain. Abraham is established in the promise of El Shaddai (Gen. 17.1), often translated as 'God Almighty'. Sarah's longings are planted in and supplanted by God. We, like Sarah and Abraham, are on the threshold, on the eve of something better.

To say that we are on the eve of something better does not mean that experiences of isolation, suffering and loss have not been real. It does not mean the wilderness is or has been a mirage. The wilderness is real, but the promise is greater. Whatever we have lived through so far this year, Lent gives us permission to bring it all to God. The message that we are on the eve of something better cannot and does not speak into our experiences to dismiss them, but rather it speaks to uphold them and to say to us all that it is one step in front of the other, in faith and hope. We take one step in front of the other knowing that our ground is love and that the light of the Easter dawn makes each step more bearable, more steady, more purposeful.

Mariama Ifode-Blease

Hymn suggestions

Immortal, invisible, God only wise; Be still, my soul, the Lord is on thy side; The God of Abraham, praise; In Christ alone.

Second Sunday of Lent   25 February
Second Service   **Calling and Blessing**
Ps. 135 [*or* 135.1–14]; **Gen. 12.1–9**; Heb. 11.1–3, 8–16;
Gospel at Holy Communion: John 8.51–end

Leaving home

I wonder how many of you have lived abroad? There is a kind of excitement about leaving your home. A frisson of adventure. Going into the unknown, full of expectations and enthusiasm. Then reality hits. You discover you don't speak another language as well as you thought. And the people you meet, well, they're – different. And they are a people. They belong together. They speak the same, they have similar values. They may think of one another as very different, but to you, the stranger, the alien, they present a united front. They may welcome you but, even after years, subtle differences would still mark you out. And when you visit home, you discover it isn't quite home any more. People there have changed. The home you remember simply isn't there, and friends have become strangers. I don't know what Abram thought when God told him to go. Whether he was excited or scared. But whatever he thought at that moment, what God was asking was no small favour. Especially in a tribal society, with strong kinship ties, where your identity depends on the strength and shape of your relationships.

Only a blessing

And God did not make it easy. God promised blessing, but God did not really specify the shape of the blessing. God is asking Abram to take him on trust, to leave everything and 'Go ... to the land that I will show you'. Hardly a Michelin atlas! I think I'd have said, 'OK, God, but can I have an itinerary, please? They're bound to ask for it at customs.' No direction, no destination. Only a promise. This land could have been anywhere. Anyone could have lived there. But God promises. God promises a future, descendants and a great name. And God promises to walk along the way, by blessing those who bless Abram and cursing those who curse him, which, by the way, means that some people would curse him, treat him badly. God isn't promising an easy ride, but he is promising to be alongside Abram.

Call and promise

This is the shape of God's call throughout Scripture: a call to trust and follow, a call to put God first, beyond other loyalties, and trust that God's word is true and reliable. So, Abram goes. Just like that. Well, maybe not quite. I suspect a little organization was involved – camels and tents and deciding who's coming and who's staying. And a few goodbyes.

Abram was middle-aged when he departed from Haran, and we know nothing of his life so far. Abram was not too old, too settled or too unremarkable for God to burst in with something new. And Abram carried with him the skills, knowledge and wisdom he had acquired through a normal life: the skills to lead a community wisely, the wisdom to deal with rulers he met along the way. His faith was built on years of walking with God through the routine of daily life – the kind of faith that has become resilient, rooted and well established. The kind of faith that is now put to the test, through both call and promise: a call to step out, and a promise of children that seems all but impossible given his age.

Journeying in faith

Abram's story is an every-person story, as well as an extraordinary story. It is the story of a man called in his mid to older years, invited to step out on a journey with God, a journey that takes him into the heart of faith and trust. A journey that tests his trust to the limits; and every time his trust is stretched a little further, Abraham's faith and relationship with God grow and mature. His journey of faith isn't linear, just as his wanderings take him round and up and down. His journey of faith will see him stumble and fall and go the wrong way. Yet God is there, ever-present, to hold him by the hand and lead him on. God doesn't give up, and God doesn't tell him just to settle for a nice cosy retirement. God fulfils his promise in Abraham.

Whoever we are, wherever we are, God's call on our lives is the same. It might be to live the kind of life that Abraham led until he was 75. It might be to lead the kind of life that he led once he had Isaac and settled in a new land. Or it might be to get up and go, now. Whatever our age or position in life, God can speak, just as he spoke to Abraham. And whoever we are, whatever the call on our lives at this precise moment, God is standing beside us, ready to walk with us and lead us on to the next step – just like Abraham. One step of faith at a time. Beyond the next hill, into the next valley. The one who has called us is faithful and will accomplish in us what he has promised.

Isabelle Hamley

Hymn suggestions

Lord, for the years; Lord of all hopefulness; One more step along the world I go; Will you come and follow me?

Third Sunday of Lent   3 March
Principal Service   God's Dwelling-Place
Ex. 20.1–17; Ps. 19 [*or* 19.7–end]; 1 Cor 1.18–25; **John 2.13–22**

On a trip to South India a few years ago I visited the Maharajah's Palace at Mysore, which was an extraordinary place. But the day was somewhat marred because we were hounded by hawkers trying to sell us wooden snakes and carved elephants, inlaid boxes, silver jewellery and sandalwood soap. They were very persistent, very hard to avoid, and it was exhausting. We'd gone for one thing but had to run the gauntlet of buying and selling to get there.

Jesus in the Temple

Perhaps it was rather like that for Jesus going to the Temple. The Temple was familiar ground to Jesus; we know he'd been there before. But this visit provoked an angry outburst from him. Imagine the scene. The Temple courts – the outskirts of the Temple – filled with traders selling cattle, sheep and doves ready to buy for sacrificing in the Temple. Then there were tables of money-changers waiting to change the pilgrims' money into the special Temple coinage needed to pay the Temple tax. These traders were there to provide necessary services, but it seemed the original good intentions were lost in the pursuit of gain. The house of prayer had become a busy, bustling marketplace.

Enter Jesus, who takes stock of this desecration and in his anger lashes, driving out all these traders. It's a scene of utter chaos, anger and disbelief. Reflecting back on this episode the disciples remember the prophecy from Psalm 69: 'zeal for your house that has consumed me'. Jesus is zealous for the house of God to the point of righteous anger. This is no Jesus 'meek and mild'. I'm reminded of the prophet Malachi:

> the Lord whom you seek will suddenly come to his temple … But who can endure the day of his coming, and who can stand when he appears?
> For he is like a refiner's fire. (Mal. 3.1–2)

True worship

John has Jesus, here at the very beginning of his ministry, purifying the Temple from sin, and there's more. Jesus suggests that true worship will no longer be dependent on the Temple – a very radical idea. The Temple he says will be destroyed and rebuilt in three days. The Jews think he is talking about the physical building, but Jesus is referring to himself. The incarnation marks a new place for God – God with us – alongside people, within people. Jesus is claiming nothing less than the reconstituting of the entire worship of God's people around himself.

We're used to that idea today: we know we are the body of Christ, we know we are the Temple of the Holy Spirit, the place where God dwells both for individuals and corporately. But this would have been a radical and potentially blasphemous suggestion at the time.

So, if this is the case and we are temples for God, I wonder what Jesus would find if he suddenly came to his temple today. Would our inner temples be places of holiness and awe where God is honoured and worshipped? What's at the very core of our being? And then the outer courts – the place where all the money-changers were, the interface with the outside world. What is going on there for us? What would Jesus find there? Are there things that Jesus would want to drive out of our lives, drive out of his temple? Are we God's house or a marketplace?

Holy living

God's blueprint for holy living is laid out in the reading from Exodus. The Ten Commandments were given to the Israelites as they emerged from the oppression of Egyptian law. Given that a new society might find a way to order itself. Given as a strategy for an enduring relationship between God and God's people.

God intends freedom and well-being for all and that starts with the need for total loyalty to God: 'You shall have no other gods before me.' We find our joy, destiny and fulfilment in God alone, not in any commodities or things. God is to be honoured, to be first in our hearts, taught to our children, worshipped and loved. That's what should be going on in the inner courts of our temple: in our heart and soul. In the outer courts are the terms for living alongside others. Some are obvious: 'You shall not murder'; 'You shall not bear false witness against your neighbour.' Others are more subtle. We're not to long for things which are not ours. We are to be content with what we have. We are to honour our family members and take sufficient rest so that we can enjoy creation and break the vicious cycles of production and consumption.

The Ten Commandments give a framework for an ordered life in God's society, and Jesus adds to them his new commandment of 'love' for one another: going the extra mile, turning the other cheek, loving your enemies, and praying for those who persecute you. These are the things, the way of living, that Jesus would hope to find in God's temple – in each of us as individuals and in his church, the body of Christ.

Jesus comes today to his temple – to each of us. He comes to purify, heal, nurture and love. Let's allow him to enter our inner and outer courts, inviting him to make the changes necessary for us

76

to become the place where God is honoured and worshipped. The place where God dwells.

Catherine Williams

Hymn suggestions

Christ is made the sure foundation; Restore, O Lord, the honour of your name; Take my life, and let it be; Before the throne of God above.

Third Sunday of Lent   3 March
Second Service   **We Choose How to Live**
Ps. 11, 12; Ex. 5.1—6.1; **Phil. 3.4b–14**, *or* Matt. 10.16–22

The world is changing, as people have said in churches for generations, maybe even for over a thousand years. They have said it in times of war when politics led to the local monastery being destroyed or the beautiful statues and wall paintings being damaged beyond repair. They have said it when mechanization changed farming for ever, and when ideas like evolution made the very idea of God tremble. This is the great sweep of history, which catches all of us, and in such moments we choose how to live.

Not because it's easy

'We choose to go to the moon and do the other things, not because they are easy but because they are hard,' said President J. F. Kennedy in 1962. Choosing a big vision that is hard was very familiar to St Paul who, against the backdrop of his history, where persecution was happening and economic uncertainty was all around, social mobility was at a standstill and life was hard, made a choice of how to live. He expresses it in his letter to the Philippians as choosing to press on to know more and more of Christ in his life, responding to the call of God.

At the beginning of 2019, the BBC showed a mini-series called *Years and Years*. It portrays the near future, some 10–15 years ahead, and was full of technological change, political uncertainty and economic collapse. The central character, Muriel Dean, makes an impassioned speech to her family, in which she tells them it's all their fault. For all their blaming of others and presumed helplessness, they did nothing. She says, 'This is the world we built.' We choose how to live. Do we hold on to our vision and our hope and learn to live as followers of Jesus Christ not because it's easy but because it's hard – and the alternative is to do nothing? Paul is clear: we choose to keep faithful.

It's all in the detail

It's the detailed choices that will matter. The things that may feel insignificant, yet the choices we make each day are the hope for humankind, the hope for each of us who seek to follow Jesus. It's about how we treat others, whom we speak to, smile at, or whom we ridicule or label or exclude. It's what we buy, what we replace, where we travel and what we eat. And above all, as people of God, as those who like St Paul bear witness to the faithfulness of God, it's about how we choose each day to live out our baptism as we pray, read, think and take action so that the impossible task of seeing God's love transforming lives, seeing truth and justice for all, seeing people set free and a world living God's way, can come into being. This is what Paul wanted the Philippians to hold on to. He wanted them to choose as individuals and as a community of believers, listening together to his words. These are words of encouragement, designed to give us confidence and courage, in all our circumstances.

Boast in Jesus, not in ourselves

We hold on to a big vision – not because it's easy but because it's hard. Paul makes that clear, as he outlines all the challenges he has faced. He also tells us all the things he could boast about – the identity that he has in his society, the things he has achieved. But all of it is as nothing compared to the choice to stay faithful to the call of Christ on our lives. We might list our achievements differently from Paul, naming our legacy in terms of our work, or volunteering, or our family and friends, our great successes. We have become familiar with such stories as we read the biographies of those whom we admire, hearing about the journeys they have made to the point where they are confident in who they are. But St Paul would tell it differently, were he to be a contestant in a modern-day skills contest, whether for baking or sport. He would tell them that all that counts for nothing compared with the joy of following Christ and being found faithful at the end. With confidence we step into the future, not passively but with the Spirit of God enabling and inspiring us to press on towards what lies ahead, choosing life and hope and the joy of knowing Jesus. Hang in there.

Sandra Millar

Hymn suggestions

Fight the good fight; All I once held dear; Father, hear the prayer we offer; Let us rejoice: God's gift to us is peace.

Fourth Sunday of Lent   10 March
(For Mothering Sunday, see p. 84.)
Principal Service   **The Serpent Lifted Up**
Num. 21.4–9; Ps. 107.1–3,17–22 [*or* 107.1–9]; Eph. 2.1–10; **John 3.14–21**

Logos and symbols

Visual identity matters: logos help us recognize a product or organization easily; but logos can also point beyond themselves to the things they represent, acting as symbols. Symbols work on different levels. Some speak for themselves. If we smile at someone, the person who sees us will know instinctively that we are being friendly. But other symbols work only if we are aware of a certain amount of background knowledge. The Remembrance poppy, for instance, to the uninitiated is simply a poppy. But to those who know about two world wars, and the significance of Flanders Fields, it has a symbolic significance: it speaks of those who died in active service.

But what might the person in the street make of the fact that many ambulance services, medical suppliers and the World Health Organization have as part of their logo a snake on a pole? I suspect that, for many, the symbolism does not register.

The serpent and the cross

A clue to this seemingly bizarre symbol is in today's first reading (Num. 21.4–9). The Israelites in the wilderness were being bitten by poisonous serpents. Moses prayed for them. He was told by God to make an image of the serpent and set it on a pole, so that anyone who had been bitten could look at it and live. The snake on a pole has, over time – and across Jewish, Greek and Christian culture – become a symbol of healing.

But symbols aren't static; they grow and develop over time. We encountered the snake on the pole twice in today's readings, in Numbers and again in the Gospel. Jesus tells Nicodemus that, 'as Moses lifted up the serpent in the wilderness, so must the Son of Man be lifted up' (John 3.14). John writes of Jesus being 'lifted up' twice: here and again in chapter 12, where Jesus declares, 'I, when I am lifted up from the earth, will draw all people to myself' (John 12.32). In the Fourth Gospel, it is Jesus' exaltation on the cross which is his ultimate glorification. Over time, then, the symbol develops: a snake on a pole for the benefit of the Israelites becomes Jesus crucified for the benefit of all.

The cross is the most powerful of all Christian symbols. Within political history, it was a favoured Roman instrument of execution. Within salvation history, it was the means of Jesus' death. And for those with faith in Christ, it has become the symbol of our salvation and the source of our life and hope. By linking Moses' bronze serpent in the wilderness and Jesus on the cross, the evangelist points clearly to Jesus as the one who fulfils the Hebrew Scriptures. The Israelites looked at the serpent in order to be healed and to live, for this world only. We look to Christ on the cross in order to receive ultimate healing and everlasting life.

But there's still another layer to be uncovered. The serpent was an ancient symbol of wisdom, more crafty than any other created animal (Gen. 3.1). Jesus himself warned his disciples that they must be 'wise as serpents, innocent as doves'. By lifting up a bronze serpent on a pole, Moses was teaching that people should look not to their own insight but to God's wisdom. Following their own wisdom during their wanderings had led to godless ways, and ultimately to death, whereas God's wisdom would lead them to right living, health and life.

The transposition of this symbol into the new key of the Christian gospel is obvious. Jesus, the one to whom we must go in order to live, is not only the one who brings healing and life, but is himself the incarnation of divine wisdom: 'Christ crucified ... the power of God and the wisdom of God' (1 Cor. 1.23–24).

A challenge for Lent

As we stand in the middle of Lent, the rich and developing symbol of the serpent on the pole offers us two challenges.

First, it calls us to stop, to 'look and live'. To remind ourselves again that Jesus, exalted on the cross for us, is the one in whom we find healing, life and peace. Passiontide and Holy Week, when we enter most fully into the mystery of God's love, lie just around the corner. The serpent is a wake-up call not to miss the opportunity.

Second, it calls us to ask, 'On whose wisdom am I relying from day to day?' The human capacity for self-deception is almost limitless, and we can easily pretend that we have more than enough innate wisdom to get by.

God's wisdom (as St Paul and the Fourth Gospel remind us) is not something intangible or nebulous but is embodied in the person of Jesus. Whatever our journey, at the end of the day, that journey should lead us to Jesus, the one in whom we see God's love and God's wisdom displayed. If Lent is about anything, it's about deepening the relationship we have with him.

Peter Moger

Hymn suggestions

Praise to the holiest in the height; In the cross of Christ I glory; O, my Saviour lifted; I heard the voice of Jesus say.

Fourth Sunday of Lent   10 March
Second Service   **Pouring Love**
Ps. 13, 14; Ex. 6.2–13; **Rom. 5.1–11**;
Gospel at Holy Communion: John 12.1–8

I imagine Paul, writing his letter to the church in Rome, pacing around, gathering his thoughts into this sentence, nailing the exact *word* with that hand gesture of his, the crunch point of every one of his sermons.

He is trying to find the words for this life, with God, with the struggling community. Standing in the grace of God. They seem to be going through the world like Israelites in the desert all over again, through sufferings, hardships and endurance, and they get stronger. He looks at the ground, at the hard work of each footstep.

The amanuensis tries to get it all down, to squeeze each word on to the parchment; then at Paul's pause, he looks up. Paul has stopped. He's gazing into the middle distance. He has looked down for too long. 'Write this,' he says, "God's love has been poured into our hearts ..." an open hand, reaching up, "by the spirit he has given us".'

Pouring love

Love breaks into the humdrum, the enduring, the difficult. Liquid, flowing love. Where there was dryness between us, something pours and flows. This fellowship, this community, has become filled with the most beautiful thing in the world. 'How good and pleasant it is', sang the Psalmist, this community of fellowship of reconciliation, of love. It is like precious oil, poured out, flowing down over Aaron's head, down over his clothes and out to others. The pouring love of God.

This love was there in our hearts. We saw it in each other's faces, and in the way this presence of Christ appeared in one another. Because this pouring love was the real presence of the Anointed, the flowing Christ oil. Any little evidence in our lives that the Holy Spirit was in residence was in fact this pouring Christ, this love.

Ordinary love

But to be clear, there may be moments of unity and bliss, extra-ordinary events and signs, but that is not what Paul is talking about. His eye falls on the ordinary, the humdrum, even the difficult – and in it, for this is his gift, he sees already the depth, the reality, the operation of the love of God.

And his struggle to find words adequate to the experience of Christ has become also a quest, to find words that might open up the hearers to the fullness, the richness, of the love and grace of God that is already operational. In their hearts, these very words become the performative action of the Holy Spirit, who pours out love.

Always 'we'

To the modern ear, the plurality of this whole passage is striking. We concentrate so much on the individual experience of God's love: Jesus loves *me*. This is not wrong, but it is probably quite alien to Paul. This writing is all about *we*, *us*. And if God's love does appear, it is not in *my heart*, but in *our hearts*, it is part of a great reconciliation – never a solitary journey.

So this suffering community becomes stronger in their endurance, and hope emerges among them because God pours in love, a love that overcomes our fragilities and weakness to make a new community of reconciliation.

And when the love between us falters, where hostility and division start, then this is our hope also – to open ourselves to this pouring, spilling, unrestrained love. The love of God that comes into our hearts if we allow it.

Of course, we need to be empty to make room for this love. The heart is a cluttered room, full of unnecessary things. We turn towards God and make room for the gift of God.

Into our hearts

Into us, this love pours. There is ambiguity in this word. It is often used for the spilling of blood, for the *bursting out* of something precious. It cannot be just a blissful flood of good feelings, but it's a pouring out, at great cost. This pouring love is profoundly eucharistic: a cup of blessing poured out for us, which is also the lifeblood of God.

The same ambiguity is there in Mary's anointing of Jesus' feet – she is pouring out love and wastefulness. She participates and demonstrates the flowing love of God.

'Hope does not disappoint us, because God's love has been poured into our hearts through the Holy Spirit that has been given to us.'

What pours into our hearts? How can we know this security in love that comes from the work of the Spirit in us? What pours out of our hearts? How can we overflow to a world in need of this love?

Andrew Rudd

Hymn suggestions

Come, let us sing of a wonderful love; Such love, pure as the whitest snow; Come down O love divine; Ubi caritas (Taizé).

Mothering Sunday   10 March
Principal Service   **It Takes a Village to Raise a Child**
Ex. 2.1–10, *or* 1 Sam. 1.20–end; Ps. 34.11–20, *or* Ps. 127.1–4;
2 Cor. 1.3–7, *or* Col. 3.12–17; Luke 2.33–35, *or* John 19.25b–27

The most evil leader

My daughter and I have a secret addiction: we love doing silly quizzes like, 'Which book character would you be? Or what animal would you be?' They're silly and fun. Once, we did a 'Which arch-villain would you be?' I won't tell you the answer. But when it comes to baddies, I think the Bible has a good collection to offer. And one of the most disturbing ones has to be Pharaoh, the man who is so afraid of the slaves he was oppressing that he started killing all their baby boys. That is taking fear of the stranger – xenophobia – pretty far. It is an act of profound evil, designed to bring the people to their knees and, eventually, exterminate them.

Hidden courage

But there is a twist to the story. Pharaoh, the most powerful man in the land, is also the most afraid. Meanwhile, Hebrew women, oppressed and persecuted, are not cowed but stand for what is right. Women, who were often disregarded and considered weak, were the ones who resisted. It was women, who give birth, who assist at birth, who were primarily responsible for endangered children, women who acted with incredible courage and saved the life of baby Moses.

The midwives must have been afraid. But they decided that a vulnerable child was more important than fear, more important than their own lives. They looked to the welfare of the vulnerable and, through him, unexpectedly changed the course of history for their entire people.

Trusting God and letting go

They did what little they could and hid him. Being able to do little is no excuse for doing nothing. They had something to give the little boy, and they gave what they had. But then they ran out of options. Hiding a baby is one thing, hiding a toddler who likes to run around is quite another. Nobody can hide for ever. Nobody can grow up to be a full person if they spend their time afraid and in hiding. Moses' mother was faced with the worst dilemma: in order to save Moses' life, the only way forward was to let him go, without any certainty about what would happen.

She decided to trust God with her baby. Instead of trying to keep him safe by hiding him, she tried to keep him safe by sending him away, hoping and praying that someone, somewhere, would look after him. Mothers all over the world are faced with similar choices, even though we rarely talk about them. Mothers who risk travelling as refugees. Mothers who send out unaccompanied minors when they themselves cannot escape. Mothers who decide that their child should be adopted because they cannot look after them, for a myriad of reasons. And even when they do not part with their children, mothers often, always, need to enlist the help of others as they raise their children. Bringing up a child is not a task to be accomplished alone, or even by two parents.

Work of many hands

Keeping children safe, helping them grow up into well-adjusted adults isn't the work of just mothers, but the work and responsibility of an entire community: parents, grandparents, extended family, friends, teachers, sitters, doctors, counsellors, churches, and even, sometimes, strangers. Parents are important. They are vital. But they were never meant to do this alone.

And the story of Moses tells us that children need an entire community, beyond the midwives and mother. We have Miriam, Moses' sister. She's only a child, but she follows the basket and speaks to Pharaoh's daughter. She spoke to Pharoah's daughter despite fear, and, thanks to her, Moses' mother could look after him a little longer, knowing that he was safe. Love doesn't go just one way. Just as Moses' mother cared for her children, Miriam cared for her mother and did what she could to make her life better. This story is one of care and kindness going in multiple directions, forming a net that catches the vulnerable and holds them safe.

And think about Pharaoh's daughter. She had incredible courage. It would have been much easier to turn aside, pretend she hadn't seen the basket and give the baby back. But she knew what was the right thing to do. She was the only person who could keep Moses safe from Pharaoh. So, she did it, even though she was a stranger, even though she didn't even belong to the community of Hebrews. Caring for the vulnerable, for those in danger, is everybody's responsibility. Caring and mothering is a collective responsibility we all share, as is the responsibility to be there when others cannot be.

We're not all in danger like Moses. Most of us don't have to risk our lives for others. But all of us have a responsibility to one another, a responsibility to care for the vulnerable, for those who cannot care for themselves. And, as in our story, all adults have a responsibility towards all children. On this Mothering Sunday, the story of Moses reminds us that mothering is not the task of mothers alone. It is the task of entire communities of love, care and compassion. Our task, together.

Isabelle Hamley

Hymn suggestions

For the beauty of the earth; Guide me, O thou great Jehovah; Even though I walk through the valley (You never let go); Some of us are big and tall (Big family of God).

Fifth Sunday of Lent (Passiontide)   17 March
Principal Service   **Sir, We Wish to See Jesus**
Jer. 31.31–34; Ps. 51.1–13, *or* Ps. 119.9–16; Heb. 5.5–10;
John 12.20–33

I was providing cover for a parish priest who was taking a well-deserved holiday. On arriving at the church, I was shown the vestry and, as is my custom, made my way to check whether the altar table was laid up and the 'pots and pans' were in their places. As I stood behind the altar table, I found a handwritten note with these words on it: 'Sir, we wish to see Jesus.' That brought me up short and made me realize what we were about to do – making Jesus real once again in word and sacrament.

They are, of course, the words that 'some Greeks' spoke to Philip when Jesus and his disciples were on their way to Jerusalem. I suspect they spoke to Philip as these Greeks probably recognized a connection: Philip being a Greek name. They felt at ease with one of their 'own'; a connection, however tenuous, is still a connection.

The Book of Glory

When Philip reported to Jesus that the Greeks had asked to see him, Jesus exclaimed, 'The hour has come for the Son of Man to be glorified.' This is a major turning point in St John's Gospel. Biblical scholars tell us that John is divided into two: the 'Book of Signs' and the 'Book of Glory'. In the Book of Signs, Jesus performs seven miracles that John refers to as signs. Throughout the Book of Signs, Jesus makes strange references to his 'hour' or 'the time' and says that it has yet to come. But when the Greeks asked to see Jesus, he knew that the hour had come, the time was near for him to be glorified.

The word 'glory' in Greek is *doxa* – that's where we get 'doxology' from: 'Glory be to the Father.' Its Hebrew root means *heaviness, substance, form*. The glory of God in the Older Testament was shown in the cloudy or fiery pillar, earthquakes and storms, Mount Sinai and even the Temple. Such events make God's presence real but they are also designed to conceal God and make God distant. For Jesus, to be glorified was to embrace the cross, the embodiment of suffering:

> Unless a grain of wheat falls into the earth and dies, it remains just a single grain; but if it dies, it bears much fruit …
>
> Now my soul is troubled. And what should I say – 'Father, save me from this hour?' No, it is for this reason that I have come to this hour …
>
> And I, when I am lifted up from the earth, will draw all people to myself.

The cross is to become 'the glory of God'. God would no longer be a distant figure concealed in fire and smoke, but earthed in the reality of Golgotha and human suffering. It was time for Jesus to be lifted up – that is, crucified – so that all people could be drawn to him, the suffering one

Giving more

For us, glory is about having more: more money, more prestige, more power. For Jesus, glory was about giving more. Jesus gives himself to his friends by washing their feet; he gives himself to the world by dying on the cross.

All around us are people who want to see Jesus. Do they see him in us? Do they see the Servant King who washed the feet of his friends? Do they see the prophet who cleansed the Temple? Do they see the healer who made the blind see? Do they see us painfully letting go, dying to the past in order that we may live for the future? If we are to let people see Jesus in us, then we must go and sit at his feet, let him heal us, feed upon his body broken, and above all stand at the cross and wonder as the glory of God lapses into silence and death. When we are closest to the cross, when we have truly embraced our death, have faith! Easter is only a step away.

If we want people to see Jesus in our actions and our words then to journey with Jesus is our only option. Journey with Jesus again through Holy Week. Score out some time in your diary to do just that this coming Holy Week which begins next Sunday.

'Sir, we wish to see Jesus,' the Greeks said to Philip. We, too, need to see Jesus, so that when others want to see Jesus, they can see Jesus in us.

Paul Williams

Hymn suggestions

And now, O Father, mindful of the love; Lift high the cross; When I survey the wondrous cross; Unless a grain of wheat shall fall (Farrell).

Fifth Sunday of Lent (Passiontide)   17 March
Second Service   Longing for Justice
Ps. 34 [*or* 34.1–10]; Ex. 7.8–24; **Rom. 5.12–end**;
Gospel at Holy Communion: Luke 22.1–13

Longing for justice

Let me introduce you to Danny. Danny leads walking tours around the city. We begin at the Cenotaph, a glorious memorial to those who died in war. Danny points out that he did not die. He suffered post-traumatic stress disorder, left the army and became homeless. He takes us to the artists' part of town; wall-to-wall artisans' shops making everything from jewellery and clothing to bread and yoghurt. But we don't stop there. Behind these shops is a doorway, where Danny slept for three years until a group of drunken men took exception to him one night, beat him up and left him with broken ribs and lost teeth. Danny takes us to two churches. Outside one is a sculpture of the homeless Christ, a metal blanket, covering a metal body, with nail-imprinted feet sticking out. He tells us that he sometimes goes into this church, and they give him tea and biscuits. He doesn't go in when people are there though. They don't like him to be in the services. He takes us to another church too. It's always open, and Danny says he meets God there.

Danny's story makes my heart cry out for justice. I want to hear that the army cares as much for the living as the dead, or that the men who beat up Danny met their demise somehow, or that the people in the church welcome him and invite him to join them. But none of that happens.

There is something in the human heart that cries for justice. If you doubt that, watch the average football crowd when a penalty decision goes for or against their team. Justice puts things right; justice restores things to how they are meant to be. If this desire for justice is inherent in being human, our faith – the faith of the church – needs to address it; and I think it's this longing that Paul addresses in today's passage from Romans.

Justice and Justification

'Hang on,' you might say. Paul talks about justification, not justice. They seem to be worlds apart. Justification appears in theological libraries and on the lips of preachers and evangelists. Justice appears on placards and on the websites of marginalized social groups. But in the ancient languages of the Bible, there is no distinction, they are both covered by the same Greek and Hebrew words.[20] Paul talks about justification in the context of sin and law, so even here they are not far apart.

A cycle of sin and condemnation

Things are not as they are meant to be, Paul explains. The law came into a confused, sinful world. The role of the law is to highlight what is wrong. Let's return to football for a moment. In the Premier League, decisions are no longer the referee's best guess. Fans of one side might fully believe they should have a penalty kick; fans of the opposite side might wholeheartedly disagree. But the law is the law. It is applied by the Virtual Assistant Referee, who looks at the incident over and over again in slow motion, takes tiny measurements, looks at the rules, and applies the law. It's possible that the players involved have no idea that they transgressed, but if the person interpreting the law says they did, then they did. That's what the law does. In Paul's terms, the law leaves us in a cycle of sin, conscious or unconscious. But by making us aware of injustice, the law also makes us aware of grace.

We have made justice/justification ordinary

I am very grateful for Peter's second letter. Particularly the bit in chapter 3 (15–16) where he says that some of Paul's letters are hard to understand! This deeply theological passage could be included in Peter's comments! So, I want to focus on one aspect of the passage as we move towards Holy Week and Easter. Placing justification, or justice, in a theological context makes it seem ordinary. Perhaps we've even interpreted it to mean that Jesus' death means we can get away with doing wrong things. But it is not ordinary. It is the activity of God in Jesus to bring about a justification that leads to eternal life in him. In the sentence before our reading starts, Paul says that through Christ we have now received reconciliation. The human desire for justice is a desire for things to be put right, and that is exactly what God in Jesus has done. Of course, we still live in a world of sin and death. But they do not have the final word.

Human justice is warped. As Danny told us on our walking tour, it honours the dead and ignores the living. It seeks to harm what does not fit in. But God's justice is essential. Without justice, we cannot live in harmony with our neighbours; without justice, we cannot live in harmony with God. Because of God's justice, we can walk in newness of life.

Liz Shercliff

Hymn suggestions

The kingdom of God is justice and joy; Send down the fire of your justice; Beauty for brokenness; God of justice, Saviour to all.

Holy Week

Palm Sunday   24 March
Principal Service   **Between Cheers and Jeers**
Liturgy of the Palms: **Mark 11.1–11**, *or* John 12.12–16;
Ps. 118.1–2, 19–end [*or* 118.19–end]
Liturgy of the Passion: Isa. 50.4–9a; Ps. 31.9–16 [*or* 31.9–18];
Phil. 2.5–11; Mark 14.1—end of 15, *or* Mark 15.1–39 [40–end]

A changing perspective

I've been to some extraordinary parties, festivals and processions
in my time. I've waved the palm branches of youthful enthusiasm,
disorder and folly at Glastonbury, Download and a dozen other
festivals. I've protested on sit-ins and demos; it generally felt good
and worthwhile, and sometimes it even changed things.

And now I am middle-aged and I am rather broken down ... a
priest, a canon, an agent of respectability. I look back on my restless
and protesting youth and I am shocked to think that, these days,
when faced with the enthusiasm and youthful passion of protestors,
I tend to worry about good order breaking down.

The remarkable events of the first Palm Sunday bring alive, for
me, this tension between the energy and protest of youth and the
small 'c' conservatism of middle age. Jesus' triumphal entry into
Jerusalem raises questions about what kind of response we would
make to it if we had been present. We might like to imagine that we
would position ourselves among those who waved palm branches
and placards of hope, proclaiming dreams and expectations of
liberation. However, I suspect many of us would – shamefacedly –
sit with those who greeted Jesus' progress with fear. Jesus' actions
threatened the status quo. As I've grown older, I've discovered that
when one has a growing stake in the status quo it is easy to react
negatively to anything that threatens it. As we live in the rubble of

91

our youthful dreams, enthusiasms and desires, do we stand with God or with our own self-interest?

A provocative procession

Perhaps part of the power of Palm Sunday is its capacity both to expose our longing for change, redemption and justice, as well as our capacity to fall away into judgement and self-interest. So, as we read of Jesus' triumphal entry, I suspect we want to be among those who cheer and welcome the revolution of love and reconciliation. We wave our palm branches. We feel our muscles grow taut as we raise our fists in solidarity. We feel lactic acid burn through our legs as we march on, and stand for hours, waiting, waiting for Jesus to be crowned king. We are proud to be in the vanguard. For into our midst has come the one who gives sight to the blind, lets the lame walk, who sets the prisoner free.

If Jesus' triumphal entry happened today perhaps some of us would wave banners that might say 'Hosanna! Hosanna! Now our King will make austerity no more, and will set the oppressed free.' Depending on our passions, we might wave placards which anticipate God setting LGBTQ+ people, global-majority people, disabled people and the whole variety of human beings free from prejudice. Pick your pet issue! God will throw the oppressor off. God will set his people free! We travel into glory and it makes us feel good. Nothing can stop us now! Nothing!

The deep challenge

If only it were that simple. There is a reason we also hear of Jesus' Passion on Palm Sunday. Among other things, that narrative reminds us that our enthusiasms for what is good and holy so readily turn into cowardice and fear. Our desire to be part of Jesus' movement of grace can all too soon be turned into betrayal and mob instincts. We may want to be in the vanguard with Jesus, our subversive King, but we can also become faces in a crowd as the implications of Jesus' way become clearer to us. Following Jesus leads to changes in our lives. If these changes are challenging, we might be tempted to stick with the status quo.

Perhaps we are already respectable … perhaps we're priests and lawyers and officers of the law. Perhaps we are on the side of property, suspicious of those who might threaten our magnificent buildings and the civility of our streets. Even as we welcome protest, we don't want anyone to threaten *our* church, *our* cathedral, our comfort. In abstract, we like the idea of revolution, of God transforming the world, but please could he do it without too much cost to us?

Inside each of us, inside our community, is a wound of grace and fragility. It invites us to follow the way of hope. It tempts us to betray or run away and hide. Palm Sunday invites us to occupy that space between the call Jesus makes on us to stand up for grace and love and the fact that, in our fragility, we so easily fall away. This is an uncomfortable place. However, it is a place I think it always wise to walk towards on Palm Sunday, as we begin the extraordinary journey of Holy Week. It is holy ground. It is the ground where we face the facts of our hopes and the reality of our weakness. It is the place where Jesus can meet us and ready us for the promise of death and life held in the Easter event.

Rachel Mann

Hymn suggestions

Ride on, ride on, in majesty; Make way, make way; All glory, laud and honour; Hark, the glad sound, the Saviour comes.

Palm Sunday   24 March
Second Service   **The Rewilding God**
Ps. 69.1–20; **Isa. 5.1–7**; Mark 12.1–12

Vineyards

For those of us living in Scotland, vineyards are not things we easily identify with or have a close connection to. Vineyards come from a world unlike our natural habitat, a world of warmth and sun and stability of weather. And the stuff vineyards produce is not a natural part of our cultural habitat. We are people of grain, not grape, malting not fermenting, whisky not wine. We, therefore, come to the use of vineyards in the biblical text at a disadvantage, needing to put in some extra steps, perhaps by dragging up memories of holidays and other cultures.

The reading from Isaiah has a really good play around with this image. It gives us space and time to get used to it and sop it up. The Gospel reading uses the image in a much more prosaic way, but

Isaiah is poetry and song. The chapter starts as a song and gathers pace as a good song, a song fit for a party where much wine has been drunk. It goes on to repeat itself, it trips over itself, it tells a story and confuses the metaphors and the characters. It creates the intimacy of dear friends and the distance of wrongs done.

The friend who owns a vineyard

The insights this short reading gives us into the nature of God are worth prioritizing, I think, as we start Holy Week. It is a picture of God that I suggest is the opposite of what we are bracing ourselves for. This is not a God of sorrow and grief, existing in moments of trauma and wickedness. This is a God primarily of good things, joyful things. The image is first and foremost of God as a beloved friend who owns a vineyard. These are two things that bring joy to life: friendship and wine; the drink which enables celebrations and social occasions. Think of the moments you have in your memory of good times with good friends. Think of what went on in those moments. Think of how you felt. And this is part of the image of God we are being encouraged to absorb. God is in the business of enabling life in all its fullness, not dullness.

Then the image extends. God, unlike the vineyard owner in the Gospel reading, is a daily worker in the vineyard not a distant owner. God does the backbreaking work of digging it and clearing it of stones, building a watchtower and a wine vat. God chooses and plants the best vines and has the expertise to make the best agronomical choices. This is the stuff of the dirt-engrained hands of peasant farmers not the gardening gloves of the landed gentry. This is the stuff of a God who is in the business for the long haul, who puts the hard graft in, expecting and believing that good things, the best of good things, are being created.

This perspective casts a whole different light on the meaning of the next few verses. The song turns to a moment of acute disappointment. The reality is that the vineyard has not produced any fruit that can be used, but instead, for some reason, produced fruit that is useless, sour and inedible. We enter into the uneasy work of sitting with God as vine-keeper and worker, producing wine, experiencing huge disappointment and instinctively taking responsibility for what has gone wrong.

Rewilding

And so, the image extends again, the vineyard owner acts in response to the new circumstances. They take away the artificial boundaries they have put in, they let the plants grow however they grow, they let the animals take whatever they want to take, and they quit hoping the weather will be favourable to growing. These days we would perhaps call this 'rewilding'; stepping back to let nature take care of itself in order to protect and restore the environment. This is still an act of extreme care and deep love, of sympathetic thoughtfulness and long-term planning. This is the stuff of a nurturing and parental God who holds faith in the ability of the world to right itself, not a managerial and angry God who lashes out with punishment.

Rewilding as a process has no definite end point. That is perhaps something else to hang on to this week. The God who gets us to Easter Sunday will get us to Pentecost and to Christmas and to another year. The God who restores one lost part of life now will restore other lost parts of life in the future. The God who has worked with humanity and all creation to heal and grow and reconnect with each other will continue to do so, over and over again.

Esther Elliott

Hymn suggestions

My God, I love thee; Ride on, ride on, the time is right; One shall tell another; I am the vine, you are the branches.

First Three Days of Holy Week   25–27 March
Six Days of Awe

(These are the readings for Monday of Holy Week but the sermon may be used on any day.)
Isa. 42.1–9; Ps. 36.5–11; Heb. 9.11–15; **John 12.1–11**

'Six days before the Passover Jesus came to Bethany,' says St John. Those six days sound like an incidental detail. But there is the hint of foreboding, a cloud no bigger than a man's hand that portends how this story will unfold. Passover is a time of freedom and festivity but also of bloodletting, the slaying of animals in memory of terrible ordeals long ago when rescue seemed impossible. And

95

Bethany – symbol of homecoming and rest for the Son of Man with nowhere to lay his head – this place has just witnessed one man's passover, Lazarus who died and whom Jesus raised. Bethany is the only place in St John's Gospel where Jesus has wept.

However, on the surface, everything seems calm and peaceful – for now. They are giving a dinner for Jesus and the house is filled with warmth and laughter and the love of friends. But then Mary does this extraordinary thing with the most expensive perfume that could be got. And as the sweet fragrance fills the room, the bitter smell of death can be scented too. Judas remonstrates: John says not because he cares about the poor but because he is a thief, another hint of what is to come when Judas will shortly go out into the night to hand Jesus over. And Jesus interprets Mary's act for what it foreshadows: 'She bought it so that she might keep it for the day of my burial.' At once we see with shocking clarity what the end will be. 'Six days before the Passover', six days before this Lamb of God must be offered up, six days before the hour of suffering, death and burial is finally here.

We are into those six days now. The Jewish community calls its solemnities 'Days of Awe'. Holy Week and the Easter Triduum are our Christian 'days of awe'. As these days unfold, we enter into the most profound mystery of the universe, that ours is a suffering God in whom we see love emptying itself, love freely given so that all creation may be redeemed. These days draw us into this movement of passion and pain that is the cost of our salvation. But because love conquers all things, love is risen too, like spring following winter. Throughout the lengthening light of Lent, we have been looking forward to this 'hour' of the Passover of the Lord. Like Jesus in St Luke's Gospel, we set our faces to 'go up' to Jerusalem at Passover time to witness this exodus he must perform there that has changed human history and saved the world. 'The royal banners forward go,' says the great sixth-century hymn of the cross. And we must go with them to see this thing that has come to pass, and gaze upon the 'Tree of beauty, Tree of light', on whose arms the weight of the world's ransom hangs.

Holy Week summons us to an act of the imagination. These 'days of awe' ask us life's fundamental question: where do we most want to travel to? How we respond to the saving events of the gospel, cross and resurrection, will decide the kind of people we shall become. That is to say: do we want to take up our cross and follow him? Do we want to make him our king? Or are we content with the easy-going, fair-weather religion that asks little and in the end gives nothing in return? For, the liturgy of Holy Week is more than a powerful spectacle. It is drama, something performed, something done, the work of God that in its very act proclaims the kingdom of God, summons us to repent and believe the gospel, and invites us to recommit ourselves to the transformation that following Jesus must mean. That will bring its share of pain, for there is a cost to discipleship. So Holy Week should change us in deep and lasting ways. For we should glimpse how we enter into God's movement of love and grace which entails being crucified with Christ so that we might be raised with him in newness of life.

It is an awesome prospect to draw near to holy ground, this blazing heart of God's passionate love for us. Yet it is good to be here, joining this pilgrimage of grace in Holy Week as we look forward to celebrating the Lord's Passover, this 'thing most wonderful'. Yes, it takes time and effort: a week is a long time not just in politics but in religion. But to invest in God, to transact the issues of death and life, to deepen and enrich our own humanity could be the most important thing we do this year. These six days of awe give us just enough time to take off our shoes.

Michael Sadgrove

Hymn suggestions

It is a thing most wonderful; O love, how deep, how broad, how high; How deep the Father's love for us; We sing the praise of him who died.

Maundy Thursday   28 March
Bending and Stooping
Ex. 12.1–4 [5–10] 11–14; Ps. 116.1, 10–end [*or* 116.9–end]; 1 Cor. 11.23–26; **John 13.1–17, 31b–35**

To serve, not to be served

In reading the New Testament, we discover that Jesus – in word and deed – tried to teach his followers about God's love. He told them plainly that he had come 'not to be served, but to serve, and to give his life as a ransom for many' (Matt. 20.28), and that he would suffer death on a cross. Yet, even those closest to him did not seem to understand what he was trying to say to them. In fact, surprisingly, as they journeyed with him towards Jerusalem and the cross, his disciples were thinking about their own status and argued among themselves about who was the greatest.

It is against the backdrop of his teaching about 'loving and serving' others that, having made their way to Jerusalem, Jesus and his disciples gathered for a meal. It was just before the festival of the Passover and, while the disciples still seemed unaware of what lay ahead, Jesus knew that he would be betrayed, abandoned and crucified. Knowing 'that his hour had come to depart from the world and go to the Father', Jesus tried once again to show his disciples what it means to love and serve others: Jesus got up from the table and, pouring water into a basin, he began to wash the disciples' feet.

Setting an example

Can you imagine the scene? Foot-washing was a dirty, dusty business, considered a menial task to be left to servants. Yet, one by one, Jesus knelt before his disciples and washed their feet. His followers must have looked at one another in disbelief. This was surely not right. Jesus should not be 'bending and stooping' to wash their feet! Peter protested, though perhaps he was expressing what all of the disciples were feeling. 'You will never wash my feet!' To which Jesus replied, 'Unless I wash you, you have no share with me.' Peter then asked to be washed all over! In reply, Jesus said to Peter, 'One who has bathed does not need to wash, except for the feet.' It has been suggested that this reply to Peter was a reference to Judas whom he knew would betray him. Yet, the truth is that none of the disciples were 'clean'. Nor are we. Everyone has made wrong choices and, though we may have sought forgiveness, in a sense often we feel tainted by the burden of regret.

After he had finished washing their feet, Jesus said to his disciples, 'If I, your Lord and Teacher, have washed your feet, you also ought to wash one another's feet. For I have set you an example, that you also should do as I have done to you.'

Learning to 'bend and stoop'

In the Appalachian mountains, there are congregations of believers who have taken Jesus' command to wash one another's feet quite literally, and they still practise foot-washing – not just on Maundy

Thursday as we might do reflectively each year, but every time they gather to share in the Lord's Supper. Indeed, when asked about their practice, one woman said that she would never 'take the bread' unless she had washed feet.

While we may not feel it is necessary to literally wash one another's feet before we share in the Eucharist, I wonder if the Appalachian Christians provide us with an important reminder: the mark of a true disciple of Jesus is the willingness to 'bend and stoop' in love and service to others. Of course, this idea does not really sit well in our 'self first' culture today. Yet, most of us have met those who, perhaps in very small ways, have 'washed the feet' of others. For instance, think of the person who often rings others to offer a word of encouragement. Or the individual who, without being asked or looking for any recognition, takes on some small tasks in the church. Or the person who, in spite of being deeply hurt, refuses to nurse a grudge towards another. In many different ways, we may 'bend and stoop' as we remember the words of Jesus: 'I give you a new commandment, that you love one another. Just as I have loved you, you also should love one another.'

Karen E. Smith

Hymn suggestions

Kneels at the feet of his friends; Great God, your love has called us here; Brother, sister, let me serve you; A new commandment I give unto you.

Good Friday   29 March
Principal Service   **Why Do We Call It 'Good'?**
Isa. 52.13—end of 53; Ps. 22 [*or* 22.1–11, *or* 22.1–21];
Heb. 10.16–25, *or* Heb. 4.14–16; 5.7–9; **John 18.1—end of 19**

The four Gospels give us very different sayings with which Jesus takes his leave of the world. In Matthew and Mark, the last words from the cross are desperate, godforsaken and stark: 'My God, my God, why have you forsaken me?' In Luke, they are confident and trusting: 'Father, into your hands I commend my spirit.' And in John, they are different again. 'It is finished.'

It's a single word in Greek: *tetelestai*. You should put an exclamation mark after it, for it is more a shout than anything else: 'It is accomplished!' You sometimes hear those words read as if they were a sigh of resignation or defeat. You could not read the text more wrongly. On the contrary, *tetelestai* is a cry of victory, of triumph that a task has been successfully accomplished.

What is that task? Nothing less than the salvation of the world. And that is what Jesus has now achieved, now that his hour has come. The cross is a throne where he is 'lifted up', where he reigns in the glory of love freely given, of a life laid down. Glory, says the opening passage in St John, the Christmas Gospel, is what Jesus has come to reveal to the world: 'we have seen his glory, the glory as of a father's only son, full of grace and truth' (John 1.14). Ask John where we see it fully disclosed, and his answer is: here, on the cross, in Christ's enthronement as king.

St John has already foreshadowed this last word of the Passion earlier in the Gospel, when, as so often, a trivial incident is used to underline some truth about the work of Jesus. The disciples are urging Jesus to eat something. He replies, 'I have food to eat that you do not know about.' They conjecture what that secret provision might be, but Jesus translates the conversation to a wholly different plane. He says, 'My food is to do the will of him who sent me and to complete (to accomplish) his work' (John 4.34). The same word.

It is a wonderful word because it leaves us in no doubt as to why we call today *Good* Friday. It is a day of dark and dreadful things, passion and pain, suffering and death. Yet it is a *good* day because of what has been accomplished in them. To the soldiers who crucified him, he was just another criminal, hoisted up and exposed to public shame and disgrace. To the crowd who clamoured for his death, he was the usurper whose false claims to kingship were mocked by the purple robe and crown of thorns. But to the few who were there because they loved him, he was the Son of God never more majestic than now, never nobler, never more regal. He has overcome the world and can go to the Father. All is accomplished.

But John also wants to remind us of an older story still, the creation story. On the sixth day, the Friday, Genesis says that God created humanity. And he looked on what he had made and pro-claimed that 'it was very good'. That Friday was the culmination of what was begun when God said 'Let there be light'. 'God finished the work that he had done' – the word for 'finished' is the same root in Greek. So, John is saying that on the sixth day – Good Friday – God finished remaking the world through the cross of his son. All was accomplished so that Jesus could rest in the tomb on the seventh day, the Sabbath. What was begun at the dawn of time was waiting for Good Friday. Only at the cross, only in his own death, could the Word of the Father finish the making, or the remaking, of the world. Only at Golgotha is creation finished and our humanity complete.

So, the cross is more than the redemption of individual men, women and children like ourselves – though it *is* that. For St John, it has a cosmic dimension, for it is the *world*, the *kosmos* that God so loved. Therefore, Jesus is lifted up between heaven and earth so that everything may be brought into one, and the whole creation, the *kosmos*, may be healed of its pain. The cross is a gateway, an open door of hope, a place of new beginnings for the world. To him, it is pain and loss. To us, it is life and grace. As George Herbert puts it in his poem 'The Agony',

> Love is that liquor sweet and most divine,
> which my God feels as blood, but I as wine.

We contemplate the cross of Christ and hear that great and marvellous final word re-echoing around the universe: 'It is finished.' All is accomplished. And we are thankful for this Friday of the year that we call *good*.

Michael Sadgrove

Hymn suggestions

The royal banners forward go; O sacred head surrounded; We sing the praise of him who died; Praise to the holiest in the height.

Easter

Easter Vigil 30–31 March
The Defining Story
(*A minimum of three Old Testament readings should be chosen. The reading from Ex. 14 should always be used.*)
Gen. 1.1—2.4a *and* Ps. 136.1–9, 23–end; Gen. 7.1–5, 11–18;
8.6–18; 9.8–13 *and* Ps. 46; Gen. 22.1–18 *and* Ps. 16;
Ex. 14.10–end; 15.20–21 *and Canticle*: Ex. 15.1b–13, 17–18;
Isa. 55.1–11 *and Canticle*: Isa. 12.2–end; Baruch 3.9–15,
32—4.4 *and* Ps. 19, *or* Prov. 8.1–8, 19–21; 9.4b–6 *and* Ps. 19;
Ezek. 36.24–28 *and* Ps. 42, 43; Ezek. 37.1–14 *and* Ps. 143;
Zeph. 3.14–end *and* Ps. 98; Rom. 6.3–11 *and* Ps. 114;
Mark 16.1–8

Start at the beginning

Like all writers, I can agonize over how to begin a new book or chapter or even a new sentence. That should come as no surprise. Writing is an act of creation. As such, it requires decision and discernment and a willingness to start over if the writing is stale or bad or heading down into a cul-de-sac. *Where to begin?* It's a mesmerising question if you think about it.

The clear-minded person might answer simply by saying, 'Don't be clever! Begin at the beginning. Start at the beginning, head towards the middle, and drive on to the end. Simple.' Indeed, the opening words of the Bible confirm God's attention to beginnings and beginning well: 'In the beginning …' This fascination with beginnings is reflected throughout the Old and New Testaments: in the beginning, God separates the light from the dark, the day from the night; in Genesis, God brings forth the rainbow promise of a new world after a great flood; in Ezekiel, God raises dry bones to new life. Ultimately, God sends his son to save us. God is serious about beginnings.

Easter represents the ultimate beginning. As we gather for the Easter Vigil, we are invited to find God's new beginning in the most unexpected place: a tomb. This beginning comes not with a birth but after a death; not at the dawn of creation but right in the midst of God's world. The ultimate new beginning is found right at the moment of grief, where all one wants to do is anoint the body of the beloved whom we know has been slain. The beginning comes at the point of the practical question, 'Who will roll the stone away from the entrance of the tomb?'

The fulcrum of God

Easter reflects the subversive, radical power of God. 'Subversive' because God comes into the midst of the ordinary run of time and history and turns it upside down; and 'radical' because, in the face of God's love and grace, the world simply cannot be the same again. In the ordinary run of things, the world – like a classic story – runs from the beginning through the middle and on to the end. However, in the resurrection of Jesus Christ, God shows that the Easter event itself is the fulcrum and the still turning point of the world. Time and reality and story do not work according to human design, but God's. To begin, even just to begin, to understand salvation history, one has to go to the empty tomb. In the resurrection of Jesus Christ, the whole of creation is reworked.

What does this mean for us? Well, one of the things it means is that we can never, ever say that death has the final word. It is worth reminding ourselves that ordinary people in Jesus' time no more believed in the possibility of the resurrection of the dead than they do in ours. They knew – as we know – that if a person is executed, that's it. A person doesn't come back from that. Death is final; and those who have the power to bring it about (empires, armies, mobs and so on) have the final word. Once you're dead, the story is over.

God says otherwise; he – in Jesus Christ – tells another story of salvation, hope and promise. The empty tomb takes us to the fundamental story of God: he has the final word. This is a story that reverberates through the Bible but is definitively revealed for all and for all time in the truth of Jesus Christ's resurrection. God is about life and hope and promise, even when the world seems to tell a different story.

The ultimate story

This is such a powerful and challenging counter to so many of our human experiences. When we lose a loved one – a friend, a member of our family or, as we saw when the late Queen died, anyone who has been part of our lives – it can seem as if the world has come to a definitive end. The story is over. Or when one has to negotiate a sense that the world has no future – because of war or economic wreckage or climate grief – our lives can feel denuded of promise. There is seemingly, under such circumstances, no open texture to the world. But the empty tomb speaks otherwise.

As we enter into the power of the Easter Vigil, we gather with all those who have gone before us – including those first women who came to anoint their Lord at the tomb – as well as all those who will come after us; together we bring our fear and doubt and anxiety that the world's violence and death has the final word. We come at the moment of dawn and we long for truth and promise. We pray that we are to meet someone who is worthy of our hope. And God greets us ... he greets us with the only story that truly matters: that Jesus is risen. And we make our response: he is risen indeed. Alleluia.

Rachel Mann

Hymn suggestions

Jesus Christ is risen today; Thine be the glory; The day of resurrection; Now the green blade riseth.

Easter Day   31 March
Principal Service   **Just Turn Up**
Acts 10.34–43, *or* **Isa. 25.6–9**; Ps. 118.1–2, 14–24 [*or* 118.14–24]; 1 Cor. 15.1–11, *or* Acts 10.34–43; John 20.1–18, *or* **Mark 16.1–8**

Do you ever wonder about how Easter faith changes things? In a world full of war and struggle, failure and fragility, how does the truth of the resurrected Jesus help? We live in an age of deep anxiety and raging anger, as a dip into the comments section on social media platforms readily reveals. The church in the West has been chastened: terrible stories of abuse coupled with rapid decline.

So how does the Easter story change anything? Is anyone even listening?

Withdraw, doubt or just turn up

We might be tempted to one of two extremes. One is for the church to withdraw into itself – speaking into the increasingly empty vaults of its own echo chamber. The other is to fall into doubt, to see the resurrection as just 'an idle tale' (Luke 24.11) and live as practical atheists. But there is another way; a bold, humble and simple way – just turn up. Do what you can with what you have, even in the face of seemingly impossible barriers, and let God be God.

The women just turn up

Mark's account of the resurrection shows clearly how the power of God breaks into the pain and brokenness of humanity. When Mary Magdalene, Mary the mother of James, and Salome turn up with the spices to anoint Jesus, no doubt they were torn apart by the trauma of all they had witnessed. That morning it might have been easier to turn over and stay in bed, folded into grief. However, they come to do what they can. They turn up. They fretted over the problem of gaining access to the tomb, having witnessed a huge stone sealing Jesus' body in. But they turn up anyway, hoping to find help, but in no way certain that they would.

They see the massive stone rolled away, but they don't know how this has happened. It's not obvious to them that God is at work; Mark makes no mention of angels – just of a man in a white robe. The ordinary in the midst of the extraordinary; God is here. The women are alarmed. The words of the young man – 'you are looking for Jesus of Nazereth, who was crucified. He has been raised … he is going ahead of you … you will see him, just as he told you' – don't bring them any comfort. Ponder that a moment. It is not immediately obvious to the first witnesses of the resurrection what any of it means. They don't leap for joy; they flee in terror and amazement, and fear binds their tongues. 'They said nothing to anyone.' This does beg the question of how the story got out in the first place, but clearly the power of God is greater than human silence.

A call to just turn up

So, what difference does the resurrection make? It reminds us that our job is to just turn up, to do what we can with what we have, even when we face seemingly impossible barriers and blockages, trusting that God will meet us. It is not all on us. Ponder that. The women did not make the resurrection happen, they just turned up with the spices – thinking they were facing death.

People don't seem interested in the church, which appears to be so disconnected from the everyday lives of most people. Many are suspicious or dismissive. That might feel like death to us. In spite of that, we need the boldness to just turn up in the public square, trusting that God will meet us there in God's good time. That means going out and building relationships in business, politics, sports, education, health care, the military, in our workplaces and social spaces. We need to simply be ourselves, listen to others and tell our stories of God – undefended and open, simply holding on to the promises of God in the muddled reality of the day-to-day. We need to just turn up as we are, with what we have, aware of our limitations, and trusting God. And …

God works Saturdays

The resurrection is God's promise to us that God is at work during the long hours of Saturday – and Sunday will come. Isaiah paints a picture of that Sunday, pointing to a movement of God from beyond into the life of the world. It's a picture of glorious provision, community and comfort. At the heart of it is the line, 'he will swallow up death for ever' (Isa. 25.8). Death cast away – and with it all the horrors of war, abuse, racism, corruption, hunger, loneliness, grief, despair and cynicism. Death done away with; all wounds healed.

In the meantime, just turn up

Paul writes: 'Christ has been raised from the dead, the first fruits of those who have died' (1 Cor. 15.20). Because of Jesus, there is more fruit to come. This is the source of all our hope. In the meantime, just turn up – do what you can, with who you are and what you have, and trust God is still at work. Always.

Just turn up.
Happy Easter.

Kate Bruce

(Many of the thoughts underlying this sermon were inspired by a sermon preached by the Bishop to the Forces, the Rt Revd Hugh Nelson, addressing the Anglican Chaplains of the RAF in June 2022.)

Hymn suggestions

In Christ alone; Now the green blade riseth; How great thou art; I surrender all.

Easter Day 31 March
Second Service **The Wide Space of Hope**
Morning Ps. 114, 117; Evening Ps. 105, *or* 66.1–11;
Ezek. 37.1–14; **Luke 24.13–35**

Heady days

They had enjoyed – and endured – a heady few days. Depending on which Gospel account you read, just a week ago Jesus had ridden into Jerusalem to shouts of adulation from the crowd; he had raised a dead man; and kicked the corrupt money-changers out of the Temple. Then – well, he had just hung around for a bit, eating with his friends, washing their feet and talking about servanthood. Finally, one of their own had handed him over to the Jews. The Jews had given him to the Romans, and the Romans had killed him. At the beginning of the week, they thought that at last Jesus their Messiah was actually going to demonstrate the power of God and kick the Romans out of Palestine, restore Temple worship and come back to be among his people. Possibilities opened out before them.

But now Jesus is dead.

Hope is gone

The two disciples walk along the road to Emmaus bereft, devoid of hope, heads down, seeing nothing but the next step in front of them. Regretting the past. When a stranger comes to walk beside them, they use those saddest of words, 'We had hoped.' They are in that constricted space of hopelessness.

We know the ending of the story, of course. But they don't. They have no concept of a God who dies, or a God who dies and rises again, and certainly not of a God who is killed.

Hope is gone.

Worse, there is the poignant pain of potentially good news. Jesus' body is gone, angels have been seen at the tomb. But it has happened to some *women* and every good Jew knows that God does not speak through women. Every Roman knows women are too unstable and emotional to be witnesses. Every Greek knows women are unteachable.

This hope was no hope. It could not lift their eyes to wider horizons.

Then Jesus comes alongside these despairing disciples and – walks with them.

They don't recognize him. We don't see what we don't expect to see. Of course, the disciples don't recognize Jesus – it's impossible he should be there.

Jesus begins to explain what's happened. He begins with the old stories of how God over and over again reaches out to people, loves them, restores them and redeems them – again and again.

Easter hope

Easter hope is a Christian virtue. Easter hope changes things. Easter hope raises our eyes to wider horizons.

I don't mean the kind of hope that is an aspiration, or a desire, or ambition, but the kind of hope that is based on what we know to be true. The kind of hope that is based on Jesus being Lord.

Up to the point where Jesus breaks bread with them, the disciples have only a knowledge of how his life might have fitted in with their Scriptures. Faith alone does not restore recognition of their Lord. But when hope is restored by the breaking of bread, faith grows. Faith is believing things about Jesus; hope is seeing what he is doing and joining in. Jesus restores hope for the two disciples, and they bring hope to their friends. Hope changes things. Hope is the business we are in.

The disciples were walking along, without hope, repeating the story they thought they knew: Jesus, a prophet mighty in word and deed, had been crucified; they had hoped he was the Messiah, but apparently not; and now some women had astonished them by finding Jesus' body gone and talking with angels about it. It was demoralizing and confusing.

But Jesus reshapes the story: remember how the prophets of old said God was going to do something new; remember how God led his people to freedom before; remember how God has come over and over again to redeem people? Remember how God never acts according to what people expect?

When the story has been retold the disciples are able to recognize Jesus; it's like scales falling from their eyes. And thinking back over their time with him, they recognize that hope had begun to grow in their hearts from the moment they met on the road. The resurrection demonstrates that hope is not blind or stupid or naive. We, like the disciples on the road to Emmaus, have been given hope to pass on to others; hope that can stand even in hard times; hope that lifts our eyes to new horizons.

In the words of Jürgen Moltmann, God is 'the wide space of hope'.[21]

Liz Shercliff

Hymn suggestions

Christ the Lord is risen today; Thine be the glory; The day of resurrection; He was known in the breaking of the bread.

Second Sunday of Easter   7 April
Principal Service   **Encounters with the Risen Christ**
Ex. 14.10–end; 15.20–21 (*if used, the reading from Acts must be used as the second reading*), or Acts 4.32–35; Ps. 133; 1 John 1.1—2.2; **John 20.19–end**

First encounter

We're a week on from Easter Sunday but for the disciples in our Gospel this morning it's still Easter Day. We find them huddled together on the evening of the resurrection, behind locked doors. Too frightened to venture out despite the news from Mary that the Lord has risen.

The doors are shut tight but that doesn't stop the risen Christ who suddenly appears in their midst. What a gracious entrance he makes. There are many things the risen Christ might have said to the disciples at this first meeting: 'Where were you?', 'Why did you betray me?', 'Why are you all hiding away here?' But he doesn't say any of those things. Instead, he greets them with 'Peace be with you'. He uses the Hebrew word 'shalom', which means 'well-being' in its fullest sense. Jesus says to the disciples: may you be whole, may you be one, may all the blessings of the kingdom of God be yours.

Jesus then breathes the Holy Spirit on them, filling them with the power of God, commissioning them to go and spread the good news of the risen Christ in word and action. We can see the difference that encounter with the risen Christ makes in the reading from Acts, where the disciples are united, hold all things in common and share their possessions and money to help those in need.

Second encounter

Back to the Gospel. Thomas wasn't there. We don't know why. But he misses the first encounter of the disciples with the risen Christ. Despite their many detailed stories of the event, he doesn't believe it, stating he won't believe until he sees for himself and can touch the reality of Christ's wounded flesh. It's not surprising he doesn't believe it: this is a completely new event. Something which has never happened before – no wonder it's hard to believe.

But resurrection is a God-event, and God is a God of new creation, of surprises, of breaking the rules. It's in God's very nature to do new and creative things. Thomas doesn't have to wait long to discover this – just a week later – in fact where we are now.

The disciples have gathered together in the house again and this time Thomas is there too. Jesus comes again with peace for the whole group but gives his individual attention to Thomas and invites him to see and touch. Thomas makes a huge leap in his faith: not only does he see and believe, he worships and proclaims Jesus as 'My Lord and my God', the first disciple to do that. His hesitancy and doubting have led to a place of firm and committed faith. We should never underestimate the place of searching and questioning in our journey with Christ.

Thomas does something else which is very important – he draws our attention to the scars and wounds of Christ. The resurrected Christ is a new creation, the first fruits of those who sleep; he is a new being – not a ghost or a resuscitated man like Lazarus, but a being who can pass through locked doors, come and go at will, eat, drink, be both recognizable and unrecognizable. Despite resurrection, he still bears in his body the marks of the cross. It reminds us that resurrection doesn't come without crucifixion. Sometimes things really do have to die in order for something new and fresh to come about. As Christians, we hold in tension death and life, darkness and light, suffering and joy.

Our encounter

The risen Christ comes to us this day and every day. We are even more blessed than the disciples because we haven't seen him face to face and yet we believe. Christ comes to us through the Scriptures, through the witness of others, through prayer, through the Eucharist, and through the many signs of resurrection in our world that we can see if we open our eyes and dare to believe.

Christ comes to us bringing peace. He does not berate us or tell us off for our failings. He comes to quash our doubting and still our fears. He comes bearing scars to remind us that where we are hurting and struggling he has been there too and will walk with us through it. He comes to breathe the Holy Spirit into our lives – to turn us from frightened lukewarm followers into committed disciples, ablaze with the love and power of God, fired up with the good news of God's love for the world. He comes to show us the new creation which is possible through the act of resurrection, and which is promised to us both now and throughout eternity.

Christ comes also to mould us into a united, loving community – his body – where people are equal and no one is needy. He comes to surprise us, to disturb us, to make us think again, to do a double-take. He comes to breathe new life into places where our lives have become stale or predictable. To challenge us to think outside the box and to remind us that nothing is set in stone.

Be challenged, be surprised, be transformed by the risen Christ and go out from here to dare to change the world.

Catherine Williams

Hymn suggestions

Jesus, stand among us; Breathe on me, breath of God; We walk by sight and not by faith; Thuma mina (Send me, Jesus).

Second Sunday of Easter 7 April
Second Service **Hope and Faith**
Ps. 143.1–11; **Isa. 26.1–9, 19**; Luke 24.1–12

Looking to the future

We are in the Easter season. The season when we focus on life and light and broken tombs. And yet, as you look around, things might seem gloomy. In this season of life, we see whole communities being wiped out by rising sea levels. In this season of light, we see the world's wealthy force the weak into the darkness of poverty and death. How can we celebrate resurrection life in the midst of death?

Isaiah begins by pointing us to the future: 'On that day ...' On that day the gates of the city will be opened, the proud and power-ful will be laid low, the oppressed will shout for joy. Isaiah's words are similar to those used by Mary when pregnant with Jesus, and by Jesus when he spoke in Nazareth at the start of his ministry. Hope for the poor and needy is a constant gospel theme. As is hope for the future. On that day things will be put right. But we have to acknowledge that we are not there yet.

Hope – hearing the whole piece

I don't know whether you know the adagio from Mozart's Clarinet Concerto.[22] If not, try to listen to it when you get home. It's a very simple piece of music, very calm. But it weaves together joy and sorrow. It reflects the world as it really is. There is no false hope in it. Francis Spufford writes that it tells you 'Everything you fear is true ... and yet ... there is the possibility of *this*.'[23] Despair and hope exist together in this world. For that reason, I don't believe we can understand Isaiah's apocalypse as encouragement to sit back and let God get on with things. We need to hear the whole music of the universe, as in Mozart's concerto.

Faith – living with the whole piece

Hearing the music that tells us pain and joy coexist is not enough. Isaiah does not limit himself to foretelling what God will do. He is clear about our role in the coming kin-dom too. Who is kept in peace? Those of steadfast mind. Who has an everlasting rock? Those who trust in the Lord. These are energetic, strong actions.

Being steadfast takes quite a bit of courage and determination. Wouldn't it be easy to allow the currents of optimism to take us to a land where things are all right really? Or the tides of pessimism to take us to a land of despair? Steadfastness means attending to the world as it is, living with the joy and the sorrow, in the knowledge that in the end life wins. Trusting in the Lord doesn't mean adopting a 'let go and let God' attitude. Trusting in the Lord might bring assurance that the Lord is with us even when we can't see it. Sometimes it will mean taking risks to point out what is righteous and just. Sometimes it might just be comforting.

It's going somewhere

Forgive me for some musical technicalities here. One of the interesting things about the piece of music I've mentioned is how it relates to the rest of the piece. It's in the middle, the second movement. It accurately reflects the world as it is, but it is going somewhere. What follows is full of life. It expresses where Isaiah is headed in this passage. At the moment, life and death coexist, but on that day this song will be in the land. The gates of the city will be open so that all the righteous may enter.

Isaiah's message is honest. At the moment there is what he refers to as a 'lofty city' that will be brought low. We know as we look around us that the world has not yet been put to rights. But on that day, it will be full of resurrection life. We have a part to play – to be steadfast and trust. To do and say what is right. To move faithfully through the world as it is. On that day, Isaiah says, the path of the righteous will be level and clear. But not yet. First, the path must be made. The paths I imagine are not gravelled or maintained paths, they are new paths, made by walking. Our challenge is to make paths that lead through a complex world to righteousness. Our challenge is to live out our resurrection faith in a world where life and death still coexist.

Liz Shercliff

Hymn suggestions

A mighty fortress is our God; Seek ye first the kingdom of God; My hope is built on nothing less; Christ our hope in life and death.

Third Sunday of Easter 14 April
Principal Service **Is It Still Easter?**
Zeph. 3.14–end (*if used, the reading from Acts must be used as the second reading*), or **Acts 3.12–19**; Ps. 4; 1 John 3.1–7; Luke 24.36b–48

The dangers of ignoring context

The story goes that a priest was invited by a local Mafia boss to take his brother's funeral. A very generous donation to the church was offered, and reluctantly the priest agreed. 'The only condition', said the Mafia boss, 'is you must say that my brother was a saint.' A few days later the priest stood at the front of the church, having had several sleepless nights wrestling with a troubled conscience. 'The man in the coffin before you was a murderer, a thief, a bully and a tyrant,' began the eulogy. 'But compared to his brother, he was a saint.'

Peter's address to his fellow Israelites seems a bit like that eulogy. He apparently has nothing good to say about them. 'You handed Jesus over, you denounced him, you made sure he was killed.' Sadly, it is an accusation that has been made about the Jews collectively and individually. New Testament scholar Amy-Jill Levine writes of a high-school friend, a Christian, accusing her of exactly that. With so much condemnation around, it's hard to remember it's still Easter, the new life season.

The first thing I want to say about our reading is that it has been taken out of context in a way that is seriously misleading. Peter is not distancing himself from the people he addresses. If 'fellow Israelites' does not make that clear enough, he later calls his hearers 'brothers and sisters'. And although the reading stops at 'Repent and turn to God so that your sins may be wiped out', Peter goes on to say, 'so that times of refreshing may come'. God is not condemning the Israelites; God wants to bring times of refreshing. It's still Easter, there is the promise of new life.

Blessing and response

What leads up to Peter addressing a crowd anyway? Peter and John healed a destitute person who could not walk. The change in the man is so profound that he enters the Temple walking and leaping and praising God. He has been given new life. It draws a crowd. A man is blessed and a crowd responds. Witness to a new life brings others to find out about the promise of new life. It's still Easter.

Perhaps it's easy to forget the season. Perhaps you, like me, have often conflated Holy Week and Easter and come up with one week, between Palm Sunday and Easter Day, or even just the two Sundays, where I remember how new life springs from death. But for the church, while we celebrate Easter on one day of the year, it actually goes on – and on. Whenever we turn to God, our sins are wiped out and times of refreshing may come. Blessing and response are not one-off events, nor are they transactional – if you do this, God will do that. They are integral to our relationship with God; where there is blessing, there is response; where there is response, there is blessing.

Rejoice and exult

Peter refers to Moses and the prophets later on in his sermon. I wonder whether any of his hearers went home to check what the prophets really had said. If they picked up Zephaniah, the prophet we heard read, they would have been reassured. 'Sing aloud, rejoice, exult, the Lord is in your midst,' says the prophet. I do not suggest that we should rejoice no matter what – I have met Christians who insist on praising God because they have a migraine, imagining that they are obeying some kind of divine injunction. I doubt that is the kind of rejoicing Zephaniah has in mind. But the fact is that because of Easter, the Lord is in our midst and, if in nothing else, we can rejoice in that. It is still Easter. The ongoing Easter season is not good in comparison to Good Friday, it is not good in comparison to anything. It *is* good. Easter has brought about a qualitative change in everything because life has burst from the tomb. Whatever we may go through, on a global, local or personal scale, we live in Easter time, when life overcomes in the end. There may be difficult times ahead because of political, economic or environmental crises. Whatever happens, our faith tells us this – it is still Easter.

I'm grateful that the lectionary reminds us Easter didn't finish after Bank Holiday Monday. The story Peter tells ends in resurrection hope that will last much longer than that. It is still Easter.

Liz Shercliff

Hymn suggestions

For the beauty of the earth; This is a day of new beginnings; See what a morning; Bless the Lord, O my soul (10,000 Reasons).

Third Sunday of Easter 14 April
Second Service **Strength in Faithfulness**
Ps. 142; **Deut. 7.7–13**; Rev. 2.1–11;
Gospel at Holy Communion: Luke 16.19–end

Strength in numbers?

What's the largest crowd or gathering you've been part of? For me, I think it was a 'Monsters of Rock' music festival crowd in the late 1980s. According to official figures, there were over 100,000 people present. It was a remarkable experience, especially when we all sang along as one to the headlining band's most famous song. I felt part of something so much bigger than myself; for that one night I felt powerful and lifted up. I guess there can, then, be strength in numbers. That's why, in times of war, nations seek to mobilize huge armies. It's also why those who might otherwise feel marginalized or vulnerable will gather together; to march or protest and, sometimes, to celebrate.

For people of faith, too, there can be something exhilarating about being part of a large congregation. It must feel pretty extraordinary to worship as part of one of those enormous megachurches. On the other hand, it can sometimes feel dispiriting to be part of a congregation or church where numbers are thin on the ground or there is a lack of resources. How easy would it be to imagine that God – the almighty and all-powerful Lord of creation – has blessed the megachurch and withheld his blessing from the struggling, tiny church? For numbers and resources are – at a human level – often recognized as a token of success. Popularity and size are often translated to mean 'success'. Perhaps, then, it's not unreasonable to assume that God is most alive in the churches and congregations which display obvious power.

Strength in vulnerability?

Our reading from the book of Deuteronomy invites us into a wider understanding of 'success' and God's relationship with his people. The words are part of Moses' sermon delivered to the people of Israel. His words remind us that if we – as humans – can become obsessed with size and scale and numbers, God is not. His agenda is centred on faithfulness and relationship:

116

It was not because you were more numerous than any other people that the LORD set his heart on you and chose you – for you were the fewest of all peoples. It was because the LORD loved you and kept the oath that he swore to your ancestors, that the LORD has brought you out with a mighty hand, and redeemed you from the house of slavery, from the hand of Pharaoh king of Egypt.

Moses' words are clear: Almighty God does not operate according to human ideas of greatness and flourishing; if he did so, he would offer his love and devotion to nations like the then superpower Egypt. Rather, there is a tenderness and intimacy about the divine. He seeks to lift up not the mighty but the readily ignored. His bonds of affection are bounded in personal relationships with our fore-bears like Abraham and Sarah. His love seeks to set the captive and slave free. One might expect the Almighty to align himself with the powerful rather than the weak. After all, in human experience that often happens. However, God turns the human order upside down. His solidarity lies with the weak and excluded.

I wonder how you react to God's priorities. I suspect much depends on where we locate ourselves: if one has a fair degree of privilege or power, I guess Moses' words might be very challenging; if one is vulnerable or part of a community that has traditionally been ostracized, I suspect there is a great deal of comfort. Given that many of us find that we occupy a complex mix of privilege and vulnerability I suspect many of us find both comfort and challenge in Moses' account of God's priorities.

Strength in faithfulness …

I sense that the deepest challenge presented by Moses' words is at the level of community. Moses insists that those who would be in relationship with God are called to obedience: 'If you heed these ordinances, by diligently observing them, the LORD your God will maintain with you the covenant loyalty that he swore to your ancestors.' In our individualistic age, we tend to see this as all about a one-to-one relationship with God. That is *my* relationship with God.

However, the call to obedience is made to the people first. In short, if we are to be the kind of people who seek after God's ways, we do that first as a community, and secondarily as individuals or persons. This raises huge challenges: while God is faithful and loving, we as the church and the body of Christ are called to make the appropriate response in turn. We are called to demonstrate real, identifiable love, grace and faithfulness. As church history has repeatedly shown, that can be challenging. Too often, the community of God has persecuted, abused and exploited those whom it is called to cherish. It has wounded itself and called it 'love'. God's priorities demand of us a holier way.

Rachel Mann

Hymn suggestions

Great is thy faithfulness; Now thank we all our God; Where he leads I will follow; The steadfast love of the Lord.

Fourth Sunday of Easter   21 April
Principal Service   **Shepherds and Sheepdogs**
Gen. 7.1–5, 11–18; 8.6–18; 9.8–13 (*if used, the reading from Acts must be used as the second reading*), or Acts 4.5–12; Ps. 23; 1 John 3.16–end; **John 10.11–18**

Have you ever met a shepherd? I met one once on a train just outside Oxford. He didn't look anything like my expectations of a shepherd. He was very young, with a shaved head. He was wearing leathers and sporting many tattoos and piercings. In the crook of his arm, he carried a tiny border collie puppy called Sweetpea, who was his newly acquired sheepdog. In conversation with him, I learned that he was expecting to spend weeks and months with his new dog 24 hours a day – alongside, tending, caring, training and loving her so that she would learn to recognize his voice, understand what he expects her to do and grow to be devoted and loyal. He was hoping that together they would make a great team for working sheep.

Jesus: the good shepherd

Jesus uses the metaphor of the good shepherd to describe himself. It's a controversial metaphor, because shepherds at the time of Jesus were tough and hard, low class and often dirty. They worked outside in all weathers and didn't have time to go to the Temple to worship. They were often seen as 'unclean', beyond the pale. On the other hand, it was through a shepherd – David – that Israel's fortunes were restored. In God's topsy-turvy economy the lowest and the least are closest to the kingdom of righteousness. Remember, it's shepherds who hear the angel's message and are the first to visit the newborn Jesus, the Messiah.

So by using this metaphor Jesus challenges the Pharisees by saying that he is both beyond the pale yet walking in the footsteps of King David. Jesus' metaphor is that of a *good* shepherd – loyal and sacrificial – who knows his sheep by name. One who looks beyond the current sheepfold to see who else can be brought in. The shepherd who ultimately gives his life to save the sheep. Jesus is painting a picture of leadership for his followers.

Peter: the good sheepdog

Peter in the reading from Acts demonstrates how that understanding of leadership is beginning to be lived out in the light of the resurrection and the day of Pentecost. Peter and John have healed a crippled man at the Beautiful Gate of the Temple. Peter speaks about the power of the risen Christ to save and heal. It's a very daring thing to do: it gets the disciples arrested.

And so they begin to show what they've learned from the good shepherd. Peter, an ordinary fisherman, declares in broad daylight – before the most learned men in Jerusalem – that power and healing come through the name of Jesus Christ, who has been raised from the dead. The last time Peter was in the Temple courts it was dark and he denied Jesus three times. Now filled with the Holy Spirit he stands and takes on the leaders of the Temple. This is no hired hand who runs away when he sees the wolf coming. This is a much loved and well-trained sheepdog working with Jesus the shepherd – standing up to the wolf and being prepared to lose his life so that broken lives can encounter the risen Christ.

Us: Jesus' sheepdogs

Today is Vocation Sunday – a day when we celebrate that each of us has been called to follow the Good Shepherd and to serve alongside him. We are not just passive sheep waiting to be led. That image of the sheepdog is more helpful. Jesus the shepherd loves and cares for us. He trains us – is alongside us 24/7. He loves us, his co-workers, faithfully and anticipates that we will serve him faithfully in return, repaying with love and gratitude what he has invested in us – his very life.

I wonder what sort of sheepdog you are. Are you a puppy, newly acquired, with lots to learn and plenty of energy, encountering many things in the Christian life for the first time with wide-eyed wonder? Are you perhaps a well-trained and faithful sheepdog, still learning new things, still listening for the shepherd's whistles, but serving the flock faithfully as you have done for many years? Are you perhaps a retired sheepdog who is no longer into all that running around, but is still much loved, and who sits and watches, passing on wisdom and support to the next generation?

You might be called to exercise your role as a sheepdog mainly in the church. But most of God's people are called to love and serve God in their everyday lives, at work, at home, at school, in the supermarket, at the polling station and even down the pub. How can you show others the love of God through generosity, service, sacrifice, truth, goodness and so on? We're all called to love people into the kingdom – searching for those outside the sheepfold and bringing them in, going the extra mile, like my shepherd with his trainee sheepdog.

So, if you are wondering how best to serve God, what God might be calling you to next, or if you want to ask for strength and courage for the next steps in your Christian life, then pray to be empowered by the Holy Spirit afresh. Pray for wisdom and guidance. The good shepherd is calling you to love and serve him. How will you respond?

Catherine Williams

Hymn suggestions

The king of love my shepherd is; The Lord's my shepherd (Stuart Townend); The Lord is my shepherd (Surely Goodness, Surely Mercy); There is a redeemer.

Fourth Sunday of Easter   21 April
Second Service   A Gospel of Challenge, a Call to Integrity
Ps. 81.8–16; Ex. 16.4–15; **Rev. 2.12–17**;
Gospel at Holy Communion: John 6.30–40

Pergamum, mentioned in today's reading from Revelation, was the provincial Roman capital of Asia for many years before it was moved to Ephesus. An important centre at the time, Pergamum was the very first city in the entire Roman Empire to worship the Roman emperor. As in many parts of our world today, life for Christians in first-century Pergamum was an incredible struggle and challenge. The Christians living and working in Pergamum were persecuted because they refused to bow to the emperor.

It is interesting that Jesus reminds the people in verse 13, 'I know where you are living', because often when people are going through a difficult time, it feels as if they are in it on their own. In this statement, Jesus assures us that he sees us and is with us in the peaks and valleys of our existences. He knows exactly what we are going through. We are never alone!

Say 'No!' to compromise

In this passage, Jesus speaks to Christians about the sin of compromise. He highlights the pervasive, corrosive and corruptive nature of sexual sin, which was a problem in Christian communities. The Christians of Pergamum would not deny Christ before the world but were tolerating worldly practices.

In our age, people are encouraged by self-empowering expressions such as, 'You do you!' 'Live life your way!' 'You only live once'. As followers of Christ, we need to be mindful not to chase idols and ideologies set by the world's standards. Because in so doing we often compromise God's benchmark. While these motivational statements can be helpful, they can also be destructive when they place the 'me' or 'I' at the centre of our world at the expense of others, living life on our own terms. We are called to flourish on our life journeys, but we are also called to seek the flourishing of others.

We are called to serve our kingdom community through a relationship with our Lord Jesus Christ. In working towards this purpose, we have to be intentional in saying 'No!' to anything that compromises our faith.

Reliance on God's promises

Psalm 81 implores: we need to repent and move towards reliance on God. We are called to trust in God's promises and provision. As described in the Exodus passage, God provided manna daily for the Israelites as they traversed the wilderness. And in the midst of their grumblings, God reminded them again and again that if they stood firm, and did not compromise their beliefs, he would provide for them. Similarly, this is the message for us today.

As I write this, we are going through many crises in our world: pandemics, economic crises, the threat of hunger, climate change, child and domestic abuse, conflict and war, political tensions and civil unrest. We find ourselves in the wilderness where there might be many temptations and opportunities to compromise our faith. But in standing firm on the purposes of God, we are promised that when we are faithful God provides.

The life, death and resurrection of Jesus enable us, through faith, to stand for him, even to death if necessary. Let's ask our risen Lord to help us guard against all kinds of compromise: to recognize that the Holy Spirit empowers us to live grace-filled lives that glorify our eternal God.

Catherine Okoronkwo

Hymn suggestions

And can it be that I should gain; God of mercy, God of grace; What wondrous love is this; How deep the Father's love for us.

Fifth Sunday of Easter   28 April
Principal Service   **Breaking Boundaries**
Baruch 3.9–15, 32—4.4, *or* Gen. 22.1–18 (*if used, the reading from Acts must be used as the second reading*),
or **Acts 8.26–end**; Ps. 22.25–end; 1 John 4.7–end; John 15.1–8

I am a Yorkshireman by birth, and an Indian by ethnicity. In cricket I support both Yorkshire and India, my experiences form part of my identity. Consequently, I was deeply disturbed by the claims of the cricketer Azeem Rafiq, not so long ago, of racism at the hands of his Yorkshire club. As a person of colour, I can testify that there is a human tendency to oppress people different from us. Race may be an easy target, but racism is intolerably painful to those who receive abuse. In the book of Acts, we witness encounter after encounter where prejudice, bias and racism are challenged so that the church becomes open to all people.

A new narrative begins in Acts 1: Jesus, at his ascension, has left his disciples with the encouragement to spread the gospel from Jerusalem (the familiar) to Samaria (the excluded) to the ends of the earth (that's all of us). In today's reading, we encounter a powerful story of Christian witness to someone who was very much excluded, an Ethiopian eunuch. In the Gospel, we explore how we are guided by the Spirit in our mission.

Who's in? Who's out?

The great persecution is in full flow. Philip, a deacon in the early church, finds himself expelled from Jerusalem. Yet through this disruptive situation, God gives Philip a pioneering ministry to proclaim Christ to excluded groups. First, he is called to share Christ with the Samaritans, a people very much looked down upon and excluded from Temple worship and pure Judaism.

Subsequently, Philip is led into dialogue with an Ethiopian eunuch, once again breaking social norms. The ancient Greek historian Herodotus describes Ethiopians as black, but here is not just someone black but also a eunuch. This was an occupational requirement to be an official to the Queen of Ethiopia, Candace.

Philip is open to God's guidance through an angel; he models breaking down social barriers. The Spirit prompts Philip to share the transformative love of Jesus with the Ethiopian, who is at that very moment reading the Hebrew Scriptures. Without prejudice. Philip helps him to understand salvation through the crucified Christ. He responds at once to God's grace and requests baptism.

Where shall I go?

Philip taps into signs of a spiritual search in the Ethiopian. We too need to discern signs of God at work. The South African missiologist David Bosch describes mission as God's mission, *missio Dei*. Where are we prompted to go? In our mission we listen for the voice of the Holy Spirit, who hovers over the world, bringing people into a love of Christ, empowering us to go out to spread the gospel in both word and deed. In my previous church, a small group of people were prompted by the Holy Spirit to offer hospitality and

English language classes to asylum seekers who were placed in the parish, often feeling vulnerable and isolated. This grew into a significant project and many beneficiaries have been touched by the love of Christ that they saw in the volunteers. Many have come into a living Christian faith; mission is following God's prompts and tapping into God's mission.

Fruitful for Christ

In the Gospel reading, Jesus declares, 'I am the true vine, and my Father is the vine-grower.' We are inextricably linked to him; as we abide in him, we become more fruitful for him. By allowing ourselves to be pruned back, we become ever more Christ-like, in our inner life and in our outer life.

Our mission as Christians is rooted in what the world sees of our fruits. This is reflected through our interactions with the world; through our acts of love. Through our compassionate service, we become Christ's ambassadors to a broken and hurting world. This involves being counter-cultural, as we welcome all who seek Christ, as Philip did without prejudice, without barriers, without assumptions. We demonstrate a love ethic modelled on Christ, which has the power to transform a broken world, reaching out to people of all backgrounds, many of whom may feel excluded by society.

May we, like Philip, seek God's guidance, through engaging in God's mission. Philip was unencumbered by human prejudice and went to those to whom the Spirit called him. Like Philip, we are called to be witnesses, through prayer and through being transformed daily into the image of Christ so that those we encounter can experience the healing, joy and love he alone can bring to a broken world.

Arani Sen

Hymn suggestions

I am the vine, you are the branches; Beauty for brokenness; Love divine, all loves excelling; God's Spirit is in my heart.

Fifth Sunday of Easter 28 April
Second Service **Christmas Points to Easter**
Ps. 96; **Isa. 60.1–14**; Rev. 3.1–13; *Gospel at Holy Communion*:
Mark 16.9–16

Is it Christmas already?

If you found that your mind drifted towards a very different part of
the church year during our first reading today, you would be forgiven. The text from the prophet Isaiah that we heard is one that we
more usually associate with the period of Christmas and Epiphany.
It turns up in those days in late December or early January most
years, and it immediately makes us think of the three wise men and
their journey towards Bethlehem, guided by a star: 'Arise, shine;
for your light has come ... Nations shall come to your light, and
kings to the brightness of your dawn ... They shall bring gold and
frankincense.' What is this text doing here, over halfway into the
great season of Easter? Are we not getting our festivals confused?

Christmas points to Easter

But, of course, what Scripture is reminding us today is that everything points to Easter. Even way back at the very beginning of
Christ's life, everything is pointing towards the cross and the empty
tomb. The whole sweep of God's wonderful plan to redeem and
save poor fallen humanity unfolds through history and culminates
in the darkness of Easter night, as death is defeated and the gates of
heaven are flung open.

And the connection between Christmas and Easter makes complete sense. Lots of the medieval mystery plays reminded their
audience of this visually, by having the staging for the Bethlehem
manger being the same stage as the cross of Golgotha. And many
of our great poets and hymn writers play with the idea of the baby
Jesus, even in the earliest hours of his life, knowing that he is born
with Easter as his destination.

Treading the same footsteps

Isaiah's vision, you will remember, is of a city whose 'gates shall
always be open; day and night they shall not be shut'. Christian
tradition has recognized in this text a description of the kingdom

that is promised in our earliest Advent prophecies, preached about by Christ in his own ministry on earth, and then realized as the door of the tomb bursts open and resurrection light spills into the darkness before the dawn on Easter morning.

And we, like the prophets of Christmas and the magi of Epiphany, are drawn to that light as well. We find our footsteps turned towards that light. We find that our life becomes a journey towards that open door. There is an awful lot about doors being opened in our Easter liturgy. Easter hymns sing about the gates of hell being opened by Jesus as he descends into the darkness and then rises again; one of our Easter prayers describes how no door is locked to the risen Christ, and the readings for the last day of the great Easter octave talk about Christ walking into a locked room and into the lives of his frightened disciples.

In through the open door

Prophecy way back in Scripture proclaims the same message as prophecy that closes the canon of Scripture. We heard in our second reading, from the Revelation to John, 'I know your works. Look, I have set before you an open door which no one is able to shut.' This glorious Easter season through which we move is telling the same story that our faith has told us from the beginning: we are going home. Easter opens the gates that once were barred before us, and we must follow through those gates.

Following that light, following that Christ, means being attentive to the gates and doors that we actively close in our own lives, and opening them up again. And the language we use for those types of gates is sin. Where are those gates unnecessarily closed in your life, or in your mind? Where am I blocking and barring the light from shining clearly? And of course, part of our Christian calling is also to spot where those types of doors are shut on God's people, through greed, exploitation, selfishness and discrimination. The language we use for noticing, and lending our weight to opening those doors is mission.

Onwards!

So we find, two-thirds of the way through our Easter journey, that everything in our faith has been pointing us in this direction from the beginning. We don't need to feel seasick when we hear Christmas readings during Easter, because the Bethlehem stable has always been pointing towards Easter night. The voices of the prophets have always been crying out for Easter light. And our lives, if we allow them to be, are shaped for the door of the empty tomb.

Tom Clammer

Hymn suggestions

Jesus lives! Thy terrors now; I cannot tell how he whom angels worship; At the Lamb's high feast we sing; Jesus is King and I will extol him.

Sixth Sunday of Easter 5 May
Principal Service **Friends of God**
Isa. 55.1–11 *(if used, the reading from Acts must be used as the second reading)*, or Acts 10.44–end; Ps. 98; 1 John 5.1–6; **John 15.9–17**

Today's Gospel sits within a sequence of Jesus' teaching to the disciples. It covers his relationship with the Father, the gift of the Spirit, the call to unity and the New Commandment to 'love one another'. These themes intertwine and phrases repeat. If we read the chapters in a single sitting, the key words begin to take root within us. In today's Gospel, the recurring refrain 'love one another' links with a new theme: friendship. It's to friendship that Jesus calls the disciples.

Friendship

Social media platforms such as Facebook have been criticized for debasing the currency of friendship. It's common to have more people in our 'friends' list' than we would ever count as personal friends. In the world of social media friendship, it's easy to 'add' someone to the list, or even to 'unfriend' them.

Jesus' words are a million miles from this. He says, 'I have called you friends because I have made known to you everything that I have heard from my Father' (John 15.15). The disciples have been taken into Jesus' confidence. He is about to leave – to go to the Father – and so that God's mission may continue, he is about to share with them the things that are closest to the Father's heart. This is the friendship of close companions: those in whom we confide.

What Jesus is saying is radical. In the Hebrew Scriptures, only Abraham is known as 'friend of God'. No one else comes anywhere near. For God's son to call his followers friends, and to entrust to them everything he has heard from the Father, is nothing short of remarkable. It's a sign that, as we approach the death and resurrection of Jesus, we are reaching a point after which nothing will ever be quite the same again.

Love

Jesus hints at these game-changing events when he says, 'No one has greater love than this, to lay down one's life for one's friends.' I wonder what the disciples made of this saying. We read it today in the light of seeing Jesus' death as the laying down of his life for his friends. For the disciples, it would have been some time before these words made any sense. But this is the nature of the friendship to which they are called. It's a friendship founded on love: not the friendly affection of *philia*, but *agape* – a self-giving, self-sacrificing love.

The disciples haven't chosen to be friends of Jesus. They did not choose him, but he chose them. As ever, the initiative is God's: 'not that we loved God but that he loved us' (1 John 4.10). And the purpose of the friendship is that the disciples bear fruit. It's not yet clear what this fruit will be. We must wait until after the resurrection and the giving of the Spirit to see that. But we are told what the mark of this fruitfulness will be: the love they will have for one another. Time and again through history, love for fellow human beings has been the touchstone of fruitful lives lived as friends of Jesus Christ. Tertullian, in the third century, imagined pagans looking at Christians and saying, 'See ... how they love one another.' Would that it were always so.

The call to be friends

So, what about us? A crucial question to ask when reading the Gospels is, 'Where am I in this passage?' The writer of the Fourth Gospel, in particular, has the ability to draw us into the narrative. We can imagine ourselves being there with the disciples, listening to Jesus. It might seem presumptuous to place ourselves alongside them. But they were a mixed bunch too: convinced believers alongside instinctive doubters, a betrayer and a denier thrown in; and that's just the apostles, to say nothing of the many others –

women and men – who formed the wider group of disciples. A motley crew of all sorts and conditions; why should we not place ourselves with them?

If, then, we are there with the disciples, it is to us too that Jesus speaks those words. We are to keep his commandments, to love one another, to abide in his love and know ourselves to be his friends.

In Catherine Fox's third novel, *Love for the Lost*, the central character, Isobel Knox, suffers a crisis in her life and seeks the wise counsel of her bishop. He asks her whether she sees herself as a child of God, servant of God or friend of God.[24] As which of these do *we* see *ourselves*? Child of God? We are clearly part of God's family, but children know their place. Servant of God? Servants are entrusted with important work but don't know the employer's mind. Or friend of God? Chosen, taken into confidence, and in a relationship so close that, like Abraham and like Adam and Eve in the garden, we walk and talk with God: the easy conversation of friends.

God chooses us not primarily as servants, nor even as children, but as friends. And God chooses not someone else but you and me.

Peter Moger

Hymn suggestions

Christ is the one who calls; My song is love unknown; Lord of all power, I give you my will; O Jesus, I have promised.

Sixth Sunday of Easter   5 May
Second Service   **Burning Passion and Cool Indifference**
Ps. 45; **S. of Sol. 4.16—5.2; 8.6–7**; **Rev. 3.14–end**;
Gospel for Holy Communion: Luke 22.24–30

Burning passion from the Old Testament

Buckle up! Maybe the lectionary compilers are wise to give us only a snippet of the Song of Solomon. It's hot stuff. The poem consists of exchanges between two lovers, celebrating their burning passion for each other. Every now and then we hear from the women of Jerusalem who act as a chorus, drawing in the reader. The poem is an unashamed celebration of the lovers' mutual desire, with some fairly unsubtle metaphors lobbed in, evidenced in the verses we've heard. You can't fail to recognize the burning passion between the lovers. Their mutual desire is intense, laser-like.

What do we do with this erotic love poem? First of all, recognize it for what it is – a celebration of sexual love, the body and human passion. Let's not get all prurient and airbrush that out.

Cool indifference in the church

If we set the reading from Revelation next to the one from the Song, we see an interesting contrast. In Revelation chapter 1, a being 'like the Son of Man' (Rev. 1.13) commands John to write to the seven churches. Our reading consists of the letter to the seventh church, Laodicea. This church is neither hot nor cold. There is a cool indifference to God in this community, evidenced by a lukewarm attitude in the way they live, leading to the potential judgement of being spat out from the mouth of God.

It's a hard read, especially when the words resonate for those of us who have a tendency to retreat into self-satisfied self-reliance: 'I've done all right. I don't need anything ...' But before we despair, listen to the voice of Jesus: 'I reprove and discipline those whom I love.' This is a word of judgement delivered from the fire of love.

Need some salve?

Let's be honest with ourselves, do we ever 'dethrone' God because we feel we have enough resources for ourselves? Do we resist God because of fear of losing independence or control, deluding ourselves that we can even draw a breath without God? Perhaps we think, 'I'm doing OK, fine and dandy, thanks.' Pray for the salve to anoint our eyes that we may see our deep need for God and that this need might be ignited into burning desire for God.

The laser-like passion of God

Like the lovers in the Song, God's passion for his creation is laser-like. He will not let us go, waltzing off into our delusional sinfulness, sauntering with cool indifference into the nearest ditch. No – the letter reveals the warmth of God, the focus of God and the desire of God. Overwhelming? Yes! God wants us to be drawn into a deep relationship of trust. God seeks our invitation. The image is of one opening the door of our home and welcoming God in to share a meal: 'I will come in to you and eat with you, and you with me.' With the same startling imagery of partnership and togetherness, John offers us the picture of God scooting over on the throne to make space for us. God comes to us; we go to God.

Handling the 'hot stuff'

This imagery of mutuality resonates in the Song of Songs. Historically, the church has handled the 'hot stuff' of the Song by reading it as an allegory of God's love for God's people. We can read it in this way, without denying that its primary focus is on sexual love and tenderness. It's important not to airbrush out the importance of the body and of physical love with an unhelpful, unnecessary and awkward embarrassment. So, let's not lose the literal sense of the poem. This can and should be warmly celebrated.

At the same time, when we read the Song as a theological metaphor for God's love, something interesting happens. In most of the Bible, there is an imbalance in the relationship between humanity and God. Reading the Song as allegory renders the relationship as a partnership. There is a parallel here with the imagery in Revelation of God making space on his throne for those who conquer the ludicrous delusions of self-sufficiency, coming in penitence, seeking the God who desires us with a fierce passion.

The choice is in our hands

Perhaps we resist this strong language and flee to a cool indifference behind the defences of self-sufficiency. Fundamentally, this is a move of fear. However, there is no need to be afraid because in God we find completeness, warmth and belonging: genuine riches, genuine security, genuine homecoming.

The imagery of Jesus standing at the door knocking in Revelation picks up a similar image in the Song of Songs, where the lover knocks on the door. In both cases, the one who hears the knock is free to open the door or not. There is no force. We can choose to bolt the door and sit in cool indifference. We can choose to throw it open, and step into the fire of God's love.

Don't stay in cool darkness, step into warm light.

Kate Bruce

Hymn suggestions

Empty, broken, here I stand (Kyrie Eleison); All-consuming fire; Come down, O love divine; Purify my heart (Refiner's Fire).

Ascension Day   9 May
Principal Service   **Endings and Beginnings**
Acts 1.1–11 (*must be used as either the first or second
reading*), *or* Dan. 7.9–14; Ps. 47, *or* Ps. 93; Eph. 1.15–end,
or **Acts 1.1–11; Luke 24.44–end**

In the days and weeks following his resurrection, Jesus had been
appearing to his disciples and then disappearing, only to reappear
again. Jesus interrupts a conversation between Cleopas and his
companion as they travel the road to Emmaus. He had stood in
the presence of the disciples and eaten with them. He was no ghost,
but the resurrected Christ offering peace and hope for the future.
In a generation where people are searching for peace in all sorts of
unhelpful places, this gift of God's peace is something the world
seeks. Jesus shows beyond a doubt to all who follow him that he is
the resurrected Christ.

It is against this backdrop that we enter this ascension scene and
become 'witnesses of these things'. Witnesses for Jesus tell others
what they know about him, the good news of his ministry among
humanity, and all that they have personally experienced through a
life in Christ.

Witnesses: God's presence in the world

The ascension is both an ending and a beginning. It is the end of
Jesus' time on earth and the beginning of our 'being witnesses' and
sharing the gospel. We do this not in our strength but by the power
of the Holy Spirit: 'And see, I am sending upon you what my Father
promised; so, stay here in the city until you have been clothed with
power from on high.' Jesus is 'carried up into heaven', or, as the
Acts passage puts it, 'he was lifted up, and a cloud took him out
of their sight'. As this is happening, the Acts onlookers watch and
note two men in white appear. These men say, 'Men of Galilee,
why do you stand looking up towards heaven? This Jesus, who has
been taken up from you into heaven, will come in the same way as
you saw him go into heaven.' It seems as if they are saying, 'Why
are you still here? Don't just stand here! Go and do what Jesus told
you to do.'

So, the ending is also the beginning. The ascension of Jesus is in
fact the commencement of the church, the ongoing presence of God
in the world. God is going to use his disciples to spread the gospel
beyond Jerusalem; in fact, to the ends of the earth.

Witnesses: instruments of transformation

The question for us as witnesses is: in the face of all the pain and suffering in the world, do Christians have a message from God to share? And how can we be used as instruments for God's transformation in people's lives?

The Christian church has an incredible message to share – that Jesus is our Lord and saviour; that Jesus has defeated evil; that humanity has the opportunity to live an abundant and eternal life because of all that Jesus did on the cross. This is the good news we have to share. We do not do this work in our own strength. The Holy Spirit is not some mystical force, but rather the Holy Spirit is the third person of the divine Trinity. Jesus promises to send his Holy Spirit to fill up his disciples and empower them for ministry.

When we are open to the Holy Spirit, God can and does use us to touch lives. Towards the end of my curacy years, I had the privilege of supporting a family who had lost a loved one to suicide. In a particular moment of distress, I had arrived at the family's home, who at that very moment had been informed the body of their loved one had been located. What a 'timely' visit! But I truly believe it was the leading and guidance of the Holy Spirit that led me to their front door at that precise time of need. The family commented that this timely visit was transformational in their trusting that God was with them.

If you are a friend of God, a follower of Jesus Christ, then the Holy Spirit resides in you – in us. And we can ask for the enabling power of the Holy Spirit to help us to reach out and share our lives and testimonies of faith in Christ with others.

Catherine Okoronkwo

Hymn suggestions

Christ, whose glory fills the skies; Crown him with many crowns; Lord, I lift your name on high; Hail the day that sees him rise.

Ascension Day   9 May
Second Service   **Leaving a Legacy**
Morning Ps. 110, 150; Evening Ps. 8; Song of the Three 29–37,
or **2 Kings 2.1–15**; Rev. 5; *Gospel at Holy Communion*:
Matt. 28.16–end

Out of sight, not out of mind

This is a strange day. Ascension Day marks the day when we see the
resurrected Jesus make his last physical appearance, but we are not
looking at that text. Instead, we are looking at the equally dramatic
last physical appearance of Elijah, and for the Gospel writers the
link between Jesus and Elijah is always important. The parallels and
differences between their lives and deaths reinforce the significance
of Jesus' identity. For Jesus' followers, this is the day when Jesus
has gone from sight, and for Elisha, Elijah too is taken from his
sight in the dramatic account of heavenly chariots that mysteriously
sweep him away.

After this incredible moment, Elisha turns and walks away ready
to get on with the task that Elijah had begun, and in the same way
the disciples turned away from the mountain from which Jesus was
taken. They are ready to live out the legacy. Legacy is that which
continues when something comes to a close – whether the ending of
our work, our relationship or a stage in life. Above all, we experience it when those we care about die, and then we might talk of
legacy. We think about how we might carry on a person's work or
live out their values.

Around the globe, beyond imagination

Around 1832 the Japanese artist Katsushika Hokusai was creating
woodcuts. He was selling them for the price of two bowls of
noodles. He died in 1849, unknown beyond his world in Japan.
But then artists from Europe began to travel, and discovered his
work, until in 1867 his work *The Great Wave off Kanagawa* was
shown at one of the big art exhibitions in Paris, where it went on
to influence van Gogh and Monet among others. Today you will
recognize his most famous work, which appears on countless cards,
notebooks and posters. He could not have known that his work
would spread across the world and down the generations, leaving a
legacy beyond his imagination.

Elijah had been challenging the people of Israel to live differently, to rediscover their priorities and discover again the God who had called them by name and was on their side. Elisha had been by his side, watching and learning, and as the end drew near Elisha longed to continue this work. As the end of his life drew near, Elijah might have been wondering whether all that he so passionately lived and prayed for would really make a difference. If you read on in 2 Kings you will find all the ways in which Elisha did similar and yet different things from Elijah as he continued to share the message of God's love and action in the world.

The continuing story

The story doesn't end there. God continues to yearn for people to discover his heart and his purpose. Prophets and leaders go this way and that ... until in Jesus the word is made flesh, and through him all of us can finally be reconciled to God and discover what it means to live God's ways in the world, empowered by the Spirit. The ascension of Jesus opens the way for the true legacy – lives changed and a world transformed.

On this Ascension Day, this is our prayer too. Jesus is no longer physically present but our calling is to follow, to do the work that he did. Often, we don't see the way in which the things we are involved with might continue, even when we are involved in something that might change lives, or even transform the world. But we are the ones who long to inherit the mantle, who want to continue the work of prayer, healing, caring, including and sowing seeds that will bear fruit as the kingdom of God becomes real.

Sandra Millar

Hymn suggestions

Jesus shall reign; Thine be the glory; Come to me, come, my people; There's a spirit in the air.

Seventh Sunday of Easter
(Sunday after Ascension Day)   12 May
Principal Service   Missio Dei – a Ripple Effect!
Ezek. 36.24–28 (*if used, the reading from Acts must be
used as the second reading*), or Acts 1.15–17, 21–end; Ps. 1;
1 John 5.9–13; **John 17.6–19**

I was studying for a Bachelor of Science in Finance at Virginia Commonwealth University (USA) when I met Jeannie Tabb who served as a missionary for Cru. She befriended me, shared the gospel over the course of several years, and 'made Jesus' name known' to me. Before I left the USA to return to the UK, I had made a personal decision to become a follower of Christ. As you reflect on your Christian life, I wonder whom you might identify 'made Jesus' name known' to you?

There is something about being 'intentional' about sharing our faith that comes through in this John 17 passage. If we are followers of Christ, that's amazing! But we're not called to be Christians for ourselves. Our Christian faith should have a ripple effect, in that the experience of Jesus in our lives compels us to make known Jesus' name to others. In what way does your faith in Christ ripple out and affect the community in which you serve?

Missio Dei challenge

Rowan Williams asserts, 'Mission is seeing what God is up to and joining in.' The dynamic of God's mission, the divine's *missio Dei*, is that he sent his only beloved son into the world to 'make his name known'. And in turn, he commissions us to continue this kingdom work through the enabling of the Holy Spirit. Thus, our calling as believers is to do as Jesus did.

As we endeavour to follow in Jesus' footsteps, a question is how did Jesus balance this 'in the world, but not of the world' dynamic? Though fully divine, he was wonderfully human. He engaged with the full range of humanity. He reached out to people on the margins of society, eating and drinking with them. He listened to their concerns, spoke into their lives, and was involved with the reality of their lives. Jesus wept, healed and prayed. Jesus offered a new way of being/doing to people, forgiveness, restoration and release from the shackles of institutional and structural injustices. As we reflect on this, I wonder what you might observe as being the concerns of our society.

Missio Dei community

To make a difference in people's lives, we are invited to be a part of God's great reaching out into the world. To do this effectively, we need to be committed to our communities. As co-participators and co-creators in our world, we share in the trials and triumphs of humanity. We are called to bring healing, hope and peace to our communities, just as Jesus did. To do this, we need to be intentional in listening to the concerns of people, because these are also God's concerns.

As I reflect on this passage, a number of questions challenge me: how do we plant trees which will yield fruit in season (Psalm 1.3)? What are the issues that most wound our communities? In recent years these have been encapsulated in movements such as: Me Too, Black Lives Matter, Eco Warriors and LGBTQ+. What does the Christian faith have to offer in these times of brokenness? What can we, as followers of Christ, put forward that might be relevant, exciting and capture imaginations for a different future?

It's important we spend time listening to our family members, our neighbours and others we come across in our communities – especially as we navigate a topsy-turvy world where people are searching for anything that will give their lives meaning, anchoring and purpose. So, let's get praying, let's get listening and let's make a difference together as a *missio Dei* community of believers.

Catherine Okoronkwo

Hymn suggestions

Amazing grace; Be thou my vision; Let all the world in every corner sing; Take my life and let it be.

Seventh Sunday of Easter
(Sunday after Ascension Day)   12 May
Second Service   **Removing the Pews**
Ps. 147.1–12; Isa. 61; **Luke 4.14–21**

Clearing the decks

The story is told of the principal of one of the Church of England's theological colleges. This particular principal had some really interesting ideas. One of them was that on the eve of Ascension Day every year the pews would be removed from the college chapel. This meant that after evening prayer on that day all the students and staff would physically lift the wooden pews up and carry them out into the cloisters that run around the garden where they would sit for the period of time between Ascension Day and Pentecost. The chapel would be left empty except for a few benches around the outside of the space, and the worshippers were encouraged to sit on the floor, lie on it, lean against the walls or use the space in any other way that they felt would be helpful to their devotions.

The reasoning for what might, at first glance, feel like a rather peculiar tradition was that it was a physical way of representing, the 'gone-ness of God'. It meant that the students and staff, who of course were very used to worshipping several times a day in this space, would be presented with a different experience. It would feel a bit odd. The same, and yet different.

The gone-ness of God

In these rather odd few days, these nine days between the feast of the ascension and Whitsunday, or the Day of Pentecost, which we will be celebrating this time next week, we get to the bit in the story where Christ has ascended into heaven, however precisely we think that might have happened. Christ has disappeared physically, but we haven't yet reached the point in the story where the Holy Spirit descends on the church at Pentecost. The disciples are told to wait. To wait, and watch, and pray. And this is where we arrive now.

It's a kind of waiting space, isn't it? A waiting room if you like. Imagine waiting at a railway station, having got off one train, but the train on to which you are connecting hasn't yet arrived. An in-between place.

That apparently slightly odd ritual of carrying the pews out of a worship space for nine days might seem a little odd, but on reflection it is a rather good symbol. There's a kind of space in which we wait for these nine days.

Expectation Sunday

Certain Christian traditions call today, this Sunday in-between Ascension Day and Whitsunday, 'Expectation Sunday'. Isn't that rather wonderful? Perhaps we should adopt that? Expectation Sunday. A time when, like the first disciples, we are told to wait, to watch and to expect God to do something. The Book of Common Prayer calls today 'The Sunday after Ascension Day', which I suppose is a bit like Ronseal: it does exactly what it says on the tin. In *Common Worship* this is 'The Seventh Sunday of Easter', reminding us that we are still in the season of celebration, of remembering that all these things are connected. The ascension of Christ into heaven, the gift of the Holy Spirit to turn a rabble of frightened people into a group of people who will turn the world upside down; these things are all part of the promise of Easter. The promise that the tomb is empty and that life, not death, wins.

But these are a messy few days as well. And in many ways, they are the days that I think most represent the actual experience of being a Christian. We *know* that Christ is risen. We *know* that God is coming to us. We hear that promise of Christ – of the poor hearing good news, the captives being released, the oppressed tasting freedom. We hear that, and yet ... and yet death still seems to triumph. Darkness still seems powerful. Illness and famine and war still wreak their havoc. Disease exists. So do fraud, child abuse and corruption. We live out our discipleship in this in-between place, full of expectation and hope, but waiting for the fullness of the kingdom.

And it is into these in-between days, into the gap between the empty tomb and the kingdom finally coming, that you and I are called to maintain, unflinching: 'Alleluia! Christ is risen!'

Tom Clammer

Hymn suggestions

Now is eternal life; Hail the day that sees him rise; The head that once was crowned with thorns; Longing for light, we wait in darkness.

Day of Pentecost (Whit Sunday)   19 May
Principal Service   **God's Honest Truth**

Acts 2.1–21 (*must be used as either the first or second reading*), *or* Ezek. 37.1–14; Ps. 104.26–36, 37b [*or* 104.26–end]; Rom. 8.22–27; **John 15.26–27; 16.4b–15**

In Acts 2, we meet the apostles grieving. Jesus is dead. They have lost their friend and teacher. It is some 50 days after the resurrection and we are told they are 'all together in one place'. The Holy Spirit fills the space and flows out of the domestic into the streets, from the private to the public, from the people as church gathered in that place to beyond its walls. The Holy Spirit fills and overflows, so much so that the apostles 'began to speak in other languages, as the Spirit gave them ability'. Can you imagine the fear? Can you imagine the discombobulation? The invitation is to listen, yes, but also to participate.

Being a witness

It is so easy to become familiar with and to allow dominant narratives to flourish. Not all dominant narratives are true. Not all that we have been told about ourselves speaks to the deeper truth of our made-in-the-image-of-God selves. Despite our best efforts, this world can sometimes make us think that our beings and bodies are not quite right, that the person we love is not quite right, and who we would like to be when we are fully alive is not quite right.

In John 15, we hear Jesus saying that we're to testify. Are we really called to testify? Surely, the Holy Spirit has got this sorted? Surely, Jesus does not need us to bear witness? The truth is that this is not a question of Jesus' needs, but a question of the needs of our world. Our society, our world needs us to testify. Our communities, our cities need us to testify. We are given the Holy Spirit so we can join a different kind of witness protection programme because evil and corruption know no bounds.

This is why we need the Holy Spirit. This is why we need that fire and why we are surrounded by this divine power. The flame has been ignited and we have been equipped to step into a new reality in which we have been liberated, liberated to imagine a better and more equitable world. A world that promotes and celebrates a sense of deep and broad hospitality that recognizes all, and gives room at the table for different voices and accents, and equal opportunities to engage with the jaw-dropping potential of creativity and light that is within us all.

The Spirit of truth

Four times in the passage from John is truth named. Through these references, Jesus' identity is intertwined with that of the Holy Spirit, and the Holy Spirit asks us to speak truth, because in doing so we bear witness to the truth of God in and within us, because of who we are, because we are known and loved and trusted. The Holy Spirit is light and wonder, but fundamentally the Holy Spirit is also truth. Truth that pierces the darkness of a lie. Our Jesus' body was not stolen, our movement has not failed.

To be a Christian is to look a lie in the face and be unafraid because we have the Holy Spirit. It is not our fault that we were abused. It is not our fault that we were betrayed. It is not our fault that someone said we weren't quite right or that we were not Christians. We do not need scandal in public life or mismanagement of public funds. What we need is more funding for social care, for education, and for our nurses and teachers to be paid the salary they deserve for their selfless service and professionalism.

God with us

We need to make room to speak God's honest truth because we have the freedom and permission of the Holy Spirit. In this truth, we travel the path together laid before us, set aflame by the resurrection of a dead body and the living breath of a loving and patient God. Jesus is alive! Jesus loves us and is waiting for us to testify against the greatest lie and to say loud and clear, and without hesitation: we are not alone, we are not abandoned, the world is upside down. God's world is the right way up. The hungry will be fed, the children will be safe. God will wipe away every tear from our eyes. There will no longer be death or sorrow. Our weeping may endure for one night, two nights, for a lifetime even, but joy comes in the resurrection morning.

The Trinitarian reality of Pentecost is that God sees in us something greater than we could possibly ever see with our own human eyes. And we are called to be that people, the people who testify to the greater good and the greater glory with our lives, with our very breath. God's honest truth is that God was with us in the beginning, when we were created in God's image, and we will be with God again at the end after we have lived out the language of our purpose and stepped into the promise of our potential as children of God.

Mariama Ifode-Blease

Hymn suggestions

Come, Holy Spirit (Veni Sancte Spiritus – Taizé); Breathe on me, breath of God; Eternal Spirit, God of truth; Holy Spirit, living breath of God.

Day of Pentecost (Whit Sunday)   19 May
Second Service   **To Begin Again**
Ps. 139.1–11, 13–18, 23–24 [*or* 139.1–11]; **Ezek. 36.22–28**; Acts 2.22–38; *Gospel at Holy Communion*: John 20.19–23

A new beginning

Right after the last match ended, the captain of the cricket team was interviewed on television. His team had not managed a single win in the series; it was, in cricket terms, a whitewash. Looking completely crestfallen, he said that they had failed and obviously change was needed. Then, wistfully, he added, 'I wish we had another chance and could play the series again.'

Most of us know what it is like to wish for a new beginning. Perhaps it was something we felt after an argument with someone, and we'd said something that we wished we had not said. Later, having cooled down, we may have thought, 'If only I could have that conversation again.' Or maybe, at some point, we've made a bad choice and looking back now we wish we could 'turn the clock back' or 'wipe the slate clean'. Most of us, I imagine, have at one time or another thought, 'Oh, to have a second chance and just begin again.'

A new relationship with God

The prophet Ezekiel realized that what the people needed was a new beginning, but the situation looked very bleak. Jerusalem had fallen, and he and the other Jews living in exile in Babylon seemed to have no hope of returning home. Ezekiel had tried to warn them that they must stay faithful to God, but the people had turned away and looked to the gods of their captors. Such was their sin that it seemed, to the prophet at least, that there was little hope of change or restoration. In fact, he had seemingly almost come to the conclusion that God had given up on the people and simply abandoned them.

Even as the people turned away from God, Ezekiel continued to prophesy and reminded them of the consequences of turning away from the covenant relationship with God. He also continued to listen to God and knew for himself not only the power of the Spirit 'entering into him', 'raising him' and 'taking him out', but also the presence of the Spirit for the people as a whole. Yet, when it came to restoring the people of Israel, it appears that the prophet was close to giving up hope, for it seemed to him there would be no second chance.

A new life in the Spirit

Just when it seemed that all hope was gone, Ezekiel proclaimed a word of hope from the Lord: God would cleanse the people and bring them to their own land. In a startling image of new life, God says to the people through the prophet: 'A new heart I will give you, and a new spirit I will put within you; and I will remove from your body the heart of stone and give you a heart of flesh. I will put my spirit within you.'

It was the promise of a second chance. Not because the people deserved it. Certainly not because they had earned it by anything they had done. Rather, we learn that God promises to do it for the sake of God's own name. In other words, God in love reaches out because God longs to be in a close relationship with the people.

As we reflect on the work of God's Spirit in our day, we might pause and ask: could this promise be true for us, too? Is it possible that even today, God as Holy Spirit continues to enter into us and is present with us, offering us a 'second chance' just because God is God? Yes. While at times we have lived for ourselves, we actually belong to God. We are created in God's image, made for relationship with God and to hallow God's own name. Therefore, continually in love, God seeks us out in order to restore, renew and remake us. It is all that love can do. It is what love must do.

Today, on Whit Sunday, as we celebrate the outpouring of the Holy Spirit upon the earliest disciples of Jesus, we give thanks for God's love and care. Like the people of old, we realize that, at times, we have gone our own way; even, perhaps, at some moments in life, we have felt that there was little hope for a new beginning. Yet, the wonder of Christian faith is that what we can't do for ourselves God has done for us. God sent Jesus into the world to show us his love, and by the power of God's Holy Spirit given to us, we may experience new life. Indeed, by the grace of God and for no other reason, we can each begin again.

Karen E. Smith

Hymn suggestions

O for a heart to praise my God; I, the Lord of sea and sky; Breathe on me, breath of God; O breath of love, come breathe within us.

Ordinary Time

Trinity Sunday   26 May
(For Trinity All Age, see p. 357.)
Principal Service **'The Whole Thing Incomprehensible …?'**
Isa. 6.1–8; Ps. 29; Rom. 8.12–17; **John 3.1–17**

The Athanasian Creed

If you are a good 'Book of Common Prayer Christian', you will know that there are certain days on which a mysterious text called the Creed of Saint Athanasius is appointed to be said. Technically it is supposed to be said on 13 days of the year. It is a rather curious and ancient statement of faith which is deeply Trinitarian. The creed includes sections like this:

> The Catholick Faith is this: That we worship one God in Trinity, and Trinity in Unity;
> Neither confounding the Persons: nor dividing the Substance.
> For there is one Person of the Father, another of the Son: and another of the Holy Ghost.
> But the Godhead of the Father, of the Son, and of the Holy Ghost, is all one: the Glory equal, the Majesty co-eternal.
> Such as the Father is, such is the Son: and such is the Holy Ghost.
> The Father uncreate, the Son uncreate: and the Holy Ghost uncreate.
> The Father incomprehensible, the Son incomprehensible: and the Holy Ghost incomprehensible.

The whole thing incomprehensible!

To which centuries of wags in the back pews of parish churches have, I am sure, muttered, 'The whole thing incomprehensible!' The text continues, stressing all the time that all three Persons of the

Trinity are eternal, almighty, Lord and so on, but that there are not three eternals, there are not three almighties, there are not three Lords, but one.

I wouldn't blame anybody here today for never having heard of this text. But it is there for a reason. It is there to try to make some kind of sense of this formula that we use all the time: 'In the name of the Father, and of the Son, and the Holy Spirit.'

Perhaps for a lot of Christian people, the Trinity exists as a concept but not something that we necessarily use in our day-to-day life. Are there moments when we are facing times of stress, or decision, sickness or profound danger, where we think, 'Oh, the doctrine of the Holy Spirit can help me'? That's probably not our immediate thought.

Perfect balance, perfect love

But there are deep truths in the Trinity. It took the early church quite a long time to get the Trinity clear in their heads. And that's why stuff like the Athanasian Creed got produced. The deeper truth is that what the doctrine of the Trinity shows us is an example of perfect balance, communion and relationship. Here we have three Persons, distinct but utterly united. Here we have the Father, the Son, Holy Spirit, all of them absolutely equal, all of them the same nature, but with their own identity and attributes, in which there is no domination, there is no power relationship, there is only absolute, beautiful, simple love.

At the heart of it all is a model of love from which we all might learn. At the heart of it all is a model of love which is supposed to form us – as we pray ourselves – into the mystery of God day by day. We are created in the image of God. And the image of God is a relationship. The image of God is three Persons and one nature. The image of God is love perfectly balanced, eternally equal, constantly giving and receiving, constantly offering, constantly blessed.

Moulded in the image of the Trinity

And because we know that we share with Christ, through his death and resurrection, somehow, mysteriously, we are drawn into that relationship of love. So, the doctrine stops being a distant, academic exercise for beardy weirdos in Oxbridge towers and becomes part of the nature of our experience. As St Paul wrote, 'We suffer with [Christ] so that we may also be glorified with him' (Rom. 8.17).

Nicodemus trips up on the teaching of Christ because he approaches it from a functional point of view: how can I be born again? How can I climb back into the womb? Christ says: no, you're not getting it, you're born again because you rise with Christ. You're born again because you are, at the heart of your being, God's child, and God is Trinity, and God is love, and God is relationship.

The Holy Spirit dwells in our hearts, and the Spirit is God. The Son is placed into our hands at the altar rail, and he is God. And stamped in our being, in the Garden of Eden, is the image of God, as we are moulded in the Father's hands: clay, infused with the Trinity's breath and fire.

And so we find that deep down, under all the mess and the failure and the infirmity, there is relationship; and there is the call upon our lives to enter into that eternal dance of three Persons, one nature: perfect, balanced, self-giving, ever-receiving love. The image of God in you, in me, in the world.

In the name of the Father, and of the Son, and of the Holy Spirit. Amen.

Tom Clammer

Hymn suggestions

Thou, whose almighty word; I bind unto myself today the strong name of the Trinity; Holy, Holy, Holy, Lord God Almighty; Angel voices ever singing.

Trinity Sunday 26 May
Second Service **The Eternal Throne of Triune Godhead**
Morning Ps. 33.1–12; Evening Ps. 104.1–10; Ezek. 1.4–10, 22–28a; **Rev. 4**; *Gospel at Holy Communion*: Mark 1.1–13

For my secondary education, I attended boarding schools in the UK while my parents were living in the Middle East. We, my siblings and I, went home only for long vacation breaks – so these were special occasions. And in adulthood, as I went on to complete my university studies in the USA, before returning to settle in the UK, I have always found our yearly family gatherings very precious. A time to catch up with news and enjoy time in each other's company.

Throughout Scripture there are many examples of people gathering around. On Good Friday, Jesus' friends gathered around the foot of his cross as they watched his execution by the people he came to save and serve. On the third day, a few of his friends gathered around the tomb only to discover that the tomb was empty. Jesus Christ had risen.

Now, imagine the Triune Godhead inviting you to gather around the throne of heaven, to celebrate Christ's victory over death. It's significant that the word 'throne' – referring to the throne of God – occurs 14 times in this Revelation 4 passage. The throne of God is introduced to us through an open door in heaven, offering us a glimpse into eternity.

Created for worship

In today's Revelation passage, we are given an insight into heaven's throne room, a place brimming with colour, light and sound. And around the throne, 24 elders and four spectacular creatures, singing ceaselessly:

> Holy, holy, holy,
> the Lord God the Almighty,
> who was and is and is to come.

If we accept the invitation to join the eternal Triune Godhead at the throne, the eternal dwelling-place, we too will be full of praise, honour and adoration. Like the 24 elders and four living creatures, we will gather around and worship the source of power and authority, the Lord God Almighty.

And the journey to the throne, our eternal home, begins in the here and now. In this earthly realm, we have been purposed and are being fashioned daily for praise and worship. As we spend time in prayer and Scripture, fellowship with believers around the Lord's Supper, we are being prepared for that ultimate gathering when all who believe are raised up to God's right hand, singing:

> You are worthy, our Lord and God,
> to receive glory and honour and power,
> for you created all things,
> and by your will they existed and were created.

Psalm 86 reminds us that we worship a God who is like no other, and that we were created to bow down and glorify our Lord's holy name, and to give thanks with our whole hearts.

Cultivating a discipline of worship

An aspect of being created to experience the love, compassion and grace of our Lord Jesus Christ is a lifelong journey towards developing a posture of worship. That is worship which oozes from every pore of our being, where our whole selves are consumed with and glorify the Triune Godhead. Have you ever experienced and enjoyed such all-encompassing worship?

It is impossible to worship God if we do not know him because true worship is a response to knowing God. It is near impossible to worship God without trust. If we want to cultivate a discipline of worship, we need to immerse ourselves fully in our relationship with God, so that we can offer authentic worship to our Creator.

Such worship happens when our hearts, minds and beings are consumed by God in prayer and we have a real desire to know God better as we meditate on Scripture. God made us for intimate communion and fellowship with the Triune Godhead. We were created so that we can flourish in relationship with the divine. Worship is about God, not about us. Worship involves the way we live our lives. It is who we are before God, both publicly and privately, internally and externally, spiritually and physically.

What does your worship look like today? How will you respond to the Triune Godhead's invitation to gather around the throne of heaven?

Catherine Okoronkwo

Hymn suggestions

Jesus, lover of my soul; Guide me, O thou great Jehovah; 'Tis so sweet to trust in Jesus; My hope is built on nothing less.

First Sunday after Trinity (Proper 4) 2 June

Principal Service **Discernment**

(*Continuous*): **1 Sam. 3.1–10 [11–20]**; Ps. 139.1–5, 12–18; or (*Related*): Deut. 5.12–15; Ps. 81.1–10; 2 Cor. 4.5–12; Mark 2.23—3.6

Hearing and seeing

In this story of the call of Samuel, we start with the juxtaposition of seeing and hearing. To begin with, in the second verse of the reading, we are told, 'The word of the LORD was rare in those days.' Making the presumption that God is always the same, that suggests people were not listening, and here follows a story about just that. Next, we are told about Eli, whose eyesight 'had begun to grow dim so that he could not see'. A man who is going blind but who can still hear, alongside a boy, called Samuel, who can hear but doesn't know who is speaking. Seeing and hearing – and yet soon Samuel will hear (and Eli will see) what is foretold by God.

Listening

Prayer is many things, but at its heart there is deep communication – 'heart speaks to heart', to quote John Henry Newman. Prayer can be like a conversation, but like all good modes of communication it involves listening as well as speaking. A school pupil once asked me, 'What does God's voice sound like?' Now there's a question! I wonder if you have ever heard God's voice? If so, what did it sound like? What did God say to you?

Understanding

I know that this might sound obvious, but it has major implications for us as human beings: God is different from us. Therefore God speaks to us as he wishes to do so, and in the ways that are true to him. That means that we have to learn, or at least ask for the grace to learn, to hear him. To search for how to understand him. Like any relationship, that can take time and our close attention. Like an old-fashioned radio or wireless, it is like tuning into the frequency: finding the ways that we can most easily come into God's presence and hear him. Psalm 139 reminds us that God knows us better than we know ourselves, and so part of listening to him can come through loving the mystery that is the person that we are.

The early hours

We know from 1 Samuel that this revelation from God happened near dawn. The lamp in the Temple burned at night (Ex. 27.21), and the fact that it has not yet gone out tells us that it must be near morning. This seems significant to me. How often do we 'know' things or discover truths in that liminal moment in-between sleep and being awake? That only half-awake moment. This is when Samuel hears the voice. A voice that he can only assume is Eli's. An old man's voice? After all, it is a voice that knows his name, so who else could it be at this time and in this place? Samuel responds.

Discernment

I find that the word 'discernment' is a rather underused word in church life. At the heart of its meaning is that because God is God and we are not, we need help in understanding what God is saying. The call of Samuel is for me one of the most beautiful depictions of that in the Bible. Samuel hears a voice: he reckons he knows whose voice it is. He goes to the person whom he assumes is the author of that voice, but finds that he is wrong. Eventually, after the third time of hearing the voice (a deeply symbolic number), Eli gives Samuel the key to discernment – to recognize the speaker: 'Lord' – and to ask for the grace to hear: 'Speak, for your servant is listening.' The one who cannot see clearly teaches the one who cannot hear clearly, to listen. Notice the companionship in discerning. Often, very often, we can only hear with the help of another.

Consequences

All calls by God have consequences. How could they not? Just when this has sounded like a rather lovely story about a young boy who finds his vocation in life, we discover that in listening and receiving his call Samuel gets to see things that he never thought he would, and he gets to tell the very person who has helped him to hear and see, some hard truths about the consequences of his own family's actions. God's call is never to a more comfortable life. He calls us out of slumber to be awake to the world, and by his grace to see his vision of how the world should be. Samuel, through Eli, reminds us that the work of discernment starts with deep listening, and he gives us the gift of this prayer that echoes down the ages for all to use who are searching to understand God's will: 'Speak, Lord, your servant is listening.'

Jonathan Lawson

Hymn suggestions

Will you come and follow me; I, the Lord of sea and sky; All that I am; All I once held dear.

First Sunday of Trinity (Proper 4)   2 June
Second Service   **The Challenges of Service**
Ps. 35 [*or* 35.1–10]; **Jer. 5.1–19; Rom. 7.7–end**;
Gospel at Holy Communion: Luke 7.1–10

Jeremiah had a tough ministry. Chosen and consecrated before he was born, the Lord appointed him as a prophet to pluck up and to pull down, to destroy and to overthrow, to build and to plant. Charged with such tasks his response in chapter 1 is to say something like, 'I really can't do that – I'm far too young!' Making excuses for not being willing to obey God's calling goes back a long way! 'I'm too young,' says Jeremiah; 'We're too old,' say Abram and Sarai (Gen. 17); 'I'm not very good at speaking,' says Moses (Ex. 4); 'I don't want to,' says Jonah as he runs and hides from God (Jonah 1). Imposter syndrome is not a new phenomenon!

Challenging people

In today's passage from Jeremiah, we meet the prophet listening to the very difficult message that the Lord wishes him to deliver. It's such a hard message that God says the words he is going to put into Jeremiah's mouth will act like a fire devouring the wooden and stubborn people. Because of the sin of God's people, their turning away from God's laws and morality, their denial of God as creator and their general 'don't really care much about God' attitude, terrible things are going to happen to them. In dramatic imagery, God indicates that wild animals, lions, wolves and leopards, will tear the people in pieces and no one will be safe.

It's not the sort of message I'd want to deliver and I expect if any of us were charged with it we too would be running up and down the streets, hunting all around Jerusalem looking for that one person acting justly and seeking truth who would ensure God's pardon for Jerusalem. Jeremiah thinks that the poor won't be able to hear the message, so he should speak instead to the rich. But the rich are too well fed to think much about God. They are living immoral lives, feasting and sleeping with all and sundry – there is no hope for them either.

Being called by God to this role is very demanding for Jeremiah. and it's all too much for the people of God to whom he's sent. Ignoring the warnings he brings, they find themselves invaded by the Babylonians. As the Lord indicated through Jeremiah, mighty warriors overrun the land, eat all the food, destroy the crops and take the people away into captivity. As the people have served foreign gods so they now have to 'serve strangers in a land that is not yours'. It's very hard to serve God and to remain faithful when the people won't listen.

Challenges within

Paul, in the reading from Romans, is struggling to serve God too. For him, the problem is rather different. He is finding that whenever he wants to do good, 'evil lies close at hand' tempting him. He perceives a battle to be going on – not an outer battle, as with Jeremiah, but an inner battle, within himself. He longs to do one thing but finds himself doing another. How often do we find ourselves in this position too – knowing what the right thing to do is, but finding it almost impossible to do it; something, somehow seems to be stopping us from doing the things of God? Paul recognizes a spiritual battle going on within himself. He has become the battleground between Christ and the principalities and powers of evil. He describes an ongoing fight between sin and grace, between death and new life. As part of the body of Christ, he senses the tension within himself of living through death and resurrection, which replays within himself over and over again.

Ongoing challenges

Being called by God, following and serving Christ, is often demanding and challenging, full of ups and downs, joys and sorrows. It's possible to fly with the Spirit at one point and be crucified with

Christ at another. In between, there are many, many hours of ordinary faithful plodding along when obedience, faith and trust are required and not very much seems to be happening. For Jeremiah and Paul, God is the priority. This is demonstrated by listening to God, being in tune with the Spirit, praying, responding to God's surprises and living alongside God's people. Being called by God means not giving up, even when serving and being faithful is almost impossible. Being called by God means remaining faithful when faced with unpopularity, ridicule, danger or even intense and demanding surprise.

Each of us is called and chosen by God, redeemed and saved by Christ and filled with the Holy Spirit. We are each called to serve God in a variety of ways – like Jeremiah, like Paul, like thousands of other Christians named and anonymous. Called to serve in exciting ways, in demanding ways, in challenging ways, in surprising ways. Throughout the challenges to remain steadfast – challenges from within and without – we can be assured that God will be faithful.

Catherine Williams

Hymn suggestions

Father, hear the prayer we offer; Just as I am; He who would valiant be; Faithful one, so unchanging.

Second Sunday after Trinity (Proper 5)   9 June
Principal Service   **Would You Adam and Eve It?**
(*Continuous*): 1 Sam. 8.4–11 [12–15] 16–20 [11.14–15];
Ps. 138; *or* (*Related*): **Gen. 3.8–15**; Ps. 130; 2 Cor. 4.13—5.1;
Mark 3.20–end

The garden

Here we are at the beginning of the Bible and therefore the story of creation. Let's recap where we have got to so far. Despite only being at chapter 3 of Genesis, we have already heard how the world has been created, including all created beings (as well as human beings), and the story continues to this scene in the Garden of Eden, where Eve has been tempted to eat with Adam the fruit of the tree of the knowledge of good and evil. This is where the passage we have been given begins. Here in the garden, the man and the woman hear the sound of God walking in the garden. This is no distant God, it is a God who is right there immersed in his creation, and God is walking. I wonder what that sounded like? How did they know that it was God?

Hiding

Next, in this rather dramatic passage, the man and the woman hide. They hide from their Creator. Later in history, when God again walks the earth in the form of Jesus, he will tell people: 'For nothing is hidden that will not be disclosed, nor is anything secret that will not become known and come to light' (Luke 8.17). Why do we hide? I guess most often it is out of shame or fear – it's because we have something to hide. Facing up to what we have done takes some courage: it's easier not to take responsibility. I suspect that there are all sorts of subtle ways that we hide from God. How hard it can be to let him see the naked truth.

Sought out

Next, we discover that God wants to know where Adam is. He searches for him. He asks, 'Where are you?' This is no disinterested God, out for an evening stroll, keen to be in his own company. This is a God who wants to be among his creation and in companionship (even communion, you might say) with the human beings that he has formed from the dust of the earth. From the very beginning, we are given the sense that God desires to be close to us, his creation, and yet we hide. The movement away is not God's movement but ours. I think that's worth noting for the spiritual life. God is the constant, and he gives us the freedom of movement – to draw closer to him or away from him. That is why this story is so archetypal: for in a few sentences the story captures the whole human story of what we do with free will in relation to God.

Nakedness

I used to be a university chaplain, and once I met a professor at the local swimming pool just as he came out of the changing cubicle. It's an incredible leveller, being unclothed. We said hello, and he told me wryly that he was of the age when he had to check that he had his swimming trunks on before coming out of the cubicle. That always makes me chuckle. The possibility of the naked professor forgetting to put on his swimming trunks. Yet, one of the earliest pictures of me as a child is in a paddling pool, ironically wearing a sun hat and nothing else, completely content with my nakedness, so it seems. Childhood innocence, which at some point changes to acute self-consciousness, as we too, like Adam in the garden, become aware of our nakedness.

Blame

Once we get past the nakedness in this passage, we are on to blame. Adam blames Eve, Eve blames the serpent. The serpent doesn't get a say. The naked truth is too hard to bear – this all has to be someone else's fault. The God who draws people and creation together begins to see it fragment. Love draws people and creation closer, sin divides and separates. Here we see sin entering the world. The huge industry of victim culture begins. The scapegoating begins with femininity and concludes with a reptile. The cold-blooded one. How apt.

Unlove

Whether you go with the doctrine of original sin or not, it seems to me to be undeniable that the world is not as it should be: that all human beings have the most remarkable ability to be tempted in the way of self-destructive behaviour – changes in our climate being the latest example of our sleepwalking into collective self-harm. One of the hardest pastoral experiences I find in ministry is that of seeing how loved some people are, and of their inability to receive that love for whatever reason. It makes me weep. Eve and Adam by their actions are cast out of paradise, but for Christians there is a path back, offered to all in the unconditional love of the new Adam, Jesus. He has come looking for us, searching us out and drawing us back into communion with God, loved sinners that we are, redeemed by another tree and a different garden.

Jonathan Lawson

Hymn suggestions

God that madest earth and heaven; Walking in a garden; Praise to the holiest in the height; Ye choirs of new Jerusalem.

Second Sunday after Trinity (Proper 5)   9 June
Second Service   **Walking the Ancient Ways**
Ps. 37.1–17 [*or* 37.1–11] [12–17]; **Jer. 6.16–21**; **Rom. 9.1–13**;
Gospel at Holy Communion: Luke 7.11–17

Dreams of life ahead

Do you remember what you wanted to do when you were a child? What was your life ambition? And as you look back over your life, what do you think? Did you make it? Do you regret your choices?

I often think of my dreams as a teenager, and how reluctant I was to listen to adults giving me advice. Thinking I knew better and would make my own way, regardless of what wisdom they had to share. And most of all, I was determined not to pursue anything similar to my parents, grandparents or very large extended family. I wanted to make my own path rather than follow what had come before.

Turning away

Turning away from an ancient path, thinking we know better, disliking the advice of others, the feeling of life being determined – all of this is common and very human. It is part of how we grow into ourselves. Sometimes it's OK, and sometimes not. Whether or not our choices are good, as life goes on, attitudes solidify, and it becomes hard to consider changing. We justify our choices, we adapt to life as it comes, and sometimes we lose track of who we were meant to be in the first place.

In our Jeremiah reading, the people of Israel had been told what to do. They had been chosen, loved and helped. They had been nurtured to take a certain path – but they turned away. We read about their turning away in Jeremiah and in Romans, and of God's sadness and frustration at seeing the people he loves taking a path that will lead them away from everything that is good and right and true. But God ... accepts their choice. He does not force, does not impose love. But he leaves the people to experience the consequences of their own choices.

In Romans, Paul is dismayed at the thought that everything had been given to Israel, yet they still chose to turn away, in myriad different ways: in choosing to live as if there was no God; in choosing to worship other gods; in choosing to seek after riches and power and forgetting justice and kindness. Or, like Paul himself, in choosing to lose themselves in the rules and rituals of religion and forget what matters most – truly listening to God and loving God's people. The demands of faith in the God of Israel are high: it is about the whole of life, all relationships, and how we relate to everyone and everything.

To follow God is to know God

And so we have Paul's famous words about the true Israel, the true people of faith. Paul knows better than anyone else how easy it is to deceive yourself, to think you are doing God's will but instead pursuing your own path. Paul had ended up persecuting Christians. Paul knew that even though he followed all the regulations, and tried very hard, he had completely missed the point, and had never really known God until Jesus appeared to him on the Damascus road. He had heard the stories, heard of the ancient path, but not listened to the voice of God; instead, he had followed his own counsel, dismissed what he did not want to hear, and clung to human traditions that had gradually come to replace relating to God.

And that makes me squirm a little bit! I wonder – what am I missing? What am I ignoring? I know how good I am at talking myself into doing silly things, and justifying my choices to others, even when they are blatantly daft. How do we know we are going in the right direction?

The power of grace

Paul gives us the answer in Romans: grace. It isn't about what we do. It is about what God does. We see this in the pages of the Old Testament – as the people get things wrong and God meets them in the places of pain and harm they have created for themselves, again and again. We see it in the Old and New Testaments, in God loving and choosing us before we even know God. We see it in God sending Jesus regardless of whether we want God or not, in God prompting others to speak to us about him, in God encouraging us to stand at the crossroads of our lives and look, and ask for the ancient paths, where the good way lies, and give heed to the sound of his voice. We have God's guide – in Scripture, in the treasure and wealth left by those Christians who came before us, and in one another, and in the guidance of the Spirit. And when all else fails, God's grace remains, calling us to be honest with ourselves and with God, and to start again. To go back to the crossroads and take the right path. Again. And again. And again.

Isabelle Hamley

Hymn suggestions

How deep the Father's love for us; I surrender all; O love that will not let me go; Take my life and let it be.

Third Sunday after Trinity (Proper 6)   16 June
Principal Service   **Living the Kingdom**
(*Continuous*): 1 Sam. 15.34—16.13; Ps. 20; *or* (*Related*):
Ezek. 17.22–end; Ps. 92.1–4, 12–end [*or* 92.1–8];
2 Cor. 5.6–10 [11–13] 14–17; **Mark 4.26–34**

Our readings today are about God at work in our world, about the reign of God being fully established in our lives, throughout our churches and communities. Jesus often used illustrations from the natural world to teach about the kingdom. Using the imagery of seeds, he reminds us that the kingdom of God is an organism – a living, growing entity not just an organization. The church, as the body of Christ, is a growing, loving community, in which all our work and worship is done in the name of Jesus Christ and through the power of the Spirit.

Jesus spoke about mustard, a tiny seed that grows into a vast shrub capable of housing and giving protection to many others of all shapes and sizes. He's drawing here on the imagery of the Old Testament prophet Ezekiel. In that passage, God takes action and plants a cedar shoot. It's planted on a high mountain – God's native soil. And though it's a tender shoot it becomes a magnificent cedar tree in which all can seek refuge.

Phenomenal growth

Ezekiel and Jesus make the point that though the seeds of the kingdom may be very small when God is in control, the growth can be phenomenal. The seed has within it all the potential to become a tree, and God gives and drives that mystery which is life, growth, reproduction, death and life again. We as Christians sow the seeds of God's kingdom all around us – by meeting together to worship, by sharing our faith in Jesus Christ with others, by works of service in our communities, by being generous with our buildings, resources and money.

We may feel that we are doing very little for the kingdom, but across the worldwide church a very impressive amount of kingdom activity is taking place. We may have one service here a week, but across the world millions of opportunities for worship take place day by day. We may be involved in volunteer activities in this community – just imagine those acts of service multiplied throughout the world, a myriad of Christians going about kingdom business, sowing small seeds that God can grow into mighty shrubs.

Building confidence

We need to have confidence that God is at work. St Paul writing to the Corinthians urged the Christians there to have confidence in the message of God's saving action through the death and resurrection of Christ. The word 'confidence' means 'with faith'. We are people of faith and we trust and believe that God is at work in our churches and in our world and that God has confidence – has faith – in each of us to help build the kingdom wherever we're placed. Where people are in Christ, we can expect to see a new creation – new energy and creative activity.

But it's no good sowing seeds and watching them grow if we are not prepared to be part of the harvesting. Traditionally, harvest time was an event when everyone pulled together to gather valuable crops. When we are engaged with kingdom work – the work of God – we can never be quite sure when the harvest will come. We need to be alert to its possibility and work together to ensure a successful gathering in of all God's good growth.

Not giving up

It's really important not to give up on the church or on our faith because not much seems to be happening, it's all too difficult, or we don't like the way things are going. Commitment to Jesus Christ and to kingdom living requires faithfulness in good times and in bad. It requires proper and responsible use of our gifts in God's service, and a sacrificial giving of ourselves and our resources, including our money and our time. We also need to celebrate the good things that are happening – the signs of God at work in our communities. We need too to celebrate and support the work which is happening across the worldwide church, where hundreds of thousands of lives are being reached and transformed by God's love and salvation.

Remaining faithful

So what can we all do to be fully committed to kingdom living? First, we need to be faithful in worship, attending church regularly and praying every day. That keeps us firmly in touch with God. Next, let's remember and celebrate that we are a part of something much bigger than our local church. Together with God and our Christian family across the world, we are making a real difference, even when we are not aware of it.

Is it time to review our giving? Both in terms of time and money. Just think what we might be able to do if there was more money available. Everything we have comes from God and belongs to God. In what ways are we using God's gifts for God's work? How are we allowing ourselves to be shaped for the work of the kingdom? What more might we do?

Above all, let's remember, however difficult times are, that God is at work in our world. God is at work in our churches and communities and in our lives too. It only takes a tiny seed to produce a vast tree. Let's offer our small seeds in the expectation that God will grow something of real substance.

Catherine Williams

Hymn suggestions

God is working his purpose out; For the fruits of his creation; Great is thy faithfulness; The day thou gavest, Lord, is ended.

Third Sunday after Trinity (Proper 6)   16 June
Second Service   A Troublesome Word
Ps. 39; **Jer. 7.1–16**; Rom. 9.14–26;
Gospel at Holy Communion: Luke 7.36—8.3

I wonder if you have ever thought about troublesome words? I don't mean words that are difficult to pronounce, like otorhinolaryngologist. (There is a reason why we refer to an ENT specialist!) Rather,

I am thinking about simple words that are sometimes difficult to say, such as 'sorry'.

No one really likes to say 'sorry'. In fact, to avoid doing so, at times people look for someone or something to blame. Even when error is acknowledged, a 'non-apology' apology may be offered: 'If I have offended anyone, I am sorry', or, 'Clearly, mistakes were made.' Without a doubt, in the words of the songtitle, 'Sorry seems to be the hardest word.'[25]

The test of the three Rs

Research on offering apologies to people and to animals (yes, believe it or not, there are instructions on the internet for apologizing to your cat!) suggests that the sincerity of a person's apology may be measured by the test of 'three Rs': remorse, regret and repair. 'Test' questions include: is there genuine remorse? Is there a willingness to take responsibility for an action? Is there a desire to make amends? Does the person promise that the offence will never occur again or, at least, that there is the intention of change?

While the 'three R test' may be one way of measuring the earnestness of an apology, there is another 'R word' – which Christian faith teaches – that goes hand in hand with saying 'sorry'. It is the word 'repent'.

Sadly, for many people, 'repentance' is a word with negative connotations. In fact, there are those who think that 'to repent' means leaving behind everything that brings joy in life. Yet, while it may grow out of the tears of remorse and regret, true repentance contributes to the repair of relationship – with God and with one another, too. Indeed, repentance is life-enhancing, not only for ourselves but also for others.

To repent literally means 'to turn around' or to have a 'change of heart and mind', and it reflects a desire to embark on a new way. It marks a new beginning and a fresh start. It begins with saying 'sorry'.

Amending our ways and our doings

There are many stories in the Old and New Testaments that remind us of both the necessity and the joy of repentance. Nevertheless, sermons on repentance have a tendency to raise the ire of a congregation! The prophet Jeremiah no doubt found this to be true when he stood at the Temple gate and called to the people to amend their 'ways and their doings' and to let God dwell with them. Can you imagine their annoyance? They were on their way to worship and bringing their offerings. Wasn't that enough? Why didn't he go and preach to someone else?

Yet, Jeremiah would not – perhaps could not – stop proclaiming the word of the Lord to them because he knew that if the people really experienced the joy of God's love and life-giving presence in worship, it would also be reflected in their lives – in their 'ways and doings'. The reality was that while the people were coming to worship, they were failing, day by day, to care for those who were most vulnerable around them: 'the alien, the orphan and the widow'. Change was needed. True worship can never be separated from daily life. The people needed to turn around and, with God's help, begin afresh. The difficulty, of course, for them and for us all today is finding the way to say the hardest word: sorry.

God's mercy and compassion on a 'messy house'

As an artist in residence at parochial schools, Kathleen Norris has used poetry to try to help children express their feelings. On one occasion, a young boy in her class wrote a poem called 'The Monster Who Was Sorry'. At the beginning of the poem, the boy said that he hated it when his father yelled at him. His response, in the poem, was to throw his sister down the stairs, wreck his room and then do the same to the whole town. The poem ended, 'Then I sit in my messy house and say to myself, "I shouldn't have done all that."'[26]

The child's poem poignantly calls us each to gaze upon our own 'messy house' and to consider the need to amend our 'ways' and our 'doings'. Of course, our faith teaches that repentance is not a momentary, single event. Rather, it is an ongoing process of daily turning and turning, again and again, to God who is rich in grace and mercy and who always stands ready to forgive. We do so remembering that while 'sorry' may seem the hardest word of all, it is a word that leads to joy, peace and life.

Karen E. Smith

Hymn suggestions

Dear Lord and Father of mankind; O for a heart to praise my God; There's a wideness in God's mercy; Lord, thy church on earth is seeking.

Fourth Sunday after Trinity (Proper 7)   23 June
Principal Service   **Stilling the Storm**
(*Continuous*): 1 Sam. 17.[1a, 4–11, 19–23] 32–49 *and*
Ps. 9.9–end, *or* 1 Sam. 17.57—18.5, 10–16 *and* Ps. 133;
or (*Related*): Job 38.1–11; **Ps. 107.1–3, 23–32** [*or* 107.23–32];
2 Cor. 6.1–13; **Mark 4.35–end**

Living on a Scottish island, I am ambivalent about the sea. It has great beauty and is a source of food, but it can also do immense damage and wreak havoc. One of my churches is cited as the place from which islanders once walked to make propitiatory sacrifices of ale to the sea-sprite *Seonaidh* in the hope of freedom from storms and an abundant seaweed harvest for the coming year.

The sea and chaos

There is a biblical tradition which treats water – and especially the sea – as representative of chaos. In the first creation story God's Spirit hovers over the face of the waters (Gen. 1.2), and in separating water and dry land God brings order out of chaos (1.9–10). At the Exodus, the Red Sea is parted as the Israelites cross from slavery to freedom (Ex. 14.21), and in John's vision in Revelation there is, significantly, no more sea (Rev. 21.1). Several psalms speak of God's power over the sea, for example, Psalm 89.8–10, where the sea monster Rahab is a personification of chaos.

Mark's account of the stilling of the storm has strong resonances with Hebrew Scripture, especially with Psalm 107. This psalm – which is very close indeed to today's Gospel – addresses several contexts in which God has saved his people, among them being the chaos of the sea (Ps. 107.23–32). The thrust of this, and of similar passages, is that it is God *alone* who defeats the chaos-monster, God *alone* who rules the waves, and God *alone* who stills storms and defeats the powers of evil. The Gospel passage ends with the disciples' question, 'Who then is this?' (Mark 4.41). It's for us, though, as hearers of the Gospel, to answer. If we read the miracle against its biblical background, then we are left in no doubt. 'Who then is this?' Jesus *is* none other than God's own self: God in human form.

Theophany

This is a significant point for Mark to make because Mark's Gospel includes no account of Jesus' birth, nor does it comment on the incarnation. Matthew and Luke record the Christ-child's birth and John affirms the Word taking flesh and dwelling among us (John 1.14), but Mark's narrative begins when Jesus is an adult. Hence the writer has to convince readers that Jesus is truly divine. And how better to do this than through a miracle in which Jesus overcomes the sea – a potent symbol of the forces of evil. This miracle is a theophany: a showing-forth of Jesus as fully divine.

Mark's context and ours

But why else might Mark have included this account, and what significance might it hold for us? It's thought that the Gospel was probably written for a church in Rome, at a time when to be Christian was almost to sign one's own death warrant – or at least a guarantee of persecution. It's possible that the Christians of Mark's community felt buffeted by the wind and waves of a hostile regime and were in grave danger of sinking. Having embraced the good news of the risen Christ, they now found themselves asking whether their faith was, after all, in vain. Was Christ with them, or had he perhaps fallen asleep and left them to sink? Mark's point is that, despite the trials of their situation, they must hold on to their faith that, with Jesus with them in the boat (the ark of the church), the powers of evil will not win.

A storm is a powerful symbol. For the writers of the Old Testament, a storm symbolized anything and everything disastrous that could come upon an individual or a community. For them, in such storms, God was their only hope; and so the Hebrew Scriptures bear witness to an unshakeable faith in God to save and protect them. The miracle of the stilling of the storm transposes that faith in God into a new key by making Jesus, the Son of God, the one whom the wind and the waves obey. It's interesting that Jesus addresses the sea as if it were a person, and when commanding the sea he uses the same word as when he binds demons in his healing miracles. In Jesus, we have not only a divine being showing his authority over the whole created order, but a divine being *like us*, fully human and able to empathize with us, able to be *with* us in the boat as well as able to save us.

Each of us faces different storms. Some of us, like Mark's original audience, might face persecution for our faith; for others, it's a storm of illness, of loss, of trauma, of separation or of loneliness. Each of us is in need of that saving love: the love which both comes alongside us and saves us – the love of God who, in Jesus, shares our life and changes it.

Peter Moger

Hymn suggestions

Fierce raged the tempest o'er the deep; Eternal Father, strong to save; In Christ alone, my hope is found; Lead us, heavenly Father, lead us.

Fourth Sunday after Trinity (Proper 7)   23 June
Second Service   **Icons and Idols**
Ps. 49; **Jer. 10.1–16**; **Rom. 11.25–end**;
Gospel at Holy Communion: Luke 8.26–39

An icon is not an idol

I love an icon. I've got quite a few dotted around my house. Each one draws in the eye to reveal to the heart something of the nature of God. Rublev's icon of the visit of the angels to Abraham and Sarah draws in the viewer as the fourth person around the table. It speaks of the hospitality and welcome of God. I have an icon of Mary and the infant Jesus, their cheeks pressed together, holding each other's gaze. It suggests something of the intimacy and nurturing love of God. Icons are designed to draw us into the worship of God. Idols, on the other hand, demand to be worshipped. An icon is not an idol.

Dangerous idols

Jeremiah has plenty to say on the subject of idols. Like icons, they are painted by craftsmen on to blocks of wood. Unlike icons, they do not point to God. An icon points through itself to a greater reality. An idol claims to be that reality. The effect of this is to give a sense of power to the one who owns the idol. If you own the greater reality, then you must be greater than it. Idolatry is simply self-worship in a loose disguise.

Jeremiah paints a powerful contrast between the living God and worthless idols. God is great, mighty, incomparable, the King of the Nations, the true and living God who is everlasting. The idols, made from that which God has already created, are like 'scarecrows in a cucumber field', draped in purple with painted eyes. They have no real agency of their own. That's what makes an idol really dangerous. Why? Because when you worship an idol, you control it. You can make it say what you want. Idolatry is fundamentally worship of the self.

If this all sounds a little distant from our everyday, just pause and reflect.

Idolatry boils down to self-worship

When I make an idol out of a car, I am worshipping my financial agency and perceived success. I'm worshipping myself. This does not mean we can't enjoy things, but it's a reminder to hold lightly to stuff. Cars rust and crumple; we age and wither. But the living God, the Creator, lasts from generation to generation.

When nationalism becomes an idol, a perceived good is worshipped. This perceived good, funnily enough, tends to look rather like the one upholding it – another form of self-worship. This generally ends badly for people caught up in the nationalist agenda of us and them. Just ask the Windrush generation, or refugees deported to distant lands for processing.

The one who makes an idol of power and position is going to seek to hold on to that, come what may. This leads to lying in public life, an erosion of trust, an increase in cynicism and, ultimately, the fall into dictatorship when truth is what the leader says it is. It is an extreme form of self-worship, often involving trappings of pseudo-religious symbolism – music, crowds, flags, mass gatherings and processions – to justify and embolden.

If I make an idol of religion, then I set up *my* interpretation of theology and practice as the only and correct way. All other ways are heresy. A glance at history shows that accusations of heresy tend not to end too well for the accused. Extreme religious idolatry is often death-dealing. Genuine faith is a form of icon, drawing the worshipper into a bigger vision of the living God. Religious idolatry, in contrast, seeks to force people to obey the person or persons wielding the power. There it is again – self-worship.

Idolatry doesn't impress God

Idolatry will always end in ruin. Jeremiah states, 'There is none like God.' In Romans, Paul reminds us of the 'depth of the riches and wisdom and knowledge of God' (11.33). Meanwhile, idolatry tries to oust God from the throne, claiming 'I am god-like'. Idolatry replaces the sceptre of love with a rod of iron to break across the backs of dissenters. As Jeremiah points out, this will not impress God: 'At his wrath, the earth quakes, and the nations cannot endure his indignation' (10.10).

Jesus Christ: icon of icons

Beware the idol. Beware the tricksy shifting self. Seek out the icon – that which draws us into worship of God. The ultimate icon is not a painting on a block of wood – as helpful as it can be. The icon of icons pulses with life. Jesus Christ in his living flesh draws us into deeper understanding of the nature of God. Here is God with fingerprints, who kneels down to serve, who seeks out the unloved and the lost, who breaks bread with sinners and lifts us up in love. 'From him and through him and to him are all things. To him be glory for ever' (Rom. 11.36). Away with idols. Seek out the icon of icons: Jesus Christ.

Kate Bruce

Hymn suggestions

The splendour of the King; Great is the Lord and most worthy of praise; Give thanks to the Lord, our God and King; All my days, I will sing this song of gladness.

Fifth Sunday after Trinity (Proper 8) 30 June
Principal Service **A Culture of Invitation and Inclusion**
(*Continuous*): 2 Sam. 1.1, 17–end; Ps. 130; *or* (*Related*): Wisd. of Sol. 1.13–15; 2.23–24; *Canticle*: Lam. 3.22–33, *or* Ps. 30; 2 Cor. 8.7–end; **Mark 5.21–end**

Traditionally, in Igbo culture, names hold significance and meaning not unlike names in biblical times which were often used to record an aspect of a person's birth or to communicate God's message. In some cases, in Scripture, a person was renamed to indicate a new beginning or direction in a person's life. My last name, Okoronkwo, locates me as a daughter of the Igbo tribe, from the Aro Chukwu clan, of the Ndi Oti Aliche family. This name tells, in part, my history and heritage.

In the last couple of years, there has been a social movement that seeks to raise awareness of violence against females using the hashtag #SayHerName – another illustration of the power of names and naming as a means of showing identity, giving dignity and affirming relationship. And in today's gospel message we meet a woman who also calls to us to #SayHerName.

#SayHerName

As a woman living a 'less than' life due to her health condition, the woman with the issue of blood not only seeks physical healing but wants to be seen, valued and affirmed in a society that has shunned her into the shadows of her existence.

Thankfully, the Scriptures are full of accounts of how God brings about his redemption in the midst of chaos, that impetus on God's part to respond to the messiness of life.

This passage in Mark's Gospel reminds us of God's incarnational response to the suffering of humanity. Through the ministry of Christ Jesus – his life, death and resurrection – we are offered a paradigm of salvation, redemption and liberation.

It is incredibly overwhelming that the whole point of Jesus' mission was to recover the personhood of those who have been lost, maligned or marginalized by human conditions, systems and structures. There is hope in the image of a suffering God; that trope of a redemptive Christ provides occasions to find God in seemingly unredeemable places. Even in that place of worthlessness, weakness and marginality, this woman 'who had been suffering from haemorrhages for twelve years' could be transformed into a new creation, a whole person.

Like the woman with the issue of blood, many in our communities are shunned for all manner of reasons. Are we silent or complicit in their plight? In the midst of a society which seems reluctant to confront the underbelly of inequalities and injustices of all kinds, do we challenge cultures and systems that maintain the status quo? Or, as followers of Christ, do we seek to offer renewal, restoration and redemption through the touch of Jesus' cloak?

Re-imagination and re-humanization

We are reminded time and again that our churches and our communities can be re-imagined through God's generous love. We are called to a God-centred model of humanity living together in a way that transcends boundaries and brings into God's kingdom-community those whom society has fenced out or rejected.

When Jesus asks who had touched him, and the woman 'came in fear and trembling, fell down before him, and told him the whole truth', Jesus does not walk off, carry on his way, as one might have expected him to do. Rather, he chooses to stop and acknowledge this woman. The manner in which he does so is significant. His love protects her personhood, dignity and identity. Jesus restores and re-humanizes her personhood, modelling a life-enhancing friendship that is invitational and inclusive. Over and over again, God starts afresh with sinful humans and demonstrates generous compassion.

We are all made in the image of God. And, if we truly believe this, then any institutional system or structure undermining the full participation and contribution of any person erodes kingdom-community. How then do we re-imagine our church through the lens of Christ?

The church has a role to play in offering a Christ-centred narrative of solidarity with people from all backgrounds and walks of life, particularly those who remain on the outside. Jesus' relationships underscored unconditional love and acceptance with those on the margins. Therefore, the truth of the gospel message is that God is found in vulnerability. His presence is revealed, and people encounter Christ when we take up the invitation to create communities where all people know a God-centred acceptance and belonging in his kingdom-family.

The challenge for us all is to open ourselves to a more expansive compassion for people who might look different from us. It should matter to us when 'the other' is bleeding, crying and dying because we are called to be an invitational and inclusive church.

Catherine Okoronkwo

Hymn suggestions

Brother, sister, let me serve you; Kumbaya, my Lord, kumbaya; Let all the world in every corner sing; When I needed a neighbour.

Fifth Sunday after Trinity (Proper 8) 30 June
Second Service **Living the Small Print**
Ps. [52] 53; Jer. 11.1–14; **Rom. 13.1–10**;
Gospel at Holy Communion: Luke 9.51–end

Small print matters

Today's readings face us with some big choices, choices that stretch over thousands of years, describing who we are and how we live. But we are also faced with some big consequences when those choices go wrong. It's a bit like trying to get to grips with the small print – all the details that most of us avoid and then discover when it's too late, like realizing that you should renew your driving licence photo every ten years or discovering that your insurance policy doesn't actually cover the things you thought it did. The small print really matters. We sign up to the big message of faith, rejoicing that God is our God, and we are his people, whether we are the exiled children of Israel listening to the prophet Jeremiah or the church in Rome struggling to establish a new way of being.

Not fear but conscience

The big words are great, for they give us confidence and courage. We believe in a God who is committed to us, and we sing praise and declare our faith. But then it turns out, like all contracts or covenants, that there is some detail and that detail is about how we live and how we behave as followers of the one true God. Paul begins by encouraging the Roman Christians to live by the laws of their community and is clear that disobeying leads to consequences. Those listening were living in harsh times, where breaking laws led to harsh penalties. But Paul takes it further, suggesting that it shouldn't just be fear of punishment that makes us keep laws, but rather a deep-rooted sense of what is right. This is the nature of the covenant, the covenant God made with his people, and Paul takes his listeners and us back to the Ten Commandments and Jesus' summary of those commandments. We are to be those who love in fidelity, who resist anger and have values that are honest, respectful and real. We are to deal justly and honestly, and in our daily realities we live out our calling, which above all is based in love. This is living out the small print.

Godly living

Research with baptism families shows again and again that parents and grandparents want their children to choose a right path and to live by good values, values like fidelity, generosity, fairness, kindness and love, and yes, these are Christian values. It's not always our focus. We often talk about what we need to believe, about who Jesus is and what his life means for us. Yet so often it is when our leaders hold fast to these values that they are applauded. We think of Archbishop Justin Welby speaking out about unfair payday loans, Archbishop Sentamu's stand on Zimbabwe, or ordinary families who speak of forgiveness after terrible events. This is the small print, this is Christian, godly living, rooted in love.

Forgiveness and grace

Yet our readings are realistic. We will fail to live up to our calling. Jeremiah paints a picture of a people who follow other gods and act dishonestly. Writing to the Romans, Paul reminds them and us sharply that failing to live by the laws of the land, and implicitly the laws of God, will have consequences. And we need to put right the things that go wrong, always acting out of love. For it is when we fail that the reality of our call is revealed. Our faith is not just about values, standards and behaviours, not simply about being good people, but it is about who we trust and what we believe. This is the small print of a covenant. God is our God and we are his people, and through Jesus he has revealed grace so that we can be forgiven. The Holy Spirit enables us to learn how to live as Jesus taught and modelled, living out the small print, rejoicing that we are God's people, living God's way, rooted and grounded in love.

Sandra Millar

Hymn suggestions

Amazing grace; Who can sound the depths of sorrow; There's a wideness in God's mercy; Dear Lord and Father of mankind.

Sixth Sunday after Trinity (Proper 9)   7 July
Principal Service   **Coming and Going**
(*Continuous*): 2 Sam. 5.1–5, 9–10; Ps. 48; or (*Related*):
Ezek. 2.1–5; Ps. 123; 2 Cor. 12.2–10; **Mark 6.1–13**

Today's Gospel is two discrete episodes placed together: first, the return of Jesus to his home, and then the sending out of the disciples in pairs to do missionary work.

Returning home

I feel sorry for Jesus in this passage as he makes his way home. He's been travelling around the lake performing many miracles and wonders. He's stilled the storm, healed the demoniacs, raised Jairus' daughter to life and healed the woman with the flow of blood. Now he comes home to Nazareth, his home town, and begins to teach in the synagogue. At first, the people are very excited. Here's the local lad made good, Mary's boy full of wisdom and learning – just look at him now.

But then they can't get their heads around it – it's too much. It's almost as if they think he's got above himself, put on airs and graces. After all, he's supposed to be 'one of us' – so what's all this authority, this power? They take offence and turn against him, just as the Pharisees and Herodians and scribes have done earlier in this Gospel. The Greek phrase 'take offence' is used in Mark's Gospel for those who begin to follow Jesus but then fall away, those who start walking but then stumble – the seed that falls on rocky ground or among thorns.

Due to the rejection, Jesus finds himself unable to do many deeds of power in Nazareth. Others' lack of faith inhibits his ability. He moves on and another group of people who should be insiders in the kingdom become outsiders through their inability to embrace change, their short-sightedness faced with the works of God.

Sending out

In the second story, Jesus, having moved on, sends out the Twelve to begin the work of mission. He sends them out in pairs, working collaboratively. They go very simply, taking the bare minimum. It's important to be lean when doing the work of Jesus. Encumbered by too much we can be distracted. Jesus gives clear instructions.

If they are made welcome, they are to stay. If they're not wanted, then there's no point hanging about – they are to shake the dust off their feet and move on. Their mission is very successful: they anoint the sick and cure them. They cast out demons; they proclaim the good news of the kingdom. It's an exciting and heady time as they witness the kingdom of God breaking around and through them.

Moving on

So, what about us, worshipping here? First, Jesus shows us that it's acceptable to move on. Sometimes God calls us to move away from home and to do something new. Jesus' rejection at Nazareth leads to the mission to the Gentiles and the empowering of the disciples to continue the work of the kingdom. By leaving home, Jesus' mission expands and grows, probably somewhat unexpectedly.

Second, Jesus empowers the disciples with his authority and sends them out in pairs to be salt and light in new places. It's a taster of what's to come after Pentecost when this group of friends will be scattered in all directions to do the work of God throughout the world. As we go out, we go in the name of Jesus – with his authority – to be his disciples in new places. And although we may go in different directions, we have the Christian community for support. The Christian journey is rarely done alone – we all need each other in the body of Christ, whether we remain at home or go out to new places.

Going lightly

Third, Jesus tells his disciples to go with very little – just a staff, no extras. To take hold of the new thing that God wants to do, we have to go with empty hands. If we hold too tightly to the past there's no room for God's new thing. We need to let things go as we are called into God's exciting future. We need to be lean for the journey ahead – with open, empty hands, ready to go where the Spirit blows and ready for the gifts she has for us.

Christ has secured our salvation by opening his hands on the cross – by letting all things go so that something extraordinary and unique could happen: the resurrection. As disciples of Christ, we are called to imitate that surrender to God's unknown but remarkable future.

God's constancy

The God we worship is faithful. Wherever we go, God will be with us – calling us into new places, into new ways of being citizens of the kingdom. At times the Christian journey is risky and scary and demanding. At other times we are led beside still waters and situated in solid, stable places. God is with us, as individuals and as a community. God calls us and equips us, goes before us, walks with us and brings up the rear. There is nowhere we can go where God is not. Whether we are coming or going, remaining or moving on, we can be sure that God holds us and will not let us go.

Catherine Williams

Hymn suggestions

Father, hear the prayer we offer; Thuma mina (Send me, Lord); Forth in thy name; Will you come and follow me.

Sixth Sunday after Trinity (Proper 9)   7 July
Second Service   **Intolerances**
Ps. [63] 64; Jer. 20.1–11a; **Rom. 14.1–17**;
Gospel at Holy Communion: Luke 10.1–11, 16–20

Hospitality

I have just been to a wedding celebration of a couple who were married in a private ceremony last year but wanted to have a celebration with as many of their friends and family present as possible this year. It was a great party and a huge amount of effort had gone into the choices people could make around the three-course meal that we shared, including whether people ate meat or not, but also any other dietary requirements that the guests might have. These days, with so many people having intolerances to various types of food, it can be quite a task to be sensitively hospitable. I was once at a wedding blessing meal when someone went into anaphylactic shock after eating some peanuts to which they were allergic. I drove them to hospital at quite a speed and luckily they made a good recovery, but it was a sober reminder of how important it is to be careful in such matters. Sometimes choices about what we eat can mean life or death.

Dietary requirements

At some pivotal points in Jewish history, most notably in exile, the Jewish faith (like all faiths under threat) has had to ponder what it is that makes someone a Jew, as opposed to anyone else. As such, a greater identity is found, and clarity is given as to what it means to be of the Jewish faith and of Jewish ethnicity. As time progressed, part of what it meant to be Jewish was defined by clear dietary laws that are contained in the Torah. As Jesus was a devout Jew, he would have adhered to these laws, but as his message spread throughout the world, it raised questions about what non-Jewish followers of his, in particular, could eat, in the same way as it raised questions as to whether Gentile Christians should be circumcised or not.

Standard class

In Great Britain, on trains, we now have standard-class carriages (which used to be called second class) and on some trains first-class seating too. It's tempting to think that in the early church there was a standard type of Christian, but that's not true. From the very beginning, Christians, as they are today, were a whole bundle of different people with a great range of backgrounds. St Paul himself, a zealous Jew who persecuted Christians before his conversion to following God in Jesus, was faced with the challenge of what to keep from his Jewish faith and background and what to let go of. In his Letter to the Romans, in this particular chapter, he is addressing Christians who do different things, eat different things and observe different things. It's not a reading that I would give from the Bible to a vegetarian exploring the Christian faith for the first time!

Welcome

When I read Scripture, I keep an internal eye out for what phrase or words jump out at me. In this passage, the end of verse 3 jumped out: 'for God has welcomed them'. That seems very important to me. It shifts the focus from those who are arguing over various matters to the fact that God has welcomed them. Indeed, the whole chapter begins with the word 'welcome'. People of faith have often quarrelled. I guess it's hardly surprising considering the nature of faith and of belief as a conviction. It's not so much the dispute that's the problem, but the respect shown (or not) to each other in doing so.

Tolerance

The one who has written this letter to the Romans, St Paul, has himself found freedom, from that which bound him, into a new and living faith. This conversion has transformed him. It is not surprising then that his relationship with laws and rules might be something he is very sensitive about. The closing verse of this reading consequently seems highly significant: 'For the kingdom of God is not food and drink but righteousness and peace and joy in the Holy Spirit.' It is a movement from the external to the internal; from the physical to the spiritual. This passage prompts me again to think about the kind of church we are called to be. How do we live with different beliefs and traditions within the church? How do we debate together well and kindly? How do we welcome others as God has welcomed them? Can we ask for the grace to see with God's eyes those who believe differently from us? Can we leave judgement to God?

Jonathan Lawson

Hymn suggestions

Let us build a house; Seek ye first; There's a wideness in God's mercy; I'm black, I'm white, I'm short, I'm tall.

Seventh Sunday after Trinity (Proper 10)   14 July
Principal Service   **The Beheading of John the Baptist**
(*Continuous*): 2 Sam. 6.1–5, 12b–19; Ps. 24; *or* (*Related*):
Amos 7.7–15; Ps. 85.8–end; Eph. 1.3–14; **Mark 6.14–29**

Speaking truth to power

John the Baptist's role is vital. In his own words he 'prepares the way' for Jesus, 'decreasing' that Jesus may 'increase'. His ministry is prophetic and sits within the prophetic tradition of the Hebrew Scriptures.

A prophet's task is to tell it as it is, warts and all; knowing that what is said will be hard to hear. One of the most difficult – but important – prophetic roles is speaking truth to power; it was this that brought about John's demise. John was not known for mincing his words. When he begins to baptize in the Jordan, he declares the Pharisees and Sadducees a 'brood of vipers' (Matt. 3.7). He remained forthright and fearless; in today's Gospel we hear his criticism that Herod's moral standards fell short of what God required.

As with many of the prophets before him, John cared deeply about those in authority, longing to change them and their situation for the better. He was motivated not by a desire to consign sinners to outer darkness but that they 'might turn from their wickedness and live' and so further God's work on earth. This motivation came from God's Spirit within him: John was a holy man.

Herod and John

Herod Antipas (a tetrarch, ruling over Roman-occupied land) had entered a relationship with his brother's wife, Herodias. This was contrary to Jewish law, and John regarded it as his God-given duty to tell Herod. Events conspired against John when, at a birthday banquet, Herodias' daughter danced before the assembled company (an action many would have seen as morally dubious) and Herod made a rash promise to grant her a wish. After consulting with her mother, she requests John's head on a platter, and John is duly beheaded.

It's not quite as simple as that, though. Mark tells us more about the relationship between Herod and John. We learn that Herod respected John: he recognized him as a holy man and liked to listen to him, but he was afraid of him. John probably had about him something of the mystery that both fascinated and terrified his hearers. A charismatic figure with an engaging message, he had a phenomenal track record in drawing crowds. His message, though, was uncompromising: the unvarnished, and unpalatable, truth. This must have been unsettling, and when delivered by a man of wild appearance must have made his hearers quake in their boots.

Herod had responded to John's challenge by keeping him under lock and key. John was arrested and put in prison, but the Greek word used here means less that he was kept in custody than he was kept 'safe' or 'under protection'. Herod was almost hedging his bets, keeping John close at hand.

Herod is a contradiction. He recognizes goodness, holiness and truth in John, and likes to hear him speak. Yet he continues to live immorally. He might be an extreme exemplar of this contradiction, but the fundamental issue is no different for anyone: a prophet's call to holiness and right living hits us hard and makes us squirm.

Mark paints a vivid picture of Herod as conflicted. Like his ancestors, he suffered from serious paranoia. Politically, he skated on thin ice – Rome could have him removed in an instant – and he couldn't afford to be seen to be weak. He had made a promise to his wife's daughter, and to renege on that promise in front of the great and the good would have made him a laughing stock. And so he gave in – and had John beheaded.

John and Jesus

This is the only section of Mark's Gospel which does not feature Jesus. Given Mark's liking for conciseness, why such detail about John? John is Jesus' forerunner, preparing his way. In this passage, he becomes Jesus' forerunner in death as well as in life. Both John and Jesus are executed for political reasons. John proclaims God's truth and points to Jesus who *is* God's truth. John is executed and points to Jesus who will himself be executed. John is buried by his disciples, as Jesus will be too. This account is as much about Jesus as John. And it's because of *this*, and because we follow not John but Jesus, that it speaks powerfully to us.

Our duty

Our allegiance to Jesus carries that same God-given duty to speak truth, and maybe sometimes truth to power. This takes courage. Any of us who has ever made a stand against illegal, bullying or abusive behaviour will know how costly this can be. We might not face death but we might very easily become the victim of a hate campaign. The beheading of John, like the persecution of the prophets before him, reminds us of the cost of discipleship.

It's often easier to go with the flow, even if we know the direction of travel to be wrong – easier to stay silent or walk away from trouble than to speak up. So do we opt for a quiet life, or are we prepared to count the cost of faithfulness?

Peter Moger

Hymn suggestions

Who would true valour see; The kingdom of God is justice and joy; O God of earth and altar; How shall we sing salvation's song.

Seventh Sunday after Trinity (Proper 10)   14 July
Second Service   **A Path to Joy**
Ps. 66 [*or* 66.1–8]; Job 4.1; 5.6–end, *or* **Ecclus. 4.11–end**;
Rom. 15.14–29; *Gospel at Holy Communion*: Luke 10.25–37

For many years, in the town where I grew up, the daily newspaper included an advice column from an 'agony aunt', Abigail Van Buren. People wrote to 'Dear Abbey', seeking advice on issues ranging from conflict with family or friends to problems with work or just disappointment with life. Anyone reading the column might have been left with the impression that people are, as the book of Job puts it, 'born to trouble just as sparks fly upward'. While we may not want to think of facing problem after problem, most of us have experienced the ups and downs of life and perhaps have searched for advice, too.

Seeking guidance from a friend

The book of Ecclesiasticus – written by a scribe around 200 BC – is an early book of wisdom offering guidance on living well. In short proverbial verses, the scribe – speaking as Wisdom – addresses topics such as proper speech, friendship, riches and poverty, honesty, diligence and retribution. The voice of Wisdom in ancient literature was perceived as the voice of God. Hence, read in one way, the proverbs might seem to be 'rules' to follow which are given by God depicted as a 'rule-giver' or judge. Yet, the voice of Wisdom offers us a different perspective: God, speaking as Wisdom, draws near to us as a thoughtful, caring friend. Wisdom speaks to us as one who knows us and reaches out to try to encourage us to discover the way of joy. With this in mind, I invite you to draw near and overhear Wisdom's warm counsel.

An appeal

Wisdom begins by assuring us that we are deeply loved. As a parent loves a child, she offers to give 'help to those who seek her'. Her speech is direct, but Wisdom's care is evident friendship and we may relax in her presence. How good it is to be with Wisdom as a trusted friend who knows all of our faults and failings but does not condemn us.

Quietly, Wisdom says that it is possible 'from early morning' to be 'filled with joy'. This is startling, though I have sometimes reflected on the words of the Psalmist: 'You show me the path of life. In your presence, there is fullness of joy' (Ps. 16.11). It seems that joy isn't mere happiness or a feeling of contentment or satisfaction with life, but true joy is discovered in the presence of God. That means that joy may be present when we least expect it – even at a funeral. We can know joy in other experiences, too, though admittedly at times it seems elusive.

Wisdom counsels that the path to joy can be 'torturous'. Fortitude and determination are needed to stand for truth. More surprisingly, the path to joy cannot be discovered by merely following religious rules. Rather, it requires openness to relationship with God, with others and with the world around us. Yet, Wisdom warns that such openness to relationship requires great sensitivity: we cannot be 'reckless' in our speech or 'sluggish and remiss' in our deeds.

As the time of reflection with Wisdom concludes, it is evident that approaching God and others with open hands and hearts is always costly. Yet, this is the path to joy.

Pondering Wisdom's advice and the path to joy

I am reminded of a drawing of a house made by Grace Sisson, aged 5, and sent by her father in 1962 to his friend, the Trappist monk Thomas Merton. Merton was so moved by the drawing that he wrote a poem noting everything that appeared in it, including a dog and a person peeping out of a window. However, he ended the poem by saying, 'Alas, there is no road to Grace's house.'[27] Five years later, young Grace – then aged 10 – sent Merton another drawing of the house, which this time included a road that she called 'The Road to Joy'.

Picture Grace's drawings. One without a path, seemingly closed to the world. Another with a clear way – we might say open to God and to others. When he received the second drawing, Merton wrote a letter to Grace saying that he hoped that they would both continue to travel their own 'road to joy', which, he claimed, 'is mysteriously revealed to us without our exactly realizing'.[28] So may it be for us all. Amen.

Karen E. Smith

Hymn suggestions

Fill your hearts with joy and gladness; Be thou my vision; Lord of all hopefulness; Forth in your name, O Lord, I go.

Eighth Sunday after Trinity (Proper 11)   21 July
Principal Service   **Restored by Love**
(*Continuous*): 2 Sam. 7.1–14a; Ps. 89.20–37; *or* (*Related*):
Jer. 23.1–6; Ps. 23; Eph. 2.11–end; **Mark 6.30–34, 53–end**

Two weeks ago we heard how Jesus sent the disciples out in pairs to spread the good news of the kingdom of God. In today's Gospel, we find that they've been very successful. They come back excited and full of stories about what's happened. Jesus takes them across the lake to a deserted place to rest because they've been so busy; they haven't even had time to eat. Jesus is looking out for his disciples so that they don't burn out. They've got a long way to go yet, and playing the long game requires rest, resilience and self-care. You can't do everything at once, however exciting and fulfilling it is.

However, Jesus is becoming something of a celebrity and as they sail across the lake the people rush around on foot and get there before them so that as Jesus and the disciples land, they find that the place isn't deserted at all – a great crowd has gathered.

Compassionate love

Jesus turns his attention to the crowd. The Gospel says he has compassion on them – and that word means he's deeply moved, right in his guts, in solidarity with the people who are harassed and helpless. They are like sheep without a shepherd and so Jesus takes on that role and begins to teach them. Later he will feed them miraculously – that's next week's Gospel.

Jesus is stepping into our Old Testament lesson from Jeremiah. He is being raised up. He is fulfilling that role of executing justice and righteousness that the kings of Israel had failed to do. The current leader – Herod – also failed. Remember, Herod has just murdered John the Baptist. Herod has destroyed and scattered the flock. Jesus gathers, feeds, heals and blesses them. Jesus is bringing about the restoration of Israel that Jeremiah foretold. He is also embodying the shepherd of Psalm 23.

Jesus can do this even though he is tired, even though he is grieving for his cousin John, even though he's been rejected in his home town of Nazareth. At this very low ebb, God is at work in Jesus and is about to perform a great miracle – the feeding of the 5,000. Jesus sees a mass of people and knows that God loves them without beginning or end. The people see Jesus and sense that even touching the fringe of his cloak will bring healing, wholeness and a fresh start. They only have to reach out to be restored by love.

Sacrificial love

Jesus will go on to die for these and all people (us too). He will suffer with and for them (and he suffers with us too). And his sacrifice on the cross will enable restoration, peace and reconciliation. As St Paul writes to the Ephesians, there will be no dividing wall, no longer hostility between races, genders, those who are far off and those who are near. All are equal in God's sight. One new humanity. And it is this ability to see people as all equally loved and precious that helps the early church to grow the holy temple in the Lord and become the body of Christ, filled with the Holy Spirit. Jesus Christ is the cornerstone and we build on his care, compassion, love and sacrifice, so that justice and righteousness may flourish

Enfolding love

But it's very much a work in progress, isn't it? And sometimes we're really not very good at it. We know that the most vulnerable in our communities are not always met with care and compassion. We are not good at sharing the world's resources equitably or caring for our beautiful planet and all its inhabitants. When we are tired or frightened, hurting or anxious it's hard to remember that everyone is a precious child of God, that everything is part of God's creation – utterly loved.

So let's look to Jesus – who listens to our stories of success and failure, who sees how hard life can be for us and calls us to rest. Let's look to Jesus who has deep compassion on us when we are frightened and anxious – when we don't know what's coming next, we aren't sure how to stay safe, or we just wish life would go back to operating on an even keel, a level path.

Jesus reminds us to eat – to feed on him – in the Scriptures and in the Eucharist. As you meet with Jesus here today, imagine yourself reaching out to touch the fringe of his cloak, the hem of his garment. Feel his love enfolding you, as his power and goodness flow through you bringing life and light. Know yourself precious and utterly loved by God – who in Jesus sees all you are carrying, has compassion on you, wraps his cloak of love around you and restores you with his peace.

Catherine Williams

The king of love, my shepherd is; Broken for me, broken for you; You never let go (Matt Redman); The Lord's my shepherd.

Eighth Sunday after Trinity (Proper 11)   21 July
Second Service   **What Use are We?**
Ps. 73 [*or* 73.21–end]; Job 13.13—14.6, *or* Ecclus. 18.1–14;
Heb. 2.5–end; *Gospel at Holy Communion*: Luke 10.38–end

Being useless

Our readings don't seem to be chosen to boost anyone's self-esteem, do they? We have certainly been put in our place. From Ecclesiasticus we have, 'What are human beings, and of what use are they?', which is echoed by Hebrews where we have, 'someone has testified somewhere, "What are human beings that you are mindful of them, or mortals, that you care for them?"' And the fact that the writer of Hebrews can't even remember where in the Scriptures the quote is from just proves the point about how useless we are! It's enough to make anyone's ego feel a little bruised.

What is it about us that is so pitiful? We can't adequately proclaim the works of God or witness all God's mighty deeds. We can't measure God's power or recount God's mercies.

'When human beings have finished, they are just beginning, and when they stop, they are still perplexed' (Ecclus. 18.7). We only live a few meagre decades and then we die, with a miserable end. And we're not as good as angels. Well, that's us told, isn't it? It would be easy to feel as if we are rather insignificant and pointless.

Bridging the gap

But just look at who we are being compared to. The one who 'created the whole universe, who lives for ever'. The one who has compassion for every living thing – and it really means every. The one who is patient, who pours out mercy, who grants forgiveness. We can never compare with God. Not in power, might, forgiveness or mercy, compassion or patience. What these passages highlight is the incomprehensible difference between us and God. Compared to God we really are utterly insignificant, impotent, pathetic.

But we don't need to go home feeling like worthless wretches. There's enough in the world to undermine our self-esteem without letting the Bible join in too. Because what these passages point to is the lengths God goes to in order to bridge that gap, to cover that distance. In fact, the distance is so great that the only way to bridge it was for God to become human. We hear in Hebrews that Jesus, despite being fully God, 'had to become like his brothers and sisters in every respect'. That means human, like us, with all our human frailties and weakness.

Sharing our flesh and blood

The great scandal is that God – almighty, powerful, eternal God – becomes one of us: weak, vulnerable, mortal. What this shows us is that God is fully united with creation. Again, from Hebrews, 'Since, therefore, the children share flesh and blood, he himself likewise shared the same things.' God becomes the same as us. And the reason? To share in our life and share in our death, so that death will have no power over us any more, and we can be free from the fear of death.

God loves us so much that God even submits to death, the immortal one submitting to mortality, to show us that God's love reaches even into the depths of death. And once we know that, that even in death we are not alone, even in death God's love can reach us, we can be free to live in a different way.

Free to live without fear

Because Jesus has known human suffering, he can help us in our suffering. Because he knew death, we know that death has no power over us. This means we can live in a way that risks suffering, risks death, without fear. We can love without fear. Because what's the worst that can happen? Nothing can happen to us that Jesus hasn't borne. And everything that Jesus has borne he has also sanctified.

God became like us so that we can become like God. If we know we are loved *by* God, it sets us free to try and love *like* God. To love like we have nothing to be afraid of. That's not easy and it doesn't come naturally – remember that we humans were so dim that God had to become human and show us how to do it. But God did it – God did it for love of you and for love of me. So please don't go out feeling, 'What are human beings that you are mindful of them, or mortals, that you care for them?' Because the answer to that question is, you are loved so much by God that God became like you. You are crowned with glory and honour. You can live without fear.

Kat Campion-Spall

Hymn suggestions

And can it be; Christ triumphant, ever reigning; Meekness and majesty; O Lord my God, when I in awesome wonder.

Ninth Sunday after Trinity (Proper 12)   28 July
Principal Service   **Where are We to Buy Bread?**
(*Continuous*): 2 Sam. 11.1–15; Ps. 14; *or* (*Related*):
2 Kings 4.42–end; Ps. 145.10–19; Eph. 3.14–end; **John 6.1–21**

The UK underwent a series of bread strikes in the 1960s. It was then that I realized that there is much in life we take for granted, only to be discovered when there is a shortage of it. I can remember queuing with my mother outside the local bakers hoping to get one of the last remaining loaves. It was serious business making sure we didn't lose our place and actively discouraging pushers-in.

Hallowing everyday things

As a Palestinian Jew, Jesus was brought up in a religion that hallowed everyday things, such as bread and wine, because they were appreciated as gifts from God. Food was a holy thing, and the Torah required people to say a prayer of thanks every time they had eaten. The rabbis taught that a meal without a prayer was a meal that was accursed. When was the last time you said grace at a meal? Perhaps it is something we need to rediscover.

Bread was the essential, basic food. 'To eat bread' in Hebrew meant 'to have a meal'. The poor ate barley bread; the rich ate the bread of wheat. Whether barley or wheat, bread was to be treated with respect: if crumbs were 'as large as an olive', it was forbidden to throw them away.

A poor boy's lunch fit for a king

A large crowd, impressed by the wonders of Jesus' healing, has followed him into the hills on the far side of the lake. Jesus turns to Philip, who is from the locality, to ask where food can be bought. Philip does some quick arithmetic and calculates that six months' wages wouldn't even make a dent in the food bill. Andrew has spotted a small boy who has five barley loaves and two fish, but this 'poor' lunch doesn't appear to the disciple to be much of a resource. What the disciples have to learn is that Jesus is not only resourceful, he himself is the resource.

There is a lesson for all of us in this young boy offering freely his tiny gift. We all have gifts we can give to the Lord and no talent or moment of time is too insignificant to be placed in his hands. Whatever we give out of our meagre resources will be accepted and multiplied beyond our greatest expectations. Like the young boy's lunch, which seemed so trivial, God uses our tiniest efforts to perform his greatest wonders. If that is true of time and talent then it is also true of our treasure, our money. Like all our gifts, money is just that, a gift from God, and we are asked to give it back in God's service and the service of God's church. The stewardship of our money shouldn't just be seen as a means to balance our books, important as that is. The giving of our time, our talent and our treasure is a spiritual discipline; just as important as reading the Bible, saying our prayers, attending church and receiving the bread of life.

With Jesus as the resource, the bread of the poor is seen to be enough to satisfy the hunger of so many people. In the hands of Jesus, shortage becomes abundance, deficiency becomes plenty, and nothing is lost of what has been given to him.

Saying 'no' to the crowd

After the crowd take the food, they want to take Jesus by force and make him king. But Jesus is not going to be tempted to exercise that kind of power and fragile authority. In the Gospels of Luke and Matthew, Jesus fights this temptation in the wilderness. Here, in John's Gospel, the temptations come not from the devil but from the crowd, his own people.

Jesus is happy to satisfy the hunger of the crowd by offering them the bread of the poor; he is not, however, happy to satisfy their hunger for power. There are some hungers Jesus refuses to satisfy:

the hunger for domination is one of them. Jesus rejects the lord-ship of domination, the destructive power which he sees all around him. Perhaps Jesus believes that the power which lords it over other people is the very thing that keeps bread from the hungry, a power that steals the community's resources to secure its own superiority.

Giving rather than grabbing

In saying 'no' to the crowd who would make him king, Jesus gives us a new model of leadership – one that must always resist the lure of secular power, because it must always be free to give rather than grab. That is Jesus' challenge: only when we share the little we appear to have will we discover how much we have left over. And with all challenges that Jesus places before us, the truth will only be discovered in the doing of it!

Paul Williams

Hymn suggestions

Bread of heaven, on thee we feed; Let us break bread together on our knees; Dear Lord and Father of mankind; Lead us, heavenly Father, lead us.

Ninth Sunday after Trinity (Proper 12)   28 July
Second Service   **Written in Stone**
Ps. 74 [*or* 74.11–16]; **Job 19.1–27a**, *or* Ecclus. 38.24–end; Heb. 8; *Gospel at Holy Communion*: Luke 11.1–13

What would your epitaph be?

'I told you I was ill.' Some of you may recognize the famous epitaph of Spike Milligan, which was voted the nation's favourite epitaph, closely followed by Oscar Wilde – 'Either those curtains go or I do'; Frank Sinatra – 'The best is yet to come'; and Mel Blanc, who voiced most of the Loony Toons characters – 'That's all, folks!'

What would your epitaph be? What would you want the words on your gravestone to say? It's one of those questions designed to get to the heart of who a person is, what's important in their life, and what they want to be remembered for. A permanent record, engraved in stone.

Memorial stones in many churches might testify to relationships – these people were beloved parents, spouses or children. Some have a verse of Scripture, reminding us of the faith in which these people died. Many are simply a name and dates, a record of a life lived, which speaks for itself.

Engraved on a rock for ever!

In our reading, Job makes a heartfelt request for his words to be written on stone. He describes at length how he feels God has turned against him: 'God has put me in the wrong, and closed his net around me ... there is no justice.' Job's troubles, his desperate circumstances, he believes, are seen by God, and are inflicted by God's hand, by God simply refusing to act to save him. And yet Job is faithful and believes in God's faithfulness. While everyone around him is abandoning and accusing him, while his friends believe he must have committed some offence against God to be suffering in the way that he does, Job wants his innocence to be recorded in stone for ever: 'O that my words were written down! ... O that with an iron pen and with lead they were engraved on a rock for ever!' he cries. It may look like God has turned against him, but Job wants the world to know that he has never turned against God.

And what is more, he proclaims confidently, in the words incorporated so beautifully into Handel's Messiah,

I know that my Redeemer lives
    and that at the last he will stand upon the earth ...
    then in my flesh, I shall see God,
whom I shall see on my side.

Faithfulness is Job's epitaph – faithfulness to God and God's laws during his life, and faithfulness that at the end he will see God at his side. Faithfulness, written in stone.

Written on our hearts

Our reading from Hebrews goes beyond what is written in stone to what is written on our hearts. It draws a comparison between the old covenant, written on tablets of stone and given to Moses, representing mutual faithfulness between God and the people, and the new covenant, brought by Jesus, which is not written on stone but is written in our hearts. Not laws, but a living relationship.

189

What is written on your heart? Because the question – what would your epitaph be? – is not quite the same. It's easy to focus on achievements, the things we have said and done, what we hope other people will remember us for. But if all that is stripped away, what is left? Job lost all that he had – everyone turned away from him. He searched deep and found faithfulness, written deep on his heart. What is written on your heart, if you search deep?

White stone names

There is a tradition that God has a secret name for each of us, known only to God and sometimes revealed to us. We find this idea in the book of Revelation, that God will give a white stone to those who have conquered, with a new name written on it. This idea of a name known to God can be a wonderful one to pray with. You may like to take some time in prayer to search your heart to find what God has written on it. Your name may be a particular gift that God has given you – 'delighting in God's creation' or 'singing God's praise'. Your name may be a quality you have – faithfulness, like Job, or joy, or nurture, or peace. Your name may be a task God has given you – teacher, comforter, truth-speaker, fighter for justice.

Whatever it is, it will be rooted in the laws of God that are written in all our hearts, and the new covenant of love that Jesus brings. But what is written deep in every heart, however our personal gifts and callings may manifest themselves, however many layers of guilt or shame, complexity or self-deception obscure it, written deep in every heart of every person, created in the image of God, is *beloved*.

Kat Campion-Spall

Hymn suggestions

All my hope on God is founded; Be thou my vision; O thou who camest from above; Take, O take me as I am.

Tenth Sunday after Trinity (Proper 13) 4 August
Principal Service **From Disparate Crowd to Diverse Community**
(*Continuous*): 2 Sam. 11.26—12.13a; Ps. 51.1–13; *or* (*Related*):
Ex. 16.2–4, 9–15; Ps. 78.23–29; Eph. 4.1–16; **John 6.24–35**

Of crowds

I live in the shadow of two large sports stadiums: Tynecastle, the home of Hearts football club, and Murrayfield, the home of Scottish rugby. I'm used to organizing my rather boring domestic life around the sudden appearance of large crowds outside my flat, the traffic congestion, the atmosphere in the air and the noise that they bring. It makes me wonder what it was like to experience the crowds that followed Jesus around. If you are schooled in the stories of the New Testament, you know that these crowds are often portrayed as a single entity, a bit like a school of fish, who tend to act as one and be astonishingly good at misunderstanding Jesus. But what about the stragglers, and the singing? What about the hassle and the harm they cause to the environment they descend upon? What about the infrastructure: the crowd control, the clean-up and the commerce?

The story in John's Gospel today is the story of a crowd with a bit of a morning-after vibe going on. They had spent the day before listening to Jesus and being looked after by him and the disciples who had fed them fish and bread. They had camped out overnight, possibly expecting more of the same the next day, only to wake up and find that Jesus and the disciples had left overnight. So they move on, and this is the story of the conversation they have with Jesus when they find him again. It's an odd conversation. Possibly one of those where really you had to be there, and, if you had just joined the crowd and not been there the day before, pretty obtuse.

The preferential option for the poor and vulnerable

Crowds of people who attend sports games or concerts all have at least two things in common: they admire and support at least one of the groups of people they are going to see, and they can afford the costs of attending the event. This crowd is different. The day before, Jesus had provided food for them all regardless of whether they could afford to pay for it or not. But this was a mixed crowd economically. Drawn together by a fascination with what Jesus was saying and doing, there were some in the crowd who were wealthy and some who were well and some in the crowd who were poor and some who were ill. On this morning after, some of the crowd would have found the camping overnight and morning journey easy, some who had found food and water along the way, and some who had found it all very hard. There would be some, no doubt, for whom the meal of fish and bread seemed a long time ago and their next meal an anxiety-inducing long way off.

I find it impossible to believe that Jesus ignored the people in this crowd that morning who were poor and ill and had no sustainable way of meeting their basic daily needs for food, water and shelter. His way is quite the opposite. And yet we far too readily fall into the trap of thinking this conversation is all about Jesus telling people not to focus on material things like a good meal, but to focus on spiritual things – 'the food that endures for eternal life'. We perhaps picture Jesus as some sort of TED talks presenter, ready to pull out a diagram of Maslow's hierarchy of needs and assume that the audience is full of people whose basic needs are consistently met. And so this is a good time to move up the scale and find ways to meet their need for personal growth and peak experiences, the things of modern-day spirituality.

The work of God

I think Jesus looked at that crowd, the rich, the poor, those who knew they were going home to full cupboards and those who knew they were going to have to beg for that next bit of bread, and longed for them all to focus on 'the work of God', or, as we would put it today, the building of the kin-dom.[29] The work of ending hunger, poverty and destitution per se. The work of ending inequality and injustice. The work of treating every single individual with dignity and love and joy because they, as they are in the moment you encounter them, are made in the image of God. The courageous work for each of us in putting ourselves out there in telling others about what we need and what we have to give. The work of turning a disparate crowd divided by access to resources and power into a diverse community united by respect and appreciation for each other. The work of giving life to the world. That was his way.

Esther Elliott

Hymn suggestions

Inspired by love and anger; For the fruits of all creation; Heaven shall not wait; Thy kingdom come, on bended knee.

Tenth Sunday after Trinity (Proper 13)   4 August
Second Service   **Crying Out to God**
Ps. 88 [*or* 88.1–10]; Job 28, *or* Ecclus. 42.15–end;
Heb. 11.17–31; *Gospel at Holy Communion*: Luke 12.13–21

The need for lament

The young woman seemed to have all of life in front of her. Having gone through treatment for cancer she was given the 'all clear'. Now, a few years on, all was well and the future looked bright. Then, suddenly, things changed. Hospital tests confirmed that the disease had returned and the prognosis was poor. A person of faith, she cried out to God, but there seemed to be no response and when she went to worship with others there seemed to be no place for her lament.

Throughout life, there are moments for tears. Sometimes they come in joy or surprise, but there are also moments of anger, deep anguish, regret or remorse. Yet, at times, we avoid any expression of lament in public worship. To bewail one's troubles to God is often considered a sign of a lack of faith and an affront to a good and loving God. Yet, there are times when the only honest prayer we can offer to God is a cry of lament.

Speaking directly to God

While there are many songs of lament within the Old Testament, the starkness of the language in Psalm 88 is troubling. Walter Brueggemann has called it a psalm of 'disorientation', which, unlike many of the other psalms, never moves positively towards a 'new orientation'.[30] The Psalmist seems to have lost all hope and accusingly addresses God in phrases that seem to cascade upon one another in despair: 'You have put me in the depths of the Pit, in the regions of the dark and deep'; 'my soul is full of troubles'; 'I am like those who have no help'; and 'like those forsaken among the dead'. There is no confession of faith or affirmation of trust, and there are no words of praise. Instead, just one petition is made – 'Let my prayer come before you; incline your ear to my cry.'

Many years ago, I went to a prayer group in a local church which was also attended by Harry, a middle-aged man 'of no fixed abode'. Evidently, he had been taught to address God in the language of 'thee' and 'thou', but beneath all the formal speech his prayers were always a very long and loud cry to God for help. At some point, in the midst of praying, he would pause and say to the gathered group, 'Sorry to be praying for myself so much, but I need it.'

While his troubles were far deeper than practical issues, and as a group we could not solve those problems, it seemed that, like the Psalmist, Harry knew that he could speak directly to God in lament. The experience was also a reminder to me that, while we must be ready to help others, there are problems that we can't 'fix' ourselves. In fact, there are times when all we can do is wait and lament with them.

Waiting with God

Twentieth-century Christian writer Henri Nouwen said that a friend wrote to him on one occasion saying, 'Learning to weep, learning to keep vigil, learning to wait for the dawn. Perhaps this is what it means to be human.'[31] Crucially, it is also at the heart of what it means to be a faithful follower of Jesus Christ. For even as we lament the problems which we, or others, may face we remember that Jesus himself knew tears of sorrow and loss. Abandoned by friends and seemingly by God, he experienced the pain and forsakenness of the cross, even as in love he waited for the world he came to save.

It is right to offer our joyous praise and thanksgiving to God in worship. However, we also bring our prayers of lament – not just for ourselves but for a world in disarray. And as we wait and lament – for and with others – we know that God is waiting with us, too. So we need not worry about offending God with our direct pleas. Rather, with the Psalmist we may say, 'Incline your ear to my cry'!

Karen E. Smith

Hymn suggestions

O Lord, hear my prayer (Taizé); Father, hear the prayer we offer; By gracious powers, so wonderfully sheltered; The king of love my shepherd is.

Eleventh Sunday after Trinity (Proper 14)

11 August

Principal Service   **On Not Being Mr Spock**

(*Continuous*): 2 Sam. 18.5–9, 15, 31–33; Ps. 130; *or* (*Related*):
1 Kings 19.4–8; Ps. 34.1–8; **Eph. 4.25—5.2**; John 6.35, 41–51

Uneven Gospels

Mark's Gospel is too short. This, at least, is the assessment of the Church of England's liturgical commission. Mark's Gospel is much more like a short story than a novel, isn't it? It goes at breakneck speed – the word 'immediately' appears 42 times – and compared to the other three Gospels it is very short. So you will notice that we have stopped reading St Mark and over about five weeks in the summer we get a repeated presentation of what is known as the 'bread of life' discourse from St John's Gospel. It started last week and it goes on until nearly the end of August. For a month or so we reflect on what it might mean if Jesus is 'the bread of life'.

We might notice some of the words in the Epistle today as well because they help us to make the connections. The first couple of verses of the reading from the Letter to the Ephesians: 'let all of us speak the truth to our neighbours, for we are members of one another. Be angry but do not sin; do not let the sun go down on your anger, and do not make room for the devil.'

In these few verses we get St Paul at his most practical. Paul is often really difficult, esoteric, complicated and densely theological. Not here. 'Be angry but do not sin; do not let the sun go down on your anger, and do not make room for the devil.' And why? 'For we are members one of another.'

Making relationships work

This passage is often used in marriage preparation, or indeed in helping people in any relationship to make their friendship work: 'do not let the sun go down on your anger.'

How do we live in fellowship together? How does any friendship work? Whether that is between individuals, the way in which a parish lives, or the way in which different parts of the church exist together. Well, we recognize that the way we behave matters. Be angry but do not sin, says St Paul. OK, yes a few verses later he also asks us to try to put away anger, but here he recognizes that relationship is difficult.

We are not Mr Spock

Any relationship is difficult. But there is a difference between anger and sin. Notice that. Lots of the great spiritual teachers of the tradition remind us that it is not our emotions that are the problem. We are not machines or Vulcans (if you enjoy your *Star Trek*). The object is not to try to suppress our emotions. But it is how we direct them that is the mark of our family living. So when I am angry with a friend or family member, or the church, what do I do with that? What do you do with it?

St Augustine says that we always have a choice. We can turn in on ourselves, we can let things eat away at us, we can obsess and stew. Or we can turn outwards, we can let the light into the parts of our lives that are festering. We can orient our frustration, our anger, and turn it into prayer.

Provisions for the journey

Jesus said to his disciples, 'I am the bread of life. Whoever comes to me will never be hungry, and whoever believes in me will never be thirsty' (John 6.35). God's provision is not contingent on our capacity. Indeed, it is the other way round. We manage because we are fed by our Father. We must come, again and again, to God's table. Because he is the bread of life. And as we gather around the communion table, week by week, season by season, we are fed. Those who have the privilege of ministering to the dying will know that one of the last things we do if we can is give a dying person communion. And when we do that at the very end of life it is called *viaticum*, which literally translates as 'provisions for the journey'.

Whenever any of us receive communion it is always 'provisions for the journey'. The journey towards the kingdom. Never confuse the Church of England, or any institutional church, with the kingdom of God. We live towards the future. And all of our relationships now are imperfect because they are shadows, sketches, of the great relationship which the kingdom will be. But, nonetheless, we live towards that ambition. So when we are angry we try not to sin. We try to open ourselves up to the light rather than closing ourselves in and starting to rot. Let the fresh air in. Let the sunlight in. We thank God, at every Eucharist, for the provisions for our journey. And we receive the bread of life, the bread of heaven, each time as if it was the last time, and we set off again, looking outwards, living kindly, trying to put our anger away before bed. Forward into the future. Eyes fixed on the kingdom.

Tom Clammer

Hymn suggestions

Will you come and follow me?; The kingdom of God is justice and joy; Bread of heaven, on thee we feed; Guide me, O thou great Redeemer/Jehovah.

Eleventh Sunday after Trinity (Proper 14)
11 August
Second Service **The Race that is Set Before Us**
Ps. 91 [*or* 91.1–12]; Job 39.1—40.4, *or* Ecclus. 43.13–end;
Heb. 12.1–17; *Gospel at Holy Communion*: Luke 12.32–40

A winning mindset

What lengths will athletes go to in order to win a race? World-class athletes are subject to gruelling training programmes, restrictive diets, a huge amount of psychological and physical preparation and exertion, pushing themselves through pain and exhaustion to keep going.

It's a pretty unforgiving process too, with mantras such as 'there's no such thing as second place, only first loser'. And for some, the need to win overrides other values like honesty and integrity – stories of doping among elite athletes are not uncommon. Competition can be very ugly.

So it can seem quite strange when we hear our faith referred to in the Scriptures as a race. A journey, yes – many people find that a helpful way of describing their spiritual life. But a race? That implies competitiveness, winners and losers. Can this be what the writer of Hebrews means?

A different kind of race

Well, it looks like this is a very different kind of race. For a start, there is already a winner, who has received the victor's crown, long before most people even started the race – 'Jesus the pioneer and perfecter of our faith'. And there are a whole host of other people who have already finished the race – that 'great cloud of witnesses' we are told surround us. And what are we to pursue in this race? 'Pursue peace,' we hear. This is already starting to look more like a primary school sports day than an Olympic sprint – the kind of race where everyone who takes part gets a medal and no one really notices who is first, second or third.

But it's also clear that the race the writer describes is gruelling. The writer describes the things that Jesus, the pioneer on this course, endured – hostility and ultimately murder. Those participating have to 'endure trials'. The runners are exhausted: 'lift your drooping hands and strengthen your weak knees', they are told.

God is described as a kind of coach, putting us through endurance tests to develop our discipline, the kind of discipline that every athlete must be all too familiar with. But this is not in order to make us faster or more formidable competitors: 'discipline always seems painful rather than pleasant at the time, but later it yields the peaceful fruit of righteousness to those who have been trained by it.'

So we have a race where everyone who participates is directing themselves towards a common goal, but one in which we already know who has won, and the aim is simply to finish. We have a race for which the participants are trained and disciplined, but to achieve righteousness, peace, holiness and grace, not a medal. Those who are exhausted are urged to keep going, not for success but for healing: 'lift your drooping hands and strengthen your weak knees, and make straight paths for your feet, so that what is lame may not be put out of joint, but rather be healed.'

It's the taking part that matters

We come back to that primary school sports day – it's not the winning that matters, it's the taking part. That kind of attitude won't win you an Olympic medal. That concept is not in the psychology of any elite athlete. But as is abundantly clear from the life of Jesus, winning isn't the point. He is the ultimate loser.

When you think of all the things God incarnate could have achieved, being executed probably wouldn't be top of anyone's list.

But God has taken part in human life. That's what matters – it's not the winning but the taking part. He has shown us how to run the race. Competitive sport of course has its place. But as a metaphor for life, Jesus shows us that it has its limitations.

Going for bronze

We can live life doing all we can to win. That might mean exploiting the weaknesses of others, doing what we can to hold others back, grabbing what we can and not caring who gets trampled down along the way. It might even mean cheating and lying our way to the front. We've probably all come across successful people like that.

Or we can look to Jesus, 'the pioneer and perfecter of our faith', and see how he ran the race. We cannot care about being seen to lose, help others who are weaker and slower, without worrying that we ourselves are falling behind. Our goal is not a podium or a medal, but righteousness, healing, peace and holiness.

At sports day, a 12-year-old girl won silver for long jump. Then came the 200 metres and she saw she was in second place. So, she slowed down to let her friend overtake and win the silver medal because she already had one. Many people, seeing they were in second place, would give it everything and go for gold. This girl went for bronze. That's the kind of race Jesus shows us how to run.

Kat Campion-Spall

Hymn suggestions

Awake, our souls, away our fears; Father, hear the prayer we offer; Fight the good fight; My hope is built on nothing less.

Twelfth Sunday after Trinity (Proper 15)
18 August
Principal Service   **Living Bread for the World**
(*Continuous*): 1 Kings 2.10–12; 3.3–14; Ps. 111; *or* (*Related*): Prov. 9.1–6; Ps. 34.9–14; Eph. 5.15–20; **John 6.51–58**

Jesus' words come from St John's story of the feeding of the crowd with the five barley loaves and two fish from a young boy's basket: 'When the people saw the sign that he had done, they began to say,

"This is indeed the prophet who is to come into the world"' (John 6.14).

In the teaching that follows the feeding of the 5,000, Jesus explains how those material loaves that satisfied the people's hunger represent 'the bread of God which comes down from heaven and gives light to the world'. He tells them not to become enslaved to the sign itself, but to focus on what it points to: 'Do not work for the food that perishes, but for the food that endures for eternal life which the Son of Man will give you' (John 6.27). 'Those who eat my flesh and drink my blood have eternal life ... for my flesh is true food and my blood is true drink. Those who eat my flesh and drink my blood abide in me, and I in them.'

This can all seem a bit rarefied until we fold into it the episode in the Hebrew Bible that Jesus is re-enacting. It goes back to when the Hebrews wandered in the desert for those years between leaving Egypt and entering Canaan. The crowd themselves remind him of it. 'Our ancestors ate the manna in the wilderness; as it is written, "He gave them bread from heaven to eat"' (John 6.31). It was a time of disaffection and trouble. So, in St John, we must imagine Jesus as a new Moses responding to the people's need and giving them the food they craved. 'I am the bread of life' – I am to you what YHWH was to your ancestors in the desert. I give you what you ask for, even if you don't know what to do with the truths that come with this gift, for you have not yet learned how to recognize the Giver.

St John tells us that the feeding of the crowd took place near Passover time. The blessing and breaking of bread was itself a central action of the Passover meal. So when Jesus feeds the 5,000, he is symbolically reaching back to that ancient story of deliverance and redemption. This is why he speaks repeatedly about God raising the dead and giving them eternal life, no longer coming under judgement but passing 'from death to life'. The movement from death to resurrection lies at the heart of that great story of how an oppressed, enslaved people were given back their lives again, were redeemed and brought out into freedom as new possibilities opened up before them.

All these layers of story and association are embedded in those simple words, 'I am the living bread.' To eat of that bread is to be taken directly to Golgotha where Jesus' body is broken on the cross, his life laid down for his friends, for all humanity. But that is only our way into what this saying means, what the Eucharist means. For throughout the story, resurrection is always in view.

'Those who eat my flesh and drink my blood have eternal life, and I will raise them up on the last day.' Even though the Lord's Supper points us to the cross, it also looks forward to the banquet of God's kingdom when the whole creation, liberated from bondage and pain, feasts before God in glad celebration.

We have the symbol, but not yet the full reality. For now, in a thousand different places of famine or warfare, the hungry still cry out as the Israelites once did. Will God, can God, spread a table in this wilderness?

The answer the Eucharist offers is yes, he can, of course he can! But it is we human beings who must be the agents of his kindness and mercy. 'Give us this bread always!' is the plea of all who are in need from that day to this – which means the vast majority of the human race. Our Eucharists only have integrity if they take account of the political and social realities of our time. We must celebrate the Eucharist: it is the Lord's command. But we can never do this in holy huddles insulated from the realities of life.

For all of life is represented in the bread that is set on the altar before God and offered for the Spirit's transformation. 'The question of bread for myself is a material question,' said Nikolai Berdyaev; 'but the question of bread for my neighbours, for everybody, is a spiritual and religious question.'[32] In the Eucharist, Jesus is among us as one who serves. He gives himself to us as the living bread. But not without asking searching questions about what it must mean for us in turn to be those who serve everyone who still cries out, 'Give us this day our daily bread.'

Michael Sadgrove

Hymn suggestions

Now my tongue, the mystery telling; Break thou the bread of life; Alleluia, sing to Jesus; When I needed a neighbour.

Twelfth Sunday after Trinity (Proper 15) 18 August
Second Service **Curiosity Leads to Encounter**
Ps. [92] 100; **Ex. 2.23—3.10**; Heb. 13.1–15;
Gospel at Holy Communion: Luke 12.49–56

Curiosity saves

Several years ago, on a beautiful sunny day, we went to the beach. Our son went off into the sea for a swim. We reminded him, 'Look where you are, so you can get back.' Time passed. More time passed. The friends we were with began mentioning coastguards and helicopters. But before they did anything drastic, our son appeared.

He had done as he was told and looked where he was. We were near a red parasol. What he hadn't anticipated was that the owners of the parasol would move. He had looked, but hadn't been curious enough. He hadn't wondered what else was around, or whether the parasol owners might leave.

Curiosity leads to encounter

Moses is preoccupied. He is on the run. He's killed a slave master in Egypt and escaped, but he must look over his shoulder carefully whenever a stranger approaches. He's constantly looking where he is! He's busy too, looking after his father-in-law's flock. Despite his preoccupations, Moses notices a burning bush. It's not an uncommon phenomenon,[33] but Moses' curiosity is aroused for some reason. He stops what he is doing and focuses on the bush, a 'great sight', we are told, which is perhaps why he notices it. Moses is curious enough to approach the bush and discover what's happening. Then notice this: 'When the LORD saw that he had turned aside to see, God called to him.' When Moses turns aside, when he is interested enough to want to see, God responds to him. I wonder whether there is something in this story that speaks to how we share our faith. I hope I'm not the only one who finds it awkward to introduce Jesus into a lighthearted conversation in the local coffee shop. It doesn't feel natural, somehow. But suppose God can speak for Godself, as in this instance. Suppose our job isn't to tell people everything we believe, but to provoke their curiosity about God. As Moses' curiosity prompts him to go to the bush, God responds. Curiosity leads to encounter. I wonder whether curiosity might be central to our following Jesus and to our relationships with others.

When Moses approaches the bush, God identifies Godself: 'I am the God of your father, the God of Abraham, the God of Isaac, and the God of Jacob.' This isn't God ticking off followers, it's God reminding Moses of what he already knows – 'I'm the one you learnt about growing up – time to learn some more.' God might have said also, 'I'm the God of your mother who hid you, and your sister who saved you', but to the male writers of the Bible that wouldn't seem important.

If we are to understand more of God, I believe curiosity is important.

Curiosity leads to communion

'Take your shoes off, you're on holy ground,' God tells Moses. Taking off his shoes, Moses came into direct contact with the earth, the holy earth. It seems to me that the further our society moves away from appreciating the holiness of the earth, the more damage we inflict on it. I wonder whether our present, and pressing, climate crisis was engendered because human curiosity was focused entirely on what human beings can achieve, instead of on God and how God sees our world, and on the earth, and what we might be doing to it. What I am commending to you is a discipleship of curiosity. Curiosity can be a character trait, but it is also a discipline. It makes us want to know more; it prompts in us the desire to investigate, as Moses did. Doesn't Jesus commend something like discipleship that asks questions, wonders how things might be, that tries to read the signs of the times in our Gospel reading?

Curiosity allows scales to fall from our eyes as we learn to appreciate those around us, our world and our God. None of us was born with a particular religious or world view. We acquire them, as Moses did from his forefathers. What we do not read in the passage is the role of his mother and sister, who saved his life, and the reason is the writers were not curious about them. They didn't count for anything.

So I pray that we might develop a discipleship of curiosity that leads us to notice and draw near to our God, our world and our neighbour.

Liz Shercliff

Hymn suggestions

And can it be that I should gain; In the wilderness for God; Take, O take me as I am; All the room was hushed and stilled (Love Each Other).

Thirteenth Sunday after Trinity (Proper 16)
25 August
Principal Service   **The 'More' of God**
(*Continuous*): 1 Kings 8.[1, 6, 10–11] 22–30, 41–43; Ps. 84;
or (*Related*): Josh. 24.1–2a, 14–18; Ps. 34.15–end; Eph. 6.10–20;
John 6.56–69

I love the U2 song, 'I still haven't found what I'm looking for'. I mentioned to a relative that I'd like this played at my funeral, and they commented that given I'm a priest people might expect a song about having found what I'm seeking. I disagree. Easy pat religious statements of the 'I've found Jesus' variety seem too flat, too complete, too finished. Jesus comes down to earth not so we can grasp him and fix him here, like a religious talisman to whip out in a tight spot, but to draw us into God, beyond ourselves.

Medicine against the mindless mundane

We are invited 'farther up and farther in', as C. S. Lewis put it.[34] So it is entirely faithful to say, 'I still haven't found what I am looking for', because there is always more of God to be found. Such a statement is one of faith, of openness to the wild more of God, which is much, much greater than my tiny mind can comprehend. There is something expansive and exciting about this idea. Medicine against the mindless mundane.

The tension between the mundane and the more of God is clear in the Gospel reading. The worldly, fixed, finite perspective is contrasted with the spiritual invitation into the adventure of eternity which begins here in the dust of the day, extending beyond the horizons of our current perspectives. It's a matter of two types of bread.

Two types of bread

Compare the reaction of some of those whom Jesus fed earlier in John 6. In the miracle of the feeding of the 5,000, they receive the sustenance of actual physical bread, so some think 'this is what we are looking for' and they come seeking Jesus for a free lunch. Their perspective is fixed on the here and now; they chase the mundane instead of seeing in the gift of that perishable bread a sign pointing to something much, much more. Jesus offers them a different kind of bread, a bread that sustains beyond the physical and into the marvellous more of God. This bread is Jesus himself, the one who said, 'I am the bread of life' (John 6.48).

Why does this matter?

Left to our own devices we easily lose that sense of the more of God, of the God who extends beyond the limitations of the now. When we lose that focus we can become weary and cynical, easily cast down. Our imaginations atrophy. We stop dreaming dreams. With a shrug of indifference, we settle for 'how it is'. Failure becomes the end, rather than a doorway to new possibilities. If the best bread we can hope for is the kind that goes mouldy, then it's all futile and death is the final full stop.

But ...

But Jesus invites us beyond ordinary bread that sustains us for the day and then passes through us. He offers a different bread, which he calls 'true bread'. He is this bread. He offers his own flesh, his very being. Eating his flesh is not some weird cannibalistic ritual. It is about partaking in his nature. When we extend our hands to receive bread at communion, we are saying 'Yes, we need you. We need more than the everyday, more than our limited and limiting worldly perspectives. We need the more of God. Jesus, you are that more.'

The Holy One of God

Simon Peter understood this. When other disciples were leaving Jesus, finding his teaching too difficult, Jesus asked him, 'Do you also wish to go away?' Peter answered 'Lord, to whom can we go? You have the words of eternal life. We have come to believe and know that you are the Holy One of God.' In other words, 'You are the one who leads us deeper into God, deeper into all that we have yet to find and long to know. There is no one else who can take us on this journey. Only you.'

More than the humdrum round

Is that all too vague, all too esoteric, all too spiritual to be much earthly use? I don't think so. I don't want a life that is only the humdrum round. I don't despise the day-to-day – but surely there is more? I want to be captivated by the more of God which runs through the ordinary and opens our eyes to the extraordinary. The more of God that sparks us to imagine new vistas of possibility:

- helps us put flesh on those dreams;
- lifts us up after falling down;
- knows our frailty and failure and loves us still;
- enables us, to quote William Blake,

> To see a World in a Grain of Sand.
> and a Heaven in a Wild flower.[35]

The more of God that sees a doorway where others see only a grave.
    We need Jesus – the more of God.

Kate Bruce

Hymn suggestions

Let all mortal flesh keep silence; Alleluia, sing to Jesus; There's a wideness in God's mercy; Guide me, O thou great Jehovah.

Thirteenth Sunday after Trinity (Proper 16)
25 August
Second Service   **Tips for Leaders**
Ps. 116 [*or* 116.10–end]; Ex. 4.27—5.1; **Heb. 13.16–21**;
Gospel at Holy Communion: Luke 13.10–17

Practical pointers

Whether you call yourself a leader or whether you think of yourself as a follower, these verses from Hebrews are almost guaranteed to provoke a reaction. The idea of obeying leaders and submitting to them, taken without any reference to the rest of the letter, has led to terrible actions throughout the church and the world. But if we want to take our church community seriously, and learn to work together, supporting one another and flourishing with joy, then there are a few tips here in this letter.

In this chapter of Hebrews, the writer has been pulling together a lot of practical thoughts, encouraging those listening to think about all sorts of topics relevant to an emerging Christian community. He has talked about prison visiting, marriage, money, contentment, leadership, and more. In verse 7 there are some words which I have always found alarming. The writer encourages the community to remember their leaders as those who spoke the word of life to them, and then advises reflecting on their way of life and imitating them. That's the alarming bit. As someone with leadership responsibility – whether a leader of a home group or as a treasurer or the worship leader – the idea that others might reflect on the way I live and then copy it is a huge challenge. It means that the way I live as a leader needs to be open and accountable. In these verses the writer returns to the theme, reminding leaders that their job is to watch over souls, souls for which they will have to give account. Accountability is not just about being accountable to others, but about being accountable for others, and for how our actions impact them.

Influential role models

In our contemporary world, leadership is often about role models or examples. Almost every day there are stories about those whom we hold up as having values or taking actions that could be emulated. Sometimes they are in the world of celebrity or sport. Recently I heard an interview with the musician Julian Lennon and was amazed to learn about his deep commitment to philanthropy through his White Feather foundation. I found myself thinking about him as a leader in the field of music, quietly influencing others. You may know someone like that in your sphere, or you may be able to think of someone who has been a role model for you in your Christian journey. For Christian leaders it is more than just being an influence – there is that two-way accountability, the time when we will have to explain the impact we had on others. No wonder that our first thought for our leaders should be to pray for them.

The prayer for leaders is a prayer for integrity – that quality which means that there is a wholeness between the words that we say, the things we believe and the actions we take. When I was a child, there was a really annoying phrase that grown-ups sometimes used, usually when something I wanted to do was being questioned. Someone would run out of arguments and say, 'Do as I say, not as I do.' It made me cross. Even then I sensed that real integrity requires that what we do and say are held together.

The purposes of God

For the writer to Hebrews that holding together comes in the person of Jesus Christ, who, although cursed, wounded and defeated, is our high priest, interceding for us at the right hand of God: the one who is damaged has the highest place, and draws with him all others who have been damaged, broken and rejected. The letter ends with a confident assertion that God will complete all that he has started, reminding all of us that whether we lead or whether we follow, it is not our own purposes that are being worked out but the great purposes of God. There is a famous prayer from Sir Francis Drake, himself known as a great leader, who asks that whenever we set out on something we might know that is in continuing to the end that true glory is given to Christ. Tips for churches – whether we lead or follow – draw us back to our first calling as disciples, who pray and trust, knowing that the glory belongs to Jesus Christ.

Sandra Millar

Hymn suggestions

All my hope on God is founded; My Jesus, my Saviour; Take my life and let it be; When we walk with the Lord (Trust and Obey).

Fourteenth Sunday after Trinity (Proper 17)
1 September
Principal Service   **Adventures with Jesus**
(*Continuous*): **S. of Sol. 2.8–13**; Ps. 45.1–2, 6–9 [*or* 45.1–7];
or (*Related*): Deut. 4.1–2, 6–9; Ps. 15; **James 1.17–end**;
Mark 7.1–8, 14–15, 21–23

When did you last have an adventure? When did you do something new or risky or scary? Something that made your heart beat fast and your adrenalin rush, that challenged your ideas and took you way beyond your comfort zone into a new place.

Many young people are really good at having adventures – off on gap years, travelling the world, working for charities, backpacking, leaving home and learning new things regularly. Many of them relish the thrill and the challenge of adventure. If only more of them could have such opportunities.

The Christian faith is an adventure – a challenge, a thrill, a quest. A journey on which new things are learnt, new places discovered. I wonder how many people who are not Christians would look at us and see the excitement, commitment and passion that adventure demands. Is that what others see in us? I wonder.

Adventurous encounters

In Mark's Gospel – just before the passage set for today – Jesus has been travelling in the area of Gennesaret and wherever he goes ordinary people rush to him, reach for him. Just by touching the fringe of his cloak, Mark tells us, they were healed. What adventures! Life-changing moments for ordinary people, not educated in the ways of the Torah, many not welcome in the Temple, many deemed unclean.

Compare this with the Pharisees and scribes in our passage: the religious leaders of the day, the educated keepers of tradition; knowing the Scriptures by heart, faithful at worship and prayer. Do they reach out to touch Jesus' cloak? No, they don't. Do they seem eager for an adventure with this man of God? It seems not. But they have noticed that the disciples don't wash their hands before eating, and they are here to challenge Jesus on the matter. Adventures with God have got lost in the pots, pans and bronze kettles of tradition.

Jesus is exasperated with them – it's not what goes into a person that makes them unclean and out of favour with God, but what comes out. Evil intentions come from the human heart and are displayed to the world in unworthy deeds. Jesus lists them: theft, murder, sexual immorality, pride, slander, foolishness. These are the things that make people unclean: unrighteous in the sight of God.

Adventurous actions

James, in his letter to the 12 tribes in the Dispersion, builds on this. It's not enough to hear the word of God, Christians must be doers of the word of God. It's no good hearing the call of Jesus, listening week in and week out to the Scriptures if it makes no difference to the way we live moment by moment. You can't call yourself a Christian, says James, and then let your tongue betray you every time you open your mouth. How often do we speak words that exclude, judge, tear down and destroy others? If we do, then our faith is worthless, says James. Acts of charity are what's needed. Acts that mirror the generous giving of God to us in his Son Jesus Christ. So we should give ourselves in service to the most vulnerable, 'widows and orphans' for James. Who are the most vulnerable in our community? Asylum seekers, refugees, the homeless, those with various addictions, those whom society has turned against. It's quite a long way from those pots and pans of tradition, isn't it? It's a challenge, an adventure with God yet to be entered into for many churchgoers.

Adventurous living

The reading from Song of Songs is filled with challenge and adventure too. There are various ways of approaching this great love poem. Some see it as a poetic celebration of love, passion and human sexuality. Others an allegory of the divine love for God's chosen people. For Christians, it can be seen both as the marriage between Christ the bridegroom and his bride the church, and a reflection of the relationship between the individual soul and God. All approaches have value.

In this passage, the lover calls his beloved to arise and come away with him. Away from the walls, and windows. Away from the lattice of humdrum life into a new and fertile place. It's a call into liberation – into adventure. It's a call out of winter, out of rain, into spring, where there are flowers and birds, blossoms and fruit – new life: the season of singing has come. The call is filled with joy and delight for lover and beloved – that adrenalin rush I mentioned at the beginning.

This is what the Christian faith should be like for us. Jesus loves us passionately and he calls us to rise and come to him, into a new place, into a fresh beginning – breaking out of our old life, those pots and pans and bronze kettles into a new way of thinking and being and doing which is Christ-shaped, fashioned by the word of God. And that often means taking risks, being flexible, being curious; willing to move deeper in and further on. Faith is a journey, a pilgrimage, a quest.

Listen to God, hear the call of Jesus, respond to the nudges of the Holy Spirit seeking you in love for a new adventure. Be brave, be courageous, take risks, try new things, think before you speak. Rise up, come away with God on a new quest and be amazed and delighted by the treasures that await.

Catherine Williams

Hymn suggestions

There's a wideness in God's mercy; Servants of the great adventure; When I needed a neighbour; Song of Solomon (Martin Smith).

Fourteenth Sunday after Trinity (Proper 17)
1 September
Second Service **Pie or Steak?**
Ps. 119.1–16 [*or* 119.9–16]; Ex. 12.21–27; **Matt. 4.23—5.20**

Pie in the sky when you die?

One of the typical and familiar critiques of Christianity is that it is 'pie in the sky when you die', as the phrase puts it. The argument is made that for a lot of people Christianity is basically an insurance policy against the misery of this life and that what it does is help you to ignore the misery of the world, in the hope of a halo, a set of wings and a comfortable four-wheel-drive cloud when you get to heaven. Christianity, goes the argument, gives Christian people the excuse of not really engaging in the reality of the world around them, because they are holding on, with gritted teeth, for the time when everything will be better when they get to heaven. The sort of person who puts forward this quite familiar argument will say that they are really not interested in 'pie in the sky when they die'. They want 'steak on the plate while they wait'. Something *real*, that helps them to engage with where they are now, that transforms the experience of the world for them and those around them. Christians have their fingers in their ears and are just holding out for the rapture.

Is there a steak option?

Is Christianity a clever way of dodging the reality of the world by holding in front of gullible people the promise of a better life in heaven?

Well, today's Gospel reading is a useful antidote to that kind of thinking. This section of the Sermon on the Mount begins with one of the most famous passages from the New Testament: the Beatitudes. As we read this familiar text, there is certainly an element here by which Jesus does seem to be saying, yes, if you're having a lousy time now don't worry, because there's good stuff coming in the future: 'Blessed are those who mourn, for they will be comforted ... Blessed are those who are persecuted for righteousness' sake, for theirs is the kingdom of heaven.'

But then he goes right on to say a lot about how that doesn't mean we just have to endure our present circumstances. Or that we should be disconnected from them. This is absolutely not 'pie in the sky' teaching being proclaimed to those gathered on the mountainside of Galilee. This is a robust connection of what we believe comes next, with where we are now. 'You are the salt of the earth ... You are the light of the world.' Keep the commandments and teach them. This is a vital part of the Scripture because it evacuates that familiar argument against Christianity of its power. It is quite clear that Christianity, that Christ, has something to say about what comes *next*, but also a lot to say about what is *now*.

Being a recognizable presence

Being the salt of the earth is about being that recognizable presence, that factor in our environment – home, school, work or wherever else – which is distinctive, is identifiable as different and drawing out the flavour. Being the light of the world is about being visible. It is not about cowering under the basket, it is about being present, confident in having something to say about he who gives the salt its taste, he whose light we carry.

What is our character?

I think it is quite helpful to read this passage in reverse: the section on salt and light first and then the Beatitudes, because then we have presented to us some truths about the deep character of the people who are called to be salt and light in the world. Lest we be tempted to arrogance or smugness or judgementalism: true saltiness, true light is meek, merciful and pure in heart.

What a tremendous calling, what a privilege, what a challenge to be called to be salt and light in the world, wherever that might be for each of us. To be distinctive, recognizable, visible, but always to be meek, merciful, pure in heart. Because of course the distinctive, visible, recognizable person to whom we point is the Servant King; our saltiness, our light, is an indicator of, and always at the service of, our humble Messiah. What a great vocation. And it's far better than even the finest steak while we wait.

Tom Clammer

Hymn suggestions

As the deer pants for the water; Make me a channel of your peace; Longing for light, we wait in darkness; Thou, whose almighty word.

Fifteenth Sunday after Trinity (Proper 18)
8 September
Principal Service   **Who Sits Where?**
(*Continuous*): Prov. 22.1–2, 8–9, 22–23; Ps. 125; *or* (*Related*): Isa. 35.4–7a; Ps. 146; **James 2.1–10** [11–13] 14–17; Mark 7.24–end

Table of grace

Do we have favourites? Is James telling us off? Possibly. But we need to know what's bothering him to be sure. He appears to be addressing a few things: first, the poor are being overlooked during table fellowship; second, the wealthy, influential and privileged are being prioritized. Into that situation, James says, 'Don't have favourites', least of all those who will give you something back.

James also seems to be bothered about people picking and choosing which bits of the law they follow. His readers are following certain rules, but appear to be missing the big stuff. It doesn't come much bigger than the commandment, 'Love your neighbour as yourself.' James knows that this gets to the heart of Jesus' vision for what should take place on the face of the earth.

The kind of community that God would have us be is one that

doesn't favour one *kind* of person over another, less still say that some *deserve* favour more than others. Many people understand the importance of not discriminating, but we still seem to be a society that rewards those who make the biggest and best contribution. That, of course, contradicts grace. James is not always known for his teaching on grace; however, it is on display here. God's favour does not rest on those who measure up to the most acceptable standard. Instead, God's favour predates any action that we might perform, any thought that we might have, any status we might achieve. God's favour towards human beings is one born out of eternity. And God's favour finds expression in Jesus of Nazareth, the one who represents *all* humanity. This same favour is offered to all as they are invited to share bread and wine at the table.

None of this means that everyone is equally easy to spend time with. James is not promising that we will find all those we meet equally life-giving and affirming. Indeed, we might have very good reasons to give some people a wide berth, not least if being with them puts us at risk of serious harm. But if we act in a way that prioritizes one group over another, we have lost contact with the gospel of grace.

It's OK to spend time with those that affirm us and help us relax. But prioritizing people for the sake of elevation and prestige can be ruled out. Social capital might be something that leads to success in life, but it is not the calling of the Christian. It nearly always counts against those born outside of privilege.

What would it take for us to become a community where the privileged are not prioritized? What would it take to address cultural favouritism? Well, we might want to remind ourselves of how grace addresses us. Are we where we are in Christ because we deserve it? Whether we find ourselves in a position of entitlement or suffering, we equally require the grace of God. If we find ourselves in a position where we get to choose who should sit where at the table – who should be prioritized – we are probably already in a place of privilege. If that's us, we might need extra grace to spot it. At the very least, we should remember the grace we have already received in Christ.

Table neighbours

Additionally, we might want to take heed of James' reminder of Jesus' command: 'Love your neighbour.' It's the simplest commandment really, but it's the most difficult to live out. Wherever we sit at the table, loving others is a difficult thing to do. We might have to make room for those who can give us no advantage, or for people who are plain disagreeable. That's what love does. We might even need to move tables and seek those we don't 'naturally' tend towards. This is a challenging step. But sometimes when we move tables, we receive life. Life comes when we get together with people from different places, races and spaces; with different economic statuses, faces and graces. We learn what it is to be one new humanity in Christ.

So, is James telling us off? Yes, and no. It's OK to share time with those who bring us life, vitality and friendship. But if we judge in advance that there are types of people who won't be able to give us that life, vitality and friendship, then we've missed grace. We've missed 'Love your neighbour'. We've missed the fact that we are called to budge up and make room for all at the table.

Mark Amos

Hymn suggestions

When I needed a neighbour; Love divine, all loves excelling; Behold the Lamb; Amazing grace.

Fifteenth Sunday after Trinity (Proper 18)
8 September
Second Service   **On the Other Side of the Sea**
Ps. 119.41–56 [*or* 119.49–56]; **Ex. 14.5–end**; Matt. 6.1–18

The parting of the Red Sea has got to be one of the greatest stories in the Bible. It has inspired movies for decades, from Charlton Heston in *The Ten Commandments* to the wonderful animation *Prince of Egypt*. The people flee from slavery, Moses prays and God parts the sea. We read the story and the parting of the Sea is what sticks in our minds because it is big, awesome, incredible. And it is.

Between a rock and a hard place

But, in some ways, the parting of the sea isn't really the most important part of the story. It is simply a gateway from one part to the next. The people had been enslaved, oppressed for many years, and cried out in despair. God heard – and responded, and brought them out of Egypt. Now they're a little band of ragtag refugees with little to their name and even less hope to go around. Moses, their leader, had seen God, but they hadn't. Moses had seen the action with Pharaoh, but they hadn't.

God had done scary things, and now they were stuck with the sea in front and the armies of a mad ruler behind. So they were scared and cried out to Moses. They expected to die and just wanted to go back where it was safe. They weren't sure this strange God could do anything for them.

Free bodies, captive minds

Their minds were captive still. Captive to Egypt and its gods and its way of seeing the world. They simply couldn't imagine something better or bigger than what was on offer in Egypt. What it meant to be safe was controlled by what 'safe' meant in Egypt, a land of poverty and scarcity. The land was owned by the Pharaoh and a small elite, while most others slaved on land that wasn't theirs. Slavery had come about in a time of famine when there wasn't enough to go around and people sold their land and bodies in exchange for grain. Now beyond famine, the country was still governed by the idea that there wasn't enough for everyone. That the earth and its produce weren't enough and so you had to grab what you could and hoard it to be safe.

The story of Exodus changes that. The story of Exodus is all about God showing that he is the master of the land, of the people, of all the forces of nature. First, with the plagues that disrupt Egypt's land. But Egyptians and Israelites alike are slow learners. The Egyptians still think they can take back control and pursue the slaves. The Israelites still don't believe that God is bigger than Pharaoh.

So it comes to crunch point – and God displays his awesome power. God protects the people from the armies with a pillar of cloud and parts the sea before them. God is master of the universe. God owns the land, not Pharaoh.

An invitation to new life

The people crossed the sea towards a new future. But that was just the beginning: they would have to learn to live with what they had learnt. They would have to unlearn the ways of Egypt and learn the ways of God.

Human beings are part of a bigger world, and God cares about the whole of that world. God had summoned the whole forces of nature to lead the slaves into freedom; now they have to learn to live in ways that care for the whole of creation and one another. The sea parts the way and invites them to a new way of life.

One of the most common sentences given to the people with new laws is, 'Remember that you once were slaves, therefore ...' Therefore, care for the most vulnerable, the orphan, the widow, the poor, the stranger; remember that you once were slaves, therefore treat aliens well; remember, therefore keep the Sabbath and give rest to people, animals and land. Do not run your community to pursue endless productivity and profit, and do not hoard land and resources. The people are invited to respond to God's liberation by letting their imagination of the common good, of life in community, be transformed.

The people are invited to step out of an imagination controlled by fear and scarcity, and towards seeing the world through the eyes of the God who has freed them. On the doorstep of freedom, the people will have to make a choice about whose ways they will follow: their own thinking and reasoning, which led them to want to go back, or this awesome and fearsome God. The choice is between Pharaoh behind and the world they know, or God ahead and a world of the unknown.

The parting of the sea is an arresting moment because it encapsulates the choices of the life of faith. Whom do we choose to follow? How do we understand our place in the natural world? How do we, individually or collectively, respond to the call to care for the vulnerable and live with generosity and compassion? Do we dare let our faith transform our imagination of the world and how to live in it?

Isabelle Hamley

Hymn suggestions

Longing for light, we wait in darkness; A new commandment; For the healing of the nations; Lord, for the years.

Sixteenth Sunday after Trinity (Proper 19)

15 September

Principal Service   **Jesus' Question**

(*Continuous*): Prov. 1.20–33; Ps. 19 [*or* 19.1–6], *or Canticle*: Wisd. 7.26—8.1; *or* (*Related*): Isa. 50.4–9a; Ps. 116.1–8; James 3.1–12; **Mark 8.27–end**

In our journey through the Gospel of Mark this year we've reached a pivotal moment – the middle of the Gospel – chapter 8 in a book of 16 chapters. At this midpoint, Mark has the disciple Peter come to the realization of who Jesus really is. Peter reveals it to the rest of us.

Journeying with Jesus

Jesus and the disciples are on the road, journeying through the villages of Caesarea Philippi. Many exciting and surprising things have happened. Thousands have been fed. The sick have been healed. Jesus has walked on the water. In this episode, Jesus asks his disciples what people are saying about him: 'Who do people say that I am?'

The disciples answer that some say he's Elijah or one of the prophets – a great holy leader from of old. Others say that he is John the Baptist, returned from the dead, a ghost perhaps. Herod had John beheaded back in chapter 6. Jesus challenges his disciples: 'But who do you say that I am?' Peter leaps in impetuously with a spectacular answer: 'You are the Messiah.'

Spectacularly right

Here in the very centre of the Gospel is the truth. The great secret is revealed. Jesus is the Messiah – the chosen one of God – spoken of down the centuries. Jesus is the one who will restore all things and bring about God's future. Peter opens his mouth and gets it spectacularly right.

Jesus goes on to explain to the disciples what all this means. He must undergo great suffering, be rejected by the religious leaders, be killed and then after three days rise again. Jesus is drawing on the prophetic tradition from Isaiah and others writing during the exile.

I gave my back to those who struck me,
    and my cheeks to those who pulled out the beard;
I did not hide my face
    from insult and spitting. (Isa. 50.6)

And a little later:

I know that I shall not be put to shame;
he who vindicates me is near. (Isa. 50.7b)

Horribly wrong

Peter, however, has taken his picture of the Messiah from other portions of Scripture. He is drawing perhaps on the apocalyptic literature of Daniel and the Maccabees, who envisaged the Messiah as a great triumphant leader who would overthrow the Romans and restore Israel to her former glory. Peter challenges Jesus. Peter opens his mouth again and this time gets it horribly wrong! Jesus reprimands him in the strongest terms: 'Get behind me, Satan!' Peter is thinking in human terms not God's terms and such thinking needs nipping in the bud. From the same mouth – Peter's – comes truth and falsehood, blessing and cursing.

James writes about this in his letter. The tongue, though a tiny part of the body, is very powerful. We use it to bless and curse. We worship God but we also run down those who are made in God's image. The tongue can be like a spark that sets a whole forest ablaze, or the rudder of a ship that though tiny and unseen directs the whole vessel, setting it on the right course.

Peter shows how easy it is to say both the right thing and the wrong thing in the space of a few minutes. We declare Jesus as Lord and then side with evil.

Jesus' question

Jesus' question is for all his followers: 'But who do you say that I am?' Who do you say Jesus is? Week by week in our liturgy we say who we believe Jesus is. We say he is Son of God, God of God, Light of Light, Lamb of God, Living Word, and so on. These are words we use in our worship.

What do we say when we are away from church? Do the people around us know that Jesus is Lord for us – in the things we do, the decisions we make, the words we speak?

Jesus told his disciples that if they wanted to follow him they needed to deny themselves and take up their cross. That means putting Christ first in all things. Not thinking about what we want but what God wants for us and for our community. It may mean travelling a bumpy road, filled with sacrifice, not quite sure what the future holds, not always being in control of things – but trusting always that God can and will bring good out of the most difficult circumstances. Jesus knew that he was destined to die at the hands of the authorities but he had hope that God's way would bring glory and victory – which it did – through the resurrection.

This week let's think and pray about the words we say in church and the words and actions we perform day by day as we live our lives. Does it all hang together? Are we people of integrity?

We all make mistakes, says James – Peter is a really good example of that. But Jesus challenged Peter and reminded him to do the work of God, not Satan: truth not deception.

Check your words, check your actions, think before you speak and hear Jesus whisper in your ear, 'But who do you say that I am?'

Catherine Williams

Hymn suggestions

Led like a lamb to the slaughter; Take up thy cross; O Jesus, I have promised; Jesus, you have called us (I Will Follow).

Sixteenth Sunday after Trinity (Proper 19)
15 September
Second Service   **You'll Wear Yourself Out!**
Ps. 119.73–88 [*or* 119.73–80]; **Ex. 18.13–26**; Matt. 7.1–14

Moses the indispensable

Moses, the leader. Moses, the man who brought his people out of slavery to freedom. Moses, the one who had access to the thoughts of God and explained them to the people. Moses, the person who might know the answer to every question, the one to get in touch with whenever there was a problem. Moses the *indispensable*. Does any of this sound familiar?

It's great when a leader leads well and people follow. And often those who follow are more than happy to leave everything to that one person – the one who is clearly doing such a good job! And sometimes the leader enjoys being the one with power, the one on whom everybody else depends. Indispensable.

But there is a cost. We try to live out our calling, to be as good as we can be in our role – in the church or outside the church – but sometimes it all gets too much. If we are successful, we will be expected to be more successful. If we give our time, people will demand more time. It's easy for our life to become a battleground of competing good things until at last we begin to burn out.

This was happening to Moses. Moses' father-in-law could see this happening. It's often the case that somebody who sees you at home, rather than in public, might have a much better view of what is really going on. They might be placed to be more honest. Do you have people whom you trust, to whom you listen, who can tell you the truth? People who can ask you the hard questions? Any kind of leadership, whether in a small group situation or something much bigger, needs people like this.

Delegate

Moses' father-in-law suggests a bit of delegation. Incidentally, he manages to set up an enduring legal system of judges in Israel. Moses changes his role – he moves from sole arbitrator to a kind of supreme judge. Now he takes on the hard cases. The discernment is outsourced. He appoints a much wider leadership of 'able men'. And each of these exercise the skill to decide if a case is *minor* or *hard*. They have to develop an 'inner Moses'. They have to find wisdom and discernment for themselves. A good idea.

So Moses turns out to be a listening leader, a delegating leader, and a leader with an awareness of self-care. I think it's fascinating that Moses, the law-giver – whose books, the Torah, give guidance and commandments for every aspect of people's lives – takes some good advice. He takes something – that he hadn't even thought of – from his father-in-law!

This says some good things about the character of Moses, who is described as *meek*. He's too busy thinking about others and their needs to be fully aware of his own problem. Maybe we all need to open our lives, to tell our story, to somebody who is outside our immediate circle. A listener, a spiritual director or companion, somebody who can hear the situation in a way that we can't. That way we can begin to discern and understand more deeply.

Do not judge

How does all this sit with the Gospel reading today, in which Jesus says *do not judge*? This deeper understanding has to exist underneath all the systems of justice and discernment. Jesus pulls out the deeper level of these transactions.

We watched Moses as he found some new self-knowledge, as he began to see clearly. And now Jesus takes the issue further. Jesus points the way to a deeper seeing, which questions all our judgement. All human judgement is provisional, partial, and has to acknowledge God's understanding – a bedrock of truth, compassion and love.

So human beings, Moses and his judges, even we ourselves – frail and flawed in our view of reality – seek to judge issues and make right decisions. But we can only do this in the safety of healthy self-doubt, in the safety of trusting God. In the end, all our judgements are provisional. We do not judge but depend on the one whose judgments are unsearchable.

Andrew Rudd

Hymn suggestions

Inspired by love and anger; Forth in thy name, O Lord, I go; I heard the voice of Jesus say; Make me a channel of your peace.

Seventeenth Sunday after Trinity (Proper 20)
22 September
Principal Service   **Wisdom and Understanding**
(*Continuous*): Prov. 31.10–end; Ps. 1; *or* (*Related*):
Wisd. 1.16—2.1, 12–22, *or* Jer. 11.18–20; Ps. 54;
James 3.13—4.3, 7–8a; Mark 9.30–37

'Who is wise and understanding among you?' asks James in the passage today from his letter. If we were trying to identify those with wisdom and understanding among us here today, who would we go for? What factors would colour our decisions? Would we look for age, learning and intelligence? Would we look for authority, leadership, qualifications, experience, length of time as a Christian, or grey hair? Whom would we consider wise?

Godly wisdom

James tells us some of the characteristics of the wisdom that comes from God – it is pure, peace-loving, gentle, flexible, full of mercy, good things come from it, it doesn't take sides, and it hangs together: it has integrity. This is the level of wisdom that God's people are to exercise in the church, with one another and most importantly in the world. But James is a realist and he knows that this is a big ask. So helpfully he points to things that get in the way of wisdom. Where there is envy and selfish ambition, disorder and evil will follow. Conflicts and disputes come from deep longings within us to have things – power, status, wealth, land, possessions. We crave things for ourselves and our families and it puts us in conflict with one another, sometimes very subtly.

Selfish ambition

We see an example of this in today's Gospel. Jesus and his disciples have come down from the mountain after the transfiguration where the glory of God has been revealed in Jesus. As they walk along, Jesus teaches them what it means for him to be the Son of Man, the Messiah. He speaks of betrayal, of being killed and then rising again. The disciples can't grasp this and don't want to ask, so they go off into their own little world with only half the information. The disciples have heard about Jesus being the Son of Man and they've perhaps interpreted this to mean he's going to take power, overthrow the Romans, become king and restore Israel. They argue about their positions in this new kingdom. Who will be chief of staff, who will run the treasury, who will be ambassador – the spokesman for the new king? Who will be the greatest? Conflict, argument and dispute – envy and selfish ambition – cravings at war within the disciples, blocking out the wisdom of Christ.

The kingdom belongs to the least

What does Jesus do? He explains the ways of God's kingdom with a visual aid: a little child. This would have been mind-blowing. In the ancient world, children were of course loved by their parents and celebrated as the closest thing to social security – if you were lucky enough to make it to old age then your children would look after you. But first-century children were very vulnerable: less than half lived to be adults. They were generally the first to fall when disease or famine struck. Socially, children were the lowest and the least; there was no children's charter, they had no rights and they couldn't own anything.

Jesus is saying that God's kingdom belongs to those who are no one and have nothing. Those the world considers the least are the ambassadors of Christ. When we welcome these then we welcome Jesus and, more than that, we welcome God. Status, power, authority, wealth, land, possessions and qualifications will not bring any of us closer to God, nor will they determine whether or not we are wise.

Practical outcomes

So practically we need to think carefully about our inner motivations, to be more aware of our habits of grasping and craving. We do that when we think, 'This is *my* church, and I want it run in the way I like, that meets my needs', rather than recognizing that it's God's church to which God invites everyone and anyone. And everyone means *everyone* – not just those we know and like, not just those with whom we share culture, language, social class or family links.

And it's not just about church life. As Christians filled with the Holy Spirit, this wisdom should naturally colour the whole of our lives. We are to evaluate every system, every power and every choice based on the outcome for the most vulnerable in our communities. That affects our politics, lifestyles, jobs, what we eat, what we wear, how we travel, what we do with our money, whom we mix with, and so on.

It's both challenging and threatening, to ourselves and to our social norms and constructs. Such sacrificial living, such wisdom, cost Jesus his life. Made in God's image and baptized into Christ's body we are called to follow in his steps – to take the teaching of Jesus seriously. These are the secret purposes of God, the wisdom and understanding that God calls forth from us. The least is the greatest in the kingdom of God, the first must be last and servant of all, and from sacrifice and death come new life and resurrection.

Catherine Williams

Hymn suggestions

The church of Christ in every age; Lord of all hopefulness; The perfect wisdom of our God; Let us build a house.

Seventeenth Sunday after Trinity (Proper 20)

22 September
Second Service   **Living on the Edge**
Ps. 119.137–152 [*or* 119.137–144]; Ex. 19.10–end;
Matt. 8.23–end

Today's New Testament lesson speaks about 'the dangerous edge of things', events that take people to the extremes of their experience. It does indeed feel edgy and dangerous. The disciples in their boat on Lake Galilee struggle against the storm. The waves crash over the flimsy craft and it threatens to capsize. Jesus, asleep, is woken by terrified cries of panic: 'Lord, save us! We are perishing!' He rebukes the chaotic wind and waves and there is a dead calm. Safely on dry land, it's the same story in another guise. Jesus takes on the chaos in human life: the Gadarene demoniacs whose lives are possessed, ruled by forces beyond their control. As on the lake, mortals clamour desperately at Jesus, hardly knowing what they shout. And Matthew asks his readers: who is this who commands even wind and water, demons, sickness and death, and they obey him?

In the ancient world, order was hard-won and precarious. There was an ever-present fear that the chaos might return to overwhelm civilization. In the psalms, YHWH is king over cataracts and floods. He has crushed the heads of the monsters of the deep; he silences 'the roaring of the seas, the roaring of their waves, and the tumult of the peoples' (Ps. 65.7). And that madness tells us that the threat is not only natural but human. The assault of the enemy is personified as an overwhelming force which only the mighty power of God can subdue: 'Why do the nations rage so furiously together?' In a bleak vision of Jeremiah, the chaos that God had brought order to in Genesis is back:

> I looked on the earth, and lo, it was waste and void;
>   and to the heavens, and they had no light.
> I looked on the mountains, and lo, they were quaking,
>   and all the hills moved to and fro.
> I looked, and lo, there was no one at all,
>   and all the birds of the air had fled.
> I looked, and lo, the fruitful land was a desert,
>   and its cities had been laid in ruins. (Jer. 4.23–26)

This is creation wound backwards from cosmos to chaos, from light to darkness, its artistry unravelling to a terrible, anarchic collapse.

Once, people thought these primitive fears had been banished by the onward and upward march of progress. But the last century dispelled the fantasy. A hundred years ago, the world sleep-walked into a Great War. After the next world war, the extermination camps revealed the unspeakable horror of what had gone on under the Nazis. A generation brought up during the Cold War learned the language of Mutually Assured Destruction. Wars, terror, disease, the climate emergency, human trafficking and the abuses that drive asylum seekers to our shores – we have learned to be afraid. Chaotic disorder, the collapse of everything we hold dear, is a present reality for us, both as a nameless fear and a felt reality, consequences most of them of what the Prayer Book calls 'the unruly wills and affections of sinful men'.

And yet … we must not be paralysed, either by the storm or by the fear of it. We must not hide in the bowels of our ship in some imagined safety. We must venture on deck to get the measure of these tempests that rage outside and within. At those times when we stand on some dangerous edge of things – in our personal life, in places where threat seems near, in the world crises that fuel our fears – the first thing is to imitate the mariners in *The Tempest* and cry out, 'To prayers, to prayers!' For the vessel we are sailing is so tiny and the sea is so terrifying and big. But as we face our fear, assess the danger, say our prayers and help one another to find strength, what do we find? That Christ was hidden in the darkness all along, and is there beside us, rebuking but also cheering us: 'Where is your faith?' Immanuel, Matthew calls him, God with us.

In our times, we can't help wondering whether our Christianity is being called to some test of resilience and maturity it has never had to undergo before. This is no time for easy religion, play-acting our Christian profession. Our faith needs to go to the heart and change us, help us cling on for dear life sometimes as our world falls apart, never despairing of the mercy of God. This is why, when big storms break against the shores of our complacency, when we are shaken by earthquake, wind and fire, we need to hear the voice that calls out to us, 'Where is your faith?', the still, small voice that gives us the strength not to be afraid. And then, God willing, our spirits are quietened and there is a deep calm once more.

Michael Sadgrove

Hymn suggestions

God moves in a mysterious way; Lord, if faith is disenchanted; As water to the thirsty; O worship the King, all glorious above.

Eighteenth Sunday after Trinity (Proper 21)
29 September
(For Michael and All Angels, see p. 336.)
Principal Service **Prayer and Healing**
(*Continuous*): Esther 7.1–6, 9–10; 9.20–22; Ps. 124; *or* (*Related*): Num. 11.4–6, 10–16, 24–29; Ps. 19.7–end; **James 5.13–end**; Mark 9.38–end

The Letter of James is full of advice on practical Christian living. With a conviction that faith must be matched by action, he writes on the need to honour the poor, care for the needy and curb the tongue. In chapter 5, James reminds us of the importance and the centrality of prayer, especially for those who are ill.

He contends that the prayer 'of the righteous' is effective and cites the example of Elijah praying first for drought and then for rain. Elijah's prayers were granted. But, we say, Elijah *was* one of the righteous, and we're not – at least, not very much of the time!

The working of prayer is one of the great mysteries of faith. Philosophers have long struggled as to whether prayer might change God's mind. More common is the notion that praying changes us as we pray, bringing us more closely in line with God's will, heart and mind. The experience for most of us is that prayer does make a difference, and so we persist in praying for God's world and for the people within it. But how do we pray?

There is a danger that prayer can become abstract: a spiritual activity detached from the physical world we inhabit. In many traditions, prayer has become tied up with words, whether a formal liturgy or extempore intercession. But prayer can never be equated with words, and – as any contemplative will affirm – is as effective when no words are uttered.

Prayer with physical objects

Within some traditions, physical objects are encouraged as an aid to prayer. Rosary beads, labyrinths and candles all have their adherents. The act of lighting a candle, for instance, is a way of *doing* something which gives concrete expression to the prayer. As the candle burns, its light reminds us that the one for whom we are praying is in the presence of Jesus, the light which no darkness can quench. The warmth of the flame, too, speaks of the fire of God's love.

Some find it helpful to carry a small wooden holding cross. As it is grasped, we are aware of connecting with something beyond ourselves – not only the physical object but what that object represents: the cross itself, the place where God's love is most fully displayed, the sign of our faith and the assurance of our salvation.

Anointing

James understood the importance of physical signs in prayer and commended the use of oil in prayer for the sick. The ministry of anointing (unction) has been part of Christian practice since earliest days. Today many churches keep supplies of three holy oils: the oil of catechumens (for baptism), the oil of chrism (for confirmation and ordination) and oil for anointing the sick. There's sometimes a misunderstanding that anointing is only to prepare a person for death – the last rites. It *can* be used at that point in a person's life, but it's also used exactly as James instructs, alongside prayer for healing and wholeness: perhaps when someone is facing a major operation or is suffering a serious illness.

The presence of a physical sign – oil for anointing – combined with words of prayer and prayerful intention is extremely powerful. As James maintains, the prayer of faith makes a difference: it is a vehicle of forgiveness and salvation. It's not the oil alone which has an effect but the prayer as a whole, of which the anointing with oil is a crucial part. Interestingly, James mentions no words; maybe he envisaged silent prayer! Over time, though, we have come to recognize the power of spoken words, such as these, which reflect James' writing very closely:

N, I anoint you in the name of God who gives you life.
Receive Christ's forgiveness, his healing and his love.[36]

Healing

But what about healing? Among those whom I've anointed over the years are some who have been restored to health, some who have continued in ill health, and others who have died. We need to be clear about our expectations when praying for healing. James writes that prayer will 'save the sick'. The Greek verb here is *sōzō*, variously translated 'to heal' and 'to save', with the two translations sometimes interchangeable. In some contexts (e.g., the woman with the haemorrhage, healed by touching the fringe of Jesus' cloak, Luke 8.48), the same word is often translated 'to make whole'. But *sōzō* tends not to be translated as 'cured'. There is a distinction here. James – and Jesus before him – offers healing, wholeness and salvation. This might involve a cure but sometimes a cure will not be possible.

A hospice chaplain once said to me, 'We're all terminally ill, you know,' and she was right. Whatever our state of health, we all share in the human certainty of this life coming to an end at some point. In the midst of that human condition, though, we are offered the promise of wholeness, and salvation, in this world and the next.

'Are any among you suffering? They should pray.' As should we all, for prayer makes a difference.

Peter Moger

Hymn suggestions

O Christ, the healer, we have come; Blest by the sun, the olive tree; We cannot measure how you heal; Heal me, O Lord (Don Moen).

Eighteenth Sunday after Trinity (Proper 21)
29 September
Second Service   **Stuck in the Middle with You**
Ps. 120, 121; Ex. 24; Matt 9.1–8

Telling it like it is

Growing up I had a little book called *Daily Light*. Each day of the year it had a selection of Bible verses to read morning and evening. I don't know how those verses were chosen – randomly, it often seemed. But more often than not, the verses from psalms were uplifting and encouraging, or so it seemed to me. And as I've gone on in the church, it has seemed that psalms mainly serve a pastoral function: Psalm 23, 'The LORD is my shepherd', for example.

So Psalm 120 can be surprising. This Psalmist is in distress. This Psalmist is being brutally honest – 'Woe is me.'

There's great value in telling it like it is, or at least as it feels. 'Deliver me, O LORD, from lying lips,' asks the Psalmist; 'I'm an alien here, I have no permanent dwelling' seems to be the meaning of living among tents. Remember when Elijah says a similar thing to God? 'Only I am left,' and God tells him, 'Actually, I have 7,000 others' (1 Kings 19). It's good to start where we are and tell it like it is.

I am for peace but they are for war

We live in increasingly troubled times – from a European perspective. While we might be forgiven for thinking that peace has reigned since 1945, the world has never been at peace. War has raged on every continent, and it is always the poor who suffer most. Christian Aid and other aid agencies highlight the devastating links between climate change and violence, the displacement of people and war. So yes, along with the Psalmist, I – and you – can say, 'I am for peace.' But what does that mean?

Am I only for peace in the sense that I think it's a nice idea? Am I only for peace in the sense that I'd prefer not to be caught up in conflict? Or am I so for peace that I am willing to change my lifestyle, examine my habits, ask what the global cost of my consumption might be? Am I so for peace that I will rejoice when the Lord rises up on behalf of the poor?

You, O Lord, will protect ...

Reading psalms such as this we run the risk of reading ourselves into the wrong bit. '*My* help comes from the LORD,' we read, and assure ourselves that everything will be fine. But let's read this as though we live somewhere else. Angola, perhaps, where land grabs by the powerful force the weak into poverty, where climate change renders more and more land unproductive, and so causes the powerful to grab even more land. Or Mali, where the land is becoming increasingly dry because of climate change. Climate change that is driven by consumption in wealthy nations like ours. We cannot be for peace while maintaining our current way of life. We are the people the world's poor need protection from.

Psalm 121 has been one of those psalms I have regarded as comforting: 'I lift my eyes to the hills.' Well, I certainly love the beauty of hills. And as I read on, the words 'The LORD will keep you from all evil' have become simply reassurance that God would keep me safe. But supposing, in light of the previous psalm, in light of the claim to be for peace, that keeping us from evil means stopping us from doing evil. Being for peace must also mean resisting evil. Being for peace must also mean fighting for the rights of others rather than ourselves. Being for peace means working with God so that our lives count for good.

Taking a stand

If we are people of peace, as we read at the end of Psalm 120, if we look to the hills and see the way may be tough but the path leads upwards, if we plant our feet firmly on the road to good, then God will not allow our feet to be moved; we will walk and stand firm in the knowledge that God is with us. People of faith are often pushed out of the way, told to keep silent, and keep religion and politics separate, for example. As things declined into political chaos recently, one Anglican bishop said, 'We are not angry enough.' If we are not angry enough, our feet have been moved. Perhaps we need to remember the assertion attributed to Dante: 'The hottest places in hell are reserved for those who, in a period of moral crisis, maintain their neutrality.'[37] While the Psalmist laments, 'Too long have I had my dwelling among those who hate peace,' we perhaps need to lament, 'Too long have we had our dwelling among those who love neutrality.'

The writer of both today's psalms appeals to God. As we look around our unjust, suffering world, we must do that too. But that doesn't mean doing nothing. Change begins with the faithful being seen. Change begins with the faithful speaking out. Change begins with the faithful being active.

As you leave church today, perhaps you might find time to reflect on how God wants you to be involved in protecting the poor and needy.

Liz Shercliff

Hymn suggestions

We seek your kingdom; Called to be partners with God in creation; How we trust and work together; The kingdom of God is justice and joy.

Nineteenth Sunday after Trinity (Proper 22)
6 October
Principal Service   Is it Lawful?
(*Continuous*): Job 1.1; 2.1–10; Ps. 26; *or* (*Related*): Gen. 2.18–24;
Ps. 8; Heb. 1.1–4; 2.5–12; **Mark 10.2–16**

Hard sayings

Our Gospel reading is often listed among the 'hard sayings' of
Jesus. Perhaps a better description would be 'painful', 'distress-
ing' or 'agonizing', as many will take it personally each time this
passage is read and heard. This is particularly so if you have gone
through a divorce, your parents have been divorced, or someone
close to you has been divorced. This results in hearing this passage
being addressed to individuals, and therefore feelings of shame or
anger or hurt or embarrassment may arise. But the more I study
this passage, the more I wonder whether Jesus was addressing
individuals. Let me explain.

Note how Mark sets up this scene: 'Some Pharisees came, and to
test [Jesus] they asked, "Is it lawful ...".' Did you catch that? This
encounter isn't a conversation about love, marriage and divorce.
It's a *test*. And it's not just a test about divorce, but about the law.
The Pharisees are trying to pin Jesus down, catch him out, trying to
label him, draw him out and perhaps entrap him so that they know
better how to deal with him later.

Relationships more than legal matters

But Jesus is having none of it. He turns their question away from
code to *character*, from *law* to *grace*, to God's hope that our relationships are more than legal matters; they are about healthy relationships. That's why Jesus turns to Genesis. Questions of marriage
and divorce, he argues, aren't simply a matter of legal niceties, but
rather about God's intention that we live in relationships of mutual
dependence, flourishing and well-being.

In fact, Jesus goes one step further and takes what had turned
into a legal convenience and pushes the Pharisees to see that this
law – indeed, *all* law – is there to protect the vulnerable. When
a woman was divorced, she lost pretty much everything – status,
reputation, economic security, everything – so how can they treat
this as a convenience, let alone a debating topic? The law is meant

to protect the vulnerable and hurting, and every time we use it for another purpose we are twisting it from God's plan and, indeed, violating it in spirit if not in letter.

Communities of love and mutual dependence

You see, Jesus isn't speaking to individuals; he's making a statement about the kind of community we should be. In fact, he's inviting us to build communities centred in and on genuine relationships, relationships founded on love and mutual dependence, nurtured by respect and dignity and enjoyed for the sake of the community's health and the protection of the vulnerable.

That's why I'm grateful that our reading includes describing the reaction of Jesus' disciples to those bringing children to Jesus to bless, and, more importantly, Jesus' response to those who tried to stop them. For Jesus, welcoming the kingdom means welcoming children, that is, the vulnerable, those at risk and those in need. This whole passage, I believe, is about community. And it's not a community of the strong, the wealthy, the powerful or the independent. But instead, this is a community of the broken, the vulnerable and those at risk. It's a community of those who know their need and seek to be in a relationship with each other because they have realized that by being in an honest and open relationship with each other, they are in a relationship with God: the one who created them for each other in the first place.

This is what the church was about originally. A place where those who had been broken by life or rejected by the powerful came to know God through the crucified Jesus: the one who met them in their vulnerability, not to make them impervious to pain but rather open to the brokenness of those around them. The One who is perfected in suffering is not ashamed to call us his brothers and sisters.

Work in progress

So can we look at this passage this way? Not so much as instructions about divorce but as an invitation to see our communities as places where God's work to heal and restore the whole creation is a 'work in progress'. Not by taking away all our problems but by surrounding us with people who understand, care and help us discover our potential and then reach out to others with love and compassion. We are communities of the broken, but we are those broken whom God loves and is healing and, indeed, using to make all things new; that's the blessing to ourselves and those around us.

Paul Williams

Hymn suggestions

Will you come and follow me? Be still, for the presence of the Lord; Just as I am, without one plea; Take my life and let it be.

Nineteenth Sunday after Trinity (Proper 22)
6 October
Second Service   **Always Read the Small Print!**
Ps. 125, 126; Josh. 3.7–end; **Matt 10.1–22**

Terms and conditions

My father was a lawyer and I fear that I have inherited his litigious mind. Certainly, he taught me never to sign a document that I hadn't read, and I guess all of us have learnt over time the perils of the small print that so often comes in the 'terms and conditions' when we purchase a product. They contain many a get-out clause. With those often come the hidden extras, the things not covered in the original purchase. No wonder the print is so often very small!

The call

Today we hear how Jesus called his 12 disciples and gave them authority. We are given their names, and it's interesting to note how some of them are defined. With Simon, we are told that he is also called Peter: he has a different name from his birth name, a holy nickname, if you like. Andrew is defined by being Peter's brother, and James as being the brother of John. Matthew is defined by his job: you can almost hear the crowd saying, 'That one was a tax-collector', in a village gossip type of way. James is defined by being the son of Alpheus, and Simon for his zeal, which is what the Greek word for Cananaean refers to. Lastly, there is Judas, who is defined as 'the one who betrayed him'. Interesting, I think, how we remember people. I wonder how you and I will be remembered? I guess it's not always in the way that we would want. How would you *like* to be remembered? What might your Christian nickname be?

Mission

Jesus is very clear with the disciples about what their work and mission are about. They are to go to 'the lost sheep of the house of Israel'. I think it might be worth resting in that phrase for a bit. Jesus' work and mission are to the lost and not to the found. How much energy is spent in church life with the lost? What does it mean to be found? Who are the lost in today's world? Have you ever been lost and known what it is to be found? There is one other part of what Jesus says that I think is worth reflecting on too. He tells them to take nothing with them. How extraordinary. Have you ever heard of being sent out with nothing? Why, I wonder, does Jesus say this? What must it be like to be totally dependent on others and on God?

Being canny

I live and work in Newcastle upon Tyne in England, where we have a whole other dialect known as 'Geordie'. I love it. Seemingly, you can get whole words out of one vowel! The Geordie word 'canny' generally means good, but it can also describe a certain wisdom. Jesus invites his followers to be canny, but not naive. They need to be 'wise as serpents and innocent as doves'. They are not to be doormats, as some people think Christians are called to be. Not just nice people. We are beginning to get a strong sense that this is a dangerous mission he is calling them to be involved in. One where they will need to have a certain emotional dexterity in how they handle people.

Divisions

When there is a vote in the House of Commons in Great Britain, it is called a 'division', because the Members of Parliament physically divide to cast their vote: those in favour to one lobby and those against to another. It is symbolic of what happens when anything of potentially significant import is debated – it causes division. That seems to come as quite a surprise to many people, and modern media has made it ever more difficult to recognize that there may be many sides to an argument. There is no small print here with Jesus though. He is very clear from the outset that being his disciple has the potential to cause division. It can and may be deeply uncomfortable to be a follower of his.

The persecuted church

Jesus is also explicit that following him will lead to persecution. In the western world, it is all too easy to forget that in large parts of the world Christians are persecuted for their faith, and that many Christians still face martyrdom today. Jesus' words are as true today as they were when he first spoke them. I believe that we should be praying regularly for our persecuted sisters and brothers in Christ. But we might also ponder, what would I be prepared to suffer for? What would I be prepared to sacrifice my own life for? Can I (or have I) answered God's call to me?

Jonathan Lawson

Hymn suggestions

Will you come and follow me? Take my life, and let it be; God's Spirit is in my heart; God forgave my sin.

Twentieth Sunday after Trinity (Proper 23)
13 October
Principal Service **Weighed Down by Possessions**
(*Continuous*): Job. 23.1–9, 16–end; Ps. 22.1–15; *or* (*Related*): Amos 5.6–7, 10–15; Ps. 90.12–end; Heb. 4.12–end; **Mark 10.17–31**

Keep your money close

In 1859, the *Royal Charter* set sail from Melbourne, destined for Liverpool, carrying an estimated £17m worth of gold and around 370 passengers, including gold prospectors, bringing home their findings from the gold rush that had taken so many people to seek their fortunes. After the cut-throat climate of the mines, they kept their riches close, with gold nuggets sewn into their belts. On the night of 25 October, with the ship only three hours from Liverpool, a hurricane blew up. The wind was so strong that the anchor chains were broken and the ship was driven towards rocks, where, pounded by waves, she broke up quickly and sank. It's believed that around 450 died, many of them pulled down into the waters by the weight of the gold they carried.

Today's reading is one of the most challenging stories in the whole of the Gospels. It's a stark challenge to examine our relationship with our possessions and our money. We all have different amounts of money and different relationships to money. Some of us may be struggling to make ends meet – if that's the case and you need help finding the right support, please do talk to a church leader. But for many in our society, that's not what's going on when it comes to our relationship with money. And that's not new, because 2,000 years ago Jesus had a lot to say about it.

Can't let go

This is the only story in the Gospels of Jesus directly inviting someone to follow him, and them refusing. And the reason he refused is that he can't let go of his possessions. He's not a bad man. He has been keeping the commandments Jesus lists since his youth. But Jesus misses out 'You shall not covet', which is all about being satisfied with what we have and not nurturing a desire for what belongs to others. Jesus seems to know that this is his weakness. Someone with many possessions probably isn't satisfied with what they have but sees what everyone else has and desires it, accumulating more and more. Jesus also adds a commandment – 'You shall not defraud.' Again, perhaps Jesus is seeing something about this man that he wants to draw attention to: could there be something unjust about his accumulation of wealth?

What do you desire?

But what does this man really desire? Because he does want something he doesn't yet have. He asks Jesus for it: 'What must I do to inherit eternal life?' We may be used to thinking of this question as meaning, 'How do I get to heaven when I die?', that having secured the resources he needs for a comfortable life on earth he's looking beyond that. But theologian N. T. Wright suggests a different perspective.[38] Eternal life isn't really about what happens when we die. It's tied up with the idea of 'thy kingdom come on earth as it is in heaven' – the possibility of a new era *here*, a world saved and transformed by God, ushering in the freedom, justice and peace promised by God. He wants to be a part of that era, of that kingdom. Perhaps he senses that his material wealth is not enough and will never satisfy.

Jesus loves him for that. This is the only place in Mark's Gospel where we're told that Jesus loves someone. Jesus loves him, and knows what he needs and tells him, 'You lack one thing; go, sell what you own, and give the money to the poor, and you will have treasure in heaven.' Wright suggests that this isn't so much about the treasure he can't have until he dies, but the treasure that he can enjoy in God's kingdom here on earth.

A shocking invitation?

So, what about us? Do we fall into the same category as this man who had many possessions? Jesus' suggestion, 'go, sell what you own, and give the money to the poor', might leave us too feeling shocked. But do we love our possessions and our money so much we would turn down an invitation to follow Jesus? Are we like those gold miners who were literally so weighed down by their wealth that they couldn't be saved?

We don't all necessarily have to sell all we have and give the money to the poor. But we do need to be ready to give, to be generous when Jesus calls us to. Like so many things, generosity needs to be practised. Perhaps this man was terrified at the idea of giving away any of his wealth because he never had. Giving financially – to the church, to charities – is part of what it means to follow Jesus. Because that is what keeps us from being pulled down by the weight of our own possessions. But more than that, it's part of how we can work with God to bring about God's era of freedom, justice and peace; how we can have treasure here and now, on earth as it is in heaven. If you are shocked by Jesus' words, perhaps money has too much power over your life. Try giving some away and see what happens.

Kat Campion-Spall

Hymn suggestions

Be thou my vision; Give thanks with a grateful heart; I will offer up my life; Will you come and follow me?

Twentieth Sunday after Trinity (Proper 23)

13 October

Second Service   **The Battle Belongs to the Lord**

Ps. 127 [128]; **Josh. 5.13—6.20**; Matt 11.20–end

Making difficult decisions

How do you go about making difficult decisions? Not just decisions about whether you want to do something, but whether it is *right* to do it. It isn't always obvious. A lot of big ethical questions have no easy answer: can war ever be justified? What economic and political system is right? Is it right to use nuclear power?

These types of questions are not new. Nor is the question, how should we, as the people of God, engage with them? Much as it would be wonderful to have a direct hotline to God, a clear sense of what to do at all times, this isn't how life works. Often, we have to make decisions without certainty or a clear word from God. We may have a general sense of what Scripture and tradition say, but no clear-cut answers.

Standing on the edge of Canaan

This is pretty much what Joshua faces in our reading. The people were freed from slavery, fled Egypt, wandered 40 years in the desert and arrived in Canaan, bedraggled refugees desperate for some- where to call home. And they look at the land, and it is good; but it is also already occupied in many places, by people much stronger, much more technologically advanced than they are. And unlikely to want to share.

What is the right thing to do? Words from God are scarce. There is a promise, yes, but few precise directions. It must have been achingly difficult. What were they thinking? What would they do? There were two equally dangerous temptations: one, to take the road of least resistance and assimilate, forgetting who they were and embracing the local culture, finding themselves once again at the bottom. The other temptation was to feel inebriated with success, certain of God's favour, turning God into a tribal God to manipulate as they make war and, ultimately, simply reproduce the patterns of life of Egypt, with Israel in power.

The Jericho episode confronts both of these, though admittedly in ways we struggle with today. We may find them difficult, particularly in the West, because we tend to associate ourselves with the wrong person. We tend to see ourselves in Israel. But of course, most of us are not in Israel's position. We, in the West, are not the bedraggled, traumatized refugees who have escaped slavery and are desperate for land. We are much more like the Canaanites, keeping Israel out, behind the walls of fortified cities.

But for Israel, what is the right thing?

Stepping out in faith

They send out scouts, who make a deal with Rahab the prostitute. Was it right to strike a deal with her? Was there space for mercy in this new land? What does being faithful look like in a world that cannot be easily divided between good and bad, between Israelites and Canaanites? Rahab had confessed faith and trust. The spies decided that ethnic boundaries mattered less than faithfulness to God.

But it was a step of trust. And now they face Jericho. The city is closed. The Hebrews are not welcome.

It may be worth wondering why. Israel – farmers and builders, women and children – aren't precisely a powerful, impressive army. What threat did they present? Why did the city shut its gates? Fear of attack? Or fear and contempt for the stranger, the poor, the needy?

Joshua now stands by the city of Jericho. He is not alone: the angelic captain of YHWH's army meets him there and confronts the second temptation. Joshua wants to know what side God is on. He wants God on his side no matter what. And that is simply not an option: the question is not whether God will be with Joshua and the people but whether Joshua and the people will be with God. Will they be faithful?

There are more tests to come. Faced with a fortified city, Israel is told to arm itself with nothing but trumpets. They must have wondered whether Joshua heard God right. And there is more. In ancient warfare, when you take a city, you take everything – slaves, booty, riches, land, houses. But here, they are told to take nothing for themselves. How hard must it have been for those who had nothing? But they are learning, as with manna in the desert: God will provide.

Mercy wins

There are exceptions. Rahab and her household are spared. True to their words, the Hebrews exercise mercy in battle. What to do with Rahab comes outside divine instruction. It is a moral choice Israel must make for itself. The story doesn't tell us whether it was right. Not straight away. The answer comes much later, in the opening verses of the Gospel of Matthew, in the genealogy of Jesus, a descendant of Rahab the Canaanite prostitute. Mercy lies right at the heart of the story of salvation.

The question for the Hebrews is, will they learn the lessons of Jericho? God cares and will provide, but they cannot assume their choices will automatically be blessed by God. How will they, like us, develop the habits of prayer, study and discernment that will enable the right choices in uncertain times?

Isabelle Hamley

Hymn suggestions

Be thou my vision; Whom shall I fear (God of Angel Armies); Strength will rise as we wait upon the Lord; A mighty fortress.

Twenty-First Sunday after Trinity (Proper 24)
20 October
Principal Service   **Tough Paths of Discipleship**
(*Continuous*): Job 38.1–7 [34–end]; Ps. 104.1–10, 26, 35c
[*or* 104.1–10]; *or* (*Related*): Isa. 53.4–end; Ps. 91.9–end;
Heb. 5.1–10; Mark 10.35–45

Have you ever had one of those moments when you're so wrapped up in yourself and your own concerns that you completely fail to notice what's going on around you and find yourself out of step with everyone else? James and John have just such a moment in today's Gospel.

Grasping status

Jesus and the disciples are on the road to Jerusalem – with all that that means. Jesus is explaining what's going to happen to the Son of Man when they reach the city. In the verses just before this passage,

Jesus says, talking about the Son of Man, 'They will mock him, and spit upon him, and flog him, and kill him; and after three days he will rise again.'

James and John rush forward at this point with their own agenda. They are concerned for their future status: 'Grant us to sit, one at your right hand and one at your left, in your glory.' What an arrogant thing to ask! In Matthew's account of this story, the request is put into the mouth of the mother of James and John – but here in Mark, it's the disciples themselves who are asking such a huge favour.

And why not? James and John, along with Peter, are in Jesus' inner circle. They've seen some incredible things – the raising of Jairus' daughter, the transfiguration. Peter is always getting it wrong, so why shouldn't James and John have the top positions in the kingdom?

Realizing the implications

Jesus doesn't rebuke them but suggests that they don't know what they're asking. Possibly they were so busy plotting their request that they missed what he was saying earlier about what's on the horizon for the Son of Man.

Jesus asks them if they are able to drink the cup he will drink and be baptized with his baptism – and they are quite sure that they will: 'We are able,' they say. Again, in their eagerness, they don't really know what they are saying. The cup is a Hebrew symbol for suffering. The cup reminds us of Gethsemane when Jesus asks for the cup to be taken away from him, begging to be released from his destiny. It is, of course, also the cup of salvation, but salvation comes with a hefty price tag – the cross. James and John don't understand what they are signing up for.

All-embracing service

When the others hear what James and John have asked for, they are angry – indignant that the brothers have been so presumptuous, or maybe jealous that they got there first. Jesus uses the occasion to give a lesson on the topsy-turvy kingdom values regarding status. Whoever wishes to be great among you must be your servant. Whoever wishes to be first must be the slave of all. The Son of Man came to serve and to give his life as a ransom for many.

Jesus' sacrifice on the cross will be the saving act which pays the price for the sins of the world – the all-embracing act of service which will bring about liberation for all. This is what it means to be truly great: to give up your life for others. True greatness comes not from being the best, not from the desire to be noticed, not from self-importance and making one's mark, but from service – being the servant of all. And service is seen by Jesus in terms of suffering and rejection, in harrowing pain and death.

Jesus, our high priest

The writer to the Hebrews reminds us that Jesus' saving act qualifies him to be seen as our high priest. Jesus is chosen from among the people to be their representative and appointed by God. Rather than a grain or animal sacrifice, Jesus gives his own body for our sins, so that we can be at one with God. The way to salvation for all is through the sacrifice of one – Jesus.

Jesus is obedient, he suffers for others, he prays, he deals gently with those who have gone astray, he is compassionate and he is humble before God. These are the qualities of the high priest – the one who represents us to God. He is both leader and servant.

The church, as the body of Christ, is called to do the same. The church is called to both proclaim and model Jesus – the high priest – for the community. The church is called to represent God to the people and the people to God – to be a bridge between heaven and earth. The church is called to deal gently with those who have gone astray. The church is called to be compassionate. The church is called to acknowledge her own weakness and failures, using these to speak humbly to the community about God's love, forgiveness and acceptance of all.

We, as the church, are called to this servant leadership – willing to be last, willing to be least and willing to serve others. It is not our calling to grab the prime places in the kingdom, to seek status in the eyes of the world. It is our calling as the body of Christ to lay down our lives for others, suffering and sacrificing so that others may see the glory of God. Baptized into Christ, this is the cup we are all called to drink.

Catherine Williams

My Jesus, my Saviour; You laid aside your majesty; Brother, sister, let me serve you; Unto your throne, we humbly come (Great High Priest).

Twenty-First Sunday after Trinity (Proper 24)
20 October
Second Service   **Wrestling with the Sabbath**
Ps. 141; Josh. 14.6–14; **Matt. 12.1–21**

Have you ever done something which seemed so natural that you didn't even think about the potential consequences?

Jesus and his disciples are walking along the edge of the fields, and they are hungry. So they do exactly what their instincts tell them and pick some ears of corn to eat. But some Pharisees see them and accuse Jesus of letting his disciples do something that is unlawful. Not unlawful because they've picked the corn; Old Testament laws tell farmers to leave the edges of their field unharvested so that those who are hungry and in need can glean. Unlawful because they've reaped, that is, done work, on the Sabbath.

Then, after leaving that place, we hear that Jesus enters a synagogue and encounters a man with a shrivelled hand. Jesus is challenged by those watching about whether it is lawful to heal on the Sabbath. After some discussion, Jesus does exactly that.

Is it lawful?

As a Gospel written to a Jewish audience, Matthew places importance on Jesus' understanding and interpretation of the law. So what's going on here? Is Jesus just dispensing with the Sabbath laws and saying anything goes? The answer is, of course, a resounding 'no'.

Instead, Jesus is doing what he does time and again in Matthew's Gospel. He is not dispensing with the law at all, but enriching it. Nuancing it. Making it ask more of us and not less, and making us work at its interpretation.

Sabbath for all

Jesus makes it clear that the Sabbath is God's day and so keeping the Sabbath *must* mean honouring God. But hunger and pain do not honour God. Sabbath is about bringing wholeness, rest and renewal, and this clearly cannot happen if you are hungry and suffering. It is near impossible to concentrate on social and spiritual needs if physiological needs haven't been fulfilled (think of Maslow's hierarchy!). What's more, our man with the withered hand was unlikely to have even been allowed to participate in Temple worship on the Sabbath, due to his disability.

Jesus is not dismissing Sabbath laws, but expanding them. Suggesting that it's not good enough just to give ourselves Sabbath rest, we must also enable and allow others to have Sabbath too.

This is what Jesus does, time and again, when he deals with Old Testament law. Looking back at Matthew chapters 5 and 6, he does this for murder, adultery, divorce, generosity, prayer and fasting. He constantly challenges listeners to do more than just follow the letter of the law and instead encourages them to look deeply and extract the real essence.

Do not think I have come to abolish the law

Despite the Pharisees thinking that Jesus was letting his disciples off lightly, this new way of looking at the law requires a far more challenging sense of discipleship. Because it means we can't just follow the rules and hope we'll be all right with God when the time comes. It requires living wholehearted lives for Christ, chewing the laws over ourselves and working out what it means for us to live them. We can find help and guidance from bishops, priests, Christian ethicists, theologians and past examples. But we also need to ask ourselves, 'Given the law, what is the most loving thing we can do here?' How we keep the Sabbath is just one example of that wrestling.

In our fast-paced and ever-changing society, it can be difficult for us to know the best way of keeping Sabbath. Many of us won't be adhering to a strict set of guidelines and it can be easy either to take pride in how well we keep it or despair that we're never going to do it properly! But the way of Jesus means that there is probably no 'perfect Sabbath', and neither pride nor despair should be our default position.

Instead, we each (individually, in families and as communities) need to spend time looking at our own version of Sabbath rest. We need to do theology and ethics for ourselves, and discern how we can each keep Sabbath in a way that honours God, is most true to Jesus' teaching *and* shows love for ourselves and those around us.

Once we've done it for Sabbath, we can do it for other areas of our lives: for the way we give to church and charity, for the way we conduct our relationships, for the way we work in our businesses, for the way we speak to people and about people ... We take each area and we turn it over in our hands, looking at the law and our own practice and deciding what our lives should look like, given the law working through a hermeneutic of love and honouring God.

Ultimately, along the way, we'll realize it is hard and that we can do none of it without God's help. At which moment, we find the best bit of news of it all. Because when we realize that following rules isn't going to sort everything, we allow space for grace and mercy to come rushing in.

Chris Campbell

Hymn suggestions

I danced in the morning; Lord of the Sabbath, hear us pray; The Spirit lives to set us free; This is the day that the Lord has made.

Last Sunday after Trinity (Proper 25)   27 October
Principal Service   **Renewing Vision**
(*Continuous*): Job 42.1–6, 10–end; Ps. 34.1–8, 19–end
[*or* 34.1–8]; *or (Related)*: Jer. 31.7–9; Ps. 126; Heb. 7.23–end;
Mark 10.46–end

How's your eyesight? Engaging with today's passage from Mark's Gospel, I find myself relieved to be living now and able to access the optician regularly. Being very short-sighted I rely on contact lenses and regular check-ups to help maintain my vision. Those who wear contact lenses or glasses or have had corrective surgery know how precious the gift of sight is and what a miracle it is to be able to see properly. Today those in our community who are blind are generally well treated, medically and socially, but for Bartimaeus it was a very different story.

There was no help for Bartimaeus when he began to lose his sight. We know he wasn't born blind because he asks Jesus to let him see *again*, but his condition leaves him penniless and outcast, begging beside the road at Jericho. Hearing someone coming he discovers it is Jesus of Nazareth. He does everything he can to attract Jesus. He shouts out, calling Jesus by name, begging for mercy. The crowd try to silence him but he screams out louder. He is not going to let this opportunity pass.

Jesus hears and calls Bartimaeus to him. Bartimaeus throws off his cloak, perhaps his only possession and a valuable one at that, because it gets very cold in high-up Jericho. Bartimaeus runs to Jesus. How different from the rich man, earlier in this chapter, who couldn't let go of his possessions to receive the kingdom of God (Mark 10.17–22). Bartimaeus comes to Jesus with empty hands ready to receive.

'What do you want me to do for you?'

'What do you want me to do for you?' asks Jesus. This is exactly the same question Jesus put to James and John in last week's Gospel (Mark 10.35–45). James and John asked for prime places in heaven: status, glory and fame. Bartimaeus answers with just four words: 'let me see again.' Sight is what he wants more than anything. He longs for renewed vision, and all that will go with it: inclusion, wholeness, acceptance and a future.

As with the woman with the flow of blood (Mark 5.25–34), Jesus tells Bartimaeus that his faith has made him well. Bartimaeus receives the gift of sight and follows Jesus on the way – not just along the road, but as a follower of Jesus himself. We know that Bartimaeus was almost certainly a member of the early church because the Gospel writers tended only to name people that their readers would know personally as fellow Christians. The blind man is remembered by name. He becomes a valued member of the community.

This fulfils the prophecy from Jeremiah 31 where the Lord encourages the people to cry out for salvation. In Jeremiah, we hear that people from all over the world will be united and become God's family and heirs. They will include the blind, the lame and those with children. God will lead them so they don't stumble and fall. Bartimaeus is a snapshot of that happening – the kingdom of God breaking through in Jesus and a life transformed by healing and inclusion.

What's your answer?

If Jesus asked you the question, 'What do you want me to do for you?', what would be your answer? Would you say, 'Oh, nothing, I'm fine, thanks' – the response we often give when people offer help and we find it hard to be vulnerable. Or would you answer like James and John, wanting to be important or special? Or might you ask for renewed vision – a new way of seeing things, growth in faith or holiness or love? Or would you ask for something else?

When we come to worship, we come with open, empty hands, wanting to receive from Jesus just like Bartimaeus. And what we receive from Jesus is everything. Through the Scriptures, through the sacraments, in fellowship within the body of Christ, we receive God's very self to nourish and save us. The passage from Hebrews indicates that Jesus' offering of himself upon the cross saves us for all time. It's a unique act that lasts for eternity. The priests in the older Testament made sacrifices on behalf of the people daily as a way of being in relationship with God. But on the cross, Jesus is the sacrifice once and for all. Jesus saves all who approach God through him. The cross heralds the transformation of all creation – life from death, relationship from alienation.

Making space for others

There's a warning to us in this passage. As Bartimaeus tries to find Jesus the crowd tries to stop him. They try to silence him, and it's not until the crowd hears Jesus calling for Bartimaeus that they allow him forward. We are not to keep Jesus to ourselves, hiding him from others, shutting others out because they make us uncomfortable.

The God we worship, the God who saves and is revealed in Jesus, loves everyone. As disciples of Jesus, we are called to make that message known and not to get in the way of God working wherever God chooses. Who do you know who is crying out for help? Stop, listen and respond. Let's renew our vision and see as Jesus sees. Let's watch for the signs of God at work all around us. Let's enable others to engage with God, who in Jesus longs to transform and save.

Catherine Williams

Hymn suggestions

Amazing grace; Open my eyes, Lord; Once, only once, and once for all; Be thou my vision.

Last Sunday after Trinity (Proper 25)   27 October
Second Service   **Behaving, Belonging, Believing and Beauty**
Ps. 119.121–136; Eccles. 11; 12; **2 Tim. 2.1–7**;
Gospel at Holy Communion: Luke 18.9–14

The values of organizations

A few years ago, I made an absolute rooky mistake at work. I was responsible for training and assessing people who were wanting to fit into a particular role in a particular organization. One of the core values of the organization was compassion and therefore one of the non-negotiable skills for staff in the organization was good listening skills. Only, I had someone I was responsible for who was hopeless at listening. So I organized a one-to-one meeting to talk about their rather flimsy active listening skills. After about 30 frustrating minutes of attempting to get my point across I realized my rooky mistake: of course, trying to get someone to listen to my opinion when they weren't very good at listening was never going to work!

It was a comical and humbling experience to reflect on with my colleagues later. Between us, we found other strategies for helping that particular person with their listening. It was also that experience which inspired me to do some deep thinking about, and subsequentially work with, organizational values and how these are embodied and lived out in workplace cultures, behavioural norms and which skills are prized, either explicitly or implicitly.

I read the Pastoral Epistles of the two letters to Timothy and one letter to Titus through this lens. They are a set of documents written to enable a particular organizational culture to flourish as it develops itself and understands what its core values are and what its purpose is. Written in the format of letters, they include details of the behaviours and skills that are expected from people and the values which are to be cherished as part of the DNA of the organization. Values which can be seen in the heroes of the organization. I suspect today they would be a set of PowerPoint presentation slides rather than letters, with vision statements, lists of organizational values and stories of successful characters and significant leaders.

Being strong

The Second Letter to Timothy is slightly different in tone from the two other letters in the set. It is the only one written from the context of prison and there are more personal touches. You can imagine being the recipient, reading how you are loved and missed. Reading that your mentor, your hero, is still in prison and that others have abandoned the cause. Over the page you skim the first sentence, 'So, my child, this is what I expect of you. Be strong.' Is this about resilience? Is this a call to arms? Is this about finding some energy to do a hard physical task, like going somewhere, or confronting someone? Is this an ask for trust, or faith, or more conviction in the cause?

There is a sense, I suggest, that this instruction is not primarily any of those things. Rather it is a big-hearted plea from one colleague and friend to another to be empowered, encouraged and inspired, by the overwhelming beauty, kindness and attractiveness of Jesus Christ. At the heart of this organization, at the core of its DNA, is this: the grace that is in Jesus Christ. Live a life dedicated to the beauty of Christ, says the writer, and then promptly runs out of words to explain what that means.

And so three images come into play – the soldier, the athlete and the farmer. Living dedicated to the beauty of Christ is all about solidarity with others, companionship, consistency, focus, dedication, diligence, productiveness, experience and the joys of being an interdependent part of creation. And just in case the recipient of the letter hadn't got the sense of pleasure and treasure of this way of life, the writer finishes with 'and openness to anything else your amazing brain and experience can understand and create out of these images'.

The truth worth surrendering to

The Irish philosopher John Moriarty, in his autobiography *Nostos*, uses a different image. It's not one of a person in a role but, as you would expect, one more philosophical and metaphysical. The utter and sheer beauty of Jesus Christ is 'not merely a speakable truth, but a truth I would surrender to'.[39] To surrender to beauty, to grace, to loveliness and kindness and to all the goodness of Christ is not a heavy burden of submission, obedience and toil. It is an act of turning, turning and turning again to open up to that which is good and lovely and let it saturate your soul. If the images of soldier, athlete and farmer don't speak of that to you, then respectfully put them to one side and explore others.

'Be empowered, encouraged, inspired, by the overwhelming beauty, kindness and attractiveness of Jesus Christ,' says the writer, swiftly followed by 'Remember Jesus Christ, raised from the dead.' I wonder what core values, cultural behaviours and skills you would want to live out, to teach and to pass on to embody this truth worth surrendering to.

Esther Elliott

Hymn suggestions

Amazing grace; Come, my Way, my Truth, my Life; Lord of creation, to you be all praise; Lord for the years.

Bible Sunday 27 October
Principal Service **What Would You Miss?**
Isa. 55.1–11; Ps. 19.7–end; **2 Tim. 3.14—4.5**; John 5.36b–end

What would you choose?

The world you know is threatened. It will fall, and with it all human knowledge, all progress, the very fabric of society and the core of all science. What would you save?

This is the premise behind Hari Seldon's Encyclopaedia Galactica project; imagined by Isaac Asimov in his staggering Foundation Series. Under threat of impending disaster, a team of encyclopaedists have to decide exactly that: what to save that would sum up the great record of human achievement and allow future generations to rebuild.

Likewise, supposing some cataclysmic event was about to remove every single Bible, not just from this church but from every other church, library, bookshelf … and from every mobile device, in every household, in every single corner of the world. What would you choose to save from this book whose narrative spans thousands of years, from this library of around three-quarters of a million words?

What would you miss?

Whatever you might choose to save, I hope that there is a lot more that you realize you would miss. Because the Bible is more than just a collection of words, it is a book with a purpose, inspired by God, not just for reproof, correction and training (as we hear in the Letter to Timothy) but to draw us closer to the one who created us, loves us and whose deepest desire is to be in relationship with us. Through the stories contained within, it exists to encourage us and equip us to deal with all the joys and challenges of life.

Despite occasionally being told that the Bible is 'irrelevant' for today, it never fails to amaze me how relevant it actually is. In the Bible we read stories of how very real people through history have lived, both with each other and with God, and there are so many resonances in those stories which help us learn new truths in our own lives. We hear stories of people who are anxious about war, sorrowful through loss, joyful in hope, and patient in times of darkness. We hear of those embroiled in family disagreements, those going on long journeys and those who stand up to power.

If suddenly every Bible disappeared, we would lose all those stories, along with the story that runs through them all. The story of a God who loves humanity so much that, despite their trickery, their hatred, their violence, their fearfulness and their unfaithfulness, gives the life of the only Son, the only human never to have given in to their temptations, to die for us and to show us another way.

Every day as Bible Day?

Just like Timothy, many of us have grown up knowing the Scriptures, but all too often we find our own Bibles sitting on our bookshelves gathering dust. We often forget that even today there are places in the world where the sale of Bibles is illegal, or their distribution is strictly limited. We take our Bibles for granted. So, what if we treated them as if they *were* going to disappear tomorrow?

If we each knew that tomorrow our Bibles would be gone, I'm sure that many of us would scrap what we've planned to do today and read again those passages of Scripture that we love, or perhaps the bits that we don't feel we yet understand, or maybe even the books that we never quite got round to reading ... like Numbers and Habakkuk and Revelation ...

If I knew that tomorrow there'd be an empty space on my bookshelf where the Bible should have been, then today I would curl up in a chair and read aloud the books of Tobit and Jonah and Ruth. I would try to commit at least a couple more psalms to memory. I would wrestle with which Gospel to read one more time, so that I could remember it all as well as I could, to tell the stories which have formed me to my children and my grandchildren and my friends and my neighbours.

The Bible is full of the potential of God speaking to us with the same voice of love and comfort and challenge and wisdom with which God spoke to all those people we read about within its covers. Through the Bible, God whispers to us and encourages us to dwell richly in those same words in which millions of people before us have dwelt. And yet so often we find ourselves doing something else, something more pressing or more socially acceptable.

But surely for us Bible Sunday shouldn't be just one Sunday a year. Every Sunday should be Bible Sunday, every day a Bible Day. God's word is precious, priceless, inspired; it is more to be desired than gold; it is sweeter than honey dripping from the honeycomb, and it deserves our best attention.

So today let's renew again our commitment to dwelling in this book, seeking the Lord in the place where the Lord may be found, and through those timeless stories allow ourselves to draw closer to the one who gives us life, the one to whom those precious words testify.

Chris Campbell

Hymn suggestions

Lord, for the years; Thou, whose almighty word; We have a gospel to proclaim; Word of God.

Fourth Sunday before Advent   3 November
(For All Saints' Day, see p. 343.)
Principal Service   The Guiding Principle
Deut. 6.1–9; Ps. 119.1–8; Heb. 9.11–14; **Mark 12.28–34**

Weaving the story

'Love the Lord your God with all your heart, and with all your soul, and with all your mind, and with all your strength' and 'love your neighbour as yourself' are well-known words of Jesus. The temptation is to assume we know what they mean. But neither life nor stories are simple. Although the lectionary has carved up this chapter from the Gospel of Mark, the writer is specific. This scribe has just seen Jesus disputing with ... someone. Some Sadducees, it turns out, if you look back a bit. This is not a simple conversation between Jesus and a scribe; it involves an earlier conversation too.

The Sadducees had asked Jesus a very specific and detailed legal question. They didn't believe in resurrection or life after death, so they set up a problem where a woman marries a man who dies. As the law requires, his brother then marries her, but he too dies. Altogether there are seven brothers who marry the woman. When she too dies, whose wife will she be in heaven? Jesus tells them they are 'quite wrong'; no wonder they didn't like him! The Sadducees were the party of the privileged and wealthy, defenders of the status quo, picky about which laws they chose to obey. They weren't keen on Jesus talking to people about rendering to Caesar what was Caesar's and to God what is God's. They wanted a bit of God's share too. They were a bit like the wealthy who legally store up money for themselves without a second thought about those who pay the price for their privilege.

Scribes, on the other hand, were practical lawyers. Every village had one. It was their job to draft contracts for local people – marriage and divorce, loans and mortgages, sales and purchases. Good scribes were more interested in justice than law, keen to apply principle instead of the letter of the law. Sometimes they were involved in reconciliation, the give and take of real human relationships. Weaving these things together gives our story a less simple texture.

The guiding principle

The Sadducees asked Jesus what they imagined was a complex legal problem. Using their logic, the problem could not be resolved. But they've missed the point entirely, Jesus says. They know nothing. On the other hand, the scribe's question was an important, practical one. In his everyday work of interpreting the law, what should be his guiding principle? For someone often called rabbi, or teacher, Jesus left us with remarkably few instructions. Instead, he left us with examples and guiding principles. He didn't tell us how to do church, or how the church should relate to its community, or who might be acceptable and who might not – though his actions were pretty clear on that one. But he is very clear that in everything we are to love God, love each other and love ourselves. Did you notice that? Love your neighbour as yourself. The guiding principle is love. How do we make complex decisions individually, in our families or in our churches? We ask first, 'What is the way of love?'

Not far from the kingdom

The scribe quickly agrees with Jesus. In his practical work in his village among his community, he knows that loving God and neighbour is more effective in bringing harmony than offering sacrifices in the Temple. Because he knows this, Jesus tells him he is not far from the kingdom. I was raised in the kind of church that told me social concerns had nothing to do with our faith. Concern for justice was deprecatingly called the 'social gospel'. Jesus has no such qualms. Mark tells us that in Jesus' opinion the scribe had answered wisely by placing love of God and neighbour above religious practices. He tells him he isn't far from the kingdom of God.

How do we understand that? I've done some research – well, googled some sermons anyway! There are several interpretations of Jesus' words to the scribe. Mainly what they seem to mean is that the person interpreting them holds correct theology! The scribe is close, but because he hasn't invited Jesus to be his Lord and saviour he isn't there. The scribe is close, but then aren't we all? The more people debate the meaning of Jesus' words the more they risk falling into the trap of the Sadducees. Perhaps it's best to take Jesus' words at face value – if you love God, love others and love yourself, you are close to God's harmonious kingdom. That, as I hope you have seen, is not an ambiguous hope or a nebulous task, it is the practical guiding principle for the daily life of all who would follow Jesus.

Liz Shercliff

Hymn suggestions

Let us build a house where love can dwell; A new commandment I give unto you; And can it be that I should gain; Be in our midst and gather us together (to use this hymn please include this copyright notice: © Ally Barrett used with permission).

Fourth Sunday before Advent 3 November
Second Service **Two Sorts of Kingdom**
Ps. 145 [*or* 145.1–9]; **Dan. 2.1–48** [*or* 1–11, 25–48];
Rev. 7.9–end; *Gospel at Holy Communion*: Matt. 5.1–12

Having nightmares

Most of us have probably woken up from a nightmare at some
point and desperately wondered what it was all about. What on
earth would cause us to dream whatever horrible scenario we have
just experienced in our sleep? And that is exactly what happens to
King Nebuchadnezzar in the long reading from Daniel that we have
heard read today. He's had a really peculiar dream and is desperate
to know what it might mean.

It will help us to remember what is going on historically. Nebuchadnezzar is king of Babylon, and he has conquered Jerusalem.
This is all set in roughly 600 BC. So we are 600 years or so before
Jesus' birth. And Daniel, together with a number of other Judaeans,
has been swept away to Babylon to serve in Nebuchadnezzar's
court. And this story that we heard today takes place about two
years after Jerusalem has fallen.

It's the end of the world!

Daniel is a book of prophecy and of 'eschatology', which is the
word we use for how we think about what will happen at the end
of the world. So Daniel is a good book to read in these dying days
of an old church year, as we prepare for another Advent and as we
begin to tell again the old, old stories of our faith. November, for
the church, is a time to think about what will happen 'at the end'.
And in Daniel we find a prophet who gives us some really quite
vivid and clear pictures.

The overriding image in this extraordinary story is how change-
able and impermanent human kingdoms are. Nebuchadnezzar is,
just at the moment, the 'big beast' in the local area. He successfully
conquered Jerusalem and Judaea. He's had a great victory and is
asserting his authority. But this vision, which forms one of a number
of highly visual prophecies and tales in the book of Daniel, reminds
the king, and all of us who read or hear the story, that our human
power is highly transient and temporary, and we do well to remember we are not ultimately in control of history, or our own destiny.

Two sorts of kingdom

'Yes, Nebuchadnezzar, you might be powerful now,' God seems to be saying, 'but just look at what is going to happen. Four other kingdoms are going to rise after yours, and each of them in turn will fall.' And the clear message of this prophecy, and of the book of Daniel in general, is that we must be very careful not to confuse the kingdoms of this world with the kingdom of God. There is a world of difference between the two. No matter how permanent, strong, dominant or secure human institutions are, God is interested in a completely different sort of kingdom. The kingdom of God is not based on power or dominance, but rather on the suffering, death and resurrection of Jesus Christ. This is a kingdom of grace, a kingdom with a Servant King. If you want to find the throne of God, you are much less likely to find it in a bejewelled throne room, and much more likely to find it in a stable in Bethlehem, or on a green hill outside the city wall.

Power play

Nebuchadnezzar's temptation, and, if we are honest with ourselves, our temptation too, is to worry about our status: how liked we are, how successful we are, how we will be remembered. But, as the reading from Revelation today reminds us, our destiny is not to be remembered here on earth. It is to join the ranks of that extraordinary choir standing around the throne of God and allow our voices to mingle in the harmony of the song of the people of the kingdom. Choirs are a really good metaphor for God's kingdom, because different voices and different lines combine to create something beautiful. We are part of something very much bigger than ourselves, in which our voice must not be strident but part of the whole.

And then of course we remember who we are worshipping. The creature on the throne is not a powerful conqueror: it is a lamb. *The* Lamb. The one whose kingdom is wrought through sacrifice. Whose authority is made perfect in the act of giving it away. We do well to remember that whenever we are tempted to worry about our legacy, our reputation or our power. These are the traps into which the Nebuchadnezzars of the world fall. Thank God that the nightmare of that sort of power is utterly transformed by the vision of a totally different sort of kingdom.

Tom Clammer

Hymn suggestions

Thy kingdom come, O God; Thy kingdom come, on bended knee; God is working his purpose out; Angel voices ever singing.

Third Sunday before Advent   10 November
(For Remembrance Sunday, see p. 262.)
Principal Service   **His Calling, Your Calling**
Jonah 3.1–5, 10; Ps. 62.5–end; Heb. 9.24–end; **Mark 1.14–20**

What is God calling me to do? What is God calling you to do? This question never seems to go away! God calls us to follow – but we rarely know what is coming next. And whatever stage of life we have reached, there is always something further, something deeper, something more wonderful – a calling, and an answering.

Jesus lived and worked for a while in the town of Capernaum. He got to know his neighbours, people who made a living from fishing.

Did Jesus keep up Joseph's business of woodwork and house repair? At the time Mark's account begins he was embarking on a different career, a different kind of building and repair altogether. Jesus seemed to be full of new ideas. He was talking more and more about the kingdom of God: a realm, a way of living that offered a better life. And he went out into other towns and started to preach.

One day, Mark tells us, Jesus walked beside the lake and met Simon and Andrew. They were throwing their net into the water. He said to them, 'Come, follow me, and I will make you fishers – not of fish but of people.' They left the net and followed him.

He came to James and John, sitting in a boat, getting the nets ready. They also followed him – and the journey began. These fishermen were becoming disciples.

Called to be disciples

How are we becoming disciples? What is God calling me to do? What is God calling you to do? When Jesus calls us to follow, it may not be a call to something completely new. It might be a call to do what we are doing, to be what we are being – but to do it, and be it, in the realm of God.

As a fisherman, Simon Peter already had many skills. He could attend to signs on the water that told him where the fish were. He could wait and be really still. He had the strength and stamina to work right through the night. All these things were part of him – and now his vocation called these skills and attributes into the service of Christ.

And although *Peter* ended up very different from the *Simon* he once was, the work had started long ago. God was always calling him and preparing him for who he was in the depths of his heart. And so it is with us.

Our deepest calling

What is your essence? What is your deepest calling? Did that lead you into your career or the work you have retired from? Could that 'secular' calling point to the shape of your future life, as a disciple, fulfilled and matured in the realm of God?

A man had retired from work long ago and had quite poor health that now limited his mobility. He loved to meet people but he was now living alone. He felt the loneliness, but he started to find a rhythm of life, of prayer and silence, of reading. He read unexpected books about unusual subjects. And although he didn't see many people, the ones he did see were really aware of meeting Christ in him, and he brought incredible blessing to others. He was finding a new way of life.

Many people come to a mid-point or a crisis and begin to change direction in their lives. Maybe they start a course or begin a new ministry. They are discovering what this call of God means now.

Fishers of people

Jesus talks about 'fishers of people', but what is this fishing? Does it mean bringing people into church? That can't be what Jesus had in mind. For a start, in those days there was no church. Jesus never seems to be interested in synagogue attendance!

Jesus described the kingdom of God as a great net – a realm of influence, spreading out, embracing more and more people, a kind of social network that gathered people into the zone of relationship with God.

It was not a conquering kingdom – not at all like the kingdoms of this world. It was not even a church, but a movement of gentleness and love.

'Fishing for people' is a disturbing idea, but these fishermen are not trying to catch or manipulate people. By what they do and say they preach good news. They want to make people aware that another way of life is possible – living in consciousness of God, the life of Jesus. Above all, they know that Jesus, the one whom they are following, has called them by name. And they understand that Jesus calls the name of every person they meet.

Good news

This good news brings other people to life and flourishing, it brings peace and love to others. This is the growing kingdom of God.

Jesus talks a lot about this kingdom. He uses images of retrieval: fishing, lost things, lost people and lost sheep. And sometimes images of growth: a great tree from a small seed, yeast in dough, a growing seed, a field growing to harvest. The kingdom is all of these – ways in which God makes an impact in our lives. And as we answer the call, God's realm becomes visible in this broken world.

'Follow me', says Jesus. Follow me – into the kingdom of love, joy and peace, the kingdom where we grow and flourish, the kingdom that is always new.

Go fishing for this kingdom, take that life to all those you meet, so that love, joy and peace can flourish, even in dark places.

Andrew Rudd

Hymn suggestions

Will you come and follow me; O Jesus, I have promised; Jesus calls us o'er the tumult; Here in this place.

Third Sunday before Advent   10 November
Second Service   **Walk a While with the Lord**
Ps. 46 [82]; Isa. 10.33—11.9; John 14.1–29 [*or* 23–29]

The voice of peace

The voice of God reaches out from this psalm and says, 'Be still.' How often do we stop everything – work, screens, movement, noise – and go properly still? In the stillness, we meet with the presence of God.

Let's be still for a moment …

The voice of God reaches out from this psalm and says, 'There's a river that brings gladness.' Rivers mean so much in the Bible:

refreshment, presence, freedom, baptism. There is something about the flow of a river that analogizes the life-giving joy of the Holy Spirit. How often do we wade into the river of gladness and get soaked? How often do we truly seek the life-giving flow of the Holy Spirit?

Let's wade out again into that river of gladness and get soaked …

The voice of God reaches out from this psalm and says, 'Wars cease.' We live in an age, replicated throughout the ages, where people have picked up arms under the direction of rulers, and have used them to harm, maim and kill. The victims of war call out from the ground and ask, 'Why has this happened?' We need to come to terms with the fact that there is no satisfactory answer to that question. However, we must continue to speak and act in a way that brings peace.

Let's bring an 'Amen' to the prayer, 'Wars cease.' Lord, might peace reign throughout the earth …

We hear the voice of God reaching out from this psalm and receive the words, 'We will not fear.' There are many things to fear in the world: war, famine, persecution, injustice. But these big things are not the only things we can be afraid of. We can be afraid of tomorrow, of ourselves, of others, of walking out of the door. We can be afraid, too, of coming home. But the presence of God casts out all fear.

Let's bring our fears and the fears of others, big and small, to the table of God …

Walking with the Lord on the road

We see that our psalm starts with a declaration that 'God is our refuge and strength, a very present help in trouble.' God is not just omnipresent in some philosophical sense of being everywhere. God is 'very' present. This has connotations of touch, smell, taste, Eucharist. It brings to mind Jesus walking along with the disciples; of them doing life together; of them sharing bread, wine, stories and trials.

We have heard the voice of God in this psalm. Now let's walk awhile with Jesus and let the pieces come together. As we walk with him, we realize that we can appreciate the stillness for a while. Although, in one sense, Jesus demands a great deal from us, he certainly doesn't tell us to be busy. We go a little further, this time to the river Jordan. We are reminded that we were soaked at baptism – taken through the waters of healing and new life. As much as we only believe in 'one' baptism for the forgiveness of sins, we would do well to get soaked in the presence of God every day.

Now we accompany Mary to the foot of the cross and look up. We see that violence is undone. We see that Jesus absorbs the anger of the world and turns it on its head. We see also that, in the resurrection, war will not have the last word. Death will cease. The last word is 'life'. Finally, we come to the table to eat, to let our shoulders drop. We come to share wine and really start to relax. We need fear no longer. When we are with Jesus, wherever we are, we are home. As we fellowship with him and his community, we tell the world a truly wonderful story – of friendship, of flourishing, of flowing and of feasting.

We come to a God who is our 'refuge and strength' and our 'very present help in trouble'. These words cut across the striving and straining of our world and our lives and invite us to share instead in the life of a God of love and in a future where all conflict will cease. This is the same God who 'makes the earth melt'. As God melts our hearts and makes them tender, let us pray that we too may have tender hearts towards each other and towards the world, while at the same time receiving the strength that helps us to stand, to act and to reach out in love.

Mark Amos

Hymn suggestions

Be still, for the presence of the Lord; In Christ alone; Abide with me; Spirit of the living God, fall afresh on me.

Remembrance Sunday   10 November
Principal Service   Beyond Words
(The readings for the day, or for 'In Time of Trouble', or those for 'The Peace of the World' can be used. Readings for the Third Sunday before Advent (Principal Service) are used here.)
Jonah 3.1–5, 10; Ps. 62.5–end; Heb. 9.24–end; **Mark 1.14–20**

The guns fell silent

At the eleventh hour of the eleventh day of the eleventh month, the guns fell silent. And so at the eleventh hour on the Sunday closest to the eleventh day of the eleventh month, just as will happen today, we fall silent too.

The Imperial War Museum has a collection of recordings of soldiers speaking about the First World War. What is striking among those speaking about the armistice is how many speak of the silence.

One soldier who was near Mons that day speaks of a silence that was almost tangible – a stark contrast with four and half years of artillery noise. Another speaks of the anti-climax – no sounds of celebration or joy, no singing or cheering, just exhausted, silent thanksgiving. Another soldier recalls his friends who were on the front line telling him that they felt flat, joyless, uncomprehending.

The Imperial War Museum also has a recording of the moment the guns fell silent, captured photographically. There are two images, one from 10.58, one from 11.00. On the first, the five lines are full of peaks, a bit like an ECG chart, each peak in the line representing artillery fire. On the second, the five lines are completely flat.

Silence. Emptiness. Flatness. Anti-climax. For many, that's what that moment represented. Because, after all, for the war to have ended, there had to have been a war.

Our silence

So, what is our silence for today? Our remembering is full of words and ritual, of music and symbolism. The power of the poetry, the liturgy, the poppies and images of our remembrance help us to start to understand the weight and cost of the wars we remember, the value of the sacrifices made. But at the heart of our remembrance there is an emptiness. Two minutes for which there are no words. No words to remember the horror of the violence that human beings can inflict on one another. No words to describe the trauma that stayed with those who came back, for the rest of their lives. No words to explain why the war to end all wars didn't end all wars.

Sacrificial following

Our Gospel reading today is a story about young men leaving everything behind to follow Jesus. Leaving their families, their work, their security; not knowing quite where they were going or what they would be doing. Today we remember those millions of men and women who left everything behind to follow orders in wars and conflicts, past and present, and those civilians whose lives have been lost or broken by war.

However it is done, to follow someone is usually sacrificial. It involves a surrender of some sort, surrender of self, surrender of will. To be a soldier is to submit to authority, to discipline, to put yourself at the service of others. To be a disciple is, perhaps, not all that different.

Remembering the sacrifice

As Christians, as a eucharistic community, we gather week in week out to remember. We gather to remember the sacrifice made by the one we follow. We have a moment of silence at the end of the Eucharistic Prayer, as the bread and wine are lifted up: the body of Christ, broken for us; the blood of Christ, shed for us. A moment of silence, beyond words, between remembering his death and receiving his life. Remembering the one who, as it says in our Hebrews reading, 'has appeared once for all at the end of the age to remove sin by the sacrifice of himself'.

Our silence of remembrance at the eleventh hour will begin with the last post, used at military funerals to honour the dead. It will end with the reveille, sounded to get soldiers up in the morning. The silence in between is a kind of Holy Saturday, between death and resurrection, a place of grief, abandonment and horror at human violence; a place of love, loss and bewilderment. A place beyond words. A place that begins in death and ends in hope. Hope that death had meaning, that the sacrifice was worth something, that we will allow ourselves to be changed by another's gift.

No words

In the silence this morning there is space for whatever we bring: pride, grief, shame, disconnectedness, horror, ambivalence; hope that the sacrifices made by so many have made a difference, or fear that they haven't. But as a Christian community, in that silence for which we have no words, we are brought back to the silence of that sealed tomb on Holy Saturday, to that silence as the spilt blood is lifted up as the cup of life in which we share.

At the eleventh hour of the eleventh day of the eleventh month, the guns fell silent.

Kat Campion-Spall

Hymn suggestions

For the healing of the nations; I vow to thee, my country; O God, our help in ages past; What shall we pray for those who died?

Second Sunday before Advent   17 November
Principal Service   **Is Big Better?**
Dan. 12.1–3; Ps. 16; Heb. 10.11–14 [15–18] 19–25;
Mark 13.1–8

What large stones and what large buildings!

If you have ever been to the Holy Land, you will know just how big those Temple stones really are. Unless you are an archaeologist, we really only have the Western Wall relatively easily accessible, but even these stones are massive and very impressive. So, what must the Temple have looked like before its destruction in AD 70? Awe-inspiring – no wonder the disciples were agog and amazed.

Bold, big and better

We love bold. We love big. We love better. That's the human motto, in every form: the bigger, the better. People of the first century were no different to us and we to them. While we tend to think that our 2,000 years of so-called 'civilization' somehow place us in a different category, Jesus calls out the truth of our humanity – past and present. Lest we think we are any more knowledgeable than those who first heard Jesus, we are not. We only know different attractions and have more opportunities of beguiling ourselves with magnificence and power.

And don't for a moment think that the Christian church is immune from all this, we're not. We love statistics, membership numbers, financial security, excellent liturgy, exquisite music, and building projects. There is no end to the large stones we seek to erect. But if they become an end in themselves rather than a means, then we are in serious trouble. Our faith, our religious life and our churches are not free from the temptation for prestige, for the desire of greatness and grandness, for a yearning for majesty beyond comparison. In fact, when it comes to faith and how we do church, our fondness for 'big is best' can be worse than the world's – and we should know better.

Tipping point

Chapter 13 of St Mark's Gospel is a tipping point: we are on the brink of Jesus' own arrest and death, and his lesson, to his disciples then and now, is crucial. Don't be tempted to compare the kingdom of God with the kingdoms of this world.

The backdrop to the ministry of Jesus was war and the fear of war. Jesus was brought up in an occupied country close to the frontier of the Roman Empire: '*When* (not if) you hear of wars and rumours of wars,' he said, 'do not be alarmed; this must take place … For nation will rise against nation and kingdom against kingdom … This is but the beginning of the birth pangs.'

Jesus tells his disciples plainly: there will be war, disease and famine. But he doesn't know when God will bring history to a close: 'But about that day or hour no one knows, neither the angels in heaven, nor the Son, but only the Father' (Mark 13.32). If the legacy of war, for the time being, is peace, we should be grateful. But we should never, never take peace for granted. In the light of all that has happened in recent human history, we need to 'stay awake'. Staying awake for us, it seems to me, includes never taking the blessings of peace for granted and doing all we can to build and strive for reconciliation while we have the time and opportunity. Because, and this is what really scares me, there may come a time when there is no opportunity to preserve the peace.

The victorious victim

Jesus says, do not be alarmed by the wars, battles and portents which are to come. Whatever the extremists say, God is not going to redeem the world through the violent events of this world. However, what he has done in Jesus is to allow the violence of this world to come upon him. And, in so doing, Jesus shows us who we really are and what we are capable of doing to each other, while also showing us who God truly is: the victorious victim, the victorious victim who, in the light of the resurrection, offers forgiveness, healing and peace to all – first to the individual and then to the nations.

Jesus knows very well that there will be wars and rumours of wars, and nations will rise up against nations. And through all of this Jesus wants his disciples to walk with care, for we cannot associate ourselves with the lie that 'big is best'. Jesus wants us to learn to believe in another kingdom, distinct from the kingdoms that are founded on such notions.

The disciple of Jesus doesn't believe in rapid and dramatic solutions to the problems of the world. The disciple of Jesus believes the good news about God, that the kingdom of God will come – but will come slowly and almost unnoticed.

What might you do this week that will advance the kingdom of God and push back the bleakness? Perhaps, by consciously choosing your words, you might sow harmony rather than discord. Visiting a neighbour who can't get out of the house may bring some light into the darkness of their day. In these small things, the kingdom will come, slowly and almost silently until that day when Christ will come again and all will be in all 'on earth as it is in heaven'.

In the end, 'what large stones and what large buildings' is a statement of faith – big is best – and it's a statement of faith that Jesus asks us to reconsider.

Paul Williams

Hymn suggestions

Jerusalem the golden; Put peace into each other's hands; Make me a channel of your peace; All my hope on God is founded.

Second Sunday before Advent   17 November
Second Service   **The Risk of Faith**
Ps. 95; **Dan. 3** [*or* 3.13–end]; Matt 13.24–30, 36–43

A world based on trust

A recent survey suggests that people trust each other less today than they did 40 years ago. It may be true. We take care to lock our houses. We have security passwords to guard our phones, computers and payment accounts. Some people have cameras on their doorbells to ensure that they are not surprised by an unknown caller. In schools, children are warned of 'stranger danger'. It seems that we feel we need to protect ourselves, our loved ones and our possessions. On the other hand, we also live in a world often built on trust. We travel on public transport with confidence that we will arrive at our destination – if not always on time – safely! We trust that the products we use will not harm us. And, generally, we place confidence in people.

In 1987, Terry Waite – working as a special advisor to the Archbishop of Canterbury – travelled as an envoy for the Church of England to Lebanon to try to obtain the release of four hostages. Unfortunately, he was himself taken hostage and then held in solitary confinement for nearly four years. After his release in 1991, in his book *Taken on Trust*, Waite described how he was betrayed by a man who had given him his hand in trust.

Taking the risk

While, on a human level, trust seems fragile and rather easily destroyed, the Psalmist reminds us that God is 'our rock': totally reliable in all circumstances. Of course, this does not mean that we will never experience trouble. Nor does it mean that we will be 'rescued' by God from every difficulty that we face in a world that is subject to change and chance. However, we can be sure that God will stand with us in 'all the changing scenes of life'.

The Old Testament story of Shadrach, Meshach and Abednego presents a picture of complete trust in God, even in the midst of trouble. However, the story also points to what we might call the 'risk of faith'. Refusing to bow down in worship to a golden statue, the king had the three friends thrown into 'a furnace of blazing fire'. Yet, when the king looked into the furnace later, he discovered that not only were they unharmed by the flames but standing with them was another figure. The story provides a reminder that while we may experience trouble in life, we may be sure that God does not abandon us but stands with us in every situation.

We ought to note, however, that according to the story, when the friends faced the king, they did not claim with certainty that God would deliver them. Rather they said,

If our God whom we serve is able to deliver us from the furnace of blazing fire and out of your hand, O king, let him deliver us. But if not, be it known to you, O king, that we will not serve your gods.

'But if not ...' The words linger in the air before us and serve as a reminder that trusting in God in every circumstance seems risky indeed.

Plunging into God

As a child in the early 1960s, my mother (who had never learned to swim) took my sisters and me to swimming lessons. I really had no idea what the lessons would entail. However, when I saw and felt the cold water, I was not sure that I wanted to continue. Nevertheless, in the shallow water, I could still feel solid ground beneath me and I felt fairly safe. All was well until the day that the teacher took the class to the 'deep end' of the pool. She pointed to the diving board and told us to jump from there into the water and swim to the side of the pool.

I dutifully lined up with the other learners, but when it was my turn to jump into the water my legs turned to stone. I was terrified. The teacher tried to encourage me by getting into the pool and promising to catch me. I did not believe her. I did not trust her. I did not jump.

Teilhard de Chardin, a twentieth-century French Jesuit philosopher and priest, wrote of the need to discover God's presence in all the world. Claiming that God is at the 'centre' and yet 'fills the whole sphere' of the world, he argued that we may know God's presence everywhere and in every circumstance. In a memorable phrase, he said that what is needed is for us to 'plunge into God'.[40]

Sometimes the troubles that come our way – bereavement, loss, broken relationships, poor mental or physical health – leave us feeling uncertain. In those moments, perhaps we need to fling all fear to one side and, taking the risk of faith, 'plunge into God' with complete trust.

Karen E. Smith

Hymn suggestions

Be still and know that I am God; When we walk with the Lord; Through all the changing scenes of life; Lead, kindly light.

Christ the King (Sunday next before Advent)

24 November

Principal Service   **Christ: Imminent and Transcendent**

Dan. 7.9–10, 13–14; Ps. 93; Rev. 1.4b–8; **John 18.33–37**

Today we celebrate the feast of Christ the King. On this, the last Sunday of the church's year, just before we plunge into the watching and waiting of Advent, into the extraordinary mysteries of the incarnation at Christmas, into the splendours of Epiphany, we take a deep breath and celebrate Christ as king over time and eternity. We remind ourselves, before we begin the Christian story again, that Christ is sovereign Lord in all things. What does it mean for Christ to be king? And what is his kingdom like? Today's readings give us a clue.

Visions fulfilled

Daniel was troubled with visions. He saw things he struggled to interpret. He had a vision of heaven with the Ancient One seated on the throne – thousands upon thousands attending him. Daniel sees a human being – one like a Son of Man coming in the clouds of heaven, one to whom is given glory and kingship, the one whom all people serve. The kingship is eternal. Visions of the Son of Man might refer to the coming Messiah, or could be a symbol for the whole people of God or the nation of Israel.

With the writer of Revelation, we've moved forward many hundreds of years. Daniel's vision has been interpreted in the light of the experience of the first Christians. The one who comes with the clouds of heaven is the risen, ascended Christ – the faithful witness, the firstborn of the dead, the ruler of the kings of the earth. The one who is and who was and who is to come – Christ the King.

Visions: imminent and transcendent

In today's Gospel, Jesus stands before Pilate. Jesus is a solitary, self-possessed Galilean. He can wrong-foot the representative of the Roman Empire – that great earthly kingdom – just by his presence. Pilate is curious and confused: is this a king before him? Whose king and where is the kingdom? The kingdom is not of this world. It has the characteristics of heaven – namely, truth. It is all beyond Pilate, for whom truth is an alien concept.

Two pictures emerge of Christ the King. One transcendent and awesome, wrapped up in the clouds of heaven, mysterious, surrounded by people without number. The other imminent: Christ the King before civil authorities, feet firmly on the ground, a personal one-to-one encounter, which shifts the balance of power for ever.

This is the Christ into whom we are baptized, in whom we are part. Jesus who is both Lord of the universe – cosmic and eternal – and also closer to us than our very self. Christ will be with us for our entire existence, whether we recognize him or not.

This is Christ the King, unlike any earthly king we're aware of. He breaks the rules of kingship. Born in a backwater to an unknown teenage mum, he becomes a refugee. He walks among his people identifying with the little and the least. He has nowhere to lay his head. He is rejected, broken, abused and killed. This is a very different king from the one in glory. This king gives up everything – even his life – so that all those over whom he rules can have life in all its fullness, claiming wholeness and relationship with God.

Citizens of the kingdom

Christ's kingdom is unlike any earthly kingdom. The kingdom of God is for all time, and beyond time – for eternity, for every place and every person. As citizens of that kingdom, we are to hold the doors wide open so that any and all can enter.

This is our king and this is our kingdom. We are called to model kingdom living wherever God places us. It's no accident that we are the people of God in this place at this time. God has called us together here so that the message of hope can be communicated to the people around us through our prayers and words, actions and lifestyle.

Christ is king

Christ is king in all things: in Sunday worship, in private prayer, in work or retirement, in relaxation or stress, when we are awake or asleep Christ is king. In triumphs and joys, in dangers or disaster. When this church is full, when it's empty, and in centuries to come when it no longer exists Christ will still be king. Whether worshipped in choral music or modern song, with voices and organ or with worship band, Christ is king. In traditional language, in modern language, in no language, in all languages, Christ is king. At baptisms, at marriages, at funerals, Christ is king.

When all is well, when all is not, when the world seems to fall apart, Christ is king – for ever, for all eternity. This is the Christ who gave himself on the cross for all people, whether they believe it or not. This is the Christ who gives himself to each of us today in his body and blood, and in the Scriptures, so that we might remain part of his kingdom of truth. 'I am the Alpha and the Omega, says the Lord God, who is and who was and who is to come.'

Christ the beginning,
Christ the end,
Christ through all things,
Christ the King.

Catherine Williams

Hymn suggestions

Crown him with many crowns; Christ triumphant, ever reigning; Majesty; How lovely on the mountains (Our God reigns).

Christ the King (Sunday next before Advent)
24 November
Second Service   **God in the Storms of Our Lives**
Morning **Ps. 29,** 110; Evening Ps. 72 [*or* 72.1–7]; Dan. 5; **John 6.1–15**

Psalm 29 opens with a call to worship and points to the power and majesty of God. We observe God's voice calling people to turn to him and recognize his power and authority. Many years ago, I had the opportunity to climb up, with a friend, the north face of Tryfan, a mountain in Wales. As we scrambled up this mountain with hands and feet (because this was not a mountain you walked up), I could feel the fear and panic rising in my throat and chest and I wondered if I would make it to the top. It was a wet and windy day and it took unbelievable focus, grit and determination to make the five-hour climb up the mountain. It was indeed an incredibly physically, emotionally and mentally challenging experience for me. But when we got to the top of Tryfan, my goodness, as I saw the beauty around us, I was so overwhelmed by the majesty and awe of God and began to sing, 'To God be the glory'. In 11 verses of this psalm, the name of the Lord (YHWH) occurs 18 times and 'the voice of the LORD' is repeated seven times. As we read this psalm, David declares our need to worship the Lord and listen to his voice.

God's voice in our lives

David begins with a call for God to be praised in the highest realms:

> Ascribe to the LORD, O heavenly beings,
>   ascribe to the LORD glory and strength.
> Ascribe to the LORD the glory of his name;
>   worship the LORD in holy splendour.

In our relationship with God, as we worship the beauty and majesty of his holiness, I wonder how we experience the voice of God in our lives. Many Christians will testify to experiencing God's voice in different ways: through Scripture, in prayer (a word, an image, an insight), wisdom from a trusted friend, an audible voice, in a dream. The main takeaway point is that God is constantly wanting to communicate with us. And we are reminded time and again that there is power in God's voice. In the wilderness places of our lives, the voice of the Lord can be heard. There is no place on earth or on the sea where we can escape the voice of the Lord. When the voice of the Lord is heard, what is our response? Is it 'Glory! Glory to God in the highest', for the power and pre-eminence of God? Because God has the last word. There is no one more powerful than him; his majesty and holiness are unmatched. There is absolutely none like him. When God speaks, the waters tremble and we should listen. What might God be saying to you today in the storms of your life?

Clinging to God's words

When we spend time in Scripture, are we expectant to receive a word of encouragement, challenge or promise from God?

Jesus came to announce the kingdom of God, the time when God would establish his direct rule over his people and all creation. In John 6, in trying to give the crowds an understanding of what this would be like, Jesus taught in parables – and he likened the kingdom of heaven to a banquet and a wedding feast. On that mountainside in Galilee, he gave 5,000 people one meal when they needed it. But there is so much more on offer. Jesus says, 'Whoever comes to me will never be hungry' (John 6.35).

As followers of Jesus, we are invited to participate in a new heavenly kingdom. Psalm 72 offers a prayer for a new king. While this psalm is intended for Solomon, it prophesies the fulfilment of a greater kingdom through King Jesus.

In the waiting for this new heavenly kingdom, in the midst of the storms of our lives, God brings his compassion, love and peace. When our days feel bleak, we are encouraged to speak to God who is in control of all things. He is here today to speak peace to our souls. All we need to do is to cling to him, the author and perfecter of our lives.

Catherine Okoronkwo

Hymn suggestions

To God be the glory; Praise to the Lord, the Almighty; How great thou art; His eye is on the sparrow.

Sermons for Saints' Days
and Special Occasions

St Stephen, Deacon, First Martyr   26 December
The Face of an Angel
2 Chron. 24.20–22, *or* Acts 7.51–end; Ps. 119.161–168;
Acts 7.51–end (*if the Acts reading is used instead of the Old Testament reading, the New Testament reading is* Gal. 2.16b–20); Matt. 10.17–22

Watching for angels

We've been travelling through Advent, watching and waiting for the coming of God. At Midnight Mass, with the shepherds, we were surprised by the angels and went in heart and mind to Bethlehem to wonder at the love of God. Yesterday we explored the meaning of the Word made flesh. Now, the day after Christmas Day, we see a man whose 'face was like the face of an angel' (Acts 6.15) killed, and we mourn with his friends as they take away his dead body.

When the Scriptures speak of angels, they act as alerts signalling that God is about to do something amazing. Yet, more often than not, we think of angels as fluffy white beings who bring 'good news of great joy'. Well, they do. But angels can also disturb and unsettle.

Only a few weeks ago, we heard of Zechariah being 'troubled' by the angel announcing the birth of his son John; the shepherds 'struck with great fear'; an angel persuaded Joseph not to leave Mary, and even Mary herself needed to be assured by Gabriel, 'Do not be afraid'.

These angels correct, educate, reveal; they make people change their plans and offer a life more closely united with God.

Speaking with passion

In Acts 6 we see Stephen, 'a man full of faith and of the Holy Spirit' (Acts 6.5), being chosen as one of the seven who would give pastoral care to those in need. So effective was his ministry that he soon came to the attention of the religious authorities. He was put on trial and, as he begins his long defence, those assembled noted that his face shone like an angel. Stephen spoke with passion, calling people to change their ways: to let go and let God. His words, like the words of angels, caused unrest rather than joy. His face, like the face of an angel, amazed those gathered. But those listening to Stephen did not (at that moment) change their minds and see that God was doing something new. Instead, when they saw Stephen's face and heard his words, 'they were infuriated' and proceeded to make him the first martyr.

The church gives us the feast of St Stephen immediately after Christmas to make something clear. Yesterday, we learned the son of God became human. Today we see the purpose – so humanity may become sons and daughters of God. Stephen's preaching and martyrdom show us what it might look like to reflect the life and light of Christ in our lives.

At the beginning of Christ's life, his mother laid him on the wood of the manger; at the end of his life, she watched as he suffered on the wood of the cross.

On the cross, Jesus prays for his enemies: 'Father, forgive them.' Stephen, too, prays for his killers: 'Lord, do not hold this sin against them.' Jesus cried to his Father, 'Into your hands, Lord, I commend my spirit.' Stephen cried to Christ, 'Lord Jesus, receive my spirit.'

As Stephen preached about the love of God in Jesus, he did not hide his face in shame. So, the Lord made his face shine with light. Stephen did not produce this light; rather, it was given to him by the one who is the light.

Shining as a light in the world

Even today, many shine the light of the gospel into the bleak places of the world. It was on St Stephen's Day in 2021 that the death of Desmond Tutu, former Archbishop of South Africa, was announced. As has been said often, if Nelson Mandela was the father of that nation, then Desmond was its soul. A recipient of the Nobel Peace Prize, Desmond's face shone in the struggle for justice as, without fear, he spoke truth to power:

I want the Government to know now and always that I do not fear them. They are trying to defend the utterly indefensible, and they will fail. They will fail because they are ranging themselves on the side of evil and injustice against the Church of God. Like others who have done that in the past – the Neros, the Hitlers, the Idi Amis of the world – they will end up as the flotsam and jetsam of History.[41]

Like so many before him, Desmond walked the way of St Stephen who fearlessly followed his Lord and Master. Perhaps you and I may never be called to follow in such an extreme way, but taking up the cross, the way of life and light that the darkness could not overcome, is not an optional extra for a Christian and comes in many different forms.

At this Christmastide, we have once again received this light. We're called to shine as lights in the world to the glory of God the Father, wherever that may lead: to the crib in adoration, to the cross in service.

Paul Williams

Hymn suggestions

Holy Stephen, Christ's dear martyr; Fight the good fight; God of the movements and martyrs; It came upon a midnight clear.

St John, Apostle and Evangelist   27 December
We?
Ex. 33.7–11a; Ps. 117; **1 John 1**; John 21.19b–end

We have seen. We have heard. We have touched.

Why does this letter start with 'we'? We expect a letter to arrive from one person. Even in the Bible, Paul sends his personal greetings to the church he is writing to, and then starts to give his ideas. But this letter starts with 'we' – there seems to be no explanation, no context. 'We declare to you … what we have heard, what we have seen … what we have touched …'

And we have no idea to whom the letter is addressed – there's no named church or group of people, just 'you'. If we are the people who are reading this letter today, then the 'you' turns out to be 'us'. Maybe that's the point!

This is a letter from those who have experienced something of the presence of Christ, the love of Christ, written in order to invite the reader into that love. And to listen deeply to the words of this letter, to receive the life it represents, can be transformative. The 'we' of this letter comes into being when we read the letter. It's an invitation to an ever-increasing circle of love, where 'you' always becomes 'we'.

The writer of this letter has a vision of the loving community of God. There is no isolation, no separation. In love, our life is lived in relationship, and there we find ourselves. *We have seen. We have heard. We have touched the word of life.* And that's the place we start the journey of faith – not believing things in our heads but making contact, seeing, entering a relationship which connects us to each other in the love of God.

Remembering John

This understanding, which lies at the heart of the Christian faith, is for ever linked to the name John.

When I was at school, I learned about the four basic flavours, about the areas of the tongue that pick up salt, bitter, sweet and sour. Much later I started to hear about umami, a taste that was different from all the rest. It had a hit of its own.

And there are some people – no longer living – who leave a memory of their character. Their personalities brought something out of the ordinary, distinctive, irreplaceable. All our lives are richer because of who they were. Could this be one of the reasons we recognize some people as saints?

John is remembered as the apostle of love. As an old man – according to legend – he always gave the same answer to every pastoral question: 'Love one another.' For him, all his life-experience had brought him to understand one thing – God is love.

We don't know for certain whether the disciple whom Jesus loved who appears in the gospel story was in fact John the apostle. We are not sure whether John the apostle actually wrote any of the books attributed to him. But when we read the writings that bear his name, it becomes clear that *we* are the disciples whom Jesus loves. It is clear that we, together, in our relationships, have the possibility of glory. We are able to show the love of God in this world. All this comes to us in the name of John.

Maybe this is the charism that he passed on to us, and which we pass on to the future – the experience, the shape of a single life called John, a facet of the diamond of God's light, a single colour of the rainbow that is Christ.

Life together

Reading the words that have flowed from John's experience, we encounter a sanctity, a holiness, an emphasis of life. This emphasis might be just what we need in our twenty-first-century world. We fall out with each other so easily. We exclude and belittle others. Our love, even after so many centuries of Christianity, too often still fails to express the glorious self-giving of God. And the all-too-necessary message of John reaches us afresh.

Maybe the medium is also the message. The truth reaches us not through theology or abstract ideas but in the vivid and personal touch of a single person who has lived in touch with Christ, the living word of God.

We declare to you. We have seen. We have heard. We have touched.

This memory of John is always there. He calls us back to the simple truth of encounter with God. John leads us gently back into the real world, the world of our experience and our senses. John helps us to recognize that this is precisely the place where the life of God appears, where the Word becomes flesh and lives among us. John helps us to look around at each other, with all our failings, and recognize, in the wonder of fellowship with other human beings, the glory of God.

Andrew Rudd

Hymn suggestions

Ubi caritas (Taizé); Beloved, let us love; Love came down at Christmas; Come, thou Redeemer.

The Holy Innocents   28 December
Principal Service   **Blood-Red Days**
Jer. 31.15–17; Ps. 124; 1 Cor. 1.26–29; **Matt. 2.13–18**

The days after Christmas

The church's calendar of seasons and special days ensures a balanced approach to Christian belief. It offers a meaningful way of ordering time, as we revisit aspects of God's creating and redeeming work year after year. The calendar in the days after Christmas illustrates this well.

The feast of Stephen is on 26 December. Stephen was among the first to be ordained deacon but was also the first Christian martyr, losing his life because of his commitment to Christ. His day enables us both to give thanks for his life and witness and to remember in prayer those of our generation who are persecuted for their faith.

The following day celebrates John the Evangelist, traditionally remembered as 'the beloved disciple' and associated with the Fourth Gospel and John's three letters. This is an opportunity to thank God and pray for Christian thinkers and teachers, especially those who deepen our understanding of Jesus as the 'Word made flesh'.

And then on 28 December is the feast of the Holy Innocents, when we recall Herod's massacre of the young male children in and around Bethlehem. Herod had flown into a rage on discovering that the magi had deceived him, going on their way without returning to him in Jerusalem. As we remember the shedding of those children's innocent blood, we intercede for the children of today's world who are victims of evil and cruelty.

But why so soon? Why immediately on two days after Christmas are we plunged into bloodshed? Why not schedule these days at another time of year, rather than destroy our festive mood? Aren't these supposed to be 12 days of celebration after Christmas? But these days belong at this point in the calendar for a reason both simple and profound: the 'blood-red' days of Stephen and the Innocents fall after Christmas lest we forget what the incarnation is about.

Incarnation

God's son came to earth to inhabit our human condition. He came to share fully in a world where persecution, murder and infanticide are (sadly) part of that world. He came to be present in the darkness and the horror surrounding us. As the great Christmas Gospel puts it, he came to shine light into that darkness (John 1.5): not to wave a magic wand to chase it away but to shine God's light into the midst of it and bring God's love to a fallen world. The incarnation means that God came to share in the life of the world *as it is*.

The world we inhabit is not very different from that of Herod. The abuse of children – infanticide even – and the maltreatment of the vulnerable are alarmingly present in a world that has lost its way. The ongoing conflicts throughout the world reveal the ever-present problems of hatred, violence and intolerance. Innocents suffer and die, and evil does its work.

It's to this 'real world' that God sends the Son to save us. But God sends him not as a strong, confident king but as a child, 'little, weak and helpless', fully human and fully dependent on the goodness and care of fragile, fallible human beings. We see how fragile God's gift is when we read of Jesus' narrow escape from Herod, his flight into Egypt and his life there as a refugee.

God with us

So how might the Gospel of the Innocents help *us* as we try and make sense of our faith within a world where things continue to go badly wrong? It helps us because it affirms the vital truth that, whatever the situation, God is in some sense already part of it; that through God's identification with the poor, the suffering, and the helpless, God is there *in* the poverty, the suffering and the helplessness.

And as God is in all these situations, God is also Immanuel: God with us. Our lot might not be as horrific as that of some, but we all struggle with something or other. We might feel that that struggle is known only to us and is not something we feel able to share. But God, through the birth of Jesus, shares our life and does so to the fullest possible extent. Recalling the death of the Innocents helps us grasp that.

But today also reminds us that the shadow of the cross lies over the crib. Jesus comes not only to share our life but shares it to change it. The cross speaks of transformation, forgiveness and the defeat of evil; it points the way to God's heart of love. And in so doing points too beyond itself towards the empty tomb of Easter.

The church's calendar makes sure we don't forget the big picture of God's work of incarnation and redemption. Year after year we

are reminded, and year after year, as we visit the truths again –
always at a different place in our lives from where we were last
year – God works in us and continues to shape us into the people
God made us to be.

Peter Moger

Hymn suggestions

*Unto us a boy is born; Lully, lulla, thou little tiny child; In the night,
the sound of crying; God of freedom, God of justice.*

Naming and Circumcision of Jesus   1 January
Name 'Alongside' All Names
Num. 6.22–end; Ps. 8; Gal 4.4–7; **Luke 2.15–21**

Parish priests have a sure way to spot shifting fashions in baby
names: baptism. In the days when I took weekly baptisms, I witnessed the rise and fall from fashion of Jacob (or, more often, Jake)
and Chardonnay, as well as the slow recovery from 'uncoolness' of
names like Elsie, Edith and Flo.

Clearly, names matter. If baptism is, of course, so much more
than a naming ceremony, it is, in the popular mind, that too. As
I've taken baptisms, I've witnessed how – at a social and human
level – the service can offer a chance for parents to celebrate the
safe arrival of a child and 'name' them in public. The names parents
choose for their children are often discussed and worried over for
weeks and sometimes months before a baby is born. The parent
or parents-to-be can find themselves asking big questions: is the
proposed name too serious or too frivolous? Will this name make
our child stand out just enough or stand out too much? In some
cultures, a name signifies deep and powerful cultural and family
meanings. In others, name choices represent a statement about
family. In my own family, I have nephews with names chosen in
honour of the great-grandparents they never knew – or even rejec-
tions of convention. I still remember how bewildered and excited I
felt when I discovered, as a child, that David and Angie Bowie had
called their son Zowie (which he later changed to Duncan!)

A usual and unusual naming

When Joseph and Mary bring Jesus to the Temple for circumcision, they follow the expectations of the law. Their action signifies the moment that Jesus, the newborn, enters the Jewish community of faith. In circumcision, he is seen, recognized and named in the covenant community of prayer, devotion and ritual.

One of the many extraordinary things about today's Gospel passage, however, is its reminder of the powerful and wonderful circumstances of Jesus' naming. Most of us have names which are chosen carefully by our birth parents. The contemporary convention in Jesus' day would likely have meant that he would be named for his father. However, we are told by Luke that 'he was called Jesus, the name given by the angel before he was conceived in the womb'.

Like John the Baptist (whom the people around Elizabeth and Zechariah expected to be named after his father), Jesus' name was given at the annunciation of his birth. Luke reminds us that Jesus' name had not been given by Joseph, but by the Angel of the Lord, that is, by the very representative and messenger of God himself. The name singles Jesus out: it declares the child's future role as the saviour of all God's people. The conferring of the name is itself an act of fulfilment.

Name above all names?

What is striking, however, are the dynamics between this divine inheritance – this clear signal that Jesus is God's saviour – and how it is held in tension with the humble requirements of a faith community which expects Mary and Joseph to bring Jesus to the Temple. For the holy family has received shepherds inspired by angels into hope and worship; Mary has treasured their words and carries with her the extraordinary knowledge that her child is the Son of God. She and Joseph have been witnesses to wonders. And yet ... they do all that is required of them as ordinary, humble members of the covenant community: they bring Jesus to the Temple for all that is right and proper so that he can take his place in the community.

And my name?

If we too are called into the likeness of Christ, what can we learn from this extraordinary blend of divine wonder and everyday humility? Well, clearly, none of us is called to be the saviour of the world. However, I think we are called to rejoice in the knowledge that we are known by God from before our birth. No human name can trump that.

Furthermore, Psalm 8 asks, 'What are human beings that you are mindful of them, mortals that you care for them?' Yet God is mindful, and he shows his care in sending Jesus who is both Son of God and one of us. Mary and Joseph know this implicitly. They do not treat Jesus, the human who is also fully God, as above the requirements of the law. The Son of God saves the world from within its fabric of obligations. He comes as a servant of all. Indeed, I am reminded of those remarkable words of St Paul in his Letter to the Philippians 2.6–8:

> though he was in the form of God,
> [he] did not regard equality with God
> as something to be exploited,
> but emptied himself,
> taking the form of a slave,
> being born in human likeness.
> And being found in human form,
> he humbled himself
> and became obedient to the point of death –
> even death on a cross.

This is the baby, the child, the adult … the God … whom we are called to follow and become ever more like.

Rachel Mann

Hymn suggestions

Name above all names (Neil Bennetts); While shepherds watched their flocks; Infant holy, infant lowly; Hail to the Lord's anointed.

Epiphany 6 January
Overwhelming Joy and Holy Awe
Isa. 60.1–6; Ps. 72 [1–9] 10–15; Eph. 3.1–12; **Matt. 2.1–12**

I have a friend who enjoys gazing at the stars at night. She told me that when her children were growing up, she and her husband would often take them outside and lie on a blanket and look up into the great canopy of space and point out various stars and constellations. Of course, looking at the stars is not new; people from very early civilizations observed the night sky.

In recent years, with the aid of powerful telescopes, astronomers have been able to draw our attention to rare cosmic events. A few years ago, a 'great conjunction' occurred which offered a chance to see two planets of the solar system, Jupiter and Saturn, come closer together. Apparently, it does not happen often – the next occurrence is predicted to be in 2040! Commenting on the conjunction of planets, a seventeenth-century German astronomer, Johannes Kepler, suggested that perhaps this is what happened when, according to the story in Matthew's Gospel, the magi saw the bright Christmas star and followed it until they found the Christ-child.

The revelation of love

Was it Jupiter and Saturn in conjunction or a comet or just a very bright star that first Christmas? I suppose it doesn't really matter since the Gospel writer is not interested in astronomy or astrology. The point of this story is not stargazing or telling the future, but the realization that God's love, demonstrated in the gift of Jesus Christ, is not just for a chosen few but for all humanity. Sometimes this is difficult for people to believe – especially in a world that seems so divided.

In the small town where I grew up, the railway line served as a kind of dividing line and it was not uncommon to sometimes hear someone described as coming from 'across the tracks'. I suppose it happens in every town; people are often separated by gender, orientation, background, social status or skin colour. Of course, none of these things matter to God. No matter who we are or what we have done or failed to do, God's love in Jesus Christ is for us all. This is what we celebrate at Epiphany: the revelation of God's love for all people, beyond all barriers we might impose.

A response of joy and awe

Often when we think about the visit of the magi, we make much of their gifts: gold for Jesus' royalty, frankincense for his priestly duties, and myrrh for his sacrificial death. Yet, I wonder if the real challenge of the story is to be discovered as we reflect on the picture of the magi who, as the Gospel writer puts it, were 'overwhelmed with joy' when they saw that the star had stopped and then, on entering the house and seeing the child with Mary his mother, 'they knelt down and paid him homage'.

Just for a moment ponder the scene: prosperous, wealthy, well-to-do people kneeling down and offering gifts to a child whom many would have considered 'baseborn'. A child from 'across the tracks', who was born in humble circumstances and with no place to call home. Yet, when the rich eastern visitors saw the child, they dropped to their knees in awe and wonder and worshipped the Christ-child. It was the only response they could make when confronted with the reality of God's immense love.

Have you had an experience of God that brought such joy? Can you imagine an experience of such awe before God? Twentieth-century Christian spiritual writer Evelyn Underhill claimed that the Christian church was in danger of 'drifting towards a religion which consciously or unconsciously keeps its eye on humanity rather than on Deity – which lays all the stress on service, and hardly any of the stress on awe'.[42] She may have been right. If so, I wonder if we can learn something from the example of the magi about attentiveness to the light of God's love and their sense of wonder in the presence of the Saviour.

Recalling the experience

The story of the magi ends as they make their way home. While the Gospel writer says no more about them, I have always wished that we knew what they said to one another on the way home. Did they laugh over fooling King Herod on leaving by a different route? Did they marvel again over the brightness of the star that had led them to the Christ-child? I imagine them speaking to one another in hushed whispers as they recalled their experience of overwhelming joy and awe in the presence of Jesus. 'Remember how we knelt down before him.' 'It was all we could do.' 'He was a child and yet a king!'

And it is to him, who is King of kings and Lord of lords, that we too bow down in worship and offer our thanks and praise.

Karen E. Smith

Hymn suggestions

The first Nowell; As with gladness; Hail to the Lord's anointed; Let all mortal flesh keep silence.

The Week of Prayer for Christian Unity
18–25 January
Clothed with Love
Readings for the Unity of the Church:
Jer. 33.6–9a; Ezek. 36.23–28; Zeph. 3.16–end; Ps. 100, 122, 133; Eph. 4.1–6; **Col 3.9–17**; 1 John 4.9–15; **Matt 18.19–22**; John 11.45–52; John 17.11b–23

In her book *Caring for Words in a Culture of Lies*, Marilyn McEntyre notes that many Old English words have fallen into disuse and, as a result, there is a danger that we will lose the original meaning of the word, as well as the experience that goes with it.[43] She mentions words such as kinsman, mirth, provident, courtship and felicity. However, even a word which we may still use may not mean what it once meant. Think, for instance, of the word charity. Today, we often refer to charity in terms of welfare relief for others or supporting agencies that provide help. We go to charity shops and put things in charity bags. Yet, charity has a deeper, richer meaning. It is an Old English translation of the Latin word *caritas* – love.

Love is generous

Genuine love, of course, may be expressed in a charitable gift, but it is not just giving away what we no longer want or need. Rather, *caritas* – love – is generous, quick to forgive and able to move beyond what may seem to be insurmountable boundaries. When Peter asked Jesus how many times he should forgive someone who had wronged him, it appears that he was suggesting that forgiving someone seven times would be very generous indeed. Surely, no one could imagine going beyond that limit! Yet, Jesus responded, 'Not seven times, but, I tell you, seventy-seven times'. In other words, there must be no limit, no boundary, to love. Reflecting on the life and ministry of Jesus, we discover that love is self-giving and not self-serving. Love will always lead us to care more for others than for ourselves.

Love breaks down barriers

Loving others as God has loved us in Jesus Christ is not a simple or straightforward experience. While Christian faith teaches that in love and forgiveness God longs to gather people together, we are often quick to judge or to place restrictions on our loving. Even in the wider church and at times in our own parish life, division and difference may lead us to open confrontation with others. Sometimes, instead of being tolerant and accepting of different views, we simply avoid or keep our distance from those with whom we disagree.

Writing to his brothers and sisters in Christ in Colossae, who were arguing over certain matters of doctrine and practice, the apostle Paul reminded them that in Christ there is no division: 'There is no longer Greek and Jew, circumcised and uncircumcised, barbarian, Scythian, slave and free; but Christ is all and in all!' Then, using vivid and wonderful imagery, he explained to them how they were to strive to overcome their divisions. He urged them to 'clothe' themselves with 'compassion, kindness, humility, meekness, and patience', and 'Above all,' he wrote, 'clothe yourselves with love.'

Love binds us together

It is noteworthy that the apostle Paul did not tell them to ignore those with whom they differed, nor to reach an agreement on all their doctrinal differences. Rather, he urged them to be clothed with *caritas*, which 'binds everything together in perfect harmony'.

Coretta Scott King, the wife of Martin Luther King Jr, wrote that when Dr King heard that he had won the Nobel Peace Prize in 1964 he was in the hospital in Atlanta having tests and recuperating after a busy schedule. While he was there, Dr King was visited by Paul John Hallinan, a Roman Catholic Archbishop. After Archbishop Hallinan offered his congratulations, he asked King if he could bestow a blessing on him. Having done so, to King's surprise, the Archbishop then knelt by the bedside and asked King to offer a blessing on him. Later, King said 'how humbled he felt and how beautiful it was that a Roman Catholic Archbishop would receive the blessing of a Baptist preacher named Martin Luther'.[44]

For a moment, just ponder the scene: two people of different colour, background, heritage and tradition perfectly united in the love of God. Of course, it can happen anywhere if we are clothed with *caritas*.

Karen E. Smith

Hymn suggestions

Come down, O love divine; A new commandment I give unto you; Brother, sister, let me serve you; Ubi caritas (Taizé)

Conversion of St Paul 25 January
Principal Service **A New Step in Discipleship**
Jer. 1.4–10, *or* Acts 9.1–22; Ps. 67; **Acts 9.1–22** (*if the Acts reading is used instead of the Old Testament reading, the New Testament reading is* Gal. 1.11–16a); Matt. 19.27–end

Who do you look up to in Scripture? I have a little list – and I am ashamed to say, Paul isn't on it! Maybe because I prefer my heroes to have a few more chinks, things that make them relatable, like Peter's bumbling-ness or Thomas' need for proof.

A man of faith

Paul has a pretty extraordinary story. It differs from the other apostles, who were called to follow Jesus as he walked the earth. Paul is different. He is educated, quite certain of his beliefs, immersed in faith and Scripture. He understands it. He knows there is only one God and to him the claims of Christians are blasphemous. He knows that Scripture curses those who are crucified. He knows you cannot make images of God – so how could God possibly appear as a human being? Paul's faith is vibrant and passionate. He cares about his country, his people and his God. He will do anything to protect them. What Christians say is dangerous, politically and religiously. So Paul steps up and becomes part of those who persecute Christians. Not out of viciousness but out of faith.

It would be easy to caricature Paul as a ruthless, rule-bound bigot, but that would be inaccurate. Paul is a man who serves God genuinely and to the best of his ability, within the culture and traditions that have been handed down to him.

A man seeking after God

It is easy to wonder, how could he get it so wrong? And see his conversion as a blinding light, God summarily intervening in the life of someone who does not really know God. Often, the conversion of

Paul is presented like this (though the word 'conversion' isn't used in the story), and Paul used as an archetype of what must happen when people come to Christ.

However ... Paul is no heathen. He already has a relationship with God. His so-called conversion is not from nothing to faith; it is from incomplete faith to something fuller, something that expands his concept of God beyond his wildest thoughts. Paul was a keen follower; he dedicated his life to God's service. God's intervention here is not uninvited. It is a response to Paul's heart's desire.

Unexpected revelations

It is dramatic, of course. But then it had to be. For Paul to accept that this Jesus is indeed one with the God of his ancestors, almost nothing but direct, dramatic revelation would do. When Paul thought he needed to defend God, God instead reveals Godself, in the style of the call of Old Testament prophets: blinding light, booming voice, overwhelming glory. Paul knows the Scriptures. He knows this is what happens when God appears. I wonder what he expected: God to commend him for his zeal? Be called as a prophet?

He has a bit of a shock. God does none of those things, but instead says, 'Why do you persecute me?' (Notice the personal note here – harming Jesus' disciples is harming Jesus himself.) Paul is confused. He thought he knew what the light meant. Now he is not so sure, and has to ask. The answer is earth-shattering: I am Jesus.

There is no condemnation, no judgement, no recriminations. A simple statement of fact. Whatever Saul thought he understood about God, whatever intellectual reasoning had led him to reject Jesus, cannot hold against the simple reality that this is God, and God has identified himself as Jesus. It is a pivotal moment for Paul, and for the early church. Paul obeys God immediately. There is no resistance, no arguing. He is not a reluctant convert. He is taking a new, albeit huge, step in his journey of discipleship.

Living the story

And so ... Paul is not a model of conversion so much as a model of discipleship. A model of openness to God, and willingness to have his entire thought system challenged and turned upside down. A model of quite how misguided we can all become, yet of God's faithfulness in helping us find our way. Paul is also a model of integration between head and heart, between theology and experience.

He shows us something of how we move on in our discipleship. His ability to respond to God's revelation stems from both his deep knowledge of Scripture and his willingness to let new experiences challenge his interpretation. His many letters display this dynamic interaction between the two. Paul is incessantly formulating thoughts and responses to experience, and interpreting experience in the light of solid knowledge of Scripture. Both are held in balance and allowed in dialogue. Paul remains grounded in Scripture, but with the humility of one who knows what it is to encounter grace in response to your most profound mistakes. The question is, for all of us, whether we are ready for such open, vulnerable and radical discipleship. Are there parts of our faith that need to be challenged, refined, rethought? And are we steeped enough in Scripture and open enough to God to do this faithfully? This is what we need to live the story – together with knowing that, if we go wrong, God can meet us with truth, grace and an offer of new life.

Isabelle Hamley

Hymn suggestions

Amazing grace; What wondrous love is this; O love that will not let me go; I stand amazed in the presence.

Presentation of Christ in the Temple (Candlemas)
2 February
Light and Darkness
Mal. 3.1–5; Ps. 24.[1–6] 7–end; Heb. 2.14–end; **Luke 2.22–40**

A liminal period is an in-between time or state, a grey area, a space of uncertainty. Candlemas is a liminal period in the church's year, the midpoint between the light of Christmas and the sombre period of Lent. The candles we will light today are a symbol of the light that Jesus Christ brings into the world, the light that is for all peoples, a light to lighten the Gentiles.

Light revealed

Isaiah foretells that the people walking in darkness have seen a glorious light, a light that is yet to come.

In Israel, Simeon is waiting in a liminal period of Israel's history, in an intertestamental period. He is waiting for light. His people are waiting for a Messiah, a saviour. Simeon, now very elderly and approaching the end of his earthly ministry, recognizes that this long-expected light has come in the baby Jesus. He and his people live in the shadow of great darkness, citizens of a holy land, occupied by Romans, ruled by Herod's court, preached at by powerful Pharisees – exploited on all sides. Great darkness is the context for Jesus' birth.

We too are called to live in hope as Christians, as followers of Jesus Christ, hope that there will be a new heaven and a new earth, that evil and darkness have been overcome through the birth, death and resurrection of Jesus.

Seeing the light

When Mary and Joseph arrive in the Temple with Jesus, a baby of 40 days, for the feast of purification, the elderly priest Simeon acknowledges Jesus to be the Christ, the Messiah, the saviour of the world. This is the moment Simeon has been waiting for, and he bursts into joyful song in the words recorded in Luke 2 and known to us as the Nunc Dimittis, the canticle sung at the monastic office of Compline, in Cranmer's Evensong in the Book of Common Prayer. The traditional words are hauntingly beautiful: 'Lord, now lettest thou thy servant depart in peace: according to thy word.'

Simeon announces Jesus as the light of the world, as well as the glory of his own people. The liminal period is ended and we have crossed the threshold. The hope for the future has arrived. This too is our future; this is the hope we live in. Hope brought through the resurrected Christ, who has conquered death, darkness and evil.

Then another elderly, wise and holy person enters the scene, Anna the prophet. She too bursts into praise. She gives thanks to God; this child will bring about the redemption of Jerusalem. Simeon blesses the baby Jesus, the saviour of the world. Jesus will be a light to the Gentiles, the redeemer of all people, and the glory of God's people Israel. Barriers will be broken down, hate will be extinguished and there will be a new world order, where all are welcome to share in the joy and joyfulness of Christ.

Living in light

We live in a liminal world, a world of uncertainty, a world where sometimes it seems that darkness prevails over light. Where suffering is prevalent still, where those who follow Christ are persecuted.

On this feast of Candlemas, we recall how Jesus was presented to God in the Temple. We too today are called to come before God in worship – to put the past and our failings behind us, and to focus on the living God who loves us and who calls us to a life of witness. We begin to look ahead to the suffering of Holy Week, to enter the darkness and engage in self-reflection, in the knowledge that on the cross all evil has been defeated.

In our faith, we live in the light of hope, just as the candles we hold today display a sense of light in an often all-too-dark world. God calls us to share in the light of Christ – to bring help and comfort to others by that message of hope and light, and to re-awaken our dedication to God in our daily lives, to be disciples committed in love and service to and for Jesus Christ. Let us also look ahead to Easter hope with expectancy. The way ahead may be uncertain and even filled with difficulties and challenges for many, but with Christ as our guide, we may be confident of his presence with us and his strength to sustain us, as we follow in his way even to the cross and beyond to newness of life.

Arani Sen

Hymn suggestions

Lead us, heavenly Father, lead us; Light of the world; Make way, make way for Christ the king. Like a candle flame.

St Joseph of Nazareth 19 March
Centre Stage
2 Sam. 7.4–16; Ps. 89.26–36; Rom. 4.13–18; **Matt. 1.18–end**

What goes before

One of the problems of reading passages from Scripture out of books rather than the Bible itself is that we lose the context. I have been encouraged in the past, especially when preaching, to look at what comes before and after the chosen passage, and today's

Gospel reading is a case in point. The passage that precedes it is the first part of Matthew's Gospel and is a genealogy. It is a passage that it is rarely read in church (in the daily eucharistic lectionary it crops up only once a year in the third week of Advent, much to the relief I imagine of many clergy). However, that is rather sad, because this passage sets the theme of the whole Gospel. I say that because it has some rather surprising people in it!

Who do you think you are?

There is a lot of interest these days in family trees and in tracing back our ancestry. In the genealogy that Matthew presents to us, he gives us clues as to the audience for whom he has written this Gospel. He includes names that we might want to be airbrushed out of our own family story, like Jacob the younger son, who stole his elder brother's birthright, and Rahab, a prostitute. This is no mistake on Matthew's part: from the very beginning of his Gospel, he is making the point that the good news of Jesus is for all people, no matter their background, notoriety or obscurity. God's grace and love are for all.

Theatre

With the Gospel introduced in this way, we come to the opening scene, with two principal actors centre stage: Mary and Joseph. Anyone who has done any acting will know that when you first look at any script, you might first check how many scenes that you are in, and if you're going to die. Having entered this story, we are not going to see a lot of Joseph, and before long he will disappear, we know not where. But what we do know is, at this, the beginning of the story, his role is crucial. His betrothed is with child and he is not the father. This is dangerous news in any society, and has the potential for shame. But Joseph, like his Old Testament namesake, is a dreamer, and he trusts that God speaks to him through dreams.

Really?

Using our imagination to get deeper into Scripture can be really helpful for obtaining a richer sense of what God is saying through it. My imagination goes a bit wild when I imagine this scene and Joseph trying to explain this situation to his family and friends. What on earth would he have said? He cannot really win, can he?

If he says it is his child, he's damned, and if he tries to explain his dream ... well really! We are very used to this story, but how would it have played out at home for Joseph? Would people have really believed him? Or was he quite literally just a dreamer? Maybe my focus is in the wrong place, for Matthew is keen to point out that Joseph is both honourable and faithful – to Mary, but also to God. He is honest and open to a God who asks surprising things of us at times, things which can lead to isolation and even disgrace and shame.

Credits

I have many eccentricities, and one of them is to stay watching a film until the end of the credits when I'm at the cinema. Maybe it's because I used to be involved in theatre lighting at school, but I am very aware that any production, be it a film, a television show, a musical or a recording, involves far more than those who are simply centre stage. A conductor cannot conduct without an orchestra, and a theatre production takes the whole team, front and back of house, for the play to happen. Joseph, whom we celebrate today, is in the spotlight of the Gospels for a brief time. We know so little about him. But it is as if Matthew gives us the meaning of each character in his Gospel through his opening passage to his book – the genealogy. What he seems to say in that is that no matter how famous, flawed or obscure a person is, they are part of the whole through which God's grace flows. Each of us is a part of the narrative, even if we find that very hard to see. From Pilate to Judas, to Joseph and Mary, each is essential in this, God's story of redemption. As such, we give thanks for Joseph today, for in the little that we know of him, God reveals that all are significant to God and all have a part to play in the bringing to birth of his son in our lives.

Jonathan Lawson

Hymn suggestions

O God, you search me and you know me; I, the Lord of sea and sky; Take my life, and let it be; There's a wideness in God's mercy.

Annunciation of Our Lord to the Blessed Virgin

Mary   8 April (transferred from 25 March)

Respite from Being a Hard-Working Icon

Isa. 7.10–14; Ps. 40.5–11; Heb. 10.4–10; **Luke 1.26–38**

Getting caught up in specifics

So here we are, post-Easter, reading a story that usually lives and breathes in December surrounded by carols, trees, decorations, presents and lots of food. Those very words, 'In the sixth month the angel Gabriel was sent by God to a town in Galilee called Nazareth', are enough to strike terror into anyone who has led or participated in a nativity play. I wonder if you were right back in Christmas as you heard the story, or if you heard it in the present moment, in spring, lodged between Easter and the ascension, on a pretty otherwise non-descript day? I wonder as well where Mary is in your mind's eye as you hear the story of Gabriel appearing to her. For me, despite years of having an icon of the annunciation on my desk where Mary is pictured on a throne, she is always in the kitchen doing the washing-up. For one of my friends, she is always walking through fields singing to herself.

This instinctive, imaginative filling-in of the details in stories that are read to us are worth paying attention to. Especially when we are given a story to be read out of its more familiar context. Particularly, when the story in hand, mouth and ear is one which has soaked up a multitude of understandings, meanings, uses and agendas over time. Mary, the peasant girl who stands doing the washing-up, and the free spirit who wanders singing through the fields, and the disciple who says yes to God, and the Blessed Virgin, and the Queen of Heaven, and the ponderer whom angels visit and chat with, and the singer and the revolutionary who plots the downfall of the powers with her female relatives. Mary has become an enormously busy character, a hard-working icon for life not just for Christmas. I wonder what it is about Mary that you prioritize from that list, and why you might do so.

The icon who takes her time

There are, of course, no right answers and there is no correct preference. All are valid things to explore to enable our faith to grow and our ability to wonder at the work of God to increase. However, being able to release Mary from the insistent pull forward of both the birth of her baby and the high feast of Christmas Day, as we can do today, does enable us to step back from specifics and see Mary from a wide and broad perspective.

From this perspective, I see a woman who takes her time because she knows that the work of God can take time. She knows that pregnancy takes nine months, not the four or so weeks we collapse it into during Advent and December. She knows that something unusual is in the air in the life of her family, so she takes time to visit them and talk with them for three months. She ponders, quickly enough in the story in front of us for her to carry on a conversation, but we know she makes a life habit of taking time to ponder and treasure things in her heart. She takes time to create and sing a beautiful song. She takes time to remember her history and her God. She does very little throughout Christ's lifetime, appearing only rarely, the opposite of a helicopter parent.

The holiness of respite

Taking time and 'doing nothing' is absolutely critical to the work of growing and healing and restoring. The writer and activist Rebecca Solnit calls this the 'holiness of respite'.[45] And it is holy, sacred time and space because it contains the work of God. Rest helps us to physically heal. Taking time out helps us to heal and grow individually, mentally and emotionally. Time out helps restore and develop relationships. Taking time, resting from a piece of work helps the imagination to be creative and ideas to form.

We have put Mary to work and made her in our own image to be hard-working and the handmaid of urgency. We use her song of praise on a daily basis in our liturgy as a manifesto and to remind us of the urgent work of the kin-dom that has been done in the day and needs doing again tomorrow. Nevertheless, here she still is, taking her time, simply singing a song of adoration, on the cusp of a lifetime of motherhood. And that, I suggest, is the real act of revolt and revolution. Taking time, daydreaming, taking respite, 'taking refuge in the beautiful stillness in which everything is happening in all the ways nothing is happening in busyness,' to quote Rebecca Solnit. This is the real path of resistance, revolution and discipleship, for it is the steady gaze of concentration on the work of God, healing, growing, restoring and liberating.

Esther Elliott

Hymn suggestions

Tell out, my soul; Sing we of the blessed Mother; Be still, my soul; Be still and know that I am God.

St George, Martyr   23 April
'God for England and St George'

1 Mac. 2.59–64, *or* Rev. 12.7–12; Ps. 126; 2 Tim. 2.3–13;
John 15.18–21

Let's not dwell on what we don't know about St George. We can be confident that he lived in Palestine 1,700 years ago, that he was a soldier, and that he was martyred under the Romans for his Christian faith. And that he became patron of England as a result of the Crusades.

We can see George as an emblem of so much that Christianity represents: destroying the dragons of tyranny and falsehood, standing for the truth against the lie, pursuing justice, cultivating virtue and nobility of character. And doing these things to the death, laying down his life for his friends out of the greater love that Jesus speaks about in St John's Gospel. This was St George the martyr, who looked persecution in the face, because 'if the world hates you, be aware that it hated me before it hated you'. A *martyr* is literally a *witness*. So the legend of St George should stir us up as God's witnesses to fight against evil and follow Christ. Three weeks ago, at Easter, we renewed our solemn baptism promises to be 'Christ's soldiers and servants' in the power of the resurrection. St George and Easter belong together.

What about England? First, let's not forget St George's cosmopolitan background – born to a Greek family in the Roman Empire in what we now call Turkey, and dying in Palestine. And remember that he is not the unique possession of England; he is also patron saint of Greece, Portugal, Palestine, Georgia, Russia and Ukraine, among other places. If George is our patron, his name should impel us to pursue those same God-given values of truth, justice and self-giving love. Righteousness exalts a nation, says the Hebrew Bible, and on St George's Day that should be our aspiration as people whose patron bids us live out of generosity and service. If we are going to 'cry God for England and St George', this is what we are raising his flag for. That much all people of goodwill can sign up for, whatever their faith: to want as a nation and society to be our best selves.

But this vision has been severely tested in recent times. The way in which the cross of St George has been harnessed to the world view of far-right extremists has unsettled those who loved England for its fairness, its tolerance, its reasonableness, its kindness and its welcome to peoples from every part of the world and of every culture and faith. But for England's hospitality to migrants, many of us wouldn't be here now. How could 'Englishness' ever be associated with a narrower vision of nationhood than St George would ever have countenanced? That our politics should be haunted by these toxic ideas is deeply worrying.

Do we need to return to the roots of our identity as 'England'? Patriotism means acting out of love for our country that has shaped our values and bestowed on us so many precious gifts. It asks in return that we play our part as a people among the family of nations, and live out all that ennobles human character. It's entirely different from the nationalism that cries 'England first!' and collapses into the self-serving accumulation of power and wealth at the expense of others. Christianity is incompatible with that idea of nation; for the church of the risen Christ is a worldwide catholic community that transcends all human identities. In the gospel, what matters is to embody mercy and truth, peace and justice, and to live together in service and mutual love.

It's a kind of death to self, a laying down of life for the sake of others. This was the spirit of St George our martyr-saint, according to the stories told about him. And it is to imitate Christ and to walk with him in the way of the cross. Jesus prayed that the cup might pass from him. Yet he drank it. As the Master is, so must the disciple be. 'Love one another, as I have loved you.' St George laid down his life as a witness to that everlasting love, and as its martyr. He held nothing back. There was no reservation and no compromise.

Could there be a better example to follow? It's a tough vocation for our church, for our nation, for any of us. But nothing less than this is the cost of good nationhood, good discipleship and good citizenship. Yet – how rewarding to live in this way! It asks everything of us. But it gives everything too. In times of trial, even at the graveside, we sing 'Alleluia! Christ is risen!' That's how we slay dragons: by worshipping our most glorious Lord of Life and living as his Easter people.

Michael Sadgrove

Hymn suggestions

Lord of lords and King eternal; Soldiers, who are Christ's below; O God of earth and altar; Ye choirs of new Jerusalem.

St Mark the Evangelist   25 April
Endure
Prov. 15.28–end, *or* Acts 15.35–end; Ps. 119.9–16; Eph. 4.7–16; **Mark 13.5–13**

Real words for real times

When Mark decided to share the good news of Jesus, I wonder what he made of these apocalyptic words. He might have been familiar with this sort of language from other places in the Scriptures. Likewise, he might have purposely selected these words for some particular pastoral issue. But really, this is some heavy stuff. So how does it fit in with the gospel? Some think Jesus was prophesying 'the end times' – cataclysmic events (earthquakes and the like) that would come before the most cataclysmic event of all, the end of the world. But as much as the language is dramatic, I think it was real events happening in real time that Jesus was talking about. Such events happened then and they happen now. Indeed, since when have wars not been a thing? Since when have famines not been a thing? Since when has being led astray not been a thing? Since when has persecution not been a thing?

Scholars suggest that most of the events prophesied here saw fulfilment within a short space of time, some by the time Mark had decided to narrate his account. After all, the Temple in Jerusalem was destroyed within 40 years of the death of Jesus, an event that would have been undeniably cataclysmic for Mark's readers, an event that would have turned the Jewish world upside down. When faced with such happenings, the words of Jesus would have felt very close, very real and very personal.

As much as these words might have been fulfilled near the time of Mark's writing, they still have bite, speaking as they do into the real world of things and occurrences that we too inhabit. Which of the words of Jesus speak with direct potency into the goings on of the world today, into our lives?

Good news then and now

The gospel is good news, but it doesn't always look like it to us, and even more to those unfamiliar with it. There is something unsettling about centring your life on this man Jesus. There is enough to object to in his teaching – often demanding, sometimes confusing, welcome for the 'sinner', judgement for the 'righteous', and the like. He was killed as one who didn't fit in the world, as one that the world did not know how to handle. Mark doesn't leave any of this out of his Gospel. Indeed, he highlights it. And Mark himself is clearly willing to go with Jesus wherever it will lead him and to let others know too. After all, he wrote this account.

In these words, we see Jesus presenting the uncomfortable truth that we will not be lifted out of times of trial into blessed escape. We find instead that we will have to endure trials. Of course, such trials vary. Some followers of Jesus know real persecution in our world, others less so. But whoever we are, we will face uncomfortable times if we seek to share the message of Jesus. Many of us will have faced such times. Responses to what we know to be good news will not always be favourable, and this can make us shrink in fear.

There are definite hints of such good news in this passage, however. We read that all nations will hear of the joy and wonder of Jesus. We are told that the Holy Spirit will give us words to say when situations seem impossible. And as we endure to the end, we can be encouraged by the salvation that Christ brings: 'The one who endures to the end will be saved.' This endurance, of course, is based on what has happened and what will happen. Christ has come and will come. The world has been made new in Christ and will be made new in Christ. The Holy Spirit has been given and will be given. Christ has died, Christ is risen, Christ will come again. There is a tension that we live with, but we do so in light of the fact that Jesus has walked the earth and walks with us now. We do so in light of the fact that the dove of peace has descended and settled upon us. Are we willing to endure to the end? And what will we say when we are inevitably asked to give account for the nature of our faith? Mark's account must have surely cost him: time, emotion, energy, even his safety. Can we endure the same? By the Spirit, I believe so.

Mark Amos

What a friend we have in Jesus; Abide with me; We are people of God's peace; Blessed be your name.

SS Philip and James, Apostles   1 May
Jesus Lays it Out Straight for Philip
Isa. 30.15–21; Ps. 119.1–8; Eph. 1.3–10; **John 14.1–14**

Which way to God?

In the middle of our passage, Philip asks for something profound: 'show us the Father'. What was he hoping for? Jesus has just said that his Father's house has many dwelling-places: a massive house with multiple rooms; a vast space, which all can inhabit, where all are welcome. He has also heard Jesus say that no one can come to the Father except through him. The house might have room for all, but it sounds difficult to get into. Philip's question, however, is not so much about who the house is for or how to get into it. No, it pertains to the owner directly.

Of course, it's a good thing to seek after the owner of this particular house. So what has Philip missed after being with Jesus for so long? The simple but startling truth that he finds difficult to grasp is that the owner of the house is talking to him even now. Accepting Jesus – this some-time refugee peasant labourer without any qualifications or recommendations – as God is no small feat. Philip clearly respects Jesus, enough to leave all else to follow him. He might have reached the point of seeing him as a prophet from God or even the Messiah of God, but it seems that he has not recognized the reality of God right in front of him.

Room for all

Not that Jesus has anything harsh to say to Philip. His words are more invitational than confrontational. In fact, if belief in Christ's divinity is too much for him to comprehend in abstraction, Jesus says, 'Well, believe in me because of my works.' It might be that Philip was taking his time to catch something about these works. This wonder-worker who seems drawn to all the wrong people is not an easy figure to accept. Many of us need time to accept him. Some have a faith that says, 'Yes – I'm in', and they jump straight in at the deep end. Some say, 'Wait, I need to weigh things up first.' Others say, 'No, thanks.' But, none of these responses are beyond Jesus. His words of invitation remain, and will remain: 'In my Father's house there are many dwelling-places.' This applies to Philip as much as it applies to anyone else. It applies to us too. We are invited into this massive house with rooms aplenty and where festive joy awaits. There should be no imposter syndrome in the household of God.

But what God do we come to? When we consider who God is, and how God relates to us human beings, where do we turn? Do we look at the Torah or the Temple, as Philip might have done? We might usefully do this. After all, God is the same yesterday, today and for ever. Do we look at a book of philosophy? Sure, there is life in philosophy yet. Do we set our thoughts on the cosmos or even each other? Yes, why not? God can be spotted in all these places. But if we really want to seek God, says Jesus, look at me: look at the refugee, the one who had no place to lay his head, the peasant labourer without formal qualifications.

If we are not willing to recognize one such as this, we may have blurred vision regarding God. We may end up with a God who is very big, very strong, very clever and even very loving. But we might still be short of God as God. That we should seek God in Jesus is an encouragement not to presume that God could only reside in a dwelling-place of glory. It is an invitation, rather, to acknowledge God's presence alongside the ostracized, the marginalized, the victimized. When we find God here, with Jesus, we find that there are many dwelling-places. For Philip? Yes. For us? Yes, we are totally welcome.

What to do

At the end of our passage, Jesus encourages us to ask for and to do great things in his name. Asking in the name of Jesus means acknowledging what he is about. What might we ask in his name? We could begin by asking that all would see that the house he is building is there to share. We could follow that up by allowing ourselves to think that there is room for us. We could then make sure we invite others in, knowing that there is room – a dwelling-place – for everyone. The Gospel begins with 'welcome' and 'many dwelling-places'. It proceeds to the more difficult call to recognize that there is space for everyone through this Jesus and that the invitation to us is to get on with the task of getting the dwelling-places ready.

Mark Amos

Hymn suggestions

From heaven you came, helpless babe; Let us build a house; Let us go into the house of the Lord; We have a gospel to proclaim.

St Matthias the Apostle   14 May
Substitute Saint
Isa. 22.15–end, *or* **Acts 1.15–end**; Ps. 15; Acts 1.15–end (*if the Acts reading is used instead of the Old Testament reading, the New Testament reading is* 1 Cor. 4.1–7); John 15.9–17

It was an extraordinary meeting. Eleven apostles, together with a crowd of followers of Jesus – Luke says 120 – all get together. They are trying to make some sense of the events that have overtaken them. They are full of joy and mystery and perplexity. They have seen their Lord Jesus – risen from the dead! So they meet together to pray and to try to understand what on earth has happened – and what will happen next.

And now, to Peter, there seems to be a horrifying gap in their number. Judas, one of their closest friends, has delivered Jesus to be crucified, and then in remorse he has gone to his own horrifying death. There's an empty place at the table.

The day of Pentecost has not yet arrived, so it's still that transitional moment. Peter sets up a process to find a twelfth apostle. Is he trying to restore some kind of normality? They choose two likely people – Barsabbas and Justus. They pray. It's a prayer that doesn't really open the situation to God but offers God a choice in the selection. And then they cast lots, toss a coin, and Matthias wins.

Filling the gap

Why did they do this? There was certainly an impulse, a strong idea among them to keep the number 12: 12 apostles who might symbolically continue or succeed the tribes of Israel. But this action doesn't feel thought through, it is not an unmixed good. It seems to be Peter's idea rather than a prompting of the Holy Spirit. They pray God's blessing on the outcome, but there is no guarantee – in a book where God's immanence and miracles are almost taken for granted – that God has answered their prayer.

Do we sometimes take decisions like this? Too quickly, too reactively? With too little openness to the larger agenda and possibilities of the kingdom of God?

What was Peter's deepest motivation for these events? Was he impulsive? Is this something that we also are very likely to do in the aftermath of trauma – to try to impose the pattern we remember from the past? In the structures and patterns of our life together as a church, the desire for safety and security can so easily lead us to a certain rigidity. It can be too painful to change.

A good choice?

Peter was looking for someone to become an apostle in the future, but was he missing those who had already seen and proclaimed the risen Lord? If the 11, looking to the future, actually did need another apostle, might this have been the moment to bring Mary Magdalene into the circle? What a different story that would have been! Maybe it would have been possible to move beyond trauma and tradition and to continue the deeply inclusive work of Christ.

And, aside from that speculation, a man called Paul was waiting in the wings. He was soon to announce his own claim to be an apostle. This was a claim that was accepted, although he was never one of the Twelve.

The overlooked

Matthias steps on to the stage of Bible history and then vanishes again without trace from the pages of the New Testament.

But in the tradition, he is remembered as a saint. He serves, apparently, as the patron saint of carpenters and tailors. He is invoked by people who need hope and perseverance as they struggle with addiction, and those who try to help them.

His number came up in a lottery over which he had no control. I wonder if maybe St Matthias can stand as patron saint for a lot of people? Maybe those who find themselves in jobs that they didn't quite choose, whose work is never completely satisfying. Maybe he can stand for those people who have to live with choices that other people have made for them. A saint for those who feel that their life has missed out on the main action. Those who would like to have been in the story, but find themselves to be a footnote. Those who find themselves in frustration, pointlessness, feeling forgotten.

The day of Pentecost was about to happen. Along with the others, Matthias was soon to be filled with the Spirit of God, empowered, loved; a vital part of that great community of God.

St Matthias may remind us that every one of us matters. We may be people who are rendered powerless but we are written in the book nonetheless, we have significance. We have our place in the story of God. Our ordinariness is celebrated among the named and nameless people that form a part of God's story.

St Matthias stands for you. Your name shall be there. You are recorded. You are not insignificant.

Andrew Rudd

Hymn suggestions

Earth's creator, everyday God; Come down, O love divine; From heaven you came, helpless babe; The highest and the holiest place.

Day of Thanksgiving for the Institution of the Holy Communion (Corpus Christi)   30 May
A Feast of Living Bread
Gen. 14.18–20; Ps. 116.10–end; 1 Cor. 11.23–26; **John 6.51–58**

Getting medieval

If I asked you to conjure a scene from the Middle Ages, what might you imagine? Perhaps you might picture knights in shining armour, or castles and kings, or scenes of squalor in which peasants live lives of almost unendurable misery. For those of us of a certain age, images from Monty Python's *Holy Grail* may leap, unprompted, to mind.

I wonder how surprised you might be to know that it was also a time of wonder, imagination and great popular festivals. Certainly, many had a very lively relationship with God. The feast of Corpus Christi, which many of us still keep as the day of thanksgiving for Holy Communion, began in the Middle Ages at the prompting of the great theologian St Thomas Aquinas. However, it was peasants and merchants and ordinary city folk who made it their own. By the time of the Reformation in the sixteenth century, the feast of Corpus Christi had become a day for performing mystery plays in York, Wakefield and countless other places. These told the story of salvation from creation to Christ, with often funny and playful effects. Often the blessed sacrament – the body and blood of Christ – was carried through the streets.

While it is possible still to witness Corpus Christi processions in England and to enjoy mystery plays in Chester and York, we cannot quite imagine the colour and devotion of those medieval festivities now (unless, of course, one heads to Italy or Spain). Nonetheless, sharing in Christ's body and blood is a founding sacrament of the Christian faith. To share in Christ's body and blood is a command from our Lord. At the Last Supper, Jesus prays thanks over bread, divides it and hands it to his disciples, saying, 'Take, eat, this is my body.' Later in the meal Jesus takes a cup of wine, prays and gives it to those present, saying, 'Drink of it, all of you; for this is my blood of the new covenant.' As Dom Gregory Dix says, 'Was ever another command so obeyed?'[46] I for one would not be who I am without regularly receiving the body of Christ.

The living bread

One of the things I adore about Jesus and his earthly ministry is how he provides feasts for those who follow him. Repeatedly, Jesus provides abundant food for the crowds who come to listen to him. In various passages, we hear how he blesses bread and fish and feeds multitudes, including, on one occasion, 5,000 people.

Ultimately, these great feedings of hungry people are a foretaste of Jesus' self-offering for all of us on the cross. As we hear in the passage from John, Jesus is the living bread that has come down from heaven. Perhaps we are as bewildered, sceptical or as frightened as the people who originally heard that claim. Nonetheless, he offers to feed the whole world from himself, making himself bread for the whole people of God. Whoever feeds on him will have eternal life. As we feed on Jesus' body and blood in the Lord's Supper, we receive God's grace and are called out into the world in service. We become ever more the body of Christ. We who follow Jesus are asked by God to make a feast of ourselves for the world.

The body of Christ

I am reminded of those famous words often attributed to St Teresa of Avila, the sixteenth-century saint whose spiritual writings continue to inspire.

> Christ has no body but yours,
> No hands, no feet on earth but yours,
> Yours are the eyes with which he looks
> Compassion on this world,
> Yours are the feet with which he walks to do good,
> Yours are the hands, with which he blesses all the world.
> Yours are the hands, yours are the feet,
> Yours are the eyes, you are his body.
> Christ has no body now but yours,
> No hands, no feet on earth but yours,
> Yours are the eyes with which he looks
> compassion on this world.
> Christ has no body now on earth but yours.[47]

St Teresa reminds us that we who follow Jesus are now the body of Christ. Jesus provides in bread and wine his own body and blood to form and sustain us; however, it is us who are called to be his feet and hands, his eyes and body in the world.

To celebrate the feast of Corpus Christi or to give thanksgiving for Holy Communion, then, is never just a pious matter. It is not something we are invited to do in order to make us feel good. It is an opportunity to thank God for his self-offering in Jesus and prepare ourselves to embody the Way of Christ in the world. As the ones who are both fed by and formed into Christ, we are called to a joyous work of sacrificial love and compassionate service for a world in need.

Rachel Mann

Hymn suggestions

I am the bread of life; Broken for me, broken for you; We will take what you offer (Wild Goose); Guide me, O thou great Redeemer.

Visit of the Blessed Virgin Mary to Elizabeth
31 May
Being God-Bearers
Zeph. 3.14–18; Ps. 113; Rom. 12.9–16; **Luke 1.39–49 [50–56]**

Of the many titles that we might use for Mary, the mother of Jesus, perhaps one of those least familiar to congregations is Theotokos, used in the Eastern Church and meaning 'God-bearer'.

It is a particularly apt title to concentrate on today, the feast of the Visitation, as we remember Mary bearing the embryonic Christ to her cousin Elizabeth. Mary's experience of carrying Jesus is something she cannot keep to herself, so she hurries to the hill country of Judaea and, in our Gospel, we witness both the wonder of Mary in sharing this miracle and the joy of Elizabeth in receiving it.

Mary the God-bearer

Although Elizabeth was the first to whom Mary carried God, she certainly wasn't the last. Mary didn't stop being the God-bearer when the birthing pangs had ended, holding up the good news to ordinary shepherds and extraordinary magi as he suckled at her breast. And from then on she continued to carry God in her heart, treasuring the things that she had been told about who and what he might be.

Mary conveyed God to the Temple, to bring light to the faithful Simeon and Anna; a light for the revelation to the nations and the glory of the people of Israel.

She bore God in her arms as they fled the country and travelled as refugees to a distant land, running from persecution and the threat of death, God held to her chest; safety in a place of fear.

She clung to God's hand through childhood: watching him grow, seeing him testing the boundaries, showing him the groundings of their faith, on pilgrimage to Jerusalem. There she found that, even when his fingers slipped away and her son was lost in the Temple, God was still in her heart.

One who never stops bearing God

Mary, the Theotokos, never stopped bearing God, not even when fully grown now he ignored her pleas, caused rejection, asking the crowds, 'Who is my mother?'

As the God-bearer, she pointed out what God was doing in the world and what more was possible; she watched over his first miracle, as she had his first steps. Go to him, do what he tells you, she said to the worried servants at the wedding in Cana.

As the God-bearer, she fed and welcomed his friends and the hangers-on, knowing that there was never quite enough with 12 hungry young men in the house. She fed them all, even the one who would later betray her son for 30 silver coins.

She held God in the pit of her stomach, as a helpless mother, watching her child struggle and sweat; reaching out, knowing she wasn't strong enough to step in and carry the burdens he carried up that long, slow walk to the place of the skull. And Mary was still the God-bearer, the Theotokos, when God, in the body of a limp and dead man, was taken down from the cross and his mother cradled him in her arms and wept in the darkness.

As she carried Jesus with her to Elizabeth, so Mary bore God throughout her life; through pain and joy, certainty, confusion and doubt; through times of comfort and fear; in moments of intimate connection and great loneliness. She never stopped carrying God.

We are God-bearers

And nor should we, for we too are God-bearers in this world.

Whether the seed of God is planted in us in one striking moment or we feel it has always been there, there are moments when we feel God working in us, and our souls want to magnify the Lord.

Like Mary went to Elizabeth, we are called to carry God to those closest to us: our family members, our friends and our community, and then beyond them, even into places of darkness, to share light on those who fear the dawn will never come.

Being God-bearers calls us to nurture that intimacy with God; through our prayer, our praise and our mindfulness of God's presence with us and in the world around us. Attuning ourselves to God in us, in our hearts, minds, bodies and souls, we too treasure all the words we hear about God, pondering them and letting them grow deep within us.

We bear God, and we point out what God is doing in the world: noticing the sunsets and spider's web glistening with dew; the laughter over a glass of wine; the little steps and the tiny miracles of everyday life; the reconciliation we thought could never happen; each prayer heard and answered. As God-bearers we commit ourselves to look back at the end of the day and see what God has done.

We are God-bearers. As we remember how Mary carried Jesus to Elizabeth, we remember that we are called to do likewise. To bear God into the world, sharing the good news with those who are waiting. Reflecting God's glory, proclaiming God's greatness, singing of God's justice and mercy and 'telling out' from our souls the wonders God has done.

Chris Campbell

Hymn suggestions

For Mary, mother of our Lord; Jesus Christ is waiting; Now thank we all our God; Tell out my soul.

St Barnabas, Apostle   11 June
Be More Barnabas
Job 29.11–16, *or* **Acts 11.19–end**; Ps. 112; Acts 11.19–end
(*if the Acts reading is used instead of the Old Testament reading, the New Testament reading is* Gal. 2.1–10);
John 15.12–17

The story of the saint we celebrate today suggests that behind every great person there's a great encourager, in this case a man called Barnabas. A Cypriot Jew, his name means 'son of encouragement'. Encouragement is a game-changing superpower and our man has it in spades. Today we remember Barnabas the Encourager.

Encouraging generosity

One of the first things we learn about Barnabas is that 'He sold a field that belonged to him, then brought the money, and laid it at the apostles' feet' (Acts 4.37). What a massive act of generous encouragement. He puts his money where his heart is, investing in the work of the gospel. How encouraging for the widows and the poor who ate because Barnabas opened his hand and gave freely.

His generosity communicates care, concern and commitment. As the ripples of his generosity flow out, who knows their wider effect?

Today is a call for us to be more Barnabas with our resources.

Encouraging words

Without Barnabas, Paul's ministry would never have got off the ground. Paul, then Saul, had been murderously opposed to the followers of Jesus; naturally, people were afraid of him. He'd looked after the coats of the mob while they stoned Stephen to death (Acts 7.58). Even after Saul's face-down experience with Jesus on the Damascus road, people were still wary of him. When Saul tried to join the disciples in Jerusalem (Acts 9.26–29) they didn't believe he was a disciple – which to be fair was a reasonable assumption. It was only because Barnabas stepped in and vouched for him that they accepted him. Barnabas encourages Paul by standing with him and encouraging the apostles to set aside their fear. He's a man who speaks up when needed, releasing Paul's ministry with an intervention which has a massive ripple effect.

Here is a call to be more Barnabas with our words.

Encouraging mission

When the apostles in Jerusalem hear that the gospel has been shared with Gentiles in Antioch – a new development, disturbing for some – they dispatch Barnabas to investigate, showing that Barnabas is trusted as a man of wisdom and discernment. When he finds that many Gentiles are becoming believers in Antioch, he rejoices. He celebrates the mission of God. He doesn't become tribal. He doesn't ring-fence the gospel for *us* and not *them*. His attitude is to follow the signs of God's mission.

If we are to be more Barnabas we will follow the ripple effect of the mission of God.

Encouraging faith

Barnabas discerns the hand of God at work and gets involved, encouraging the believers to draw closer to Jesus and to stick with their new-found faith. Luke writes that Barnabas 'was a good man, full of the Holy Spirit and of faith'. His superpower of encouragement flows from his faith in God. He is not just a nice chap, his goodness is grounded in God. That doesn't come about by chance.

He has soaked himself in God's presence, and that presence flows through him – the effects rippling out.

Let's be more Barnabas in our relationship with God.

Encouraging cooperation

Many people were coming to faith in Antioch. Barnabas heads to Tarsus to look for Paul. That's a journey of 150 miles each way. Why does he do this? He's looking to share the ministry of nurturing the church in Antioch with Paul. They do this together for a year. A different person might have wanted to be the big-shot leader, to run the show alone. Not Barnabas. He shares the work with Paul. He's a team player, not a lone wolf.

Let's be more Barnabas in cooperation with others.

Encouraging practical care

The thing about encouragement is that it can be contagious. Remember how Barnabas sold his field and gave the resources away? Notice how Barnabas has had a key role in shaping the church in Antioch. When they hear news of a coming famine, they give according to their means in order to send practical care to the church down south in Judaea. Taught by an encourager, they become encouragers. Encouragement ripples outwards.

Be more Barnabas!

Make us more Barnabas

Barnabas is a son of encouragement. In him we see the love of God rooted and expressed in many acts of encouragement. Barnabas epitomizes the love Jesus calls his friends to inhabit in the reading from John.

Encouragement is a superpower, a game-changer. Let loose it gathers momentum and can achieve far more than we can ask or imagine. In a world so often divided, mean and tribal, encouragement can unite, bless and build up.

Who knows the reach of that gift of money?

Who knows the effect of a supportive tweet, comment, card or letter?

Who can fully grasp how a kind word in a bitter moment can salve and heal?

What tremendous results are achieved when people work together, harnessing the effect of various gifts, rather than flying solo.

God, make us more Barnabas!

Kate Bruce

Hymn suggestions

Take my life and let it be; Come, thou fount of every blessing; As the deer pants for the water; May the mind of Christ my Saviour.

Birth of John the Baptist 24 June
Pointing the Way
Isa. 40.1–11; Ps. 85.7–end; Acts 13.14b–26, *or* Gal. 3.23–end; **Luke 1.57–66, 80**

A popular saint!

John the Baptist is pretty popular! If you look up how many church buildings in the Church of England are dedicated to John the Baptist, he comes eighth in the overall rankings. Unsurprisingly, St Mary comes top with, at the time of writing, 2,368 churches dedicated to her in this country. If you drift off into thought during the rest of this service, you can try to guess who fills slots two to seven. And, yes, St Peter is in there somewhere! But there are an awful lot of churches dedicated to St John the Baptist. Unusually, John the Baptist also has two feast days each year. This one, today, which commemorates his birth, and another one at the end of August which remembers his death. It's quite unusual for a saint to have more than one feast day. And the number of churches dedicated to John, together with the fact that he has multiple special days, ought to tell us there is something quite important about him.

John's highlights

John gets three big moments in the course of the Bible narrative, three things for which he is particularly well known. The first one is when he leaps in Elizabeth's womb when Mary and Elizabeth, those two pregnant cousins, meet and the unborn Baptist, even in his prenatal state, recognizes the coming of the King. The second of course is the 'main event' as it were, as he appears, shaggy and unkempt, wearing his leather belt and his camel's hair, out there in the wilderness preaching repentance: those stories that we always read in Advent. And then there is the story of his death as a result of a set of mind games between Herod and his family. His beheading. His death for standing up for a set of principles.

And there are of course other stories: he is there to baptize Jesus; he communicates with his own followers from prison as they engage with Christ's ministry. And there is the story of his naming, the story that we remember today, when even as a tiny infant he is able to fill the neighbourhood with fear and wonder.

Pointing the way

What's interesting is that in almost all the art, John is depicted in the same way: pointing. You can appreciate this either by going to the National Gallery and looking at some of the finest examples of the Masters, or by sticking John the Baptist into Google (other search engines are available!). Either way, you will see the same thing: a forefinger, often elongated by the artist, pointing. Pointing. Pointing the way. A lot of iconography works this way: Mary, winner of the 'most church dedications' in this country, is also often depicted pointing to Christ. Pointing to her son.

The saints, ultimately, are there to reorient us towards Christ. Some of them by their lives, some of them by their deaths, some of them in extraordinary miraculous acts, some of them by constant, humble, almost invisible prayer and faithfulness. John the Baptist stands right on the 'hinge' between the Old Testament and the New. He is the last of the prophets and arguably the first of the martyrs, although he doesn't get that title because he dies before Jesus' death and resurrection, so Stephen gets that particular gong.

Revisiting our priorities

But the Baptist dies as he lived: provoking, trying to shift the focus from the worldly and political games of powerplay to something more, something radically different. All those Advent prophecies, one of which we hear on this great feast day, are about where our focus is found, what our priorities are. 'A voice cries out: "In the wilderness prepare the way of the LORD"' (Isa. 40.3). It is so desperately easy to be seduced by ourselves: our own status or lack of it, our own prospects, our ambitions, thwarted or otherwise. John the Baptist ends his life in the way he begins it: pointing away from himself and towards Christ.

It's that kind of language that is spoken to those who are ordained, often at about this time of the year. It's that kind of language that we hear in the confirmation service, and in the baptism service as well. It's that kind of language that we should be using day by day in our own congregations, churches and parishes, whether or not we are dedicated to John the Baptist. It's that kind of language that we are invited to make our own on this feast day. Being a Christian is absolutely not about us. It is about discerning in which way God is calling us, each in our own way, with our life rather than our finger, to point the way to Christ.

Tom Clammer

Hymn suggestions

On this high feast day, honour we the Baptist; On Jordan's bank; O Jesus, I have promised; Thou didst leave thy throne.

SS Peter and Paul, Apostles 29 June
Open to God

Zech. 4.1–6a, 10b–end, *or* Acts 12.1–11; Ps. 125; **Acts 12.1–11** (*if the Acts reading is used instead of the Old Testament reading, the New Testament reading is* 2 Tim. 4.6–8, 17–18); Matt. 16.13–19

After Stephen was put to death, the Christians in Jerusalem faced severe persecution. It was, to say the least, a difficult and dangerous time for the church. Many of the believers were scattered through-out Judaea and Samaria and then moved out even further afield into Phoenicia, Cyprus and Antioch. Yet, even under the threat of death, the Christians continued to meet together for prayer and they boldly proclaimed 'the good news about the kingdom of God and the name of Jesus Christ' (Acts 8.12).

Prayer in the midst of persecution

In spite of their earnest prayers, however, the persecution continued as King Herod ordered the execution of James (the brother of John) and had Peter arrested. Confronted by such opposition and what must have seemed to be 'unanswered' prayer, it would not have been surprising if some of the Christians had started to question the efficacy of prayer. Why pray if God does not respond? Why ask God for help when prayer seems to be met by silence? Yet, according to the story, in spite of ongoing persecution, the Christians did not cease to meet together and 'prayed fervently to God' for Peter.

A surprising response

Meanwhile, in prison, Peter was bound in two chains and surrounded by guards. To any onlooker, the situation would have seemed hopeless. Knowing he might be put to death, we might imagine Peter would be kept awake all night by worry. So it is with surprise that we find Peter – as he is described in the story – 'sleeping between two soldiers, while guards in front of the door were keeping watch over the prison'. Peter was not lying awake fretting; he was snoozing! In fact, he was sleeping so soundly that he needed to be tapped on his side by an angel before he stirred!

If you, like me, have ever spent a restless night lying awake worrying over what has been in the past or what might be in the future, perhaps you will be wondering how Peter could have slept in such dire circumstances.

Confidence in God

The simple answer I suppose is that Peter knew that his brothers and sisters in Christ were praying for him and he was confident that God would answer prayer and that all would be well. Yet, as the story is told, it does not appear that Peter was expecting a miraculous delivery from prison. In fact, he was startled when eventually he realized he was outside rather than inside the jail and free to join the other believers again.

Thinking of Peter's response, it seems that, like us, he knew that life is often filled with all sorts of difficulty from which there is no prospect of immediate release. Genuine faith is formed and exists in a world of chance and change, and prayer is never simply about asking God to step in and remove all trouble. Instead, perhaps prayer might be better understood as a way of surrendering ourselves to God in trust that God will stand with us in the midst of both the best and the worst that life brings.

Giving ourselves to God

In 1984, a well-known author, evangelist and Anglican priest, David Watson, was interviewed on the radio. Aware that he had been diagnosed with terminal cancer and also that it was widely publicized that people were fervently praying for his healing, the interviewer took the opportunity to question Watson about his faith and the effectiveness of prayer. Rather bluntly, he asked Watson what his own response would be if their prayers were not answered and he was not healed of the disease. With quiet assurance, Watson said that he hoped that he would experience physical healing. However, he added that whatever the future might hold, he had given himself to God in trust and he believed that he would know the peace of God's presence always.

Confidence in God does not mean that we never have any doubts or moments when we wonder if our faith might be mistaken. Nor does trust in God mean that we will never have disappointment, heartache, sorrow or worry. We offer our prayers believing that, as we give ourselves to God, we will become more aware of God's presence in the midst of all of life and we shall not be overcome by whatever besets us. Indeed, it is in that knowledge that we may claim with the fourteenth-century mystical writer, Mother Julian, that whatever happens, 'All will be well, and all will be well, and all manner of things will be well.'[48] Thanks be to God.

Karen E. Smith

Hymn suggestions

O God of Bethel; Have faith in God, my heart; Be thou my vision; I am trusting you, Lord Jesus.

St Thomas the Apostle   3 July
Space to Breathe
Hab. 2.1–4; Ps. 31.1–6; Eph. 2.19–end; **John 20.24–29**

Feeling low

The reading from John's Gospel often sits in the middle of a longer reading used for the Sunday after Easter, or 'low Sunday'. When I first heard it called that I thought it referred to the mood of the disciples gathered after the death and resurrection of Jesus. In particular, grouchy, mistrusting Thomas. These are people full of fear, confusion, lethargy and doubt. They have gone back to the house where they used to meet, locked the doors and hidden themselves away, not doing much it seems. No doubt there was a bit of arguing, sniping, blaming and shaming. They aren't people who are full of Easter joy, happy and celebrating, and eager to get on and live life to the full. Of course, we can explain this by saying that they were too close to the events to know what they really meant and understand that these were people who had been through trauma. Later on, when some of them do get out for a bit of fresh air by the sea of Tiberias and decide to go fishing, that too is a depressing disaster and they catch nothing, even though they fish all through the night. It's all a long way from the mood of the women who first discovered the empty tomb and saw Jesus. They are described as having 'great joy' and running to tell the other disciples that they have seen the Lord. And let's not forget that the women doing this running were not youngsters.

In need of certainty, then peace be with you

Each time Jesus comes to these disciples he says, 'Peace be with you.' It's a really odd thing to say in this context. The disciples aren't arguing or fighting with each other. There is no hefty discussion going on where they are struggling to understand like the disciples on the road to Emmaus. Yes, they are fearful enough to have locked the doors, but they aren't portrayed as sitting there fretting or fizzing with anxiety with someone on guard duty. Thomas has had his major grump the week before and now is simply 'with them'. So why 'Peace be with you'? Why not 'Joy be with you', or 'Strength be with you', or 'Reassurance be with you'? Why peace? Of course, 'Peace be with you' is an old form of greeting, a bit like saying hello. But then why doesn't John have Jesus say it every time he appears? He doesn't, but John does have Jesus say it three times to this bunch of disciples, so it must be important.

'Peace be with you.' Peace, tranquillity, harmony, quiet, an absence of conflict and hostility. That was Jesus' first wish when he sees a bunch of his followers together, including Thomas. Peace be with you, all of you who are brought so low. For those of you who could do with some joy – peace. To those of you who could do with some strength and energy – peace. To those of you who could do with some courage – peace. To those of you who could do with some assurance – peace. To those of you who could do with some certainty – peace.

Peace, the bringer of room and space

Peace is a space creator, a room-giver. How many times have you said you need a bit of peace in order to be able to think? People who are arguing need the space created by peace and calm to be able to start to sort out their problems. That's often the thing trained mediators bring. The police often create a bit of physical space between people and groups in an emergency situation and we call them peacekeepers. We need the room, and the space peace gives us, to be able to take the next steps on our journey, to do the next thing. And here is Jesus creating that space and that room. If you struggle with finding words to talk and think about Jesus after he has died and risen again, perhaps using the language of the bringer of room and space might help.

There's one last thing I want to draw your attention to and it's about the way Jesus speaks. He speaks about the present moment. He doesn't speak of peace as something for the future, something to be hoped for, something which will be given when the disciples have pulled themselves together, something for Thomas when he has stopped doubting and started believing. 'Peace be with you,' he says. Peace be with you – creating the space and room for you to take the next steps regardless of how you feel, what's happening in life, what you want, what room you've managed to lock yourself into, or what group of people you are spending your time with. This is the gritty reality of peace, peace felt, peace offered, peace given, peace present, peace accepted in each and every moment, whatever else is being felt said or done. Whatever the past or the future may hold. Peace be with you.

Esther Elliott

Hymn suggestions

Make me a channel of your peace; Saviour, again to thy dear name we raise; Dear Lord and Father of us all; Forth in the peace of Christ, we go.

St Mary Magdalene   22 July
Who Are You Looking For?
S. of Sol. 3.1–4; Ps. 42.1–10; 2 Cor. 5.14–17;
John 20.1–2, 11–18

Mary Magdalene is probably one of the favourite biblical women of western art and imagery – though not always for very good reasons. Her reputation as a loose woman has inspired painters and writers alike, and she was made even more famous by the *Da Vinci Code* novel a few years ago. Most of what we see in art, however, is complete fiction; most of it is also unfair fiction. She has been depicted as a sinner, a prostitute, the archetype of the fallen woman, in contrast to Mary the mother of Jesus, the virgin, the archetype of true womanhood. Yet there is nothing in either Scripture or history that warrants this portrayal. We are told that Jesus touched her life very deeply, but with no details of her past. The Gospel of Luke alone mentions her past and says that seven demons had come out of her, which is quite enough to be getting on with, but nothing more. In contrast, the Gospels mention her presence at the cross, with other women, while the Twelve had fled, and again at the tomb the next day. What matters, therefore, is her extraordinary devotion and love for Jesus, and her commission as a witness of the resurrected Christ.

Journey to the empty tomb

So here we find her, alone at daybreak, coming to the tomb, presumably to finish the task of embalming the body which had been interrupted by the Sabbath. She is alone and weeping. She expects to do the last thing she can for the man who had changed her life beyond recognition, for her teacher, for someone she expected to carry on leading and teaching her and the disciples for a long time yet. Her expectations, her dreams, her hopes were shattered. The Jesus she is coming for is still the same as the man she knew. Then she discovers the empty tomb, and even the comfort of dressing the body appropriately is taken away from her.

After that, we have a scene with a slight touch of comedy, but deep meaning running beneath. She runs for help, and she's eclipsed, while Peter and his friend examine the practical details. Those details are important. They tell us what has *not* happened. Jesus has not been brought back to life the way his friend Lazarus had been.

The grave clothes are folded, whereas Lazarus had to be disentangled from them. The empty tomb and the wrappings lead the beloved disciple to believe ... but we have no idea *what* he believed! He may have believed that Jesus had been taken up to heaven, like Elijah, not resurrected, alone. Resurrection is not mentioned until the appearance of Jesus later on. The empty tomb does not prove the resurrection. Meeting Jesus does.

Turning away from the empty tomb

How often today do we still look to the empty tomb for proof? If you look at books on Christianity, or discipleship courses, there is often a whole section on 'proofs of the resurrection' – examining the empty tomb, examining the possibilities, rationalizing, trying to make the resurrection appear logical, rational, believable. But this isn't the thrust of this story. The empty tomb only leads the disciples to go home. And it is only when Mary turns away from the empty tomb that she finally sees Jesus. It is her encounter with Jesus that transforms her and the rest of the disciples to whom she witnesses. Her initial message of the empty tomb was not enough. Her second message, of meeting the risen Jesus, sets off the chain reaction that will see the birth of the Christian church. The resurrection, just like the incarnation, is not logical, believable. It is totally, utterly, un-believable, something no one could ever have expected, dreamt or comprehended. Something that completely broke with the normal order of creation, with what normal, sensible people expected God to do. While it is fair to examine the historicity of our faith, we need to remember how outrageous its claims are, learn to turn away from the empty tomb to encounter the risen Christ, and ask ourselves, where do we usually look for Christ in our lives?

When we do so, like Mary Magdalene, we are invited not to cling to a Jesus we can understand, but instead take a step of faith into new life: turning away from the tomb, turning away from the past, not clinging to a Jesus we can reduce to human understanding, and instead stepping into resurrection life and becoming partners with God in creating the future.

Isabelle Hamley

Hymn suggestions

Take my life and let it be; Go, tell it on the mountain; Led like a lamb; Morning has broken.

St James the Apostle   25 July
That Which is Good, Right and True
Jer. 45.1–5, *or* **Acts 11.27—12.2**; Ps. 126; Acts 11.27—12.2
(*if the Acts reading is used instead of the Old Testament reading, the New Testament reading is* 2 Cor. 4.7–15); **Matt. 20.20–28**

In Finland, upon completion of your PhD, you are given a black hat, similar to a top hat, and a sword. We learn that 'the Doctor's Sword is a symbol for the doctoral student's fight for what he or she, in rigorous research, has found to be good, right and true'.[49]

A question aired

In Acts 12 we read that James, the brother of John, is killed with the sword. The symbol that the Finnish academic system uses to represent the fight to find what is good, right and true is the instrument that kills the apostle James and simultaneously speaks to that to which he belonged.

To try to hold on to and believe in what is good and right and true in a world that regularly reminds us of what is evil and wrong and false is not at all easy. When someone expresses beliefs based on falsehoods and narrow-mindedness, how do we teach and respond without shaming them? How do we educate someone when they ask a question or make a statement that is born out of ambition, selfish desire, ignorance, precise planning or hate? How do we hold on to and believe in what is good and right and true when someone is saying things that challenge our very being, our values and our knowledge derived from lived experience?

In Matthew 20 we read the request of a mother who wants to plan and safeguard the future of her sons. As she approached Jesus, were her sons delighted that their brave mother dared to ask what deep down they knew they were desperate to have, but could not? Were they ashamed that their mother would expose their ambition? Did they put their mother up to it? Were they embarrassed and wincing as their mother spoke? We cannot say for certain, but what we do know is that the question was aired and brought into the open for all to hear. And Jesus responds to her.

A response without shaming

It is important to recognize the message of servant leadership that Jesus is presenting here. But perhaps what is equally important for our age is to hear how Jesus responds. He did not shout. He did not rage. He did not mock, and he certainly did not shame. What is good and right and true is that, in full knowledge of the end of their lives, he holds mother and sons in the present moment and speaks truth to them in a way that punctures their hope with the future reality, but somehow leaves things intact. James and John are not removed from the group of followers and Jesus does not lie to them either. This is divine skill, and it asks a lot of us if we are to model it.

We are living in an age of deep mistrust and polarization. We are not all on the same side. We are not all fighting for what is good and right and true. We are not all interested in the dignity of others. This means that we are not necessarily able to educate, teach and learn without shaming others. We want to shame who voted for this and for that party. We especially want to shame those who say to us that we are not right, that we have imagined it, that we could not possibly be equal and we have no right to think that we are. We want to shame those who post dreadful things on social media and those who incite hate. So perhaps we all need to make space for the grace to educate without shaming.

A Christian pilgrimage

When the mother of the sons of Zebedee came to Jesus and knelt before him, there is the sense that she knows that something bigger is happening, something which does not deny her lived experience but pierces through with a new sort of light. She is crystal clear about Jesus' place in and beyond the cosmos and she recognizes his authority. Things have slowed down into a sacred clarity of who is before her, and she has her moment. She has seen Jesus' pilgrimage and now she wants to know how it will end.

We think of James and also of Santiago de Compostela, in northwest Spain, and the pilgrimage to his remains in the cathedral there. The walk of Christian pilgrimage is about embarking on the unknown and exploring what is good, right and true. This comes through a one-step-at-a-time, daily discovery and rediscovery of a lived reality that points beyond ourselves, beyond a competitive sense of supremacy to inclusive history and storytelling, to a reconstitution of what power shared across societies and communities could look like.

To find and hold on to what is good, right and true demands so much of us, and so much of others too. This is a collective effort to reimagine a different way of living and being together as a people. As a pilgrim people that is all that is asked of us, to keep on walking towards that higher purpose.

Mariama Ifode-Blease

Hymn suggestions

Guide me, O thou great Jehovah; Fight the good fight with all thy might; O Jesus, I have promised; For all the saints.

Transfiguration of Our Lord   6 August
Shall We Move in Together?
Dan. 7.9–10, 13–14; Ps. 97; 2 Peter 1.16–19; **Luke 9.28–36**

The incredible revelation

The dawn comes and the morning star rises – such an evocative phrase, as we think of watching for that first glimpse of something extraordinary in the sky, hinted at by bird song, mysterious and wonderful. The planet Venus, known as both the morning star and the night star, is seen throughout the world as a symbol of love and eternity, but in today's readings the morning star is an image of Christ whose glory fills the skies. This is the one they saw that day, revealed on the mountain in all his majesty, perfection and glory.

Peter is caught up in this most incredible revelation, seeing the possibility, the breadth and enormity of Jesus, and then asks one of the most embarrassingly awkward questions ever, as he says, 'Shall I build a shelter here?'

Settling down

It's the stuff of fiction and sometimes of real life that people have a moment when they think, 'This is the one.' This is the moment when someone declares, 'I've met the one I'm going to marry, spend my life with, make a home with, raise children with.' There is a very natural, human desire simply to be with those we love, to settle and to build, to create family and community. So I just wonder if in that moment Peter has seen the person he wants to spend the rest of his life with, and the question 'Shall I build a shelter?' becomes, 'Shall I create a home, stay and be with you all of my life?'

Shelters and homes and dwelling are part of the language of our faith, alongside the language of love and family. Throughout the Old Testament, we know that repeatedly God's desire is to create a people, and a people with a place to belong. Conversely, the people carry God with them, finding a place for God to be in the tabernacle or tent. And this is exactly the same word that Peter uses in his question: he wants to create a tabernacle, a place where he can be with God and where God can be with them.

In his teaching, Jesus often talks of houses and dwelling. In the words from John 14 that are often used at funerals, we hear of the Father's house with many rooms, and that Jesus came that we might find a dwelling-place with him, just as he has found a dwelling-place with us. If we return to the great Christmas Gospel in John 1, we hear that the Word became flesh and dwelt among us, and as the book of Revelation ends we are promised that the Holy City is the dwelling-place of God with us.

The cost of the vision

So Peter sees Jesus, the man whom he is following, and sees him for who he is and wants to be with him, knowing that 'this is the one'. Yet somehow in his seeing, he stopped hearing and failed to grasp the implications and the cost of the vision, the challenge of actually choosing to spend the rest of his life with this person. Some of us have lived this out down the years as the choice we made that this is the one becomes real in the outworking of the years, staying there 'till death us do part'.

There is a moment in *Lord of the Rings* when the hobbits Pippin and Merry glimpse past Strider, their friend, and see him for a moment as Aragorn the Prince, not knowing the terrible journey they will all make before he is fully revealed and can take up his kingdom.

Peter didn't want Jesus to make the journey to Jerusalem. He didn't want Jesus to go there: he didn't want to hear that suffering is an integral part of the story. This is what Peter has to discover as he listens to Jesus. It's good to want to stay with Jesus, to explore what relationships mean, taking time to see Jesus in all his beauty and grace. But we also need to take time to be with Jesus and hear his word as we discover that following his way will mean accepting the journey that he will make before we can dwell with him for all eternity.

Sandra Millar

Hymn suggestions

At the name of Jesus; Jesus on the mountain peak; Will you come and follow me? All I once held dear, built my life upon.

The Blessed Virgin Mary   15 August
A Magnificat for Climate Justice
Isa. 61.10–end, *or* Rev. 11.19—12.6, 10; Ps. 45.10–end;
Gal. 4.4–7; **Luke 1.46–55**

A prophecy of justice

Mary's Magnificat offers us one of the most beautiful biblical depictions of God's justice – a prophecy about what is possible with God: what God's kingdom looks like. A kingdom where those who are powerless are given a voice; where those who already have more than enough leave something for those with too little. So how does it speak into the great injustice of our generation – the climate crisis?

The climate crisis is not just environmental or physical, and the solutions are not simply to be found in science or engineering – causes and solutions are as much to do with politics and finance. Reports have shown that the richest 10 per cent of the global population (a group which includes the top half of UK earners) have been responsible for more than half of global emissions over the last 25-year period. The climate crisis provides the single biggest threat to people in poverty around the world. The global political and financial systems that keep people in poverty are inextricably linked with the climate crisis – and that's a matter of justice. It is at the heart of why we as Christians need to take the climate crisis very seriously.

Whose shoes are we standing in?

Most of us, probably, when we read the Magnificat, cheer inwardly for the lowly and the hungry, and perhaps feel a sense of satisfaction at the just deserts of the powerful, the rich and the proud. However, if we are intentional about reading the Bible through the lens of the climate crisis, we may come to an uncomfortable realization. The realization that we are powerful. We are rich. We may even be proud. When we read the Magnificat as people from the West, those are the people whose shoes we need to put ourselves in. The shoes aren't comfy.

But it's clear in Mary's vision that justice for the hungry and the lowly is inextricably linked to outcomes for the rich and powerful. There is a connection between the wealthiest and the poorest on this planet, the powerful and the powerless. And, if we read this standing in the shoes of the rich and powerful, we can see that these outcomes don't have to be punishments. They can be choices.

When we read 'he has filled the hungry with good things, and sent the rich away empty', we can choose, more often, to walk away with nothing, to use less of the world's resources. When we read, 'He has brought down the powerful from their thrones, and lifted up the lowly', we can choose to use our power to give a voice to those who are powerless or even to give away some of our power. When we read, 'he has scattered the proud in the thoughts of their hearts', we can take that as an invitation to re-evaluate how we perceive ourselves in our narrative of the world – in our society we tend very much to see ourselves at the centre, but are we? Do we have to be?

Throughout all generations

Mary's Magnificat connects us not just across socio-economic boundaries but across generations. She talks about the promise God 'made to our ancestors, to Abraham and to his descendants for ever'. Our handling of this climate crisis, as we know, will shape the world for future generations as yet unborn. We are not acting as individuals but as a community that is connected across space and time. What we do now makes a difference to others in the future. And thinking, praying, acting on this as churches, with our neighbours, has power and impact.

The Magnificat reminds us that the climate crisis isn't really about what we drink our coffee out of, it's about how we inhabit the world. Acknowledging our power and privilege can be hard.

But Mary's song is a song of joy. 'My spirit rejoices in God my Saviour.' Her vision of a better world is rooted not in fear but in hope and delight. For us, this journey doesn't have to be about shame and guilt. Responding to climate crisis isn't simply about doing more good things, helping more people.

It's about understanding more deeply who we are in Christ, who our neighbour is here and around the world and throughout time, and about allowing our relationship with our neighbour to change us, to change our thinking, our self-understanding and our actions.

Each of us has a part to play. Each of us is called by God to love our neighbour, to participate in the coming of God's kingdom. If our generation manages to reverse climate change and save God's creation for future generations, then perhaps all generations will call us blessed too.

Kat Campion-Spall

Hymn suggestions

My soul will magnify the Lord (Magnificat with Wexford Carol); Oh, the life of the world is a joy and a treasure; Tell out, my soul; The God whom earth and sea and sky.

St Bartholomew the Apostle   24 August
In Praise of the Famously Obscure
Isa. 43.8–13, *or* Acts 5.12–16; Ps. 145.1–7; Acts 5.12–16
(if the Acts reading is used instead of the Old Testament reading, the New Testament reading is 1 Cor. 4.9–15*);* **Luke 22.24–30**

Learning to be a 'supporting artist'

When I was young, I was theatre-struck. I fell in love with every aspect of theatre and 'show business'. However, the aspect of theatre I most especially enjoyed was acting. I was a good enough actor to be able to land prime parts in many productions at school and university. I loved the applause and the attention. To my shame, like all prima donnas, I was self-obsessed. Indeed, I thought the success of a production was mostly down to me and my fellow leads.

Now I am older, I have a better appreciation for all the cast and for what TV calls 'supporting artists' (or 'extras'). If there are leads and protagonists, there is always a much wider supporting cast in the background. As I've taken my place among life's supporting cast, I've grown to appreciate that if there are 'stars' and those who take centre stage, creating something worthwhile takes a community.

St Bartholomew's Day grants us an opportunity to bring the supporting artists of the kingdom centre stage. For while St Bartholomew is mentioned as one of the original 12 apostles, that's all we know about him. Historically, Bartholomew has often been identified with Nathaniel, who appears in John's Gospel, but that reading has rather fallen from favour in recent years. St Bartholomew is one of those most trusted friends of Jesus who will take the message of God out into the four corners of the earth. Yet, unlike the 'big names' – Peter, James and John, or Judas or even St Paul – we know practically nothing about him.

Faithful anonymity

I am encouraged by the fact that Bartholomew is both a central figure – for surely all of the original apostles can claim a certain sort of centrality – and yet effectively anonymous. In the Gospel reading set for today, Jesus says, 'You are those who have stood by me in my trials; and I confer on you, just as my Father has conferred on me, a kingdom, so that you may eat and drink at my table in my kingdom, and you will sit on thrones judging the twelve tribes of Israel.' There is something deeply moving about this statement, especially when we remember that Bartholomew fades into anonymity. He, who was with Jesus in the days of his obscurity and – in terms of the Gospel record – is granted little more than a mention, will be among God's most hallowed ones. If we have no accounts of the works of grace undertaken by Bartholomew, he is called to be a judge in the kingdom of God. He, rather than one of the countless famous folk in Christianity's history, is honoured and treasured in God's topsy-turvy kingdom.

There is a story, a myth if you will, that Bartholomew took the Christian faith to Armenia. It was while on this evangelistic mission that he was martyred. According to legend, he was flayed alive. I will not dwell on the details of this horrifying way to die – it involves being, effectively, skinned – though there are many paintings which depict Bartholomew's death.

Whether Bartholomew died in this horrific manner or not, the story speaks of his faithfulness unto death. Here was not a simple death – if death is ever simple – in which a person dies in old age or in the ordinary run of things. There is spite and malice and torture woven into the manner in which Bartholomew died. There is humiliation and degradation. Whoever took Bartholomew's life wanted him to die in agony and, because it was a slow death, to be given every opportunity to recant.

Who is blessed?

I've often wondered whether Christianity is right to lionize martyrs like St Bartholomew. To focus on them too wholeheartedly can seem to give pain and suffering too much credit. Should we not as Christians be seeking to lessen violence and suffering? Sometimes those who make much of martyrdom can appear to use it as a spur to us ordinary Christians to show greater fortitude in the face of the challenges we confront in our own lives; Christian tradition can give the impression that being a martyr is the peak identity for someone following Jesus.

For me, the power of Bartholomew's story ultimately lies in the humility of this apostle and early disciple. He is not remarkable because of his letter-writing and theological genius like a St Paul, nor because he was a bold front-runner like St Peter; he is remarkable in his anonymous faithfulness. He is very much one of us. He could be one of us. He invites us to be steadfast in our status as God's 'supporting artists'. I pray that none of us faces the horror of his mythic death. Whatever we face, I pray that we have a small modicum of his quiet fortitude and determination to stay with Jesus Christ.

Rachel Mann

Hymn suggestions

Will you come and follow me? From heaven you came, helpless babe; Lord, Jesus Christ, you have come to us; Where you go, I'll go (Chris Tomlin).

Holy Cross Day   14 September
The Paradox of the Cross
Num. 21.4–9; Ps. 22.23–28; **Phil. 2.6–11**; John 3.13–17

Last Wednesday marks 23 years since the horrific attack on the Twin Towers in New York. I visited New York in 2004 and I recall the structure of a metal cross lying on the ground. It was highly moving. It has now been placed as a permanent memorial to the suffering of 9/11 but above all it is a symbol of the cross of Jesus Christ which overcomes all evil. As Pope Francis said on his own pilgrimage to this cross,

> This place of death became a place of life, too, a place of saved lives, a hymn to the triumph of life over the prophets of destruction and death, to goodness over evil, to reconciliation and unity over hatred and division.[50]

Holy Cross Day

Today the church calendar marks Holy Cross Day; our readings give us an opportunity to spend some time reflecting on the cross of Jesus Christ. Holy Cross Day traces its roots back to the fourth century, when Helena, the mother of Constantine, the first Christian ruler of the Roman Empire, was overseeing some archaeological digs in Jerusalem. She unearthed what she believed to be the true cross of Jesus, a relic which quickly became an object of pilgrimage

The cross and humility

The paradox of the cross is described in words of immense beauty from St Paul's Letter to the Philippians. This hymn reflects Jesus' self-emptying death on the cross. Though fully God, and omnipotent, Jesus willingly humbled himself, becoming fully human. He humbled himself further still, for he, of his own accord, willingly gave himself to a cruel, brutal and painful death on a cross. But the story does not end there.

An instrument of brutality becomes the means of our salvation. Jesus humbling himself even unto death becomes a symbol of hope and glory, of the power of love against evil; the way of death is transformed into the way of life. This, St Paul reminds us, is the paradox of the cross. This is the mindset we are to have.

St Paul reminds us to model ourselves on Jesus Christ, with an attitude of humility and servanthood. We are called to imitate this attitude of Jesus Christ in our daily lives; we look towards Jesus who humbled himself, even unto death. Jesus takes on the form of a servant, serving others rather than exerting power. This is deeply challenging, as people vie for position and recognition, often hurting others in the process.

The cross sets us free

Jesus knew that his earthly journey would lead to the cross – to humiliation and death. In the Gospel we hear Jesus speaking to Nicodemus, 'And just as Moses lifted up the serpent in the wilderness, so must the Son of Man be lifted up, that whoever believes in him may have eternal life.' Jesus foretells his crucifixion. Here is an image of perfect love – Christ our Lord nailed to the cross and raised up, drawing all people to himself, offering forgiveness, if we ask him, and new life.

A recent survey found that 88 per cent of people could identify the iconic McDonald's Golden Arches logo, as opposed to only 54 per cent who could name the Christian cross. This is shocking at one level, a symbol of secularization, but equally we are challenged. After all, this was the world of St Paul; he did not swerve from the message of the cross as our means to salvation. Jesus becomes a seemingly frail human being on the cross, he is fully human, while fully God. On the cross, he shows his humanity to the full, suffering pain, torture and agony. Through his suffering, he has borne in his body our sinfulness, our evil, our selfishness. Through the cross alone can we receive eternal life.

The cross speaks of Jesus, God who came into our broken world, to live alongside us, to feel our joys and empathize with our own pain; he is compassionate towards us because he understands from his own human experiences whatever we are experiencing. In times of distress, anxiety, temptation or confusion we can approach the foot of the cross, rest awhile there, be still and meditate on what the cross signifies for us. It is through the cross that we come to the realization of how much Jesus has suffered for us.

The cross on which Jesus died is for us a symbol of our salvation, the reassurance of God's love and forgiveness, but it's also a reminder of our calling to commit ourselves – body and soul – day by day to the loving and forgiving way of the cross, the way that leads to eternal life in Christ.

Arani Sen

Hymn suggestions

From heaven you came, helpless babe; When I survey the wondrous cross; Beauty for brokenness; Crown him with many crowns.

St Matthew, Apostle and Evangelist   21 September
Someone Has to Do It
Prov. 3.13–18; Ps. 119.65–72; 2 Cor. 4.1–6; **Matt. 9.9–13**

The worst job in the world

A friend of mine, who is a priest, had a recurring nightmare that the bishop was going to ask him to look at a job that no one else wanted to do. In reality, he never was asked and he didn't ever get to minister there! I guess there will always be work that is just not appealing but is still necessary for some of us. For society to function, we need people to do those jobs, and in Great Britain at least, post-Brexit, it is clear that there are jobs that people simply don't want to do. Often the vacancies are low paid and hard manual work. Sometimes they are positions that come with some form of stigma, like the work of a traffic warden. I wonder what work you would hate to do?

Different worlds

A few years ago, I was asked to do jury service. It was an interesting experience, particularly for a priest, as we were exempt from this in the past in the UK. Entering the court and watching what happened there introduced me to a whole new world, one that I had only really ever heard about before, but not seen for myself. I found myself captivated by those employed day by day as judges, barristers and clerks, and how their lives must be. I have found myself imagining similar things as I have visited prisons and met prison officers, prisoners and prison chaplains. Then there are those who work at sea. Have you imagined what it is like to be a submariner, living under the sea with no company other than your fellow sailors? Or what it is like to be displaced from your own country or people, where you do not speak the language or understand the culture?

Taxation

Israel in Jesus' day was not a happy place. How could it be while the country was occupied by a foreign power, namely the Romans? There are many signs of people's discontent, both in the New Testament and in the history books of the time. The Roman governors could be cruel and violent. Matthew's own Gospel begins with that reality, as the holy family flee to Egypt to avoid a ruthless king, Herod. A focus of that discontent, as it has been through the ages (particularly through occupation by foreign powers), was taxation. Matthew's job as a tax-collector was, therefore, to use modern parlance, toxic. His work was unpopular not only because taxation is so often disliked but also because it represented the very people that most Jews despised: the Romans.

The call

In Matthew 9.9, in two sentences, we have the call of Matthew. It seems so brief. Almost casual. Jesus is walking along, sees Matthew and invites him to follow him. As we mull over this call, we might wonder: why Matthew? Was no one else there? Why him in particular? Why did Matthew simply get up and follow him? I wonder how others reacted to this call? Were they envious, jealous, scandalized? How interesting that Jesus calls him from his place of work – to a meal.

A different world

Some years ago, while sharing Godly play with some primary school pupils about Jesus' baptism, I asked the young people what it might be like to be underwater. A child answered, 'I think it's like being in another world.' I love that. Today, as we remember Matthew and Jesus' call to follow him, I am reminded that Jesus is calling Matthew into a whole new world. A world, I would guess, that he could barely imagine. A place where he is accepted just as he is, and where what he does as a job is not judged. The fact that the Pharisees have a phrase that joins tax-collectors and sinners together (verse 11) suggests that they regarded his job with disgust. But Jesus' invitation is to a new world, which he calls 'the kingdom of heaven', where those who need healing and acceptance find a home (and food). This is a very different world from that which the religious people of his day could imagine. Which might (and probably should) disturb us. For Matthew reminds us today that, in Christ, those who think it unimaginable can be called, the excluded are included, and the meal provided by God is for those who feel least likely to be invited. I wonder how churches can reflect that way of being today? I wonder where God is calling you from and to?

Jonathan Lawson

Hymn suggestions

Will you come and follow me; He sat to watch o'er customs paid; I heard the voice of Jesus say; Jesus Christ is waiting.

St Michael and All Angels   29 September
Who is Like God?
Gen. 28.10–17, or **Rev. 12.7–12**; Ps. 103.19–end; Rev. 12.7–12 (*if the Revelation reading is used instead of the Old Testament reading, the New Testament reading is* Heb. 1.5–end); John 1.47–end

Michael. That name asks a question in Hebrew: 'Who is like God?' Angels are the Bible's great questioners. When an angel appears to Daniel and strengthens him, it is with the question, 'Do you know why I have come?' When the mysterious shadowy figure wrestles with Jacob in the dark, he asks him his name. An angel in the book of Zechariah pesters the prophet with a full-scale catechism: 'What do you see?', 'Do you know what this is?', 'Do you not know what these are?' It's as if God sends angels to tease mortals with questions.

'Who is like God?' The book of Genesis says that we are made 'like God', in his image. From the way it tells the story, the image of God is closely linked to the idea of oversight. 'God said, "Let us make humankind in our image, according to our likeness; and let them have dominion over the fish of the sea, and over the birds of the air ... and over all the wild animals of the earth"' (Gen. 1.26). To be human means having care of and responsibility for the world. If ever we needed to take seriously the thought that we are stewards of this good earth, it's now. The climate emergency is teaching us how fragile our planet is, and how easily the human race could wreck the delicate fabric of the life it sustains.

336

In the book of Revelation, the archangel Michael is the mighty warrior who 'takes dominion' against evil. He stands for salvation, truth and justice against evil and falsehood, all that comes from the adversary Satan, 'the deceiver of the whole world'. By throwing the dragon out of heaven, Michael re-enacts the creation battle of ancient myth where monsters are defeated and the world comes into being. So, there is a new creation: the universe is saved from chaos and destruction and restored to order and goodness. By the one who is like God, what was lost in the Fall is won back, put right.

Now come down to earth. In Revelation, the victor's crown also belongs to the 'comrades' whom Satan accused before God. They 'have conquered him by the blood of the Lamb and by the word of their testimony, for they did not cling to life even in the face of death'. It's a beautifully drawn parallel between the apocalyptic events in the sky and the human scale of what is happening on earth. We can imagine how this picture of evil defeated in dimensions unseen would strengthen those facing persecution at that time. So, the question, 'Who is like God?' is answered in those who follow Jesus in the fiery ordeals of passion and death, who 'bear witness' at the cost of their lives.

Discipleship, said Jesus, is to be so focused on the kingdom of heaven that you can contemplate losing your life in order to find it. And whatever the way of the cross holds, it means having the inner soul of a martyr, which is what a 'witness' literally is. We could say that the New Testament sees every disciple as a potential martyr: to be baptized is to be ready to bear witness to Christ wherever it leads, whatever it costs.

In the early church, when persecution subsided, many chose what came to be called 'white' martyrdom, by entering monasteries as a way of dying to the world. Perhaps baptism is a kind of white martyrdom, where being a Christian offends against the lazy tolerance that doesn't like the idea that truth is something you might not only live by but die for. Think of St Francis embracing poverty and kissing the leper; St Martin giving his cloak to the beggar; St Cuthbert going to live alone on the Inner Farne and fight evil through his prayers; St Thérèse of Lisieux, the 'Little Flower', full of simplicity and purity, a young girl's life offered to God's love; Mother Maria Pilenko stepping into the queue outside the gas chamber in place of a frightened old woman.

You become like the gods you worship, said a Roman philosopher. So this question, 'Who is like God?' is for anyone who is serious about Christianity. How do we live up to our name and bear witness to Jesus so that our way of life reflects his own everlasting reign? For if the demons that stalk this world are to be conquered, and the storms that threaten to overwhelm it are to be stilled, if people are to seek after God and find him, so much turns on how we live out our discipleship.

God looks for us to bring in the just and gentle rule of Christ. He asks us the archangel's question, Mi-cha-el, who is like God? Who will take the dominion of Jesus and bear grace and truth to our world? He waits for our answer. Only God knows what it will be.

Michael Sadgrove

Hymn suggestions

Christ, the fair glory of the holy angels; Around the throne of God a band; Ye watchers and ye holy ones; Ye holy angels bright.

St Luke the Evangelist   18 October
Healing
Isa. 35.3–6, *or* Acts 16.6–12a; Ps. 147.1–7; 2 Tim. 4.5–17;
Luke 10.1–9

Cure of souls

I am not sure how often Collects are referred to in this publication, but they are often beautifully crafted and very often based on those from the Book of Common Prayer. Today's Collect for St Luke is a case in point, where both *Common Worship* and the Book of Common Prayer refer to Luke as being 'an evangelist and physician of the soul'. What an amazing description – physician of the soul. This sets the scene for this feast day, for Luke not only wrote the Gospel that takes his name but also the Acts of the Apostles, and Scripture tells us that he was a Gentile doctor (Col. 4.14). When a Church of England ordained minister is inducted into a parish, they receive the 'cure of souls' for that ministry which they share with the bishop. It's an extraordinary job description: the cure of souls. Luke is a useful reminder of its ancient precedence.

You don't know what you've got until it's gone

The four Gospels have very different perspectives and emphases. Without Luke's Gospel, we would have very little knowledge of the birth of Jesus and of the annunciation to Mary from Gabriel. We would not have the parable of the prodigal son nor the story of the resurrection appearance on the road to Emmaus. Like all of us, Luke's writing gives us a sense of his own character, and his focus is very much on the poor, on women and on the lost. As a Gentile, we might guess that he easily felt empathy towards those who felt excluded. As a doctor, we might assume that he was interested in wholeness and healing. He appears to have been close to St Paul (as seen in today's Epistle) and he shares with us Mary's song, which suggests some closeness to her too. Certainly, women feature far more in Luke's Gospel than elsewhere in the New Testament.

Calling

Today's Gospel reading comes after a story when Jesus calls individuals but they find excuses not to follow, and the passage after this one includes the parable of the good Samaritan and the short passage about Martha and Mary. In between, we have the appointment of the 70, today's chosen Gospel reading. They are to be forerunners to Jesus' ministry, as John the Baptist has been, and they have a very clear job description. Notice that the harvest is plentiful. With Jesus, there is always an abundance and incredible generosity. The only thing that is lacking is labourers – an interesting thing to ponder for Christians today. Where, I wonder, is the plentiful harvest today and who (and where) are the labourers?

Peace

When I take communion to the housebound, the service begins with these words: 'Peace to this house and all who live in it.' It is a very similar greeting to that instructed by Jesus today: 'Peace to this house!' The word 'peace' stands out for me in today's Gospel. Peace is both a greeting and something to be shared (or not). Following the Covid-19 pandemic, it has been interesting to see where sharing the Peace has got to in church life. Very often now, in the churches that I have attended, a gesture is made rather than hands shaken (or hugs given) as before the pandemic. Peace is not just peace and quiet, though. To be at peace is a far deeper way of being. How do we find peace, particularly when there is no peace? What is the peace that passes understanding (Phil. 4.7)? What does it mean to be at peace with a person, situation or infirmity?

Healing

The 70 have a clear mandate and one of its elements is to 'cure the sick'. I have had several operations in my life and I have found it extraordinary to see how healing happens. So often it just requires time and rest, and yet it just occurs, without any action on my part. Modern medicine, and the ministry of doctors and nurses, are perhaps graces we too often take for granted. It is the ministry of Christians too to bring God's healing, and I am struck that very often that can be as simple as being present to a person, either in listening or by just being there. Regularly, healing comes when we can find God's peace in a situation: a sense of acceptance. Perhaps then we also know that the kingdom has come near to us. I wonder what needs healing in your life. What do you need to be at peace with and about?

Jonathan Lawson

Hymn suggestions

Saviour, who didst healing give; At even, when the sun was set; Peace, perfect peace, is the gift; Be still and know that I am God.

SS Simon and Jude, Apostles 28 October
Communicating the Communion
Isa. 28.14–16; Ps. 119.89–96; **Eph. 2.19–end**; John 15.17–end

Misfiling the post

Anyone who uses electronic communications on a regular basis will have experienced the cold fear that runs through the veins the moment after you hit 'send' on an email or a text message and then realize that you have sent it to the wrong person. Or indeed hit 'Reply all'. The embarrassment accompanying retracting the email, or explaining the circumstances that have led to you telling your grandmother something that was really very particularly meant for someone very different!

Sending a message to the wrong person can be embarrassing. For the Christians of the medieval period it seems that there were even dangers inherent in accidentally sending a message to the wrong person. Poor old St Jude, whom we celebrate today together with Simon the Zealot, carries the dubious title of being the patron saint of 'lost causes'. These two men languish here in the dying weeks of an old Christian year for a number of reasons. On all four of the lists of the various disciples of Christ which appear in Scripture, Simon and Jude invariably appear in tenth and eleventh place, with precedence only over poor old Judas Iscariot. Simon is described as 'the Zealot', and he only turns up in the New Testament in those four lists. There is absolutely no account of him doing anything at all. Jude, who is probably the same person as Thaddaeus, very quickly develops a cult of not being prayed to except in cases of desperate need because of the fear that, having sent your prayer to Jude, it might get misfiled, or opened by accident by Judas Iscariot!

The communion of saints

Those biblical lists of the apostles are really helpful, because the whole point is that the saints are a communion. Individual saints may have more or less to inspire us depending on who they were, or how much we know about them. The majority of our parish churches are dedicated to a saint, and so we might have a particular relationship with our patron. But probably what we take most importantly from the lesser-known or the historically dubious or the almost-anonymous saints of the calendar is exactly that they exist in communion. They are reminders to us of the nature of family.

Does the currency of family, of community, of communion, have any value any more? I think it does, and I think there are moments, perhaps like those moments of worldwide pandemic, or the invasion of one country by another, or perhaps a local disaster or humanitarian crisis, when community really does manifest itself and our identity as a family of people issues forth. But what seems to be frightening is the fact that you have to look quite so hard sometimes for those examples, and that more and more the world seems to be defaulting to a model of society where the individual is more important than the group, and the individual's identity is often largely defined by the ways in which we are better, stronger, louder, richer or more successful than someone else – and where the other, the other people or person against whom we define ourselves, becomes almost dehumanized. Sometimes they become an apparently legitimate target for – in the worst cases – murder, hatred and abuse, bullying, discrimination and, increasingly in a discourse largely dominated by tweets and social media, disrespect and lack of courtesy. Communicating in a set number of characters is never the best way.

The language of family

Simon and Jude, like the patron saints of our churches and chapels scattered across the land, are there to remind us that we are a family. A community. A communion, even. Look again at the words of today's Epistle. Note the nouns: 'citizens', 'saints', 'members', 'structure'. Note some of the verbs: 'joined', 'grows', 'built'. The Christian is never alone. The Christian is always surrounded by the communion of saints. Some of them great, some of them anonymous, some of them pretty dodgy, to be honest. Some of them with international patterns of veneration, like the Blessed Virgin. Some of them almost unknown. Some who didn't get on with each other.

People who identify as a family, as a communion, people like Christians, are called to challenge the prevailing culture in which conversation is largely aggressive and derogatory. We need to explore 'common ground'. Our churches must be places where we can disagree well, and respectfully. Where we can hold very different viewpoints and still love one another. I hope that you welcome the reminder, on this feast of Simon and Jude, that you are a member of a family that extends backwards and forwards in time as well as all over the globe, and in which we can stand with all the saints and resist the temptation to give up the community and to stand against the prevailing tendency to settle for something so much less than communion.

Tom Clammer

Hymn suggestions

Rejoice in God's saints, today and always; Brother, sister, let me serve you; For all the saints; Hope of our calling.

All Saints' Day   1 November (*or* 3 November)
God Will Wipe Away Every Tear
Wisd. 3.1–9, *or* Isa. 25.6–9; Ps. 24.1–6; **Rev. 21.1–6a**;
John 11.32–44

Today we commemorate All Saints' Day, the day in the life of the church when we remember those saints who have gone before us. A little history about why we commemorate All Saints Day: in the early church, the martyrs were remembered on the anniversary of their death; the first three centuries after Christ witnessed widespread and often brutal persecution of Christians. Many died by holding on to their belief in the risen, ascended Christ and not recanting under trial. By the fourth century, we can trace the roots of a tradition to commemorate all the saints who could not be fitted into the liturgical calendar; the lesser saints became part of the 'communion of saints' who were remembered on All Saints' Day.

On All Saints' Day, we are reminded to look towards the future hope that God promises us, when mourning, crying and pain will be no more and God will wipe away every tear from our eyes. We remember those we love but who are no longer with us on earth, whose names are written on our hearts and whose presence is still deeply missed.

Hope for a broken world

The book of Revelation provides us with a beautiful vision of what the new heaven and the new earth will look like: a great multitude of people of every tribe, nation, people and language. They are wearing white and holding palm branches in their hands, praising God for all eternity (Rev. 7.9). These people in white have been persecuted for their faith in Jesus; they have shed blood and died for their faith, but now they stand in glory, dressed in white – all their blood stains have been wiped away. As Christians, they have followed Jesus at great cost, even unto death. We recall Jesus' own words on the cost of discipleship: 'If any want to become my followers, let them deny themselves and take up their cross and follow me' (Matt. 16.24). This heavenly realm will be a place where all who believe and follow Jesus will be welcome.

The evils of this world will be no more. All who suffer tribalism, racism, all victims of nationalism will be set free. This is the new earth we strive to create; this is the focus of our hope and our earthly endeavours. All suffering and all evil has been wiped away through Jesus' own sacrificial death.

Death for Christians is a beginning, the Christian witness of funerals, a place of joy. I recall the first Christian funeral that I attended, of my vicar, a man of deep faith and mission. He had served for many years as a mission priest in Pakistan. The church was packed, as we worshipped, remembered and committed the vicar to God; there was a real sense of joy, a realization for me that death was a beginning not an end.

Jesus' hands and feet

We are witnesses of the glory of God, not just looking to the future but now. We remember today of all days that this life is a gift; it is given to us by God for a purpose. How will we use the time that has been given to us for God's purposes?

St Teresa of Calcutta was often described as a living saint. When asked this question, the unassuming nun, in a white and blue sari, asserted that saintly ministry is not for heaven, it is for now. St Teresa was the hands and feet of Jesus to the people most marginalized in Kolkata, the destitute and the dying. This is my family city of origin, so close to my heart; a city of immense poverty and immense wealth. In multiple visions, Teresa felt the words of Jesus speak to her: 'Come be my light. I cannot go alone.'[51] We too are called to be the hands and feet of Jesus in our communities, in our churches, in our relationships.

On All Saints' Day, we recall that every tear shall be wiped away. We look forward to the new heaven and the new earth. We share in the new life granted us through the death and resurrection of Christ. We thank God for the saints who have gone before us, and we remember their lives and serve others as Christ's hands and feet on this earth. We are called to live out the kingdom of God here and now, symbols of his light and his joy amid the pains, suffering and hardships of this world.

Arani Sen

Hymn suggestions

When I survey the wondrous cross; Praise to the holiest in the height; For all the saints; Ye watchers and ye holy ones.

Commemoration of the Faithful Departed
(All Souls' Day)   2 November
In the Shadows of Glory

Lam. 3.17–26, 31–33, *or* Wisd. 3.1–9; Ps. 23, *or* Ps.
27.1–6, 16–end; Rom. 5.5–11, *or* **1 Peter 1.3–9**; John 5.19–25,
or **John 6.37–40**

What vision of heaven do you hold? What does it look and feel
like? We start with heaven because it is the unsaid for many of us.
We have heard the words of Peter speaking about the resurrection
in his epistle. He underlines the idea of inheritance and brings to the
fore the notion of heaven. Whether we believe in it or not, whether
we have imagined it in any detail or not, the notion of heaven is
predicated on the fact that this time and this world, this space that
becomes place because we, our bodies, minds and, yes, souls, give it
meaning – that all this is not the end. All this is not the end, because
we are standing in the shadows of glory.

The mystery of life

But why do we have to experience death? Why is it the door through
which we all have to pass to see something of this unblemished
and unaffected inheritance? There are no answers that would suf-
ficiently match our need for clarity. We cannot understand why we
have had to 'suffer various trials', and especially that of living and
continuing to live after someone we love has died. In periods of
mourning, we do feel that we are standing in the shadows of glory.

Within what we live, legitimately live and experience and record
in our hearts and souls and bodies when someone has died, within
all that, we can aim to grasp and hold on to the truth that there is
yet still something that we cannot see. There is yet still a force that
loves us back, even as we crawl through the valley of the shadow
of death, even as we pitch our tent and make our home there for
a while, there is yet still something to which our hearts are called.
Even when, and especially when, we stand in the shadows of glory.

Peter's words in 1 Peter 1.8 resonate with undiluted confidence
that this mystery of life eternal and love immortal is real and it is
for us. It is for us. It is for us to believe in, it is for us to believe
in this glorious mystery. It is for us to hold, yes, when we are on
the mountaintop, but so much more when we are in the valleys of
mourning and pain.

Our living hope

Chimamanda Ngozi Adichie writes movingly following the death of her father in her work *Notes on Grief*.[52] In reading her words, we recognize that in death we are undone and that our hope is pinned down and mocked. And we feel that. This brings our earthly, embodied experience of death in parallel with the soul's reuniting with the central heartbeat of love that is God. We return to the Creator who made us in love and for love, and we are home.

You see, God gives something of God's identity to us in our creation and birth. As it was with Jesus, so it is with us. As John writes in the Gospel (John 6.39), we are asked to see Jesus, to see Jesus and believe. We are asked to see Jesus not just on the cross but in the garden at dawn, and on the shore of the lake and on the road to Emmaus. Because if we focus just on the cross, we forget that we are children born out of an empty tomb. We forget who we are, but we need to remember that we are standing in the shadows of glory. We can rest in the knowledge that we have a 'living hope' that cannot die. And to live within that hope means that when someone we love has died, we have the permission to see their life as continuing beyond our human sight.

Love beyond death

The reality, of course, is that our loved ones are not able to report back as easily as we would wish, to tell us what eternity is really like, but we can be reassured as we jointly recognize that death is not a barrier to love. Because we love still in death and, beyond what we can see, eternal love whispers back to us a different song.

In the anthology *Women of Spirit* we find the poem entitled 'Shadows of glory' by the irrepressible mid-twentieth-century Roman Catholic writer Caryll Houselander,[53] whose words inspired this sermon. We must hold on to the truth that in eternity our names are written and our souls are known. Today, we remember those our hearts will never forget. They are transposed, moved from one key to another, their lives transformed, resplendent within a cosmos, parts of which we cannot yet see. In our grief and mourning, we stand in the shadows of glory, but they who are no longer with us on earth, they, they are already there.

Mariama Ifode-Blease

Hymn suggestions

I heard the voice of Jesus say; Let all mortal flesh keep silence; O God, our help in ages past; My redeemer lives (Nicole C Mullen).

St Andrew the Apostle 30 November
Leaving Our Nets
Isa. 52.7–10; Ps. 19.1–6; Rom. 10.12–18; **Matt. 4.18–22**

The call to follow

They were out fishing – just going about their everyday business – when Jesus called to them saying, 'Follow me!' He did not coerce or pressure them to be disciples. There were no promises of a 'good life' or more money than they could earn fishing. Rather, according to the story, he just called out to them and then waited for their response. According to the Gospel writer, they did not hesitate: 'Immediately they left their nets and followed him.'

Told in that way, the call to be a disciple of Jesus sounds straight-forward: a simple invitation and an immediate response. Yet, as followers of Jesus across the years have testified, responding to the call of Jesus is not only life-changing but it is costly and demands single-minded commitment to Christ.

They left their nets ...

Those who knew Simon (also called Peter) and Andrew must have been quite shocked when they heard that the two brothers had left their father and their work and had followed Jesus. We can imagine some of the conversations within the community as word spread that they had left: 'Did you hear about Peter and Andrew?' 'Apparently, they just left their father in the boat.' 'How could they leave the security of their work and home life so suddenly?' 'Why would they just drop everything and follow Jesus?'

Across the years, and in many different contexts today, there have been those who have felt that the call to discipleship meant they should change jobs, move house or travel to a different part of the world. For others, 'leaving nets' behind has meant that they must look carefully at their values and priorities in terms of time or money. Discipleship is costly: at times even close friends and family do not understand our choices. In a real sense, we must be prepared to 'leave our nets' – whatever we have clung to for security – in order to follow Jesus.

Dietrich Bonhoeffer, the twentieth-century writer and martyr for the faith, claimed that when Christ calls a person the call is to 'come and die'.[54] While he himself was put to death in a Nazi prison camp, Bonhoeffer was obviously not speaking simply of physical death. Rather, in the way that the apostle Paul wrote to the Colossians about the need to let go of our old selves, Bonhoeffer meant that in turning to Christ we must turn away from things that we have depended upon for security in life. Money, status, position and influence, friends and family – no other commitment must come before the desire to follow Jesus.

They followed him

When the early disciples 'left their nets' and followed Jesus, they had no idea what would be required of them and, in many instances, leaving their fishing nets may have been the easiest part of following Jesus. As they listened to the teaching of Jesus, they must have been very surprised to learn that being a disciple of Jesus required a change of mind and heart as well. That is to say, they suddenly realized that Jesus was calling them to re-examine the teachings and traditions they had been taught since they were children. For instance, if they followed the religious law, they were very aware of who was considered 'clean' and 'unclean'. They believed that they were to 'love their neighbours and hate their enemies' – and so much more. However, Jesus said that he had not come to abolish the law: rather, he had come to fulfil it and, in effect, his teaching turned all their religious beliefs upside down.

As it was for the early disciples, so it is for us today. While it is at times much easier to think of Christian faith in terms of attending a certain church or believing certain doctrines, true discipleship is never measured by church attendance or doctrinal labels: I'm Anglican, I'm Methodist, I'm Baptist or I'm Catholic. Nor is commitment linked to holding certain doctrines or particular practices of faith, living ethically or giving money to charitable work. Rather, our commitment is to a person, namely, to Jesus Christ.

The clarion call to single-minded commitment to Jesus is in many ways quite daunting. This may be why speaking about 'being called' to follow Jesus leads some people immediately to think in terms of a special vocation for ministry, such as serving as a priest or a missionary. Yet, what is clear from New Testament teaching is that

Christ calls 'one and all' to leave our nets of security – whatever these may be – and to follow him.

Karen E. Smith

Hymn suggestions

Master, speak, your servant's listening; I, the Lord of sea and sky; Take this moment, sign and space (Iona); Take my life and let it be.

Harvest Festival
Do Not Worry
Joel 2.21–27; Ps. 126; 1 Tim. 2.1–7, *or* 1 Tim. 6.6–10;
Matt. 6.25–33

Jesus sits on the side of a mountain, his disciples sitting close to him, the crowds spreading out before him, hoping also to hear his teaching. All have been holding on to his every word. Words which have brought good news to those commonly shamed: the poor, the hungry, those who are grieving ... Words that have brought challenge to those commonly honoured: the rich, the righteous, the keepers of the law ... Words which have touched deeply their hearts.

Jesus has both confronted and deepened their understanding of the law of Moses. He has taken them beyond the expected practice and into a greater relationship with their God through prayer and their relationships with their fellow human beings. And then, he says to them, 'Do not worry.'

Do not worry about what you will eat. 'Look at the birds of the air; they neither sow nor reap nor gather into barns, and yet your heavenly Father feeds them.' He goes on, do not worry about what to wear: 'Consider the lilies of the field, how they grow; they neither toil nor spin, yet ... even Solomon in all his glory was not clothed like one of these.'

I wonder how many of the meek, the hungry and the poor wondered then at his words. He had told them they would be comforted, filled and shown mercy. Now he has told them to consider the lilies. Could *they* clothe themselves in petals and be warm? Could *they* peck at the meagre berries on the mountain shrubs and be filled?

Was this the good news the restless crowds on the mountainside had come to hear?

Do not worry?

Perhaps you wonder the same. Questioning whether Jesus, who says 'Do not worry', really understands that there are bills to pay, hospital appointments, rising damp, and a son whose marriage is on the rocks.

When Jesus said, 'Do not worry', hadn't he read the news – 24-7 headlines of the latest murder; of world leaders that don't take climate change seriously; of famine and drought and desperate unrest both at home and overseas?

If you're anything like me, then sometimes Jesus' command not to worry, to consider the birds of the air and the lilies of the field, can be a reassurance to trust in God when times are hard. But sometimes they can seem glib and empty words, and I want to ask Jesus if he really thinks birds and flowers are going to fix things!

Consider the lilies

But what if Jesus' message wasn't that 'everything is OK, so don't worry', but was instead 'everything is not OK ... so consider ...'?

Jesus knew, like each of us know, that there are occasional moments in each of our lives when something beautiful makes us stop everything we are doing, takes us out of the moment and makes all the worries and anxiety slip away like a mantle from our shoulders.

What was it for you? What was the last thing that was so stunningly beautiful that it took your breath away and made you forget everything that weighed you down? Perhaps it was a sunset or entering a beautiful ancient church. Perhaps it was the last bars of a piece of music that was so achingly and echoingly perfect that you stopped still and just listened. Perhaps the sight of a rainbow arching over the fields in magnificent technicolour.

Harvest thankfulness

Today we are celebrating harvest, a time for us to be thankful. To give thanks to God not just for all that the earth richly provides but for the beauty of creation that reminds us that there is something brighter, more wonderful, glorious and bigger than all the things we hold on to and worry about. It is a time to recognize that we are not just allowed, but commanded by Jesus, to take the time to consider things of beauty; for in doing so, for a moment, we do not worry but bask in the glory of God.

But, of course, it doesn't stop there. Because as we gaze at the world with awe and wonder, we find ourselves compelled to respond with thankfulness to the good things we have received. As we see the beauty of an ancient sacred building, we want to preserve it faithfully for years to come. As we see the beauty of human life, we want to join with charities that seek to end human suffering, and we respond generously to both local and national need. As we see the beauty of the natural world around us, we commit ourselves to do more to preserve our environment.

So, this harvest, let us consider the birds of the air and the lilies of the field. Let us consider the beauty of the earth and of the skies. And let us raise our voices in joyful praise, to a God who commands us to consider, to stop and rest in the glory of the world around us, from which we respond with thankfulness and through acts of generosity and love.

Chris Campbell

Hymn suggestions

All things bright and beautiful; For the beauty of the earth; Seek ye first the kingdom of God; We plough the fields and scatter.

All-Age Services

Baptism
Invisibly Marked
Isa. 43.1–7; Ps. 66.4–11; Rom. 5.6–11; **Mark 1.9–11**

Props

For this all-age sermon, you need a UV ink pen (or a UV ink pad, with a stamp) and a UV light/torch that can detect it, both of which are readily available from stationery shops and online retailers. This works particularly well in a small to medium-sized congregation, as you need to mark everyone with the UV ink (e.g. a cross on their hand) when they come in.

Script

I wonder if anything strange happened to you on the way into church today?

Did anyone else get drawn on by our welcome team?

It's very strange, I thought they drew on my hand, but it seems to have disappeared.

Well, if you were thinking the same, then I've got something that might help us. Would anyone like to volunteer to help me?

(*Use the UV torch to 'detect' their invisible mark on their hand. If there are a number of children, you'll probably need to go around most of them!*)

So, this morning, we've all been marked by a cross, but it was invisible. Until we used the torch, we couldn't see it, even though we knew something had happened.

An invisible sign

Today, our service includes a baptism. During it, I will mark the sign of the cross on (*insert name of those being baptized*)'s forehead. We'll be using some special oil, which has been blessed at the cathedral. When we make the sign of the cross, it is a symbol of our belonging to God's family, a family that is much bigger than those gathered here today.

Later in the service, we will pour water over their heads, baptizing them in the name of the Father and the Son and the Holy Spirit. It is a sign of the beginning of a new journey and reminds us that nothing we can ever do can separate us from God's love.

After the service, no one will be able to tell, by looking, what has happened. On the outside, *they* won't have changed; there will be no visible cross on *their* forehead, and *their* wet hair will quickly dry. But those of us who have been here will know.

Jesus' baptism

We've just heard a wonderful story of Jesus' baptism. The story comes from the very beginning of Mark's Gospel, and it happens right at the beginning of Jesus' ministry before he does anything very special at all. We heard that at the baptism, just as Jesus was coming up out of the water, the heavens opened and something like a dove descended on him. Then there was a voice coming from heaven, which said, 'You are my Son, whom I love; with you, I am well pleased.'

After Jesus' baptism, no one would have been able to tell those things had happened either, although those who were there would have passed on the story. But Jesus would have known that whatever happened to him during the rest of his life, he was loved by God, his Father in heaven, and that God had given him a special sign of that love. Everything that Jesus was later able to do started with the fact that he was known, loved and empowered by God.

A sign for life

The same is true for each of us who have been baptized. Even though no one can tell by looking at us what has happened, our baptism stays with us for ever. Knowing that we have been baptized gives us strength and reassurance in both the good times and the more difficult ones; and even when life is tough, we can remember that

God knows us, loves us and empowers us too. Part of the promise that parents and godparents make today is to keep reminding their godchild of their place in God's family so that they might know God's love as they walk their journey of faith.

Finally, we have one more symbol that we use today. Because when we are baptized, we are commissioned to grow in love and friendship with both God and God's people. As a sign of that, those being baptized receive a lit candle and are called to shine as lights in the world.

(At this point, you might like to ask people for ideas of how they could bring Christ's light into the world.)

Just like our invisible marks on our hands, no one can tell if you've been baptized or not. But the way we act, the love we show in the world, is like the torch. And as we each shine like lights in the world, we make our invisible sign of belonging to God's family visible to everyone we meet.

Chris Campbell

Hymn suggestions

Christ be our light; O Jesus, I have promised; One more step along the world I go; Take, O take me as I am.

Epiphany
Choosing Our Own Journey
Isa. 60.1–6; Ps. 72.[1–9], 10–15; Eph. 3.1–12; **Matt. 2.1–12**

This all-age sermon draws from the traditional Russian folktale, Babushka. If you have a keen group (of children, young people or adults), you could get them to tell (or even act out) the story. Alternatively, I have included a simple retelling of the story here.

Once upon a time, there was a woman, whose name was Babushka. Babushka was always busy; her house was the brightest, cleanest, neatest house in the whole village, and she was keen to keep it that way.

One day, as Babushka was busy around the house, there came a loud knocking at her door. At her door were some travellers, clothed in the finest furs. They told her that they had travelled far and asked if they could come in, to rest and eat.

354

Babushka quickly hurried them into her warm and welcoming home. They rested, and as she began to prepare them a meal, the travellers told her of their journey. How they had seen a star shining in the east and decided to follow it, to find the place where a baby had been born; a baby who was the King of Kings and the Prince of Peace. They were going to take the baby some gifts.

Soon they had eaten all they could, and the travellers got ready to set off once more. But before they left, they asked Babushka if she would like to go with them. Babushka smiled wistfully: the adventure sounded amazing and she loved children very much but she had far too much to do at home.

Babushka's journey

That night, when she went to sleep, Babushka had a dream. She dreamt of the warm smell of hay; of a baby who shone like light; and of a mother who held him in her arms. When she awoke, she looked out of the window and saw a bright star shining in the sky. She felt sad that she had let the travellers go without her and decided that she too wanted to take a gift to this special child.

In the morning, she went round the house and collected all the things that a child might need: wonderful toys she had carved and sewn; warm clothes that she had knitted, and all sorts of sweet treats she had baked. Soon, she was ready to go.

But as she went to leave, she found that the travellers' footprints had disappeared under a blanket of snow, and she didn't know which way to go. So, she followed her heart and started walking.

It wasn't long before she met a child, picking firewood by the edge of a forest. She asked her if she knew the way to find the King of Kings. As the child shook her head, Babushka noticed how cold she was and so gave her a warm shawl from her bag before going on her way.

The next day Babushka met another child. As she approached him, she heard his stomach growling, so she gave him some of the nuts. But he didn't know where the baby was either.

This happened again and again. Babushka kept walking and every time she met a child, she gave them exactly the gift they needed. But although she met all sorts of children, in many different places, she never met the Christ-child.

Knowing her own path

I wonder what you heard in the story of Babushka? I wonder what you thought was the most important part? (*Get feedback.*)

One message could be an encouragement to pay attention to what's important. The travellers (who are the magi from our Gospel reading) drop everything to follow the star, taking the risk of a long and dangerous journey, in order to meet Jesus. By contrast, Babushka left it too late and missed out.

But did she?

Sometimes we can't just drop everything, and Babushka knows some important things too. Her care for her home meant that her visitors were welcomed into a wonderful place where they could rest and be refuelled. Some of us are called to go out on an adventure, but some of us are also called to care for those on their adventures, and the gift of hospitality is an important one. Likewise, in the Bible, Jesus tells us that when we do something for others, we are doing it for him. The magi only give a gift to the Christ-child, but Babushka gives a gift to every child she meets, as she asks her question about the King of Kings. She knows that every child is special.

What is your journey this year?

Who are you in the story today?

Do you identify with the magi, those travellers who felt ready to step out on an exciting adventure to discover more about God?

Or are you more like Babushka, someone who wants to show Christ's love by serving others in small ways, through gifts and love and hospitality?

Or perhaps, today, you feel like one of the children in the story, grateful that someone has noticed your need and ready to respond in smiles and words of thanks.

(*You might like to give the congregation the opportunity to talk to each other about their response, before closing with a prayer that, whatever our journeys are this new year, we are both true to our own paths and able to see Christ in the people we meet.*)

Chris Campbell

Hymn suggestions

O worship the Lord in the beauty of holiness; We three kings of orient are; What child is this, who laid to rest; When I needed a neighbour.

Trinity Sunday   26 May
What is God Like?

Isa. 6.1–8; Ps. 29; Rom. 8.12–17, **John 3.1–17**

Preparation

You will need to prepare a variety of different images of God. These might include art that depicts more traditional images of God the Father/Creator, Jesus and the Holy Spirit, but also images that are more abstract or might convey characteristics of God (e.g., something that represents comfort, love or peace). Depending on your context, you might display these on a screen, give everyone a 'handout' with various pictures on, or have people sitting in groups, in a more 'cafe church' style, with images in front of them.

Script

I wonder what God is like.

I wonder which of these images is most like God for you today?

(*Give people a chance to look through the images and respond, either feeding back to the whole congregation or talking to those near them.*)

Perhaps you wanted to pick more than one ...

Perhaps you didn't think any of them represented what you think God is like.

Perhaps God is so big and beyond our imagining that we need all the different pictures together to show us even a tiny bit of what God is like.

I wonder if what we think God is like changes with us.

Nicodemus' view of God

In our Gospel reading, we've just heard about how one man – Nicodemus – met with Jesus.

Nicodemus thought he knew all about God. He was a Pharisee and a leader; he was meant to be the person with all the answers and was an expert in the law. He knew that God was holy, enthroned high above all creation; so holy that God was dangerous to get close to; so holy that those who did come close were for ever changed. God was like Isaiah's vision, and also God as described in the Psalms; God who was the creator of the world; God whose voice roars with thunder, a glorious voice, which breaks trees in half, splits the flash of lightning and shakes the wilderness. That was the sort of God that Nicodemus thought he knew.

(*At this point you might like to get to look at the pictures again and pick out one that they think might be similar to Nicodemus' view of God.*)

Nicodemus visits Jesus

But one day, everything that Nicodemus thought he knew about God changed. He had heard rumours about Jesus, and he decided to go and meet him for himself.

Did you hear when he went?

Yes – because he was worried about what people would think of him, Nicodemus went out at night.

(*You might like to give the congregation an opportunity to imagine what it would have been like at night and to reflect on whether they have ever encountered God at night.*)

As Nicodemus came to meet Jesus, he said, 'Rabbi, we know that you are a teacher who has come from God. For no one could perform the signs you are doing if God were not with him.'

Perhaps he hoped that Jesus would give him some simple teaching; like the stories we know and love about seeds and wheat and sheep. But instead Jesus and Nicodemus got into a deep conversation about God and what being in a relationship with God is like. A conversation so confusing to Nicodemus that Jesus even teased him, saying, 'You are Israel's teacher and do you not understand these things?'

But during Jesus' conversation with Nicodemus, the Pharisee would have discovered something else about God. He might not have realized it straight away, but we know that eventually he did because he came back later to openly approach Pilate and ask for Jesus' body.

Nicodemus discovered that God is also Jesus, the Son of Man, who that night predicted his own death on the cross and his own ascending into heaven. A God who is Saviour and who loves the world so much he was willing to die for it.

(*Get the congregation to look at the pictures again and pick out any they think show this idea of God.*)

God as spirit

And there's more ... As Nicodemus listened to Jesus, he might have become aware of another aspect of God. God who is like a wind, going wherever she chooses, whom you might hear or see for a fleeting moment, but never really know where it's come from or gone to. God who is the breath of God, hovering over all creation, and whose holiness doesn't burn, but fills our hearts, warming, renewing, sustaining all creation and drawing us closer into relationship. A God who encouraged Nicodemus, and God encourages each of us, to go out into the darkness, to meet Jesus and find out more!

(*Get the congregation to look at the pictures one final time, and pick out pictures that might represent the Holy Spirit.*)

Trinity Sunday

Today is Trinity Sunday. It's the day when we celebrate God who is Father, Son and Holy Spirit. We celebrate God as Creator, Redeemer and Sustainer, that God is three parts and yet one whole. The idea of the Trinity is hard for all of us, whether we are 8 or 80! But really, it's just a day for doing what we've been doing; thinking about the many ways that we have encountered God, the many pictures that we have of God, and giving thanks for them. It's also a day for doing just what Nicodemus did, asking questions, having conversations and being ready to find out more. So, as we finish, just take a moment to think quietly, or talk to your neighbour if you prefer, about what you have discovered about God today.

Chris Campbell

Hymn suggestions

Christ be with me (Prayer of St Patrick); Father, we adore you; Holy, holy, holy One; Holy, holy, holy, Lord God Almighty.

Notes

1 Søren Kierkegaard, *The Sickness unto Death*, trans. Howard V. Hong and Edna H. Hong (Princeton, NJ: Princeton University Press, 1988), pp.102–3.

2 See William Brosend, *The Preaching of Jesus: Gospel Proclamation, Then and Now* (Louisville, KY: Westminster John Knox Press, 2010).

3 See, for example, Walter Brueggemann, *The Word Militant: Preaching a Decentering Word* (Minneapolis, MN: Fortress Press, 2007).

4 See, for instance, Jennifer Kavanagh and Michael D. Rich, *Truth Decay: An Initial Exploration of the Diminishing Role of Facts and Analysis in American Public Life* (Santa Monica, CA: Rand Corporation, 2018).

5 Harold C. Syrett, ed., *The Papers of Alexander Hamilton*, vol. 12, July 1792–October 1792 (New York: Columbia University Press, 1967), pp. 229–58.

6 For example, Mark Oakley, *The Splash of Words: Believing in Poetry* (London: Canterbury Press, 2016).

7 Walter Brueggemann, *A Gospel of Hope* (Louisville, KY: Westminster John Knox Press, 2018), p. 14.

8 'Remaining Awake Through a Great Revolution', sermon delivered on Passion Sunday, 31 March 1968, in James Melvin Washington, ed., *A Testament of Hope: The Essential Writings and Speeches of Martin Luther King, Jr.* (San Francisco: HarperSanFrancsico, 1991), p. 268.

9 Maggie Shipstead, *Great Circle* (London: Doubleday, 2012).

10 C. S. Lewis, *The Chronicles of Narnia: The Voyage of the Dawn Treader* (London: Geoffrey Bles, 1952).

11 Anne Lewin, 'Watchet Auf', in *Candles and Kingfishers* (Foundery Press, 1997).

12 R. Coggins, 'Isaiah', in John Barton and John Muddiman, *The Oxford Biblical Commentary* (Oxford: Oxford University Press, 2000), pp. 433–86.

13 Corrie Ten Boom with John and Elizabeth Sherill, *The Hiding Place* (London: Hodder and Stoughton, 2004).

14 Sheila Cassidy, *Audacity to Believe* (London: Darton, Longman & Todd, 1977).

15 Helmut Thielicke, *Facing Life's Questions*, trans. H. George Anderson (London: William Collins, 1979), pp. 99–100.

16 Graham Greene, *The Power and the Glory* (New York: Vintage, 2010), p. 98.

17 Charles Wesley, *Hymns for the Nativity of Our Lord* (Charles Wesley Society, 1745).

18 Gerald Manley Hopkins, 'As Kingfishers Catch Fire', in *Poems and Prose of Gerard Manley Hopkins*, ed. W. H. Gardner (Harmondsworth: Penguin Classics, 1953), p. 51.

19 Walter Brueggemann, *Spirituality of the Psalms* (Minneapolis, MN: Fortress Press, 2002), p. 51.

20 *Diakaiosune* in Greek and *sedaqa* in Hebrew.

21 Jürgen Moltmann, 'The Hope for the Kingdom of God and Signs of Hope in the World: The Relevance of Blumhardt's Theology Today', *Journal of the Society for Pentecostal Studies* 26.1 (2004).

22 If possible, you might play part of it here.

23 Francis Spufford, *Unapologetic: Why, Despite Everything, Christianity Can Still Make Surprising Emotional Sense* (London: Faber and Faber, 2012), p. 16.

24 Catherine Fox, *Love for the Lost* (London: SPCK, 2015),

25 'Sorry seems to be the hardest word' is a song written by Elton John and Bernie Taupin.

26 Kathleen Norris, *Amazing Grace: A Vocabulary of Faith* (New York: Riverhead Books, 1998), pp. 69–70.

27 *The Road to Joy: The Letters of Thomas Merton to New and Old Friends*, ed. Robert E. Daggy (London: Harcourt Brace Jovanovich, 1989), p. xiii.

28 *The Road to Joy*, pp. 352–3.

29 Kin-dom as an alternative word to kingdom was first written about by the theologian Ada Maria Isasi-Diaz. She recalls hearing a friend use it as a substitute to the language of kingdom, fraught as it is with colonial oppression and imperial violence. Kin-dom is an image of La familia, the liberating family of God working together for love, justice and peace.

30 He discusses the psalms in terms of poems of orientation, poems of disorientation and poems of new orientation. Walter Brueggemann, *The Message of the Psalms* (Minneapolis, MN: Augsburg, 1984), p. 78.

31 Henri J. M. Nouwen, *Reaching Out: The Three Movements of the Spiritual Life* (London: Collins, 1976), p. 36.

32 Nikolai Berdyaev, *The Origin of Russian Communism* (Ann Arbor, MI: University of Michigan Press, 1960), p. 185.

33 Joe Schwarez of McGill University, among other researchers, nominates the *Dictamnus albus* plant, also known as the gas plant. It exudes a range of volatile oils that readily catch fire. The problem with the theory is that the oils need a spark in order to ignite, and they don't burn for long.

34 C. S. Lewis, *The Last Battle* (Harmondsworth: Puffin Books, 1974), p. 146.

35 William Blake, *Auguries of Innocence*, in *Collins Albatross Book of Verse* (London: Collins, 1960), p. 289.

36 *Common Worship: Pastoral Services* (London: Church House Publishing, 2011), p. 93.

37 The quotation has often been attributed to Dante. John F. Kennedy used it in several speeches in the late 1950s. The first writer to attribute the quote in its popular form to Dante was Henry Powell Spring, *What is Truth?* (Winter Park, FL: The Orange Press, 1944), p. 227.

38 N. T. Wright, *How God Became King: The Forgotten Story of the Gospels* (London: SPCK, 2012), pp. 42–6.

39 J. Moriarty, *Nostos: An Autobiography* (Dublin: The Lilliput Press, 2001).

40 Pierre Teilhard de Chardin, *The Divine Milieu* (London: Harper & Row, 1960), p. 115.

41 See Allister Sparks, Mpho A. Tutu and Doug Abrams, *Tutu: The Authorized Portrait* (Johannesburg: Pan MacMillan South Africa, 2011), p. 79.

42 Evelyn Underhill, *Concerning the Inner Life* (London: Methuen and Co., 1926), p. 13.

43 Marilyn McEntyre, *Caring for Words in a Culture of Lies* (Grand Rapids, MI: Eerdmans, 2009), pp. 29–33.

44 Coretta Scott King, *My Life with Martin Luther King Jr* (London: Hodder and Stoughton, 1969), p. 17.

45 Rebecca Solnit, @RebeccaSolnit, 'On Rest as Resistance', Twitter, 23 August 2022.

46 Dom Gregory Dix, *The Shape of the Liturgy* (London: Dacre Press, 1945), p. 744.

47 https://catholic-link.org/quotes/st-teresa-of-avila-quote-christ-has-no-body-but-yours/ (accessed 26.01.23).

48 Mother Julian of Norwich, *Revelations of Divine Love*, ed. Halcyon Backhouse with Rhona Pipe (London: Hodder and Stoughton, 1992), p. 55.

49 See www.oulu.fi/en/conferment-ceremony/hat-and-sword (accessed 21.07.21).

50 See www.catholicnewsagency.com/news/32701/full-text-pope-francis-speech-at-the-911-memorial-and-museum (accessed 04.08.22).

51 Mother Teresa and Brian Kolodiejchuk, *Mother Teresa: Come Be My Light: The Private Writings of the Saint of Calcutta* (London: Rider, 2008).

52 Chimamanda Ngozi Adichie, *Notes on Grief* (London: Fourth Estate, 2021).

53 Dorothy M. Stewart, *Women of Spirit* (Oxford: Lion Publishing, 1997), p. 60.

54 Dietrich Bonhoeffer, *The Cost of Discipleship* (London: SCM Press, [1948] 1959), p. 79.